Pensacola Days

Irv Smith

This is a work of fiction. Names, characters, and events are products of the author's imagination or are works of fiction.

Text Copyright Published © 2024

By Harold I Smith

Dedication

This book is dedicated to Sandy, my beloved wife of 53 years. Our life together began in Pensacola after a series of unlikely, even unbelievable events. There is no doubt that our being together was meant to be. It was our destiny, the same as what happens to the characters in this story.

Pensacola 1969

In the late 1960s and 70s, Pensacola and Pensacola Beach were Navy towns whose permanent residents were mostly active duty and retired Navy and Marine Corps personnel. Other than logging and farming, the main industries of the Pensacola area were paper mills and factories. Big-time tourism was still in its infancy. In Pensacola Beach, small cottages and a few hotels were scattered along Via De Luna Drive. There were long deserted stretches of sugar-soft, ultra-white sandy beaches, which bordered the beautiful azure blue Gulf of Mexico. There were also miles of dunes where dune buggies recklessly raced up and over sandy hills. On any given day, dozens of fledgling Naval Aviators spent their free time lounging on the beach or in popular watering holes like the Pier Lounge and Dirty Joe's Saloon. However, the most popular place for Naval Aviators was the legendary Trader Jon's in Pensacola's Seville section.

In contrast to Pensacola Beach's beauty and glamor with its bars and revelry, much of the area north and east of Pensacola was plagued by high unemployment or minimum wage jobs. The factories and paper mills provided jobs but spewed foul exhaust and poisoned water. In an attempt to find a better life, many young people, especially women, looked to the Navy and Marine Corps for a way out; a lot of them succeeded.

The Naval Air Station was called the "Cradle of Naval Aviation." It was the home of the Aviation Officer Candidate School (AOCS), where Marine Corps Drill Instructors honed thousands of college boys into men and Naval Officers. It was there that virtually every Naval Aviator earned their "Wings of Gold," but it was also the home of the Barrancas National Cemetery, where thousands of Navy and Marine Corps personnel (and their spouses) chose to be buried. Not far from the cemetery was the Navy/Marine Corps Memorial Chapel, where a wall was covered by hundreds of wings and placed in honor of the Naval Aviators who earned them.

On any given day, the skies over the base were crisscrossed with roaring aircraft taking off and landing from outlying airfields. On the base, the sound of Marine Corps Drill Instructors barking orders to AOCS candidates running and marching in formation could be heard everywhere. There were several barracks, referred to as "barns," where officer candidates lived and trained. One of the oldest barns, "Splinterville' was the home of Battalion I, Indoctrination (INDOC) Battalion. Beginning the moment they walked into the INDOC's door, the newly sworn-in officer candidates, called "poopies," were subjected to ten days of relentless harassment, little sleep, and exhausting PT. Often, more than 50% of the poopies who started INDOC quit before the ten days ended. Those who made it through INDOC could look forward to newer, air-conditioned barns, but first, they still faced at least fourteen more weeks of rigorous training and harassment. Not far from the barns was the obstacle course where officer candidates struggled to climb up and down rope ladder walls, across hanging hoops, and through a sandy maze, all while Drill Instructors screamed at them to go faster and harder. To the east of the obstacle course were the Mustin Beach Officers' Club and its legendary "Ready Room" bar, where legions of Naval and Marine Aviators partied. It was also where busloads of young women from the area were brought to weekly "mixers," an opportunity to party and dance with newly commissioned officers. Further east was the home of the legendary aircraft carrier, USS Lexington, the "Lady Lex," which was used for years to train hundreds of student pilots how to land safely on an aircraft carrier.

The Pensacola NAS was the heart and soul of Naval Aviation and a national treasure. It was a sacred place, revered by every Naval Officer who wore Wings of Gold.

A Personal Note

The inspiration for this work of historical fiction is based on three parts: my days in Aviation Officers Candidate School, finding my future wife, and a chance encounter with Major Stephen Pless. Now, more than 50 years later, I combined those memories into this story.

I was stationed at the Pensacola NAS in 1969 and 1970. Like in this book, it is where I met and married my wife, but this is not our story. A major part of this book is a fictionalized version of our days in Pensacola. I have tried to give an accurate description of AOCS training and the impact it had on me and my fellow officers. My chance meeting with Major Stephen Pless, USMC, actually happened like it did in this book and led to further research into his life and death. Though my research, I was able to share my findings in a copyrighted biography about Major Pless, entitled Conspicuous Gallantry. Sections of this story, including the description of Pless' heroic mission that earned him the Medal of Honor, are taken from that biography and public records.

What happened in AOCS is an essential part of *Pensacola Days,* but it is only the beginning of the story. Most of the story is about the pursuit of happiness after a life-altering tragedy and the inevitability of destiny. It is not a war story; it is about the lives of Naval Aviators as they lived and trained during a time of war. Some readers may recognize some of the events that are described in the story, but except for Major Pless, all the characters are works of my imagination or loosely based on people I knew. In addition, anyone who attended AOCS knows that the language of Drill Instructors was very "colorful," to say the least. If for no other reason than to reduce the length of this story, I have refrained from using the most colorful of Drill Instructors' vernacular.

Table of Contents

Chapter 1

Striker Leaves for Pensacola

As Striker rode in a Navy shuttle from the campus recruiting office to Andrews Air Force Base, a wave of despair began to engulf him. Everything he owned was in a weathered satchel that he found at a church thrift shop. He had not had a date for several weeks and certainly didn't have a girlfriend. He felt totally alone and was going to a place where he would not know anyone. His father had given him a hundred dollars as a graduation gift. Otherwise, he was penniless. In his last semesters in college, he sold virtually everything he owned, including his books, hunting guns, and musical instruments, to pay for tuition and books. He even had to borrow money from his family to pay his rent. Now that he had graduated from college, he was broke, lonely, and on his way to an uncertain future in the Navy, a place where he knew no one. It was Pensacola, Florida, where he hoped to become a Naval Aviator.

Striker was tall, 6'1", with light brown hair, and weighed about 160 lbs. He had two sisters, Lizzy and Anne Marie. Lizzy, who was two years older, had finished college and was a schoolteacher in suburban DC. Anne Marie, who was four years older, lived with her husband in Prince Frederick, Maryland, about forty miles northwest of their mother's house.

Jonathan Emmett Striker was born near the Patuxent Naval Air Station in Southern Maryland. It was where his parents, Andrew and Francesca, met, married, and eventually bought a house. Out of all of the places they had lived, this was the only house he and his sisters called home and where his mother still lived. His father was a career Naval Aviator who had enlisted in the Navy in the midst of World War II. He was a "Mustang" officer with no college education, but through hard work and a willingness to accept any assignment, he rose to the rank of Captain.

Even though he had moved often and changed schools several times, Striker was a good student. Because of an inadvertent error at one of the schools, Striker was wrongfully assigned to a higher grade, but he still did well, and he remained with the class. He was just sixteen when he began his senior year at St. Charles Catholic High School in Lexington Park. Like a lot of boys his age, his features were not yet filled out, making him look even younger. So, until he was in his early twenties, he was almost gaunt, making him less attractive to most of the girls his age. His weight did not affect his athletic ability; he was an all-state runner in high school, and later in life, as his features matured, women found him much more attractive.

Unfortunately, Striker's family paid a dear price for his father's success in the Navy. His mother and siblings only had a part-time husband and father, whose military duty meant being frequently absent for many months. Jonathan's father loved the life of a Naval Aviator, but his mother eventually tired of it. Her relationship with her husband was eroded by the chronic worry and loneliness that military wives endure. As with many Naval Aviator marriages, after twenty-three years, it ended in divorce. But the Navy and its vagabond life was the only life Striker knew, and he was on his way to begin it; he believed it was his destiny.

Chapter 2

First Day of INDOC

"Are You Eyeballing Me?"

On the afternoon of March 9, 1969, Striker left Andrews Air Force Base on a Navy R5D Transport aircraft. After arriving at Pensacola four hours later, he was taken to the San Carlos Hotel in downtown Pensacola. The old building was the aging queen of Pensacola hotels, but with its elegant bar, grand lobby, and spectacular stairway, it was still a local favorite. While he waited in line to check in, Striker took out his orders and hotel vouchers. When Striker saw two other guys show their orders to the room clerk, he went up to them and introduced himself. One of them was Jeff Weld, from Richmond, Virginia, who had just graduated from James Madison University. The other was Alan Stewart from Pittsburgh, Pennsylvania, a graduate of Duquesne University. As the three of them took the elevator to their rooms, they agreed to return to the hotel bar to eat and have a couple of beers.

Fifteen minutes later, they were all sitting at a table and ordering drinks. Soon after they sat down, a fourth young man walked in and sat at the bar. He heard Striker and the others talking about AOCS and walked over to their table. He asked them if they were also reporting to AOCS the next day. Weld shook his head yes and asked him to pull up a chair. After he sat down, the fourth guy introduced himself as Steve Hickey, but his friends called him 'Sticky.' He joined the others as they talked hesitantly about the coming days in AOCS. Most of their conversation centered on the horror stories they had heard about the ruthless harassment AOCS candidates received from Marine Corps Drill Instructors. In a moment of wishful optimism, they all agreed that the stories had to be exaggerated; there was no way all those things could have happened. They talked about girlfriends, cars, airplanes, and anything but AOCS. When the bar closed, they were almost convinced that AOCS could not be all that bad. None of them had much sleep that night, and in the days ahead, they would find out that most of the stories they heard were true.

Striker requested a wake-up call so he would be ready for the 7 am bus ride to the base. But he was already up and downstairs before the call. He was too nervous to eat breakfast, so by 6:30 am, he was waiting for the bus in front of the hotel. When the Navy bus arrived, there were already about twenty people onboard. About twenty more people, including the guys he had met the night before, were now lined up behind Striker. Almost everyone there was clean-shaven, in coat and tie, and carrying a suitcase. But, just as the bus driver started the engine, Sticky ran out of the hotel in cut-offs, a tee shirt, and an old backpack draped over his shoulder. He was unshaven, and his hair was a mess. When he stepped onto the bus, he stopped, waved his orders at the driver, and saluted everyone before he sauntered to a seat. As they would find out later, Sticky was just being Sticky. After he sat down, the bus began the short ride to the base, but to everybody on the bus, it seemed like hours. Everyone was silent during the ride except for a smattering of nervous conversations. When they arrived, two other buses were unloading about sixty more people.

INDOC was in Battalion I, "Splinterville," a World War II-era wooden building, but it seemed to be in good condition, with a coat of fresh paint and well-kept landscaping. To a

5

casual observer, it looked more like a museum than a place where Marine Drill Instructors would relentlessly sift out those they believed would not be able to become Naval Aviators from those who would. Making it even more stressful, INDOC was not air-conditioned; it had oscillating fans in the upper corner of almost every room. So, as the new candidates soon discovered, cooling off after a day in the hot Florida sun would be very difficult.

As Striker got off the bus and walked towards the entrance, he saw two signs in front of the building. The biggest one was a blue and gold sign that read, *Welcome to the Cradle of Naval Aviation*. Then, over the front door was a second sign; *Through these doors walk the future of Naval Aviation*. Striker would soon know that before the next ten days ended, at least half of those welcomed so warmly that morning would abruptly be sent home. Striker's dad was right when he told him that the Marine Corps ran AOCS in strict Parris Island style. In 1969, the Drill Instructors assigned to AOCS were battle-hardened veterans who showed little patience and virtually no mercy. Within thirty seconds of walking into INDOC, Striker began to understand what his dad had tried to tell him.

The screaming began when each new candidate entered a large room known as the quarterdeck. Six Drill instructors and six senior (final week of AOCS) candidates were directly in their faces, yelling insults and rapid-fire questions at anyone they wanted to harass. "Are you eyeballing me? Where did you get that pretty tie? I like how you did your hair; what did you put on it this morning? Did your mommy make your lunch? If she doesn't, I can reserve dinner for you at the Officers' Club. Can I help with your bag and show you to your room?" Most of the candidates were stunned by the sudden verbal attacks and did not know how to react. In a mocking voice, one of the drill instructors quietly asked them if they were ready to pin on their wings and climb into an F-4 Phantom. Some new candidates were naive enough to say they were. The Drill Instructor singled them out and said he would arrange for that to happen. Then he screamed, "Prove it to me, maggots, drop and give me twenty pushups, then a hundred jumping jacks, then fifty squat thrusts. When you finish, start over again. And do it by the numbers, counting each exercise loud enough that everybody in this building can hear you. And when you finish with two sets, get your fat asses up against the bulkhead and sit like you are in a chair. Remain in that position until I tell you to stop. Do it now, maggots." To the surprise of those who said nothing, they were ordered to do the same thing as those who said "yes."

While they exercised, the Drill Instructors and senior candidates walked to every candidate and harassed them, screaming that they could not hear them count or that they were doing pushups or squat thrusts like a "lame-ass girly boy" and to start counting over again. They continually called them "pussies and wimps." Those who were struggling were told they were never going to make it through the program. They were called "wimp ass pansies" and told that they should DOR (Drop On Request) now before the program got tough. All they had to do was say, "This candidate DORs." They would be taken away and allowed to serve two years as an enlisted man or return to civilian life. The Drill Instructors told them, "DORs are final, with no appeals. You say it once, and your ass is outta here, period." Four candidates suddenly yelled that they wanted to DOR, and senior candidates quickly took them away. They had been in AOCS for less than half an hour.

Finally, when the last candidate finished his Physical Training (PT) and was up against the wall gasping for air, the senior Drill Instructor walked to the center of the room and ordered them to listen carefully. He was First Sergeant Jesse Sullivan, who was well-known and respected by the Marine and Naval Officers who served with him. He was a big man built like a pro linebacker at 6'5" and about 230 pounds. His scar started on his right cheek and curved across the side of his face to just above his ear. He had a cigar in his mouth and a swagger stick in his hand. Striker learned later that Sullivan had received a Navy Cross, three Bronze Stars, and four Purple Hearts for his bravery in combat. About two years earlier, he had been on the Sergeant Major's selection list and should have been promoted on his anniversary date. But he was passed over after he got into a fight with a drunken civilian who had insulted his Puerto Rican wife. Sullivan easily won the fight and put the drunk in the hospital but lost the promotion. Sullivan often said he would gladly do it again; nobody insulted his wife. His action earned him the admiration of the entire Pensacola community.

Sullivan squared his shoulders and looked around at the new candidates as if he were sizing up the enemy. Then he ordered them to form a shoulder-to-shoulder line as he called out each of their names. When they were in line, he pointed to the first one on the right and ordered them to count individually and remember their numbers. Then Sullivan told them to look to right and left and said, "Take a good look, maggots; one or both of the people you just looked at will be gone in less than ten days." Sullivan then ordered them to turn right and get as close to the person in front of them as they could without touching. Then he yelled, "Maggots, do it now, move your dead asses; you're not in your daddy's house anymore, and your mommy isn't here to help you. Get so close to the maggot before you that your toe touches his heel."

After everyone turned, he said, "I am First Sergeant Jesse Sullivan, United States Marine Corps; I can out-run, out-drink, and out-fight any of your baby-soft asses. I'm thirty-five years old, and I can drink a bottle of Jack Daniels, smoke a cigar, then kick the cowboy dog shit out of any three of you before you can pull your thumbs out of your asses and figure out what just happened and I have the scars and the stripes to prove it." Then he stared at them and said, "You maggots are now in AOCS Class 569, the fifth class of 1969. Do not forget your class number. From now on, you will refer to me as 'the Drill Instructor' or 'the First Sergeant' and nothing else. If, for some wild ass reason, you call me 'Drill Sergeant,' I will PT you until you pass out in a puddle of sweat or wish you were dead."

Then he introduced the other Drill Instructors: Gunnery Sergeants Wilson and Johnson. Each of them, he said, spoke for him when he was not present. Then he said, "Until you finish AOCS or DOR, you are the property of the United States Marine Corps. You will do exactly what the Marine Corps Drill Instructors order you to do immediately when you are ordered to do it. Any failure to do so will result in your receiving demerits, motivational PT, or expulsion from the program. If you accumulate ten demerits, you will be expelled from AOCS. In addition, there will be an anonymous candidate peer review at the program midpoint and in the final week. If you receive three downvotes from your classmates, you will be expelled from the program unless I overrule the expulsion, and I have never overruled a peer expulsion. In addition, for the duration of the program, you will probably get less than four hours of sleep at night, be told how to make a bed, store your clothes and gear, what razor and toothbrush to use, and exactly how to store them, what to wear and how to wear it, how to salute, how to march in formation, field strip and clean an M1 Carbine, when and where to go, when to get up, to eat, to sleep, to shower and to shit. Whenever a Drill Instructor, a senior candidate, or anyone else walks in this passageway, you will immediately face the passageway, brace up against the bulkhead, and look straight ahead until ordered otherwise. You will be covered when you are in formation, so you wear a hat. In addition, floors are now decks, walls are bulkheads, halls are passageways, bathrooms are heads, stairs are ladders, and ceilings are overheads. They will not be called anything else during the program, but there is good news. You will not be told how to comb your hair. Your heads will be shaved in about twenty minutes. All this is to teach you to pay attention to detail, the cardinal rule of flying a Naval aircraft. You will also have to pass all the academics and the PT standards, complete the obstacle course in ten minutes or less, be able to swim a mile in a flight suit, and complete *Dilbert Dunker* training and many other requirements. If you are ordered to report to the Drill Instructor's office or are crazy enough to go there without being ordered, you will precisely follow the 'Pound the Pine' procedure, which you will memorize. You will also have to memorize the General Orders, the daily password, the officer of the day, and the chain of command from your poopy ass up to the Chief of Naval Operations and be ready to recite any of them at any time. If a Drill Instructor orders you to speak, you will only look straight ahead, speak in the third person, and never use the pronouns 'you' or 'I.' Until you complete INDOC or quit, you will refer to yourself as 'This officer candidate' and only speak in the third person, and you will be referred to as *Maggots, Poopies*, or *Shitbirds*." Finally, he told them the AOCS program was evenly divided into three segments: Academics, Physical Training, and Leadership. Each segment would be graded and then combined with the other two. The higher the total of the grades, the higher the class rank. Those with the highest class rank will get the highest priority for future training. A failing grade in any of the three segments will result in expulsion.

First Sergeant Sullivan turned Class 569 over to Gunnery Sergeants Wilson and Johnson when he finished. Wilson was about 6 feet tall, stiletto thin, and had a baritone command voice that could scare the dead. Johnson was a black man who was about 5'8" and 180 lbs. He was heavily muscled with a thin mustache and a stare that could melt ice. All three of the Drill Instructors had at least two combat tours in Vietnam, and they sometimes acted like they had never left.

Johnson ordered the candidates to line up in a single file and follow him to the barbershop. After cutting their hair, they marched to the Supply Office to be issued uniforms and toiletries. After they returned to the barn, they were taken to the mess hall for lunch and then to the medical center to begin their physical examinations. Later, they were taken to the mess hall and then back to the barn.

Next, Gunnery Sergeant Wilson barked, "The First Sergeant just gave you a quick and dirty summary of the AOCS program. If it isn't what you thought it would be, or you are unsure it's what you want, DOR, now." Six more candidates were asked to DOR as the class left for the barbershop and were removed from the building. They had been in INDOC for less than one hour.

Chapter 3

The First Day of INDOC Continues

It was still the morning of the first day of INDOC, and ten candidates had already DOR'd. There were now ninety candidates left in the class. With Gunnery Sergeant Johnson in the front of the line of the remaining candidates and Gunnery Sergeant Wilson at the rear, Johnson ordered them to walk, single file, out the front door to the parking lot in front of the building. Then he told them to form nine rows of people with ten people in each row. Wilson rearranged the rows to have the tallest candidate on the left side of the row and the shortest one on the right. Every time they were ordered to 'fall in,' they were told to assume this formation. Then Drill Instructor Sullivan said, "Each of you maggots, raise your right arm, touch the left shoulder of the maggot on your right, then look right and left and move back or forth to straighten the line. You should only be able to see the head to the right and the head to the left. Now, when I say 'forward, march,' you will begin marching with your left foot, then the right foot is 2, the left is three, and the right is four, and so on. Then Gunnery Sergeant Johnson will call a cadence which sounds like, 'hut, or one, two, three, four, hut, two, three four.' You will continue marching forward until I say, 'ready, halt,' and you will come to a complete stop and remain in formation. Later, you will learn to turn in formation, quickstep, and double time, followed by more complex drill maneuvers. Until then, when you are marching, you will follow the road as it turns right or left unless you have orders to do otherwise."

Gunnery Sergeant Wilson then marched the candidates to the barbershop. When they arrived, they were ordered to form a single line in their numbered order and enter the barber shop when there was a vacant chair. There were four chairs and barbers in the shop. The barbers greeted each candidate with a smile and asked him how he wanted his haircut. No matter how they responded, the barber shaved all their hair off and said, "Next." All ninety poopies were done within thirty minutes.

As they exited the barbershop, Gunnery Sergeant Wilson ordered the poopies to fall in and marched them to the supply office. When they arrived, they were given large baskets and asked by the supply clerk what their sizes were. Then they were each issued two "poopy" suits (green heavy-duty button-up overalls), bed linens, skivvies (white tee shirts and boxer shorts), socks, a "fore and aft" cap, one pair of shower shoes, and a pair of "boondocker" boots. As they would find out later, some candidates received the correct sizes, and some did not. When they left the supply office, they marched back to INDOC with the baskets.

Back at INDOC, they again formed a single line inside the quarterdeck, and Gunnery Sergeant Johnson handed each poopy two storage boxes, one small and one large. He then ordered them to strip and put all their clothes in the large boxes and all their jewelry, including rings and watches, in the small ones. The poopies then put the small boxes in the larger ones, wrote their names, class number, date, and social security numbers on the box, and secured it with Wilson's tape. After all the boxes were taped, the poopies were directed to put on the skivvies, poopy suits, and boondockers and take the boxes with their belongings to the storage room.

After they finished, Gunnery Sergeant Wilson called out their numbers and assigned every four poopies to a room. Then he announced, "At my command, you will take the baskets of toiletries and other uniforms to your rooms and put them away according to the directions listed on a sheet of paper lying on one of the beds. You have twenty minutes to get it done and form in front of the barn." Then he screamed, "Now get your poopy asses to your rooms. Hurry, hurry, hurry."

All ninety poopies, carrying baskets, stormed down the halls and up the stairs to their rooms. Each room had four single beds, four dressers, four small metal lockers, directions, and a ruler. Striker, Stewart, and two poopies, Stanford and Snowden, were assigned to the same room. They only whispered brief comments as they hurriedly put things away as best they could. With about a minute to go, Striker and his roommates believed they were ready and left to get into formation.

Gunnery Sergeants Wilson and Johnson were waiting for everyone. Two poopies were about ten seconds late. Gunnery Sergeant Johnson angrily barked, "Listen, carefully, you worthless shitbirds. AOCS Class 569 trains like a team, follows orders as a team, and pays the price when some dumb shit screws up as a team." Then, for the next two grueling hours, Gunnery Sergeant Johnson taught Class 569 close order and formation drill. During the first thirty minutes, the other poopies marched; Gunnery Sergeant Wilson PT'd the two late poopies in the sand pit, a pile of sand between the buildings.

Later, Drill Instructor Wilson marched the class a mile and a half to the mess hall. Along the way, he continually barked orders at the poopies, telling them to straighten up and get in step. Twice, Gunnery Sergeant Johnson stopped the class and started screaming at two out-of-step poopies. Johnson told the first poopy that if he did it again, he would be PT'd so much he would beg for mercy like the candy ass he was. Then he

made the second poopy get out of formation, do fifty squat thrusts, then run circles around the class until they reached the mess hall.

When Class 569 arrived at the mess hall, Gunnery Sergeant Wilson told them they could move around, talk freely, and take all the food they wanted inside. But then he stressed that they only had twenty minutes to eat and return to formation outside the mess hall.

It was in the mess hall that Striker first spoke since beginning INDOC. Sitting across from Stewart, he saw Weld and Sticky nearby. He had seen them all during the blur of activity earlier that day but didn't dare say anything. They now looked very different, with their heads shaved. Striker asked Stewart how he was doing. He grinned and said, "Just another day at the beach, how about you?" Striker responded, "So far, I've kept all my faculties and haven't broken any bones, so I guess I'm doing OK." Then Sticky, who was further down the table, said, "If I knew it was going to be so much fun, I would've signed up earlier," everyone around the table laughed. A couple more poopies nervously tried to convince each other that the worst was probably over. Then they quietly returned to eating what might be their last meal in AOCS.

After everyone was finished eating, Gunnery Sergeant Wilson ordered the class to march in formation to the rear of the mess hall and stand at attention next to the garbage dumpster. He disappeared into the mess hall for a few minutes, then reemerged with a bucket in his left hand. When he came to the front of the formation, he said, smiling, "Any one of you maggots need a smoke break? If so, fall out and stand in a line next to me." Unwittingly, three poopies fell out and quickly did as they were told. Wilson took a pack of Camel cigarettes and a Zippo lighter out of his pocket and handed a cigarette to the first poopy in line, told him to put the cigarette in his mouth, and lit it for him. Then Wilson put the metal bucket on the poopy's head. After he lit the cigarette for the second poopy, he ordered him to climb into the dumpster and close the top. Finally, he gave the rest of the cigarettes to the third poopy and ordered him to put all of them in his mouth, and then Wilson lit them. After the three poopies coughed and wheezed for a few minutes, Wilson ordered them to remove the bucket, get out of the dumpster, put out all the cigarettes, and return to formation. No one smoked a cigarette for the rest of INDOC.

Chapter 4

First Day of INDOC Ends

Gunnery Sergeant Johnson marched the remaining poopies to NAMI (Naval Aerospace Medical Institute)) for their physicals. Along the way, he barked, "Once you arrive at the hospital, you will form a single file line according to your assigned numbers. When a corpsman calls your number, you will follow him to the exam room and follow his directions exactly. After you finish your physical, you will return to formation where you presently stand. When the last poopy is finished, we will return to the barn in formation." Then he went on, "Your physicals will determine if you meet Naval Aviation standards. You will be declared medically ineligible and removed from AOCS if you do not meet every standard. Some of you will not continue in the program after today."

As many as 20 poopies at a time were taken to an examining room where they removed their clothes. Several corpsmen and physicians gave each poopy a general physical exam, then directed them, one at a time, to separate rooms where they had their eyesight and hearing tested. Striker and his roommates were among the last poopies to complete their physicals. He and Stewart passed all the standards except uncorrected 20/20 vision in both eyes. The doctor told them that although they could no longer become pilots, they could become Naval Flight Officers, the F-4 "guy in back." Disappointed but still wanting to stay in the program, both accepted the change. Unfortunately, Stanford had a heart murmur, and Snowden was colorblind. Both were disqualified and medically separated from AOCS. Striker assumed that

17

Weld had also failed the physical because he never saw him again.

When Striker was in line to get vaccinated, he saw the corpsmen using air guns to shoot pressurized serum into each poopy's upper arms. He chuckled to himself as he recalled that air guns were normally used to inoculate farm animals. But here they were, being used to inoculate poopies, the farm animals of AOCS. When the poopy in front of Striker got his first shot, he went down, face first, on the floor. Alarms sounded, corpsmen put him on a gurney, and he was taken away. Striker instinctively yelled, "Holy Shit," and momentarily considered DOR'ing. He dismissed the thought, stepped forward, and got his shots. He never saw the poopy who went down again.

There were eight fewer poopies when everyone was outside. Gunnery Sergeant Wilson ordered them to count off and rearranged the formation. Then, knowing that everyone's arms were sore from the shots, he ordered them to hit the deck and do twenty-five pushups. Many poopies struggled to finish, but in a rare moment of compassion, Wilson did not PT them any further. He just smiled and said, "If you think you're hurtin' now, shitbirds, just wait until tonight, and then oh, dark thirty tomorrow morning and the days after that. This isn't a picnic in the park like back home with little Susie the sweet tooth. It's going to get harder and harder, and that is just the beginning." Then, he strutted to the front of the formation and led Class 569 to the mess hall for dinner.

Inside, Striker saw Sticky near an empty chair and sat down. Sticky looked up and asked Striker if he was still having fun. He shrugged his shoulders and responded, "Not as much as before my eyes were examined. I didn't qualify for pilot training, so I can only be an NFO now. I almost DOR'd, but

18

after the Doc explained that I could still be in F-4s, I agreed to stay in the program." Sticky shook his head and said. "The same damn thing happened to me. I knew I didn't have a 20/20 vision, but I hoped to still be a pilot. It turned out that the NFO pipeline was the best I could qualify for, so here I am." Now silent, both of them finished eating and got back into formation.

Gunnery Sergeant Wilson ordered Class 569 to march double-time back to the barn. When they arrived at the entrance to INDOC, First Sergeant Sullivan was waiting for them. He stood in front of the formation and, in his most powerful command voice, barked, "Welcome back to INDOC, poopies. Your physicals are done, and now you begin serious INDOC training. At my command, you will fall out, go to your rooms, finish storing your uniforms and toiletries, and make your beds precisely as detailed in the written directions you have been given. You will have thirty minutes to get it done." Then Sullivan blew a brass whistle that had been hanging around his neck. Without any hesitation, the remaining eighty-two poopies of Class 569 frantically ran to their rooms.

Striker and Stewart were now the only two left in their room, so they thought correctly placing things would be easier. It wasn't. They seemed to be going in two different directions. They decided that Striker would read the directions, Stewart would follow them, and Striker would help. Just making the beds was very complicated. The sheets and blankets had to be tightly placed on the mattresses with a six-inch fold at the head of the bed, the pillow must be parallel to the folded sheet, six inches away, and there had to be a 45-degree angle fold where the blanket and sheets were tucked in at the foot of the bed and a quarter had to bounce if dropped anywhere on the bed. The uniforms were placed on hangers and in the lockers, so arranging bath soap, adjustable razors, shaving cream, deodorants, toothbrushes, and toothpaste in each medicine cabinet in exact positions was time-consuming. The adjustable razors had to be set on number 5, and the toothpaste tubes had to be inflated after each use to return to their original shape. At the end of thirty minutes, they and many others still weren't done.

Suddenly, a blaring PA system startled everyone in Class 569, "This is your three-minute warning for a room, locker, and personnel inspection." After each minute passed, the warning was blasted again. Then, there was total silence, but it was not comforting. It was unnerving, making the poopies even more anxious. Suddenly, all three Drill Instructors started pounding on the walls with their fists or hitting the doors with swagger sticks before they stormed into individual rooms, got directly into the faces of poopies, and ordered them to recite the general orders or the chain of command, or one of the other many things they were supposed to have memorized. Few poopies could recall the information they were ordered to recite, some because they hadn't memorized it, but mostly because they were so scared. Then, all of them were ordered to get into the hall, where they were told to do 100 squat thrusts, four to a count, and to count them loud enough for the Drill Instructors to hear. Others were told to assume the sitting position against the wall and stay that way until told to stop. Then, they went back into the rooms and started inspecting the lockers and beds. They used rulers to measure the distances to see if everything was aligned and dropped quarters on every bed to see if they bounced. Virtually none of the lockers were without fault, and the beds did not pass the bounce test. The Drill Instructors, now in a rage, proceeded to take every item out of every locker and threw all of it on the floor. Then, they took off the sheets, blankets, and pillowcases and threw them into the same piles.

They returned to the hall and started screaming that the poopies were the stupidest shitbirds on earth and that they were lower than whale shit with no chance of finishing the program. All of them should DOR now before they were a disgrace to the Navy and Marine Corps. Then, they continued to PT the poopies for the better part of an hour. When they stopped, Sullivan ordered them to return to their rooms and prepare for another inspection.

Twenty minutes later, the Drill Instructors went through the same routine with only slightly improved results. This time, Sullivan ordered the class to file into formation in front of the building. Then, the other Drill Instructors led the class on a three-mile run around the base. During the run, a few poopies fell down from exhaustion and were taken to the hospital. Two of them DOR'd and were never seen again. When the eighty remaining poopies returned to the barn, they were ordered to stand at attention and wait for further orders.

Even though everyone in Class 569 was extremely thirsty and tired, they stood motionless. Thirty minutes later, Sullivan barked, "Listen, shitbirds, as soon as I blow this whistle, you will again return to your rooms and prepare for another inspection, this time in fifteen minutes. And the warning for the next inspection will be reduced by a minute. After that, there will be unannounced inspections with no warnings at any time of the day or night. Shitbirds, you will get little or no sleep for the next two days, and you will face more and more inspections and PT. You will get so tired you fall asleep while standing at attention. The next nine days will not be easy; you will do things you never thought you would be able to do, even though every muscle in your body aches, and all you can think about is getting some sleep. If you are unwilling or unable to do this, do not waste my time or yours, DOR." Then he blew his whistle. Only seventy poopies went back to their rooms; the other ten DOR'd.

Striker and Stewart began putting their uniforms and toiletries into the required positions as soon as they were in their room. They had memorized the instructions for the most part, so getting everything done correctly was easier and quicker. They didn't have any quarters, so they dropped a toothbrush on the carefully made beds to see if it bounced, and it did. When the one-minute warning was announced, they were done and spent the last few seconds rechecking their measurements.

The Drill Instructors again pounded on the walls and doors and then screamed questions in the faces of poopies. But this time, only about a third of the rooms failed, and only three or four poopies couldn't recite what was demanded. The PT that followed was less demanding and took only fifteen minutes. For the totally exhausted poopies, it was a much-needed break. At about 2145, they were ordered back to their rooms to prepare for the next day. At exactly midnight, the lights were turned off, and Taps was played on the PA system. All seventy poopies in Class 569 were instantly asleep.

Less than two hours later, the Drill Instructors suddenly turned on all the lights and started beating metal trash can lids together, screaming, "Get up, get up, get up, get out of bed." Followed immediately by, "Get under the bed, get on the bed, get out of the bed, and get under the bed." After about ten minutes, the poopies were allowed to catch their breath for a few seconds and then were abruptly ordered to "get on your bellies" and then suddenly, "get on your backs." They stopped a half-hour later, and the poopies returned to bed. Later that night, they were awakened in the same manner, but this time, they were ordered to fall into formation and march around the base in skivvies for half an hour. When they returned to the barn, they were ordered to line up against the bulkhead. Drill Instructor Johnson pointed at one poopy and told him to recite the general orders. He got it right to the immense relief of the class, and they were ordered to go to bed.

Chapter 5

Wendy, Leah, and Jane Explore Pensacola

Wendy Carmody and Leah Jenkins were raised in Overland Park, Kansas, and were roommates at the University of Kansas in Lawrence. Both girls were very pretty but in different ways. Wendy was tall, about 5'8", very fair, with blue eyes, and long streaked blonde hair that reached the small of her back. Leah was darker, much shorter at 5'2", with brown eyes and shoulder-length brown hair. Both girls met on their high school track team in their sophomore year and have been inseparable ever since. While Wendy tended to be quiet and shy, Leah was outgoing and often impetuous. Both of them loved children and had known that they wanted to be teachers since they were children. They graduated in May 1969: Leah as an elementary school teacher and Wendy as a secondary school science teacher.

Sadly, at only twenty-two, both were recovering from recent terrible heartbreaks. Leah had ended a long-term relationship, and Wendy's fiancé, Roger, had been killed in a car accident the previous May, right before he was supposed to graduate. Wendy was devastated but decided to remain in college. With the help of her family and friends, especially Leah, she continued in school. Now they had both graduated and decided the best thing they could do would be to start new lives somewhere else. They wanted to leave Kansas and find teaching jobs in another part of the country.

One of the places they were interested in was Gainesville, Florida, where Wendy's older sister, Jane, was working on a PhD in mathematics at the University of Florida. Wendy had visited Jane several times while she was in college. She liked the area, especially the many nearby beach towns. So, they decided to go somewhere far away from the frigid winters of Kansas to the welcoming sun of Florida. Without any regrets, they left three days after graduation.

Two days later, on a Thursday evening, they arrived at Jane's apartment in Gainesville. She had a two-bedroom apartment, but a few months earlier, her roommate graduated and moved home. There were still six months left on the lease, so Jane decided to stay alone in the apartment until the lease ended. She hoped to finish her dissertation by that time.

Jane was three years older than Wendy but looked a lot like her. Like Wendy, she was very pretty, about 5'8", with dirty blonde hair. She kept a trim figure by running and doing yoga several times a week. Jane was too busy when the girls arrived to show them around that part of Florida. Wendy and Leah went by themselves to several beach towns; when they found a place that interested them, they stayed a day or two.

Jane didn't have any classes one week on Friday and Monday, so she suggested they go to the Florida panhandle, about three hundred miles west. She also suggested they first go to Panama City and Pensacola Beach. After she finished on Thursday afternoon, they took her convertible to Panama City. Almost six hours later, they had stopped to eat and checked into a motel to get some sleep.

The next morning, they drove into town and looked at potential places to work and live. It looked promising, but they decided to look at the beach. They found a beautiful public beach but saw mostly teenagers, families, and very few men their age. They decided to continue their search.

They headed west but didn't stop at Fort Walton Beach; they would return if things didn't work out in Pensacola Beach. They drove along Route 98 and saw the azure blue Gulf and long stretches of deserted beaches. It was even more beautiful as they got closer to Santa Rosa Island and Navarre. They arrived in Pensacola Beach at about noon, stopped at a parking lot that had the most cars, and followed people to the beach.

As they walked on the beach, they were amazed by how much the sand looked and felt like sugar. It even squeaked when they walked on it. More importantly, there were men their age scattered everywhere. After looking around for about an hour, they were getting hungry. Jane took them to the Tiki Bar, one of her favorite places. Both girls instantly loved the place; it was on the beach with an unobstructed view of the Gulf. Wendy said, "This place is gorgeous; let's grab that table close to the water." As she looked around, Leah could not help but notice that most of the people in the bar were young men, some in uniform. She asked Jane if there was a military base nearby. Jane smiled and replied, "Sure is, Pensacola Naval Air Station. It's where the Navy trains new officers and pilots. All of them are college grads and are in great shape. I'm sure you've already noticed that. Most will only be here for a couple of years, then be transferred elsewhere. I dated one of them for several months. His name is Tim Connors, and he brought me here often. We met at a party in Gainesville. He had earned a Master's degree in aeronautical engineering and was in Navy flight training. He's a great guy; we were crazy about each other. We broke up when he was transferred to San Diego because neither of us wanted a long-distance relationship. I had just started working on a PhD, and he would soon be going to sea for a year or more. He was so proud; he'd been selected for F-4s, the aircraft he had worked so hard to get. I was happy for him, but it seemed like a doomed relationship from the beginning." Then Jane paused for a few seconds, "If things had been different, I know we would have gotten seriously involved. I still think about him all the time, and I miss him." Then she looked at her sister, smiled, and said, "That's one of the reasons why I brought you here, Wendy. If you're looking for a beautiful beach, great nightlife, and lots of young single guys, you can't beat Pensacola Beach. I'm sure you could get teaching jobs here." Wendy and Leah both smiled, and Wendy said, "I love this place; let's find somewhere to stay for a couple of nights and take a look around." An hour later, they found some beachfront cabins and checked into one.

As soon as they brought in their bags and cleaned themselves up, Jane showed them some of the places at the beach, including Dirty Joe's Saloon. Later, they drove past the Pier Lounge, over the Santa Rosa Sound, and the Three Mile Bridge into Pensacola.

Once in town, Jane showed them the Seville Quarter section of downtown, with the nearby Rosie O' Grady's, Phineas Phog's, and Trader Jon's; then further out of town, Shakey's Pizza, Lum's, Morrison's Cafeteria, Al's Castle Bar, and Mrs. Hopkins Boarding House. Finally, she drove them to the base and pointed out the Mustin Beach Officers' Club, the aircraft carrier Lexington, Barrancas Beach, the Blue Angels' hangar, the Chapel, and the Barrancas National Cemetery. Along the way, they saw dozens of officer candidates running or marching in formation while Marine Corps Drill Instructors yelled orders at them. When they left the base, it was almost 8 pm, and they stopped at McGuire's Irish Pub to get a sandwich and a couple of beers and to listen to a tenor named Tommy

27

O'Shea singing sorrowful Irish folk songs. After a great day, they headed back to the cabin.

Chapter 6

Jane, Leah, and Wendy

After a good night's sleep, Jane, Wendy, and Leah went to a small nearby diner for breakfast. When they finished eating, they planned their day and drove into town. On a map Jane had in the car, they found the location of the Escambia County Board of Education and decided to start there. Since it was Saturday, they knew it probably wouldn't be open, but there might be a bulletin board somewhere with a list of teaching vacancies and how to apply. After some errant turns, they found the main Board of Education Building, parked in a nearly vacant lot, and walked to the front door. There was an unlocked lobby with a glass cabinet and sign entitled 'Personnel Vacancies,' Wendy had pen and paper in hand when she read over the list with Leah. There were only temporary or substitute teaching positions available at both the secondary and elementary schools, but the bulletin went on to say that any interested person should apply for both full and part-time positions for the next school year.   There was a stack of application forms in a box below the list.

As Wendy was copying down the information, a woman walked in the front door, carrying a bulging briefcase. She saw the three women and asked if she could help them. She introduced herself as Sarah Feldman, the Director of Educator Recruitment for the school district. She explained, "I've been on a statewide recruiting trip and just got back. I came into the office to sort through some of the applications. Are you three looking for teaching jobs?" Jane replied, "I'm not, but my sister Wendy and her roommate, Leah, are. I'm Jane, and I'm in grad school at the University of Florida." Sarah waved at them and said, "Y'all come with me to my office, and we can talk about what's available." Then she unlocked the door and led them down the hall to a conference room near her office. She said, "Go on in and have a seat, and I'll be back in a couple of minutes. I'm going to unload these apps on my desk." All three young women went into the conference room, and Wendy said, "Talk about being in the right place at the right time. What a stroke of luck."

Sarah was back with some information packets and blank applications. She sat down at the end of the table, introduced herself again, and gave each of them her business card. Then, she asked Leah and Wendy about the types of jobs they were interested in. Leah said she was interested in an Elementary School teaching job, and Wendy said she'd love to have any available Secondary School Science teaching vacancy. Sarah thought for a minute and said, "There is bad news and good news, first the bad news. Our staffing levels are currently full, but we will need substitute teachers in both areas. I can almost guarantee that you will both be in a classroom at least four out of five school days a week. The good news is at least fifty teachers in the district will be eligible for retirement in the next four months, and we have about ten teachers whose husbands are in the Navy or Marine Corps who could be transferred soon. Finally, in addition to those anticipated vacancies, there is usually at least a five percent attrition rate every year. So, if you want a job this fall, it will probably be a substitute position until full-time positions become available. There is no doubt that substitutes have a head start over most other applicants when vacancies do become available. So, if you are interested, fill out an application and give me your address and phone number. As soon as I can, I'll get back to you. You can use this room to complete the applications and leave them on the table.

The front exit door locks automatically as you leave. I'll probably be here two or three hours, so if you have any questions, just come to my office."

Jane then asked Wendy, "Well, what do you think?" Wendy smiled and said, "I think I'm going to fill out an application and look for an apartment." Leah, "I'm with you." They spent the next hour and a half filling out applications. The salary scale and benefits package were comparable to those in Kansas, but here, they had warm weather, a beautiful beach, and a lot of young single men. They turned in their applications.

Chapter 7

Connors and Riley Deploy

Timothy Connors was born and raised in Melbourne, Florida, where he grew up watching many NASA launches from Cape Canaveral, about twenty miles north. He dreamed of being on one of the giant rockets he saw lifting off. He was a good student in high school and played on the varsity baseball team. He was an all-state player and even thought about pursuing a professional baseball career, but math and science were his priorities. After graduating from high school in 1961, he went to the University of Florida to become an Aeronautical Engineer. He excelled in college and earned a full scholarship and assistantship to pursue a master's degree. While finishing his Master's degree in the spring of 1967, he read the biographies of the Mercury Seven astronauts and noticed that many of them were Naval Aviators who had attended the Navy Test Pilot School. When he finished his Master's degree, he went to a Navy recruiter to find out how to become a Naval Aviator. The recruiters told him about AOCS, and he decided to apply. Before the week ended, he passed the exam, physical, and interview, and ten days later, he was accepted. He began AOCS in mid-September 1967. His class officer was a highly decorated helicopter pilot who had just returned from his second tour in Vietnam. His name was Marine Captain Stephen Pless.

Connors was commissioned as an Ensign in January 1968. About a year later, he had completed primary and advanced flight training, earned his Wings of Gold and was an F-4 pilot. As he waited for orders, he was assigned to the Replacement

Air Group (RAG) at Miramar Naval Air Station, 15 miles north of San Diego. Two weeks later, he was in VF-125 and would soon be assigned to the USS Kitty Hawk, CVA 63, whose home base was North Island NAS, San Diego.

While he was in the RAG, Connors reunited with an AOCS classmate, Clint Riley, a fellow engineer from Texas Tech University. Riley was 6'2", razor-thin, and a proud Texan who preferred bootcut jeans and rode a Harley-Davidson. He spoke in a slow southern drawl and chose his words carefully. Even though he was a son of Texas, he had an Irishman's sparkle in his eyes and a devilish sense of humor. Like many candidates, he attended AOCS expecting to be a pilot, but the ophthalmologist found scar tissue in his retina during his eye examination. Riley confided to Connors that he knew he had a vision problem. His older brother had accidentally hit him in the eye with a BB, and it was never the same. He was medically disqualified from pilot training but decided to continue AOCS to become an NFO.

Riley and Connors were roommates beginning the week after INDOC, and Riley finished third to Connors first in their class rankings. He received his NFO wings as an F-4 RIO before Connors received his, but a backup in the RAG delayed his assignment to a squadron. When Connors found out, he asked the Commanding Officer of the RAG if Riley could be assigned with him to VF-125, and the CO agreed.

In early November 1968, VF-125, along with the 70 aircraft of the Air Wing, was assigned to the aircraft carrier Kitty Hawk. The carrier's mission was to be part of Task Force 81 to support Marine and Army combat operations on targets in North Vietnam.

In mid-November, Kitty Hawk steamed out of San Diego. Except for a brief layover at Subic Bay, Philippines, the Kitty Hawk sailed directly to Yankee Station and began combat operations. Even during bad weather, the Kitty Hawk launched dozens of combat sorties every week. In the next few months, the number of American soldiers deployed to Vietnam was at its highest, and the number of sorties increased enormously. Connors and Riley completed nearly 100 combat sorties and 200 carrier traps during that period.

Missions over North Vietnam usually required pilots to evade anti-aircraft gunfire and missiles. One of the missions assigned to Connors and Riley was to destroy a new North Vietnamese air base and its surrounding anti-aircraft missile sites. As they approached the target, Riley's radar lit up, indicating that they were being tracked by a surface to air missile emplacement. Riley quickly told Connors to watch for incoming missiles. Seconds later, Riley yelled, "Two bogeys locked on and launched." Suddenly, about 5000 feet below them, what looked like two burning telephone poles were streaking toward them. Immediately, Connors deployed chaff and flares to counter both heat-seeking and radar-controlled missiles. Then he pushed his yoke back, and his F-4 went into a steep dive toward them. Less than five seconds later, they passed the missiles going up as they streaked down. Almost simultaneously, Connors kicked into the afterburner and pulled the aircraft into a high-performance climb, nearly straight up to 30,000 feet. Then he suddenly dove down again, leveled out at 20,000 feet, and cut their airspeed back to 500 knots. For the next few minutes, Connors and Riley closely scanned the sky and radar for any sign of bogeys. When they saw none, they resumed a heading to the North Vietnamese target.

It was a clear day when they approached the NVA base. They descended to 5000 feet where they saw two aircraft taxiing towards the runway. Connors advised the other two F-4s in the sortie that he was going to engage the enemy aircraft while they engaged the base and anti-aircraft emplacements, then as one aircraft, a MiG-19, was nearing the runway. Riley said. "That son of a bitch is coming up after us. Let's take him out, Connors. It's an easy kill." Connors reminded Riley that the rules of engagement prevented them from engaging enemy aircraft on the ground; they had to be airborne and in their line of sight. So, at the enormous risk of attracting more missiles, Connors climbed and circled the base while the MIG approached the numbers. Riley, now pissed, yelled, "Damn, politicians don't know combat from cow shit. I sure don't see any of them here putting their pansy asses in danger." Just then, Connors saw the first MiG fire up its afterburners and begin to make a high-performance takeoff. "He's mine now." Connors said as he turned the F-4 so that it would be on the MiG's tail. Riley screamed, "I got him, target locked on, let's rock and roll." Connors immediately fired two sidewinders. About five seconds later, the first missile hit its target, and the MiG-19 was a tumbling ball of fire. Then the second MiG fired up its engines, and Connors wrestled his F-4 around and fired two more sidewinders, which hit the second bogey after it lifted off. Riley hooted, cheered, and then quickly checked to see if any radar was tracking them. Confident that they weren't, but seeing they were at Bingo fuel, they returned to the carrier.

Twenty minutes later, they were safely on the Kitty Hawk. After climbing out of the cockpit, they high-fived each other and the ground crew. Back in the ready room, the CO congratulated them, awarded them combat air medals, and told them he had recommended them for bronze stars. There was no further celebration; combat operations continued the same

35

as they had for weeks. In late May 1969, the Kitty Hawk departed Yankee Station and headed back to San Diego.

Chapter 8

The Second Day of INDOC

The second day of INDOC began at 0400 as the Drill Instructors ran up and down the halls screaming, "Get up, get up, get up, get out of bed." They then banged trash can lids and screamed, "You shitbirds have ten minutes to fall into formation in front of the building." Four poopies suddenly DOR'd, reducing Class 569 to sixty-six. Unfazed, Drill Instructor Wilson led the remaining class on a four-mile run around the base. When it ended, First Sergeant Sullivan ordered them to clean up and be back in formation in fifteen minutes. Twenty minutes later, they marched to the mess hall for breakfast. When they finished eating, the class marched to the 'grinder,' a wide concrete tarmac about a half-mile from the USS Lexington.

Sullivan led them past battle-damaged and wrecked aircraft waiting to be taken to the Naval Rework Facility. Sullivan barked as they went by them, "This is a place of honor. Naval and Marine officers were wounded or killed in these aircraft. They were doing their duty, what they were trained to do. They were Naval and Marine Aviators, the best the world has ever seen. It is my job to mold some of you shitbirds into officers like they were. It is my high honor to be chosen to do that, and I will do everything I know to succeed in that mission. Whenever you think the program is too hard or you hurt too much to go any further, think about this place, the aircraft, and the men who flew them. Most of them were here, in this program. They stayed in the same barn, ate the same chow, and marched in the same places, including where we now stand.

They had the same doubts, felt the same fatigue, the same pain, that you feel, and they made it. They had the right stuff. Some of you do, too. I will do my best to find out which maggots have it and which do not." Sullivan then drilled the Class near the damaged aircraft for an hour, then double-timed them to the Water Survival Tank.

At the water survival building, Sullivan ordered Class 569 to line up inside the building on the right side of the tank. On one end of the twelve-foot-deep tank was the Dilbert Dunker, a facsimile of an aircraft cockpit, complete with an instrument console and canopy. On the opposite side of the Dunker were two platforms, one 3 meters high and the other 10 meters. On the left of the platforms was a ladder up to a catwalk leading to a small platform over the center of the tank.

The Dilbert Dunker was sitting on a platform about twelve feet above the pool. It was on a diagonal ramp with rails, allowing it to roll into the water, sink several feet underwater, and invert. Candidates in flight suits, helmets, and masks had to strap in, close the canopy, and roll down into the water. It inverted as soon as the dunker was three or four feet underwater. The candidate had to pull back the canopy, unstrap, climb out, and swim to the surface without any help. Surrounding the dunker, divers were ready to help anyone who got into trouble. About half of the candidates had to be pulled to the surface and taken out of the tank. Those candidates who reached the surface without help were rewarded by having to tread water for a minute with both index fingers held above the surface. Everyone had three attempts to complete the process. Failure to do it without assistance meant automatic disqualification from the program.

On that day, they would only have their swimming skills evaluated. Dilbert Dunker testing was scheduled for the week after they completed INDOC. After everyone had lined up on the deck, Sullivan began, "Every Aviation Officer Candidate must be a good swimmer, including completing the Dunker and swimming a mile in a flight suit. If you do not want to or cannot successfully meet these requirements, DOR now before we begin. Anyone who knows that he cannot swim, but does not want to DOR, stand aside now. At my order, the first twenty-two poopies will remove your boots and line up across the side of the tank without the Dunker. When I blow my whistle, you will jump in and swim, any way you can, to the other side of the tank and back, then tread water until I blow my whistle again. This is not a race, and it will not be timed. At my command, the second group of twenty-two poopies will do the same thing. The process will continue until everyone is out of the pool."

Before he blew his whistle, six poopies DOR'd, and four more stepped out of line and said they could not swim but wanted to remain in the program. Swim instructors took the six who DOR'd to a separate room. The four who could not swim were held back from the class and given a week of intensive swimming instruction in "Stupid School." If they learned how to adequately swim in that week, they would join the next class. Class 569 was now 56 poopies.

Everybody made it without assistance, but Stewart struggled the entire time he was in the water and had a difficult time getting out. Sullivan began to doubt that he would be able to swim the required mile.

There was no rest. The class had to climb up the ladder and follow the catwalk to the small platform above the center of the tank. When the first candidate reached the platform, Sullivan barked, "You will cross your arms diagonally over your chest and cross your legs. When I blow the whistle, you will jump, swim at least fifty feet underwater, swim on the surface to the edge of the tank, and tread water until I order you to stop." Sullivan blew his whistle, and the first poopy jumped. He waited until the poopy swam on the surface before he blew the whistle again. Stewart, who was in front of Striker, hesitated a few seconds before he stepped out onto the platform. Striker growled, "Get on the platform." Stewart whispered, "Dear God," and trembled on the platform. When the whistle sounded, Stewart jumped into the water and went straight to the bottom. For a few seconds, it looked like he would have to be pulled out. But somehow, he thrashed 50 feet, clumsily swam to the side of the tank, and started to tread water. He sank several times before Sullivan ordered him to stop. When he got out, Sullivan yelled, "You OK, Stewart? That was some crazy shit you just did. You can't swim very well, can you?" Stewart stood up, came to attention, and said, "Not too good. Drill Instructor Sullivan." Sullivan replied, "Then why in hell did you jump in the water? You almost drowned." Stewart, with tears in his eyes, "Because this Officer Candidate didn't want to be held back. This Officer Candidate wants to finish INDOC with Class 569 and continue in the program." Silently, Sullivan responded, "Stewart, I'll be watching you real close whenever you are in the water. If you show any more distress, I will immediately disqualify you. No candidate is going to drown on my watch. And you won't make it through AOCS if you can't swim better than you did today. Do you understand?" Stewart responded, "Yes, sir," and quickly joined the Class against the bulkhead.

Sullivan ordered the class to get in formation in front of the building. As soon as they did, he stood in front of them and said, almost in a normal voice. "Some would call what Stewart did reckless, even crazy. But I saw it as his complete dedication to making it through AOCS to become a Naval Aviator. He went about it in a dangerous, even stupid way, but his intention was clear. He was willing to risk his life to stay with the program, to become a Naval Aviator. I'm willing to bet my career that he will. He has the right stuff."

Sullivan marched the class around the base until their poopy suits began to dry. Although not totally dry, he finally led them to the mess hall. After they ate, the class marched back to the barn, where Sullivan ordered them to prepare for an inspection in fifteen minutes.

As they walked back to the room, Striker asked Stewart if he knew how to swim. Stewart answered, "I do, but I am still terrified of being in the water. I panic as soon as I get in. I even took a swimming class in college to overcome my fears, but it still happens, especially in stressful situations. I know that I can beat it, especially after what the Drill Sergeant said today." Striker gave him an encouraging pat on the back.

Once in their room, Striker and Stewart saw that the instruction sheet was gone. They looked at each other, and Stewart shook his head and moaned, "We are in a world of hurt." Striker said it was done on purpose and started to put things in place as best as possible. Ten minutes later, they looked the place over. Striker, "It looks pretty good, but I'm sure we screwed up something." With nothing left to do, they stood at attention at the foot of their beds and waited for the inevitable.

There was no warning, and the wait went on seemingly without end. Then they heard screaming and footsteps up and down the hall and then silence. They flinched when Sullivan suddenly smashed his swagger stick on the door and entered the room. He looked around, went to the locker, measured the distances between every item, and looked at the razor to check if it was set on the right number. Then he dropped a quarter on the bed behind Stewart, and it did not bounce. "In the passageway, now, maggots brace up against the bulkhead." They both ran through the door and flattened against the wall. Striker saw that many poopies were already there. Then he got into Stewart's face and screamed at him. "Can't you follow simple ass directions, maggot?" and Stewart remained silent. Sullivan screamed even louder, "Answer me, shit bird, can't you speak? Are you mute or just a stupid shit?" Stewart, beginning to get rattled, yelled back. "Yes, Drill Sergeant, this candidate can speak, and I just screwed up." And Sullivan went ballistic, "Drill Sergeant? Are you suicidal, maggot? Don't you remember my instructions? I broke both legs of the last dumb shit who called me that. You also used the forbidden word 'I.' Give me five hundred squat thrusts, four to a count, now, before I turn your scrawny ass inside out." Stewart immediately began counting squat thrusts while Sullivan screamed at him, "I can't hear you, maggot. Count louder." Then Sullivan ordered the entire class to get in the hall and do 100 side straddle hops, four to a count. When they were finished, they were ordered to assume the sitting position against the wall. They stayed there for over 30 minutes. Then Sullivan went into Stewart and Striker's room and threw all of Stewart's linens outside the window. He next told Stewart, who was nearing exhaustion, to stop, get the linens, and then run around the barn until he was ordered to stop. Sullivan then ordered the rest of the class to get into formation next to the sand pit.

When Stewart arrived, Sullivan ordered him to stop running, dig a hole in the sand, and bury all the bedding. When that was done, Stewart had to get on his hands and knees, put his head back, and howl like a dog. Then he had to dig up the linens, take them to the laundry, get clean ones, and rejoin the formation. The rest of the class could not restrain their laughter, especially when they could hear Stewart howling in the barn. After Stewart returned, Sullivan ordered him to stop howling and start barking.

Sullivan then ordered the class to return to their rooms and prepare for another inspection in 15 minutes. Stewart kept barking even when he made his bed, and his roommates could not help but chuckle. Fifteen minutes later, Sullivan came to their room and dropped a quarter on Stewart's bed. To his relief, the quarter bounced. Sullivan ordered Stewart to stop barking and left. From that day on, Stewart was known as "Hound."

At 1600, Sullivan led them to the grinder, where they marched for two hours. At about 1800, they stopped and went to the mess hall for dinner. Several poopies barked at Stewart as they went by him. Always good-natured, Hound couldn't help but smile. After they finished eating, the class marched to a large field near the grinder. Striker noticed there was an ambulance parked next to it and wondered what more the Drill Instructors could do to make their lives miserable. He would soon find out.

After they halted next to the field, Sullivan told them that Gunnery Sergeant Johnson would now be in command of the class for some "recreation." The huge field looked like a football field but was almost twice as big. The only lines on it were at the ends, the sides, and in the middle. Gunnery Sergeant Johnson stood on the centerline next to a heavy rubber ball that was about four feet in diameter. He ordered them to form a single file and count off. When the counting ended at fifty-six, Johnson barked as loud as he could, "Listen carefully, Maggots. You are now going to play a game invented by the Marine Corps. It's called murder ball. The first twenty-eight poopies will put on one of these red vests, and the rest will put on yellow. This is how you play the game. The red team will line upon the left end line of the field and the yellow on the right line. When I blow my whistle, each team will run as fast as they can to the ball and attempt to get it, any way they can, across the center line and to the opposite side of the field. You will continue trying until I blow the whistle again. Here are the rules; there are no damn rules." Then he blew the whistle.

In less than ten seconds, 56 poopies were engaged in a giant free-for-all in which they were pushing, shoving, and tackling each other with little effect on the ball. The giant scrum became a brutal melee each time one side seemed to move the ball closer to the opposite end line. Tempers flared, and punches were thrown. The mayhem lasted another 10 minutes and was rapidly getting out of control; poopies began to seriously hurt each other. Neither team had moved the ball anywhere near the opposite side of the field.

Finally, Johnson stopped the violence with a blast from his whistle and ordered the Class to get back in formation. Four poopies remained on the ground with injured limbs, and three had nosebleeds. Nearly all of them had bruises and cuts. Three more ambulances arrived, and corpsmen rushed to the injured poopies. Those with nosebleeds were treated on the field and released, but the four with more serious injuries were taken to the hospital. No one who was taken to the hospital returned to Class 569, reducing it to 52 poopies.

When the remaining class returned to the barn, Sullivan rearranged some of the room assignments and put Sticky in with Striker and Hound. He then ordered the class to line up outside the shower room, "Sullivan, on my command, you will remove your boots, place them directly against the bulkhead, then march in close order behind the poopy in front of you into the shower room. The first poopy in line will turn the water on each shower. Then, everyone else will follow until the line gets back to the first shower. Then, you will begin again until you have been around twice. As you march through the showers, you will remove your clothes, wash them, put them back on, and then exit the shower room. Then you will return to your boots, pick them up, and await further orders."

Striker, like everyone else, had a difficult time marching, removing his clothes, washing them, showering himself, and then putting his clothes back on, all at the same time. It was his first shower in almost 30 hours of intense physical activity, and it felt great. When everyone had their boots, they were ordered to return to their rooms, hang up their wet clothes, and put on dry ones. When finished, they were told to stand at attention in front of their beds and wait for further orders.

Ten minutes later, Sullivan ordered the Class to report to the quarterdeck. Several corpsmen were there to treat blistered feet from ill-fitting boots and minor cuts and abrasions caused by playing murder ball. Since virtually all the poopies needed some form of treatment, it was almost 2130 when everyone was done. Everyone was allowed to sleep until Reveille the next morning when they returned to their rooms. It was the first time they slept through the night in INDOC.

Chapter 9
INDOC Ends

The harassment increased over the next eight days. On several occasions, poopies collapsed after being PT'd for using a forbidden word, being out of step, or forgetting an item that they were supposed to have memorized. Inspections were unannounced and almost always included PT or forced marches. The constant fatigue and endless harassment became too much for several poopies to endure, and they DOR'd. When INDOC ended, Class 569 had 42 candidates.

Striker woke up to Reveille on March 21 at 0400. It was the second time in INDOC that Class 569 was not suddenly awakened by a Drill Instructor screaming orders. Reveille was now almost reassuring, a welcome greeting at dawn. His good mood was quickly ended by the all too familiar barking of First Sergeant Sullivan, "Get your worthless dog asses out of your racks and in formation in fifteen minutes. There are empty baskets in the quarterdeck. Each one of you will get one to take to your room. Then you will place your second poopy suit, skivvies, and toiletries into the basket and immediately take it downstairs and get into a formation at the front of the barn."

Striker looked at Sticky and said, "I think we're getting out of this place; we made it through INDOC. There were times when I thought I couldn't make it one more hour of this shit. Now I think I can make it through the next fourteen weeks." Then they both smiled and slapped high fives. As Hound put his gear in a basket, he said, "I have a mantra that I began in the first few hours of INDOC. I just repeat to myself, "They may make me feel like I want to die, but they can't kill me."

Then he looked at his roommates and said, "And they're gonna have to kill me to get me out of this damn program." They picked up their baskets, ran downstairs, and got into formation.

In front of INDOC, Sullivan barked, "At my command, you will march to the Supply Shop, where you will leave the basket of clothing. Then a clerk will ask your size and hand each of you AOCS uniforms, gym clothes, covers, and shoes. Then we will proceed to Building 200." While they marched, Striker stole a last look at INDOC and said to himself, "If I had known what happened in that hell hole, I probably would not have volunteered for AOCS."

Chapter 10

Wendy and Leah

Sarah Feldman notified Wendy and Leah that they were both selected to be substitute teachers. Wendy would be substituting high school science at a school near the Pensacola side of the bridge to Gulf Breeze, and Leah got a job substituting at a new Elementary school in Gulf Breeze. Feldman also told them that she was relatively certain that both would be offered full-time jobs in the Spring, probably at the schools where they were substituting.

They found an apartment on the bay in Gulf Breeze. Their two-bedroom, two-bath apartment was in a three-story complex that had a community swimming pool and balconies on the bay. It was on the second floor with an unobstructed view of sunsets. Most of the other people who lived there were Naval and Marine Aviators, many with families. It was a quiet complex, close to work and the beach, and exactly what they needed.

During the first few weeks, they lived in Gulf Breeze, they didn't feel comfortable going to unfamiliar local bars or clubs. So, Wendy called Jane and asked if she could recommend a few places where she and Connors used to go. Jane immediately suggested the Ready Room and Trader Jon's as the most popular place for Naval Aviators. She also told them that her favorite place on the beach was the Tiki Bar, and the wildest place was the nearby Dirty Joe's Saloon, which was a cross between a college bar and a biker joint. The only difference was the bikers were Naval Aviators acting like college kids.

One Friday, Wendy and Leah decided to check out Trader Jon's. Leah got off at 3:30 pm, but Wendy's high school was on a two-shift system that ended at 5. After Wendy got home and changed her clothes, they drove to the Seville section of town in Leah's Mustang convertible. When they arrived at Trader Jon's, they didn't realize there were two entrances; one was to the bar, and the other was to a theater that advertised a 'Vaudeville' show. They bought tickets and went in without paying much attention to the billboards that displayed the night's acts. It didn't take long for them to realize that the main act was a magician who made her clothes disappear. Mortified, they quickly left, laughed as they got into Leah's car, and headed to the Ready Room.

They easily found their way to the entrance to the Naval Air Station. When they stopped at the visitor's gate, Leah smiled at the Marine guard and sweetly told him that they were meeting dates at the Officers' Club. The Marine looked them over, smiled, and waved them in, saying, "Have a good time, ladies." As Leah drove away, she giggled and said, "He was really cute. If the guys at the Ready Room are as cute, this could be a very good time."

Mustin Beach Officers' Club was just as they remembered it, except that the cars were parked everywhere, many of them new Corvettes, the preferred car for newly commissioned officers. After they parked, they walked in the club's front door and immediately saw that the Ready Room was packed. A lot of men were standing outside the ballroom or by the swimming pool, waiting to enter.

As she looked around, Wendy noted that the room was filled with young men in white or khaki uniforms. They looked like they were all cut from the same mold. She smiled and thought they looked like a flock of penguins standing together

49

on an island. She learned later that the uniforms were the "Class A" uniforms required by the club.

As they waited to enter the bar, a waitress asked if she could get them something to drink. They each ordered a glass of white wine. Before the waitress got back, a young Marine, who was standing close by, came over to the girls and said, "Hi, my name is Fred. What's yours?" Before either one of them could answer, he asked if he could get them something to drink. Leah thought he was cute, but he looked like he had just turned eighteen. He had gold bars on his shirt collars, so she assumed he was an officer. Leah just smiled and said, "Thanks, but we just ordered something." Undeterred, Fred immediately asked both for their names again. Leah smiled and said, "I'm Leah, and my friend is Wendy. We're looking for our dates. Do you know Lt. Lewis or Lt. Anderson?" Fred frowned and said, "No, I don't, but if I see them, I'll tell them you're here." He turned and left. Wendy then whispered in Leah's ear, "Who are Lewis and Anderson, and why did you tell him that?" Leah smiled and said," I just made them up. My dad told me never to pick the first horse out of the gate, and Fred was the first horse. From what I've seen so far, there are a lot of horses in this race, and I'm going to wait and find a real stud." Wendy turned red, and they both laughed.

Soon, they squeezed into the Ready Room near the bar. Luckily, the waitress saw them and brought them their drinks. As she began walking away, Leah asked if she was from Pensacola. The waitress stopped and said that she was and would graduate in May from the University of West Florida. Then she said her name was Gina Martinez, and she had worked her way through college at the Ready Room. Leah introduced herself and Wendy and told Gina they recently graduated from college and moved to Pensacola to teach. Then

she added, "Could I give you a call sometime to talk about the area, especially the night life?" Gina said, "I'll do better than that. My shift ends after happy hour is over, and we can talk. Then it would be better to go elsewhere because the guys here will endlessly hound you. I'm sure you've noticed it's about twenty men to a woman, and it's like this every night. There's plenty of time to find Mr. Wonderful." Then she showed them her wedding ring. "I'm not married, but the ring scares most of them away. Otherwise, I wouldn't be able to walk across the room without some brand-new ensign who thinks he's Paul Newman hitting on me. By the way, I am engaged to a Navy pilot who is now at Yankee Station. His tour will be over in about two months, and we're getting married in July." Leah said, "Congratulations. We'll finish our drinks; when you're ready to leave, we'll meet up outside." Gina gave them a thumbs-up and went back to work.

Forty-five minutes later and about a dozen unsolicited drink offers, the girls saw Gina wave. As they followed her out, Wendy noticed several people standing around a Marine officer sitting at the bar. She thought to herself that he must be somebody important.

Chapter 11

AOCS Starts

When they arrived at the Supply Shop, the class formed a single file line inside the building. A clerk asked each poopy what their sizes were and placed the appropriate uniforms, visored hats, and shoes in their basket. Twenty minutes later, they were approaching Building 200, the Third Battalion, their home for the next fourteen weeks.

Sullivan brought Class 569 to a halt in front of Building 200 and barked, "At my command, you will form a single file and count out from the first in line to the last. I will then assign every four of you to a room, where you will put the poopy suits in the basket and put on khaki uniforms. Place the other items precisely where the instruction sheet indicates. When you are dressed, take the poopy suits to the meeting room. put them in the indicated area and prepare for a room, locker, and personnel inspection in twenty minutes." Sullivan then blew his whistle.

Striker, Hound, Sticky, and a candidate named Joshua Schnider were assigned to a room. Schnider was from central Pennsylvania and had graduated from West Chester State University located outside of Philadelphia. He was shorter than the other three, about 5' 6" and 160 lbs., but was heavily muscled. Striker later learned that he was an all-state wrestler in high school and an All-American in his junior and senior years in college. After the three other roommates introduced themselves to Schnider, they carefully changed their uniforms.

They soon realized that wearing khakis was much more complicated than wearing poopy suits, but wearing a uniform was encouraging. It gave them a reason to believe they could make it through the program. There were no mirrors in the room, but the roommates smiled at each other when they saw them in their new uniforms.

The screaming and pounding began with no warning, and Striker's heart momentarily raced. A few seconds later, he calmed down; ten days of INDOC harassment trained him how to control his anxiety. He was ready for the inspection and the consequences.

Sullivan surprised Striker and his roommates by entering their room silently. He slowly walked around the small room dropped a quarter on Striker's bed, and it barely bounced. Then he looked into Schnider's locker, checked the razor, and measured the distance between each item. Still silent, he got in front of Sticky and checked the length of the belt in front of his buckle. Because it was a half-inch short, he suddenly got in Sticky's face and barked, "Can't you follow directions, Mr. Hickey? Haven't you learned how to pay attention to detail after ten fun-filled days in INDOC? Do you want to repeat INDOC shit bird? I can arrange that right now, but I will give you another chance to redeem yourself. What is today's password? What are the general orders?" Sticky, without any hesitation, answered the two questions as if he were giving his phone number and address to a friend.

Back in his face, Sullivan screamed, "I understand that you are called Sticky, Mr. Hickey. Why is that? Do your fingers ooze some sticky shit? Are you a kleptomaniac? Do your feet stick in your shoes or your pants to your legs? Or do your lips stick together when your mouth is shut? Tell me now before I get sticky, too." Sticky answered, "Drill Instructor Sullivan, this candidate believes he is called Sticky because his name is really Steve Hickey, and Sticky just stuck," Sullivan, almost smiling, said. "That sounds like bullshit to me, Mr. Hickey. Even Mr. Stewart knows why he is called Hound and is dog-ass stupid. Prove it Mr. Stewart, start barking." And Hound began barking. Then Sullivan continued, "Mr. Hickey, I think you need to take some time to recall why you are called Sticky and how to properly wear your web belt. Get your ass in a sitting position up against the outside bulkhead. Now." Sticky bolted out the door and got against the wall. About forty-five minutes later, Sullivan came back. Sticky was shaking and involuntarily slipped down the wall. Sullivan ordered him to get to his feet and get back to his room. Sticky could barely stand up straight, and he hobbled into the room as fast as he could. Sullivan stuck his head in the room and barked, "Next time, Mr. Hickey, if you do not pay attention to detail, you will go back to INDOC for a ten-day refresher course." He then ordered Hound to stop barking and for the entire class to fall into formation in front of the barn in fifteen minutes. When Sullivan was gone, Sticky sat on his bed for a few seconds, got up, stretched his legs, and said, "Now that was fun."

When everyone in Class 569 was in formation, First Sergeant Sullivan walked out of the Third Battalion with a Lieutenant who had Naval Aviator Wings. Sullivan stood on the front porch of the barn and said, "Gentlemen, welcome to AOCS. You're not poopies anymore, you are finally Aviation Officer Candidates. From now on until you finish, you will be called Mister or Candidate, followed by your last name. But, life in AOCS will not get any easier for at least fourteen more weeks. You will be tested in every way possible and will endure the same inspections, PT, and lack of sleep you experienced for the last 10 days. INDOC was just the introduction to the main act. I can assure you that I will continue to do my job with Marine Corps precision, just as I did in INDOC. As time goes on, some of you will be unwilling or unable to meet the challenges, and you will be separated from the program."

"Now, I want to introduce my boss and your class officer, Lieutenant Charles Emmet, who is an F-4 Pilot. He just finished an eight-month WestPac tour, completing 85 combat sorties, mostly over North Vietnam. He is also an instructor in VT-4, where some of you will learn how to fly Naval aircraft if that is humanly possible."

Then Lt. Emmet stepped in front of the class and said, "Welcome to AOCS, gentlemen. This is a special place, one where you will make lifelong friends and great memories. Whenever you come back here, you will be at your Navy home, the place where you became a man and a Naval Aviator. I know what I am talking about. I finished AOCS almost four years ago. I lived in the building behind me, the same place you will live starting today. I know what happened to you in INDOC and what will happen to you in the weeks to come. I also know that some of you will not finish. Almost seventy percent of my class did not. Just remember this. Every day I was in AOCS, I did the very best I could. I expect nothing less from each of you. As you were."

Chapter 12

Connors and Riley in Subic Bay

On the way back to San Diego, the Kitty Hawk stopped for two days in Subic Bay to refuel and replenish supplies. The officers and crew were given a forty-eight-hour liberty, the first time anyone was allowed to go on shore during the cruise. Connors had heard a lot of stories about Olongapo, where Subic Bay Navy Base was located. Most of those stories centered on the anything-goes bars and clubs in downtown Olongapo and the outrageous behavior that occurred in the legendary Cubi Point Officers' Club.

About two hours before the Kitty Hawk tied up in Subic Bay, Commander Michael Phelan, commanding officer of VF-125, called a meeting in the ready room. Phelan, "At ease, Gents. I know a lot of you have heard what I am about to say, but many have not. So here it is. Subic Bay is one of the world's largest and best-equipped Navy bases. Certainly, it's the biggest in this part of the world. There are lots of things to do on base, so take advantage of them. As you probably know, there is no other Officers' Club in the US Navy like the Cubi Point Club. I'm sure your shipmates have told you some of the crazy things that go on there. Take my word for it. The stories are all true. You cannot have a bad time there. Again, take advantage of it. Outside the base in Olongapo, you can get almost anything you want, and some things you certainly do not want, in less than an hour. It is also one of the most dangerous ports of call you will ever visit. There is no reason to wander aimlessly in Olongapo. It is not Disneyland. It is a minefield. If you do venture off base, be extremely careful and be smart. Do not, I repeat, do not go into any off-limits establishment. Be careful wherever you go. Even in the approved places, people have been robbed, mugged, drugged, and beaten. Pickpockets, hustlers, pimps, hookers and predators are everywhere. And Gents, as sweet and pretty as some of the hookers look, they are only after your money. Anyway, they can get it. Even people who believe they know their way around are at risk. Some have even been killed. About two years ago, a twenty-seven-year veteran Master Chief Petty Officer was found floating in the Shit River just outside the gate. It's called that because it's no more than a raw sewage canal. The chief's throat was cut. He had been to Olongapo several times and thought he knew where to go and where not to go. He was wrong, just once. With that, Gents, use your heads, have a good but safe time, and do not be late returning to the Kitty Hawk. As you were, Gents." Then he left the ready room.

Connors, Riley, and several other members of the squadron decided to go to the O Club to have lunch and a few beers. The CO had arranged for a shuttle to provide transportation to and from several places on base, including the BOQ and the O Club. Connors and Riley got off at the BOQ, checked into rooms and walked to the club, only a block away.

The club looked like a scene from the movie South Pacific, complete with bamboo walls and a rattan ceiling. It was in the process of being renovated and included a "safer" catapult that was being built to take a mock aircraft down a ramp. If the "pilot" missed a trap near the bottom of the ramp, they went into a 3-foot pool of water. Naval and Marine Aviators still entertained themselves during construction by "catapulting" down the stairs to the dance floor on a rolling chair. Few made it down without a tumbling crash. Almost all of them had cuts

57

and bruises, and some were seriously hurt. But risking life and limb on the catapult wasn't the only attraction. There were also USO shows on weekends, gambling, and watching hard-partying aviators find new ways to be outrageous. Pretty local girls were somehow always allowed in the club. Otherwise, only an occasional nurse or female supply officer was ever seen there. The male officers easily found girls just outside the gate.

Connors, Riley, and the others sat down at a large table and ordered lunch and draft beers, the first beer they had in months. Sitting next to Riley was the VF-125 air intelligence officer who had briefed them before every mission. Jack Gordon was a 1966 Naval Academy graduate who wanted to be a pilot but didn't meet the physical requirements. Unlike most squadron mates, he was quiet, even introverted. A couple of beers later, he loosened up and joined the conversation.

Two or three veteran WestPac officers were swapping horror stories of Olongapo nightlife. Gordon, now on his third tour, said that on his first cruise, he had gone to an approved dance club owned by an American expatriate. While he was drinking a beer, a well-dressed young Filipino woman walked in with three other women and sat at the bar. He casually began talking to the woman closest to him and introduced himself. She smiled and said she was a twenty-one-year-old student nurse. Then, with tears in her eyes, she told him that she was engaged to a Marine helicopter pilot two years before, but after he deployed, she never heard from him again. She felt betrayed and wanted nothing to do with Americans, especially Marines. Two years later, she came with friends to celebrate one of their birthdays. It was the first time she had been to the bar since the Marine left. Gordon said that the Marine's behavior was terrible, apologized for the behavior, and asked her if he could buy her a drink. She smiled sweetly and nodded her head. Twenty minutes later, she finished her drink and went to the lady's room. The American bartender saw her leave, came over to Gordon, and whispered, "Which story did she tell you, the Marine helicopter pilot, the one about the Navy Ensign or the one about studying to be a nurse? I don't know what she said her name is, but most people call her Liz the Machine. She's only eighteen, has been on the street for years, and has had every STD known to man. I'm told that she's bragged about doing six tricks on a single Saturday night. If I were you, I'd get on my horse and ride as far away from her, as fast as I could." Then Gordon said, "I just thanked the barkeep, paid the bill with a hefty tip, and caught a cab back to the O Club."

Sitting across the table was a burly Lieutenant Commander, a Limited Duty Officer (LDO) who oversaw all ordnance management. He was a mustang who had risen from an E-3 Ordnanceman up the ranks to an LDO commission. He had been on multiple cruises and almost as many marriages over a twenty-five-year career. He was a big man, nearly 6'6", around 240 pounds, and a legendary barroom brawler. He had been a star high school heavyweight wrestler who had maintained his muscular physique by pumping iron and martial arts training. Not surprisingly, his nickname was Moose, and his shipmates revered him.

Moose shared, "About two years ago, I was on another WestPac cruise. We had a two-day liberty here in Subic Bay, just like we have now. I had just split from wife number three and was feeling down. So, in a moment of weakness, this other fool and I decided to go to an off-limits dump known for cheap San Miguel and good-looking ladies. When we got there, we discovered its reputation was only partially true. It had cheap San Miguels and cheap ladies, but they were so ugly that they had to sneak up to the barstools. So, me and my buddy Manny I decided the only thing to do was put on some real thick beer goggles and try to make the ladies look better. After slamming down at least ten beers each, the ladies still didn't get prettier. So, I grabbed Manny, who was really shitfaced, and told him that if we stayed any longer, we'd probably get some incurable form of the clap and maybe even get rolled. So, I dragged his ass outta' there. Manny could barely walk, and I didn't feel like carrying him about a mile and a half back to the boat, so I made my second bad decision of the night. I waved down a pirate cab that was parked across the street from the bar. It was a Jeepney, which looked like a British Hackney crossed with a Jeep. It had two jump seats facing the back seat, so I got Manny into the back seat, and we left."

Moose continued. "About three blocks down the street, the cab stopped, and two Filipinos opened the Jeepney doors and got on the jump seats. Suddenly, both of them pulled long knives out of their pant legs and held them against our throats. The one across from Manny told him to hand over his wallet. Manny, barely able to talk, slurred that the wallet was in his waistband. He held up his left hand, and with his right hand, he pulled out a 38-caliber pistol, not his wallet. Manny pointed the gun at the guy across from him and shot him right in the middle of his forehead. I had no idea that Manny had a gun. I sure as shit didn't know he was going to shoot the bastard, and neither did the guy who was holding a big-ass knife against my throat. His eyes almost bugged out of his head, and he looked away for a second. I grabbed the knife with my left hand and hit that son of a bitch with my right fist as hard as I could, right on his temple. At the same time as I hit the bastard, Manny shot him. He went down, out cold and bleeding, on the car floor. I was scared shitless. So was the Jeepney driver, who had to be involved in the scam, and he jumped out and hauled ass into

60

the dark. At this point, Manny and I had sobered up a lot, and we got out of the Jeepney and left the thieves where they were. Without a word spoken between us, we walked back to the base. As we got close to the front gate, Manny threw the pistol into the Shit River."

"Later, when we got on board the boat, I went directly to the XO's stateroom, woke him up, and told him what happened. The XO, an old friend of mine, listened, shook his head, and told us that unless he heard something from the local police before we left, the event never happened. He went on to say that he suspected that no one would ever hear a word about it. "In Olongapo, no one gave a rat's ass about two thugs being found unconscious or dead in a pirate cab. It was just another night in town." Then, after a pause, Moose looked at us and said, "That's a true story, Gents. As the CO told us this morning, be careful out there; it's dangerous as hell." And he got up to get another drink.

There was a prolonged silence at the table. Connors finally said to Riley. "I don't know if that's a true story or not, but from what I have heard about Moose and Olongapo, I suspect that it really happened." There was loud cheering and hooting from the top of the small stairway leading from the second floor to the nearby dance floor. The cheering was quickly followed by what sounded like someone screaming in pain while pounding the walls and steps with a club. Then, a Marine Aviator face-planted on the floor at the bottom of the steps. Simultaneously, a wooden desk chair with wheels landed on his back. The Marine looked up and felt around his body. He was bleeding from his nose, forehead, and both elbows, but he was smiling and cheering as if he had completed a marathon. Several other Marine Aviators came to his aid, but he shrugged them off, wiped the blood from his nose, and limped to the bar.

The barkeep dutifully poured him a double shot of whiskey, which the Marine tossed down.

The spectacle wasn't over. Soon after the Marine came careening down the stairs, there was a second, followed by two more. Riley, "If this is what goes on in this place in the middle of the day, I can't wait to see what happens tonight."

An hour later, Connors said he was exhausted and was going to get some sleep. Riley and several squadron mates remained at the club to drink a few more beers and plan their evening in town. Weeks of little sleep and dangerous missions had taken their toll, and soon Connors was sound asleep in his BOQ room. He was very groggy when he woke up but soon recalled where he was and put on a swimsuit. Then he put some toiletries and a change of clothes in his flight bag and walked to the pool. Since it was after 5 pm, he swam laps in a nearly empty pool for about a half hour.

After he climbed out and walked toward his chair, he heard a woman's voice calling his name. Connors looked around and saw a familiar woman waving at him. He was sure she was Jane's cousin, Lisa Thomas, whom he had met in Pensacola. He remembered that Lisa was a nurse and her husband, Tony, was a Navy Surgeon. Both were previously stationed at Mayport Navy Base in Jacksonville, Florida, before Tony transferred to the Naval Aerospace Medical Institute (NAMI) in Pensacola. Three months later, Lisa joined him, and the two settled into an off-base apartment. Lisa knew that Jane often visited Connors in Pensacola and told her to call the next time she did. Jane did a couple of weeks later, and the two couples got together several times.

"Long time, no see. How are you?" Connors said as he came closer to her. She smiled and hugged him as he continued,

"Imagine meeting again on the other side of the world. What brings you here, is Tony with you?" She sat down and waved to him to sit on the chair next to her. She looked at him no longer smiling, "A lot has changed since I last saw you. Tony and I are divorced, and I've changed my name back to my maiden name, Scalise. In fact, the divorce and name change were final just last week." Connors quietly replied. "Lisa, I'm sorry, I didn't know. Jane and I stopped seeing each other over a year ago, and I haven't heard a word from her or from me since. We split because we were each going in two different directions with no end in sight. I was going to sea for an unknown length of time, and Jane was in the middle of getting her doctorate. There was just no way we could do both things and still maintain a relationship that would be fair to either of us. So, as much as we cared for each other, we decided to split. I still miss her very much and hope to find her again."

Lisa, now with tears in her eyes, said. "Our split was much more awkward. Before I joined him in Pensacola, Tony had an affair with a nurse who worked with him at NAMI. It continued after I arrived. He explained his long hours at work by telling me he was involved in complicated procedures, which I totally believed. Well, he was into something complicated, but it wasn't heart surgery. He finally told me that he had been having an affair with another nurse for several months; he was in love with her, and she was pregnant. It's the same old story; she was younger and prettier, and he was like a teenager in love. Plus, I can't have kids, and she was going to have his. He could only see one way forward and took it without me. Tony moved in with her almost immediately after he told me that she was pregnant. I filed for divorce the next day. It was the hardest thing I ever had to do. I was pushing thirty, and for six years was happily married (I thought) to a man I adored. It all ended in one night. I was crushed, apparently beyond repair. The only thing I knew to do was turn to my work for comfort and distraction. But I soon realized that I had to leave Pensacola, even though I loved living there. Tony and his pregnant girlfriend were impossible to avoid."

"About two months after we split, I was selected to be in a newly established Pediatric Nurse Practitioner training program at Bethesda Naval Hospital. I immediately accepted, but the training wasn't scheduled to begin until early July. Since I saw Tony and his girlfriend almost every day at work, I volunteered to come here to the Philippines for a six-month TDY. They really needed help in their pediatric unit, which was a perfect transition for my training. I needed to escape Pensacola, so it was a godsend. I arrived here in January and will report to Bethesda in July. Since then, I've been working twelve to eighteen hours a day, seven days a week, but I took this weekend off. I do get out and run, then go for a swim. That's it, that's my story. In fact, I just got back from a run before I went for a swim." Then she looked at Connors and said, "Please join me. We need to do some catching up." Connors agreed and moved to the lounge chair next to her.

After talking for about an hour and a half, Lisa said, "Are you as hungry as I am? I was planning to go down by the bay to a little pub as a break from the O Club. It's on the base, has decent food, and a great view. Want to go?" It took Connors about three seconds to say, "Sure, let's go."

Connors and Lisa had just changed their clothes and were leaving the pool area when Riley and some other VT-125 aviators walked in the door. They saw Connors and Lisa and walked over to them. They were all obviously very drunk. Riley, unsteadily weaving, began to talk, "Hey Connors," then looked at Lisa, "Hi, I'm Riley, Connors' RIO." Then, looking at Connors, he said, "I see you didn't waste a lot of time."

Connors chuckled and said, "Riley, this is Lisa, an old friend of mine from Pensacola. She's a nurse stationed here at the hospital. We're going to get some dinner and talk about old times." Then Riley, struggling with his words, slurred, "No, I can't go with you. I and some of the boys are going to a place called Arleens or some damn place like that. You guys wanna go?" Lisa said, "Not this time, Riley, maybe some other time." Connors looked at Riley and said, "You boys better watch you sixes out there. I hear the place is full of bogeys." Riley gave him two thumbs-up and stumbled away.

Connors and Lisa took a shuttle to a bayfront bar and grill called Bay View Club and Cabins. As Lisa promised, the restaurant had a spectacular view and offered American fare as well as dishes Connors had never tried. They ordered drinks, and then, looking at the menu, he told Lisa. "You better order for me. I'd like to try Filipino food, but I don't know what this stuff is." Lisa smiled, "I'll be happy to, but I'm only familiar with about half of it. I'll do my best, but let's talk for a while before ordering." Lisa said, "Tell me about yourself, Lt. Tim Connors. I don't know much about you. I know that you are a dedicated Naval Aviator, but that's it. Tell me your story right up to the time you met Jane."

Connors looked at her and said, "OK, I will, but you start first." Lisa began, "I am from a large, traditional Italian family. I'm the youngest of six siblings: two brothers and three sisters. We were raised Catholic in Jacksonville, and all of us attended Catholic schools. It was a happy childhood filled with the love of a stay-at-home mom and a dad who was home every night. He was a dentist who had been in the Navy. After twenty years, he retired and started a private practice outside of Jacksonville, where my parents still live. After high school, I started at Belmont Abbey College in North Carolina for my freshman year then I transferred to the University of Florida School of Nursing where I received my RN. After I graduated, I joined the Navy, largely because I grew up as a Navy brat, and it was the only life I knew. My first duty station was the Navy hospital in Jacksonville, where my father was once stationed and where Tony was just beginning his first year of surgical residency. We met in the hospital operating room and dated for about a year. We often visited my parent's house during that time, and Tony loved my big family. He often said he wanted to have a large family like mine. My family loved him almost as much as I did. From the first time we went out, I knew I wanted to marry him. We were perfect for each other, or so I thought. We got married on my twenty-second birthday. Two years later, when he finally finished his residency and fellowships, he was a board-certified thoracic surgeon on staff at the hospital. Soon after that, he got his dream transfer to Pensacola and NAMI. You already know what happened then, and I don't really want to revisit those bad memories. So now it's your turn." For the next hour, Connors detailed his life story from when he grew up in Melbourne to the day he arrived in the Philippines, and he didn't leave out anything about his relationship with Jane.

Finally, Lisa said she hadn't eaten since breakfast and she needed to order. Connors agreed, and she asked him, "Do you like spicy seafood?" Connors, "Sure, but habanero is almost too hot." Lisa, "There's a Filipino dish that is a fish stew like Cioppino, but spicy and tart. It's Americanized here with more shellfish and less heat. I like it." Connors. "Sounds good to me." Lisa got the waiter's attention and ordered for both of them.

When the food came, Connors ordered more drinks. Lisa picked up her drink and said, "If I finish this, I'll probably need a stretcher to get out of here. I haven't had this much to drink in months." Connors said, "Don't worry, I'm an expert at helping sloshed folks out of bars. After all, I'm a highly trained Naval Aviator." Lisa laughed, saying, "I bet you assisted a few tipsy ladies as well." Connors smiling, said, "My lips are sealed." Lisa looked at him, raised her glass, and said, "Here's to discretion in an era of brazen indiscretion."

The food was delicious. It was giant prawns, clams, and crab in a thick vegetable broth. Connors ate every bite. After they finished, she asked him if he wanted to sit on the veranda and talk for a while. Connors said it sounded great, paid the bill, and they went outside.

Later, Connors got another drink for each of them. When he got back, Lisa smiled and said, "Lt. Connors, I believe you are trying to take advantage of an older woman." Connors, "I don't see an older woman, but I do see a beautiful lady who I would never take advantage of." Lisa blushed as she replied, "You aren't taking advantage of anybody. I have already planned to stay here for two nights, hoping you might stay with me. I made the reservation while you were changing your clothes. Will you stay with me?" Connors smiled and said, "I could never turn down an invitation from such a sexy lady."

While they walked to the cabin, Connors said. "Lisa, you should know that I still have very strong feelings for Jane. I would have asked her to marry me if the situation were different. If I get back to Florida, the first thing I will do is try to find her. I'll never leave her again if she's still single and wants me. But I can honestly tell you that when we first met, I envied Tony when I saw how much you cared for him. If Jane has found someone else, I want to see you again." Lisa, almost crying, "Tony was the love of my life. It has taken me almost a year to get over our split, but I still haven't forgiven him for how much he hurt me. It doesn't make any sense, but somehow,

I believe that if it doesn't work out between him and his new wife, I could forgive him and try to restart our marriage." After a brief pause, "I know that is only a pipe dream, and I must continue my life the best I can without him." Now crying, she said, "We've both suffered from lost loves, but here we are. Let's enjoy our time together, no matter how long it lasts, with no strings and no regrets. You are one of the nicest and most attractive men I have ever met. Even if we go separate ways with different people, you will always have a special place in my heart."

Connors opened the blinds in the cabin and looked at the bay shimmering beneath a nearly full moon. Lisa had already taken off her clothes and was reaching around his waist to remove them. Connors turned and said, "Are you sure?" She replied, "As sure as I have been about anything I've ever done."

That night was one of the most passionate times either of them had ever experienced. When dawn broke and the morning sun awakened them, they got up, showered together, and then returned to bed. They stayed there until nearly 10 when they got up and showered again. While they were dressing, Connors said he had only brought a bathing suit and the clothes he had worn the night before. Lisa, giggling, said, "Connors, you have all the clothes you need. If I get my way, you won't need any clothes at all." Then, blushing, "We better go eat before we end up back in bed."

When they finished eating, they decided to go to the beach. They found a cabana and sat on lounge chairs in the shade. Connors. "Lisa, I couldn't help but notice the large surgical scar across your abdomen. What happened to you?" Lisa, touching the scar, said, "When Tony and I had been married for about four years, I had just turned twenty-six, we decided it

was time to have children. We had often talked about having two or three, so we couldn't wait any longer. We tried for several months, and then I thought I was pregnant, but I wasn't. I had an ectopic pregnancy. It was diagnosed as an ovarian cyst by an OB/GYN in Jacksonville. It wasn't, and it grew very quickly, ruptured the wall of my cervix, and caused sepsis. Tony came home for dinner and found me semiconscious and bleeding badly. My temperature had skyrocketed, and my blood pressure was dangerously low. He called an ambulance, and I was rushed into the OR. The surgeon, who Tony knew, explained to him that I had a massive infection, I was hemorrhaging, and to save my life, he needed to do a complete hysterectomy. Tony reluctantly concurred. A month after the surgery and some heavy-duty antibiotics, I was much better, but I could never have children. Our marriage was never the same after that. I didn't know it then, but it was the beginning of the end for Tony." She was crying as she stopped talking. Connors hugged her and said, "I am so sorry I asked. I wouldn't hurt you for the world," His words brought even more tears to her eyes. Then she said, "Connors, there's no reason to apologize, but I love you for caring."

After swimming and talking for a while, they both fell asleep in the cabana. When they returned to the cabin, they made love and showered. They finished at almost seven, and they went to the restaurant. Connors ordered a bottle of wine while Lisa again chose a seafood dish resembling a New England lobster boil. It was delicious but very spicy. After dinner, Connors bought another bottle of wine and they again went to the veranda. As they watched the moon over the bay, they talked about their experiences in the Navy and the plans they had made for after their Naval careers were over. At 10:30 pm, they left the veranda and returned to the cabin. That night was much the same as the previous one, but with the knowledge that it was probably the last time they would ever be together, they took their time making love.

The next morning, they grabbed a quick breakfast and took the shuttle to the BOQ so Connors could report to Kitty Hawk by 10. Lisa was crying as she told him that she would remember that weekend for the rest of her life. She said goodbye, and the shuttle left for the nurses' quarters.

Chapter 13

Jane Carmody Completes Her Dissertation

After returning to Gainesville, Jane had been very busy completing the final edits of her dissertation. She hoped to have it ready to submit to the Math Department Academic Standards Review Committee by the end of the week. She wanted to meet with them in mid-June, but there was a chance the committee could meet earlier.

Dr. Sandler, Jane's PhD adviser, held an endowed chair in mathematics at the University and had worked with her since she began her research. He had already read her draft dissertation, thought it was well done, and would be easily approved. He even wrote a recommendation letter, which she sent to prospective employers. Dr. Sandler had already offered her an instructor's position, but Jane wanted to try for an assistant professor's position at a local university.

Dr. Sandler received a call from an old friend and colleague, Dr. Williamson, who had been hired as the Dean of the Mathematics Department at the University of West Florida. He asked Sandler if he had any promising doctoral candidates interested in an Assistant Professor's position; he had three positions available in August. Sandler immediately recommended Jane, who had already applied for a position there. Dr. Williamson indicated he had read her application, but he wanted to see what Dr. Sandler thought of her in case there was someone else he wanted to recommend. After Dr. Sandler said there wasn't anyone, Williamson added that he was considering offering her a job. Dr. Sandler assured him that he had read the final draft of her dissertation and was positive it would be approved. Dr. Williamson, "That's good enough for me. I'll call her and offer her the job."

Later that day, Dr. Sandler called Jane and told her about the job offer. "This may not be your ideal place, but it's a great place to start your career. As I've told you, assistant professor positions are very difficult for new PhDs to obtain anywhere. You should think very seriously about taking it." After a brief silence, Jane responded, "There is no doubt in my mind I'll accept. I have a sister in Pensacola, and I've been there several times. I absolutely love the Pensacola area. Thank you so much." He replied. "Jane, you've earned it. You are the brightest doctoral student I've advised in years. Congratulations."

Chapter 14

Wendy and Leah Explore Pensacola

Once Gina Martinez left work, she met Wendy and Leah at Al's Castle Bar. As they had drinks, Wendy asked if anyone else wanted to eat; she was starving. Gina said, "This place has the best-steamed sandwiches you've ever had." Leah replied, "That'll be easy. I've never had a steamed sandwich. What is it?" Gina answered. "They make huge roast beef, corned beef, pastrami, Reuben, or just about any other cold cut sandwich you want, and they steam it for about five minutes. It makes the meat warm, juicy, and delicious. And they have a great choice of draft beer." Wendy immediately said, "You sold me, let's eat."

While they ate, Gina started by saying, "The best place to go is the Ready Room Bar and the weekly mixers. If you want to meet young men, especially Naval and Marine Officers between 23 and 26 years old, you need to go to those places. But let me give you a word of caution. The Navy recruits risk-takers and high-spirited alpha males for AOCS and flight training. Less than half of those who start AOCS finish, and even fewer get their wings. When they finish AOCS and are commissioned, most haven't been near a female in weeks. They aren't looking for a lasting relationship when they come to the Ready Room. They are looking for a quick and dirty, wham bam, thank you, mam, roll in the hay. All they want to do is fly airplanes and chase girls."

Gina continued. "To make it worse, many local girls are perfectly willing to accommodate them any way they can. Most of your competition will be college girls from as far away as Mississippi and South Carolina, local high school girls and mill workers. Some of the girls that go to the mixers are barely sixteen years old, which is the age of consent in Florida. They act, dress, and look like they're much older. Believe it or not, local girls consider these Naval and Marine Officers to be their Prince Charmings coming to take them away. Amazingly, the Navy allows it to happen and sponsors it. The base social director hires buses to bring girls from various locations to the mixers. When they get in the Ready Room, there is absolutely no effort to ask any of them for an ID, no matter how young they are. I admit that I have never asked any girl for an ID, even though I knew they were underage. So, while the Ready Room is the best place to meet young men, it's also a place you better believe only a smidgen of what the guys tell you." Leah then joked. "You convinced me, Gina. What are we waiting for?"

Gina wanted them to start at the Pier Lounge, and they could hear the loud rock and roll music as soon as they pulled into the parking lot. It was ladies' night, so every girl got a coupon for two beers or glasses of wine. The music inside was almost painfully loud, and the dance floor was packed. There seemed to be two guys for every girl, and every girl appeared to be dancing while the guys watched. A lot of the men were in uniform, mostly Navy and a scattering of Marines.

"Well, we might as well join the crowd," Leah said as she led the others to the bar. They ordered drinks, but three guys in uniform asked each of them to dance before they took a sip. All of them declined, saying they wanted to finish their drinks, but the guys didn't give up. Leah introduced herself but told them they were waiting for their boyfriends to arrive. Then the guys gave up and went to the other side of the dance floor.

They looked for a table but saw none. Wendy did see a man she recognized from the Ready Room. He walked towards a table where several people were waving to him. Wendy asked Gina who he was, and she immediately recognized him, "That's Steve Pless, the Marine you saw at the Ready Room. He's the guy who won the Medal of Honor last January. He is a living legend around here, and for good reason. How he got the medal is one of the most heroic and chilling stories you will ever hear. He's seen all around town. His picture is in the newspaper and stories about him are on TV virtually every week. There are many stories about him, and you'll hear them all at the Ready Room."

An hour later, they decided the Pier Lounge was too crowded, and they went to take a look at the Tiki Bar. It was almost empty when they had been there with Jane, but this time it was packed. It had a live band and a small dance floor and gave every girl a free drink.

Later, two guys in civilian clothes, but looking like Naval Officers introduced themselves. As suspected, they were recently commissioned but were refreshingly low-key. Impressed, both Wendy and Leah talked to them for a few minutes, and Leah gave one of them her number. After they left, Leah told Wendy that both might be interesting to date. Before Wendy said anything, Gina warned, "Meeting guys is a lot like fishing. After you catch one, you can always throw it back, especially here where the fishing is always good."

Chapter 15

AOCS Continues and Schnider is Renamed

Class 569 was now 36 officer candidates; eight candidates DOR'd and four couldn't complete the Dilbert Dunker training. In addition, each candidate was given an "in test" to determine how his abilities compared to the required standards of the "out test" given the final week of AOCS. Those standards included vertical and horizontal jumps, forty-yard sprints, rope climbs, pushups, pull-ups, three-mile runs, obstacle course, and mile swim.

The second half of AOCS had become relatively routine but not any easier. In addition to early wake-ups, near-constant harassment, repeated inspections, and exhausting PT, they went to class. Included in the academic requirements were math, extensive instruction in military and Naval history, Naval aircraft and ship recognition, the biographies of important Naval Officers, and leadership. Striker found the math to be a rehash of what he learned in high school, but military and Naval histories were often compelling narratives. The hardest part of the classwork was staying awake, no matter how interesting it may have been. The constant fatigue was often overpowering; Striker almost fell asleep several times in class, but he still managed to get some of the highest grades on all the final exams. Sticky failed the math final and had to go to stupid school.

As time went on, the Drill Instructors became more demanding during inspections and more ruthless with candidates who screwed up. To make AOCS even more difficult, candidates were issued M1 Carbines. In addition to having to learn the manual of arms, candidates had to keep their weapons perfectly clean. The Drill Instructors now had an almost unlimited source of flaws.

One moment of levity occurred on a late Wednesday afternoon at the obstacle course. First Sergeant Sullivan singled out Schnider when the class finished running a time trial. He had just finished first in the grueling run, apparently ready to go again, just as he did every time Sullivan was present. Sullivan ordered the class to fall into formation and directed Schnider to fall out and come to attention in front of the class. Sullivan noticed that Schnider was the only candidate in Class 569 who didn't seem to tire, no matter the exercise or how much Sullivan PT'd him. He also did not seem to have a normal threshold of pain, and he had the will to continue even if he was in severe pain. Schnider was the best in almost every standard except swimming and he finished first in the obstacle course.

Sullivan told Schnider that he reminded him of "Chesty," a Bulldog he once owned, and speculated that Schnider was part bulldog. Not only did he have the "never give up" attitude of a bulldog, but Schnider was short and muscular like one. To prove his point, Sullivan ordered Schnider to bark like a dog while he did twenty-five pushups. Schnider easily did it without getting winded. Sullivan, now almost convinced Schnider was a part bulldog, asked him if he had a relative who was short, bow-legged, drooled a lot, and was really ugly. He then asked, "Did you ever have a strange urge to bite dogs or other people?" Schnider, "No, Drill Instructor Sullivan, this candidate never knew of a relative who was short, bow-legged, really ugly, or drooled a lot. This candidate never wanted to

77

bite dogs, but this candidate was once disqualified in a wrestling match when this candidate bit this candidate's opponent's shoulder." Sullivan, almost laughing, asked. "Mr. Schnider, did you howl after you bit his shoulder?" Schnider replied, stone-faced, "No, Drill Instructor Sullivan, this candidate did not howl after biting this candidate's opponent's shoulder, but this candidate's opponent sure did." Sullivan, now laughing, asked, "Mr. Schnider, if you are not a bulldog, why did you bite your opponent's shoulder?" Schnider responded, "This candidate did not intend to bite this candidate's opponent's shoulder. This candidate was trying to bite this candidate's opponent's ear but could not reach it." Now laughing loudly, Sullivan said, "That settles it, Mr. Schnider. You are not only part bulldog; you are a purebred champion bulldog. From now on you are Bulldog, not Schnider. Gentlemen, we now have two dogs in the class, Hound and Bulldog," and he told Hound and Bulldog to bark. Later he ordered the rest of the class to bark, which they did until Sullivan ordered them to stop and to hit the showers before they went to the mess hall.

Chapter 16

Jane gets a Job Offer

When Dr. Williamson called Jane early on May 22nd to offer her an Assistant Professor's position at the University of West Florida, she immediately accepted. He then told her she needed to complete an employment contract, which they would send her, or she could come to his office to pick one up and complete it there. Jane wanted to meet him and explore the campus, so she made an appointment to meet Dr. Williamson at his office at 10 a.m. Wednesday, May 28. She then called her parents in Overland Park and her sister in Gulf Breeze.

When she talked to her sister, Wendy was overjoyed and immediately invited Jane to stay at their apartment in Gulf Breeze. Jane said she appreciated her offer but would only stay with them until she found an apartment closer to campus.

Jane needed to complete the final draft of her dissertation, so she decided to drive to Gulf Breeze the next morning. She also had to reserve a small one-way rental trailer that would hold the few pieces of furniture she owned.

Jane had dated several men in the many months since she had broken up with Connors and even slept with a couple, but she wasn't serious with any of them. On her drive to Pensacola, Jane realized that she had not given up hope that she would somehow see Connors again, and she wondered how he would react if they did find each other.

Chapter 17

Connors Heads Back to Pensacola

Connors walked up the ramp to the Kitty Hawk, saluted the flag, and was welcomed aboard by the duty officer. He went to his stateroom and then to the Officers' mess to see if Riley or any of his squadron mates were there. He heard Riley's deep voice calling him from the other side of the room and went towards him. Riley slowly drawled, "Hey man, how was your weekend? I vaguely remember you with a pretty brunette at the pool before we went to town. Was that some girl you just met?" Connors smiled and replied, "No, I've known her for a while. She is the cousin of my ex-girlfriend, Jane, back in Pensacola. She is a nurse stationed here at the hospital. It was a big surprise for both of us to run into each other. We got together both nights and talked about old times. How about your weekend? Did you have a good time?" Riley grinned sheepishly and said, "I'm told I did, but to be honest, I only remember waking up this morning. All the rest is either a crazy dream or it really happened. I'm just not sure. All my parts seem to be working properly, and I'm ready to return to work." Connors chuckled, and the two of them drank a cup of coffee before reporting to the ready room.

Two days before he left the Kitty Hawk with his squadron, Connors met with his CO, Commander Phelan, regarding his next assignment. Phelan asked him, "Mr. Connors, what would you like to do next? Before you answer, let me tell you that instructors are needed badly in all levels of flight training located in Pensacola, Mississippi, and Texas. With the recent increase in North Vietnam combat operations, a lot more Naval

Aviators are in the pipeline, so you have a choice of any training location you want. As you know, you can stay with VT-125 for another tour in WestPac, but it won't be on the Kitty Hawk, which is going into dry dock. I have also received a training bulletin that the Patuxent River Test Pilot School is recruiting pilots, especially those who are aeronautical engineers. They are gearing up to assist NASA with upcoming launches in Cape Canaveral. Some of the people who complete the program may be assigned to NASA as advisers. After looking at your record and education, I think you should consider it. If you do, I'll be happy to write a recommendation for you. However, the Pax River program will not select any pilots until next year when the funding starts, but they are accepting applications from now until the end of the month. Connors, with your credentials, I think you have a really good shot at being selected. If you choose Pax River, you will have to be assigned somewhere else until next year. So, you need to decide what you want to do. If you choose the Pensacola-based training command, you will report to VT-4 by June 9, and the assignment is for a minimum of a year unless you are selected for the Test Pilot School. The other assignments range from a year to eighteen months. Any questions?" Connors answered. "No sir, none. I have dreamed of going to test pilot training and even being an astronaut since I was a kid. It's why I became an aeronautical engineer and why I wanted to become a Naval Aviator with flight training. Without any hesitation, I want to apply for the test pilot program. Ever since I left Pensacola, I've wanted to go back, so being a VT-4 instructor in Pensacola is easily my first choice." Phelan smiled, looked at Connors, and said, "Mr. Connors, pack your gear. You are going back to Pensacola. I will see to it that you get an application for the program. Fill it out and give it back to me before you leave. I'll write your letter of recommendation and submit it as well.

Good luck, Mr. Connors." Connors saluted and thanked Phelan. Two days later Connors dropped off his application as he left the Kitty Hawk.

Soon after they arrived at Miramar, Connors and Riley checked into the BOQ and were scheduled on a military transport flight to Pensacola the next morning. Riley was reassigned to VT-86, Glynco NAS, as a Radar Intercept Instructor, but he had to go to Pensacola to get his Harley, which was in storage.

That night, VT-125 had a cruise party at the O Club. Before it started, Commander Phelan announced that several aviators, including Riley and Connors, had been promoted. When the Task Force 81 commanding officer pinned on their full lieutenant bars, he also awarded them both Bronze Stars. The party afterward lasted until late that night, and Connors had to drag himself out of bed the next morning to make the flight to Pensacola.

Chapter 18

AOCS Continues and Striker Meets Pless

The only times candidates could not be harassed were during meals and religious services. Striker, who had not been practicing his childhood religion for years, started going to Mass again. At first, he went because it was an hour of peace and quiet, but later on, it became more meaningful to him.

Unlike the rest of the week, the candidates were awakened on Sundays at 0530 but still went for a four-mile run. Once they showered and dressed, they marched in formation to the mess hall for breakfast. When they returned, some of them marched to the chapel for separate services. When the services were over, they returned to the barn to resume regular training.

On Sunday, June 2, Drill Instructor Sullivan surprised the class by giving them a six-hour on-base liberty, which began at 1000. Before they began the liberty, they had to prepare for an inspection. Striker, Hound, Bulldog, and Sticky now worked as a team to quickly put everything where it needed to be. After a few minutes, they finished and quizzed each other with questions about the general orders, chain of command, password of the day, and all the other information they had to be able to recite. Since the sixth week of training, the class was also required to read a printed article on leadership, which would be handed out to them every day at lights out. Any candidate could be ordered to give the class a synopsis of the daily article at any time. The last thing Striker and his roommates did before the inspection was to recap the article for each other.

Promptly at 0915, Sullivan beat his swagger stick against a wall and entered each room. But Sullivan did not inspect anything. Instead, he ordered at least one candidate in every room to recite a required memorization or to brief him on the daily leadership article. The inspection lasted forty-five minutes, but, amazingly, every candidate was able to do as he was ordered. Striker was ordered to brief Sullivan on the article, and Sticky had to recite the chain of command all the way up to the president. Striker and Sticky both nailed the answers. Then Sullivan smiled slightly and left the room.

When every room was inspected, Sullivan ordered the class to brace against the passageway bulkhead. Then, they were ordered to pat each other on the back, turn to each other, and take a bow. Sullivan then said, "Gentlemen, this morning's inspection proves that even blind hogs can find a puddle of shit to wallow in. Good job. Your liberty now begins. Be back in formation at the entrance to this building at 1600. Dismissed."

Striker and his roommates decided to walk to a new base, gedunk, which served burgers, sandwiches, and packaged goods. While it wasn't a fancy place, it was a welcome change from the mess hall's repetitive fare. When they finished eating, Hound and Bulldog wanted to go back to the barn and get some much-needed sleep. Striker wanted to take a walk around the base, and Sticky said he would go with him. First, they headed to the harbor where the Lexington was moored. On the way, they laughed at each other when they automatically walked in step and saluted every moving vehicle that had an officer's blue decal on the windshield. They even saluted parked cars that had blue decals. Sticky, laughing at their acquired habits, said,

"Before we finish AOCS, we will be saluting bluebirds, blueberries, and blue-eyed girls."

When they arrived at the Lexington, there was an open house, which allowed the public to walk onto the carrier's massive deck and see three aircraft that were temporarily parked there. When the two of them got aboard, it was the first time either one had been on an aircraft carrier. The first thing that Striker noticed was that the deck was made of wood planks and not some sort of metal or asphalt.

Crossing the deck, Striker walked as close as the barriers would allow to an F-4, an A-4, and an A-6, the current workhorses of Navy and Marine Corps aviation. It was the first time he had seen any of them on the ground and fairly close. All of them looked like something out of a science-fiction movie. There was a sign in front of each aircraft that described their individual missions and flight capabilities. The F-4s description, among other things, listed the records that it held, including a maximum speed of Mach 2.5 and, incredibly, a maximum altitude of over 98,000 feet. Flying in the F-4 was the main reason he was in AOCS, so being this close to the 'Flying Anvil' made finishing AOCS much more important.

After they looked at the aircraft, Striker and Sticky walked through the damaged aircraft waiting to be repaired. Most of them showed the scars of war, including bullet-ridden fuselages and shrapnel holes. They paused there in silence, wondering if they were ready to face the same dangers as these aviators had done. They both walked away more committed than ever to continue their work in the Navy. Then they walked across the base to see VT-10, the NFO training squadron they would be assigned to if they completed AOCS. It looked like an ordinary office building, except it had NFO wings and a *Welcome to VT-10* sign in front of the building.

There was not much else they wanted to see, so they walked back to the Mustin Beach Officers' Club. Both of them had heard a lot of stories about the club, especially the infamous mixers. They had to see the Ready Room Bar, where Striker's father and virtually every other Naval Aviator had partied. Striker didn't know if AOCS candidates were allowed in the club. When they got to the entrance, there was no one around to stop them, so they just walked in. The main ballroom was spacious and beautiful, something out of a different era. The Ready Room was very different. It was designed as a place to party, to drink, to swap war stories and to release the stress that comes from doing the dangerous job that Naval Aviators do. Striker couldn't wait to be able to go to the bar and have a beer, just as his father had done. They could see only one person in the room, sitting at the bar and drinking a beer. He was a Marine officer in dress whites. He was wearing a saber, complete with a sash, on his side. Striker was puzzled to see someone in a formal uniform drinking at this time of day. When the Marine turned around, Striker could now see the huge array of medals on his uniform and the Medal of Honor around his neck. Striker immediately recognized him as Major Stephen Pless, the legendary Marine Aviator who won the Medal of Honor in Vietnam.

Striker and Sticky were both anxious about what Pless was going to do. One word from him and they both would be gone from AOCS, stationed somewhere else as enlisted men. But Pless didn't get angry or even ask them what they were doing in the club. Instead, he waved for them to come closer and have a seat. He briefly introduced himself, shook hands with both, and asked them their names and where they called home. He also asked them what they wanted to do in their Naval careers. Both said they wanted to be NFOs, preferably RIOs. Then Pless told them a little about himself, his enlistment in the

Marine Corps while he was still in high school, then his acceptance to AOCS, and finally becoming a Marine Aviator. He stressed to them how important the discipline and stressful training he received in AOCS was to him in combat situations. "You have to be able to simultaneously pay attention to the many details of flying an aircraft while engaging the enemy in combat. That is the cardinal rule of survival in any combat mission. The constant fatigue and extended levels of stress that you are now experiencing in AOCS will train you to automatically pay attention to what's going on around you, especially in the aircraft, when things get ugly fast. If becoming the best aviator in the world is what you want, you're in the right place. It may not seem possible to you now, but if you make up your mind to do it, you will accomplish it. Gentlemen, if I could do it, you can too. Now, Gents, I have to be at a reception in an hour, so I have to leave. Best of luck to both of you in AOCS and your Navy careers."

Pless then downed the rest of his beer and left. A few seconds later, they followed him out and went back to the barn. As they walked, Sticky looked at Striker and said, "Holy shit. What an incredible day. In one morning, we see two legends, one a legendary aircraft, the F-4, and the other a Medal of Honor winning Marine."

Chapter 19

Jane Heads to Pensacola

Jane accepted the assistant professor's position at the University of West Florida as soon as it was offered. The next morning, she packed her belongings in a one-way trailer and left for Pensacola. The trailer had to be returned to the rental company within 24 hours, so she planned to take a few things into Wendy's apartment, and the next day store her furniture somewhere, and return the trailer. As soon as she got to the apartment, Wendy welcomed her to Pensacola and showed her the apartment. Jane could either double up with Wendy in her queen bed or sleep on a sofa bed in the living room. Jane chose the sofa bed, at least for the next few days. Wendy, "In about an hour, we're going to meet Gina for dinner, want to go? Or you could follow us there, eat, then head back to the apartment." Jane said, "I'm starved. Give me a couple of minutes to clean up, and I'll follow you."

They arrived at Al's, got a table, and ordered drinks. Gina walked in fifteen minutes later, saying, "Sorry I'm late. I ran into an old friend of Jake's, my fiancé, at the O Club. He just returned from WestPac, and I had not seen him for about a year." Wendy introduced Jane and they all ordered mugs of draft beer. A few minutes later, they ordered the specialty of the house, steamed sandwiches. As she ate, Jane said, "This place is great. I never came here with Connors, but he told me about it. There's no doubt that I'll be coming back a lot more once I'm settled into an apartment." Then she looked around and noticed there were a lot of men in uniform. "It looks like this is also a favorite hangout for the guys from the base. I know the food at the Officers' Open Mess is supposed to be excellent, but I'm sure it does get old eating all your meals there. This certainly would be a welcome change. The men here must easily outnumber the women, especially at the bar. The next time you're here, you should try sitting there. You might meet a few."

Later, Wendy, Leah, and Gina left for the Pier Lounge, and Jane went back to Wendy's apartment. Thirty minutes later, she was asleep on the sofa bed.

The next morning, Jane slept until she heard someone in the kitchen and smelled coffee brewing. Wendy walked out of the kitchen with two cups of coffee and handed one to Jane, saying, "If I remember correctly, you like cream and sugar," Jane, now sitting up on the sofa bed, replied. "Thanks, I really needed this. I haven't slept that hard in weeks. I've got to get all the cobwebs out and find somewhere to store some things and look for an apartment." Wendy, "We have a six by ten storage bin in the basement. Since the apartment came furnished and neither of us brought our furniture, it's empty. We are waiting to see where we're working this fall before we get our stuff. I'm thinking about leaving for Kansas the week after July 4th and returning around the 18th. Dad told me that if we drove there, he would rent a moving van and drive our stuff down here. You're welcome to use the bin until then." Jane, "Thank you, that sounds perfect. I'll put my things there."

An hour later, the three of them had eaten and were carrying Jane's furniture to the basement storage bin. Most of the stuff was small furniture and boxes, so they were done quickly. As soon as they finished, Jane left to take the trailer back to the rental agency. Leah and Wendy went shopping, then to the beach.

After Jane returned the trailer, she drove to the campus. She read that there were about 9000 full and part-time students at UWF, including those in night and weekend classes. She easily found the Math Building and the campus housing office. Even though the housing office was closed on Saturday, there was a list of available off-campus housing posted in the foyer. After she wrote down a few phone numbers and addresses, she started checking out nearby neighborhoods. She first saw an older section of town with large homes, many of which were in the process of being renovated. There were also older apartments that looked like graduate student housing and a couple of complexes that appeared to be nicer. After taking some notes, Jane drove back to Gulf Breeze; she felt that she had accomplished at least one thing that morning; the distance and traffic to Gulf Breeze from campus eliminated any chance of her living close to the beach.

Chapter 20

Connors Begins His Search

Connors and Riley arrived at Pensacola NAS in the afternoon and caught a shuttle to the BOQ. When they checked in, they both took another shuttle to the storage depot to get their vehicles and then met at the Ready Room. While Riley retrieved his treasured Harley, Connors got the Camaro Z28 he bought after he was commissioned. He had considered getting a Corvette, as many Naval Aviators did because it was a "chick magnet." But almost every time he drove to Pensacola Beach, Connors saw the two-seat Corvettes being pulled over. His Z28 could carry four passengers, and it had a lot more luggage space. More importantly, he never had any problem meeting girls, even without a Corvette.

The Ready Room looked the same as the previous year, packed with hard-partying Naval and Marine Aviators and only a few women. The obvious difference was the people in the bar were strangers, mostly newly commissioned officers. Most officers his age were stationed elsewhere. The few girls in the bar looked younger than before, perhaps because Connors was older and had relationships with women his age. Connors did recognize one of the bartenders, but he didn't see the pretty waitress, whose name he believed was Gina. After he deployed, he heard that she was dating one of his classmates, Jake Zimmerman.

By the time happy hour ended, they both ate and drank for less than five dollars. Riley raised his glass, "Ain't it great to be back in Pensacola at the Ready Room. Now, let's hope our good luck continues, and there are some good-lookin' ladies looking for studs like us."

Connors said he wanted to go to the BOQ to call his parents and sister. Riley said. "I'm gonna stick around for a while in case a lonely lady comes in looking for a lean, mean Texas stud hoss." Connors could only laugh as he walked out of the bar.

When he got back to the BOQ, Connors talked to his parents for a half hour. Then he called his sister Sheila, his closest confidant, and they talked a lot longer. Towards the end of the conversation, Sheila asked him if he was going to try to find Jane while he was in Pensacola. He answered. "Sis, I have thought about Jane every day since we split up. I would not be able to live with myself if I didn't try to find her. If I don't, I'll always wonder if she still cared about me and if we could be together again. Tomorrow will be my first day of looking for her."

Chapter 21

Jane Meets with Wendy and Leah

Early the next morning, Jane followed up on the list of available housing and went to look at three of them. Jane loved living in college towns, but she knew from experience it meant putting up with a lot of noisy partying. The places she saw were clearly not what she was looking for, so she extended her search to places farther away from campus. First, she had to meet Dr. Williamson at their 11 am appointment.

Dr. Williamson was a brilliant mathematician who was well-known in the exclusive field of Theoretical Mathematics, Jane's area of study. Jane was familiar with his published papers, some of which were groundbreaking research. She told him it was an honor to work with him and he replied he was lucky to find such a promising new PhD. Then, he took her on a brief tour of the campus and her new office.

Back at his office, Williamson told Jane that she would begin teaching four undergrad classes, and as she progressed, she would get graduate and post-graduate assignments. Finally, he gave her an employment contract and told her that as soon as she returned it signed, she would be on a provisional basis until her dissertation was approved. Williamson, "I have no doubt that your dissertation will be approved. You will officially start work on June 16." Jane asked if she could use her assigned office to review and sign the contract. Williamson, "Of course, as far as I am concerned, it's already your office." A half-hour later, she returned the signed contract to Dr. Williamson, thanked him again, and left.

As Jane drove away from the campus, she decided to go to the beach. Earlier, Wendy said that she usually went to Tiki Beach, in front of the Tiki Bar. Forty minutes later, she had changed clothes and was on her way to the beach.

The Tiki Bar was the only place on Pensacola Beach that served drinks to people on the beach. Since it was well known that IDs were never checked, many underage girls gathered there. Where the girls went, the guys went. The bar also set up two volleyball courts where young officers played almost continually, and further down the beach, many of them played touch football.

Most days, three or four guys were clamoring to sit and talk, uninvited, with any girls they saw. Wendy and Leah were no exception. On this day, men repeatedly offered to buy them drinks or just sat on the blanket and asked their names. They quickly grew tired of it and moved farther away from the bar, but the men still came, but not in an endless line.

Tiki Beach was crowded when Jane arrived, and it took her a few minutes to find Wendy and Leah. When she did, two guys who looked about 21 were sitting on the sand next to them. Wendy and Leah were being polite to the guys, but Jane could tell they were not really interested in either one.

When Jane squeezed between Wendy and the two hopeful guys, they gave up and left. Jane, laughing, "Sorry, I didn't mean to scare them away." Wendy, "Jane, you didn't scare anyone away. We were probably the tenth blanket those guys have gone to today. You're late for the grand march of men in search of their true love, or more realistically, a one-night stand. The daily routine is just ending, but it'll start here again tomorrow morning. If we were willing to go out with guys who would say or do anything to get a date, we would already have dates scheduled for every day this month. It's simultaneously irritating and ego-building, but ironic that having so many available men in one place can become a pain in the butt. I know you can sort out the keepers from the throwbacks after ten seconds of talking to them." Jane, "I can. I'm ready to face the onslaught.

Chapter 22

AOCS is Almost Over

As usual, Class 569 was awakened by Reveille blasting on the PA system, but after the morning run and showers, First Sergeant Sullivan ordered the class to stand in formation outside the Battalion for a progress report from Class Officer Lt. Emmet. Sullivan and Emmet were on the front porch as the class fell in. Lt. Emmet began, "Good morning, Gentlemen, First Sergeant Sullivan and I first want to congratulate you on your progress in the AOCS program. You have made it through almost thirteen weeks of little sleep, high stress, rugged PT, and strict discipline. There are now only thirty-six officer candidates remaining in Class 569. More than sixty people who began AOCS with you are no longer here. You still are, so you have a good idea of what it takes to become a Naval Aviator. There are two weeks of AOCS and one week of senior candidate duty remaining. At the end of the next two weeks, those of you in stupid school will have to pass your exams, and all of you will have to successfully complete the "out" test. But the next two weeks will not get any easier. There will be more inspections, more PT, more long days with little sleep, and more Drill Instructors getting in your face. Make it through those two weeks, and you can make it to the end."

He continued, "During the last week in AOCS, each of you will be given an assignment in one of two staggered classes and INDOC. In effect, you will be in command of three AOCS classes, and your leadership will be assessed by the Drill Instructors. Remember, leadership is one of the three equal segments of AOCS, along with academics and physical training. So, my message to you today is to not let up and keep doing what got you to this point. After what you have already been through, the rest is yours to complete. Good luck, gents. As you were." As Lt. Emmet went into the building, First Sergeant Sullivan marched the class to the mess hall for breakfast.

Carrying his tray of food, Striker sat next to Bulldog, who said, "It's hard to believe there are less than three weeks left. I never expected to make it this far." Striker, puzzled, said, "Bulldog, you're acing it. You're finishing in the top three in every PT category and winning most of them. No one can stay up with you." Bulldog replied. "Yeah, I know, but I'm not much of a swimmer, never have been. I've trained as a wrestler since I was twelve years old. For the last ten years, I have dedicated myself to keeping my body fat at an absolute minimum so that I could meet weight limits. Now, I'm paying the price. Floating is almost impossible for someone with low body fat. I float like a rock, so swimming is really difficult. Except for the breaststroke, I tend to sink if I have to use any other stroke. I only passed the tower jump by swimming underwater most of the way. In Dilbert Dunker training, I barely passed my third attempt. I trapped some air in my flight suit, so I managed to tread water for a minute. I think the instructor looked away for a couple of seconds and didn't see what I did. Even if I make it through the next two weeks, I don't think there is any way I will be able to swim a mile without sinking." Striker replied, "Bulldog, you can do the mile swim. You've made it this far; you've proven you can gut it out. Like I told Hound, who is also a weak swimmer, do the mile by relaxing and slowly doing the breaststroke. The goal is to swim a mile any way you can." Bulldog responded, "I hope you're right. They'd have to tie an anchor to me to get me to quit now."

97

Chapter 23

Connors' Search for Jane Continues

Connors got up early and went to the front desk to check his messages. He had one from Ted Marx, a former AOCS and VT-4 classmate. A month earlier, Marx had finished a WestPac cruise on the Coral Sea and was now stationed at Alameda NAS. Marx had heard from their former AOCS Drill Instructor, now retired, First Sergeant Wardlaw. He was trying to put together a class reunion, including their former class officer, Major Pless. About twenty guys from the class of thirty-five were in the States, and most of them could arrange a flight to Pensacola. Marx had already tentatively reserved the small ballroom at the O Club in late July. Connors said he would help any way he could, and Marx gave him a list of ten people, including Riley, to contact. Pless was at the top of the list.

After he ate breakfast, Connors went back to the front desk and left a message for Riley. Then he started to call the others on the list. Within an hour, Connors left messages for all of them except Pless. He planned to go to Pless' office the next day.

Connors found phone books for Gainesville and Pensacola. He found a J. Carmody in Gainesville, but when he called, it was disconnected. There were no listings for Jane Carmody in the Pensacola book, but after he looked at the print date, he saw that the book was a year old. He then called the operator for Overland Park, Kansas. The operator didn't find J or Jane Carmody, but she did find eight other Carmody's. He couldn't remember what Jane's parents' names were, so he wrote down all eight numbers, thanked the operator, and hung up. Connors thought to himself, "I guess I won't be going to the beach for a while." and he started calling all the Carmody numbers in Overland Park.

Later, a woman answered and told him that she was Jane's mother, but when Connors identified himself, she didn't recognize his last name. She did remember Jane talking about dating someone named Tim, but she wouldn't give him Jane's number or address. She did tell him that the next time Jane called she would give her Connors' message and phone number.

With no other option, Connors left his name and phone number, thanked her, and hung up. He thought, "Well, I've made a little progress finding Jane, but now I wonder where the hell Riley is." He went back to the front desk, but there were still no messages from Riley. Then he asked the clerk for Riley's room number, and Connors went to wake him up.

Connors banged on Riley's door for about ten minutes with no response. He thought that Riley was either really hung over or he was not there. Or, maybe he got lucky with some lady he met at the Ready Room and was now at her place. Connors decided he would try again later. He went back to his room to get ready for the beach. When he returned to the front desk, there was a message from Riley that read, "Got real lucky at the RR. I am at the beach. Try to be at Tiki Beach this afternoon; if not, at the BOQ this evening. Riley."

Connors left for the beach at about eleven and walked to Tiki Bar. He hadn't been there in over a year, and the place was just as he remembered. The bar was crowded, so instead of going in, he walked down the beach looking for anyone he recognized but saw none. He put his blanket in a large open space between the beach and the Tiki Bar so he could see most of the people there. Then, for over an hour, he sat and looked at anyone who walked nearby. With no luck finding Jane, he decided to take a swim.

He remembered the day when he was snorkeling nearby, and a couple of guys were shark fishing on the pier. The two guys had taken a case of beer, a couple of lounge chairs, and a deep-water fishing rod to the end of the pier. They put a large piece of raw meat on a heavy-duty hook, attached a couple of floats, and threw it as far from the pier as they could. Then they sat down and drank beer.

About an hour and several beers later, a 300-pound shark took the bait. Apparently, one of the guys was a skilled fisherman, so he managed to keep the shark on the hook. After half an hour, he brought it close to the pier. It was too big to get on the pier, but someone from a nearby boat brought a gaff and rope to them. The two fishermen gaffed the shark, got the rope looped around it, and pulled it along the side of the boat to the shore.

By then, a huge crowd of people on the beach immediately surrounded the shark. Dozens of terrified people got out of the water as fast as they could. The two guys quickly got some of their buddies to help carry the big fish off the beach and over to Dirty Joe's Saloon, where it was laying on the bar with a Jax beer in its mouth.

After his swim, Connors went back to his blanket to take a nap. Later, he started walking up and down the beach, but there was still no trace of Jane. It was approaching four, so he went into the Tiki Bar to get a beer and look around. He didn't recognize anyone, so he took his beer back to his blanket, where he remained until after 5 pm without seeing any sign of

Jane. It was time for happy hour, so he went to the BOQ, cleaned up, and headed to the Ready Room.

When he got there, it was not as crowded as the night before, so he easily got a seat at the bar. Beer was free again, and oysters and shrimp were specials, but they also had fried red snapper sandwiches, his favorite. Connors ordered a beer, a dozen oysters, and a snapper sandwich.

Just as he sipped his beer, Major Pless came in and sat next to him. Connors started to stand, but Pless stopped him, saying, "No need for formalities. I hear you're not only a hot shit F-4 pilot; you got two MiGs over North Vietnam. Now we're colleagues, so call me Steve. How are you, and how long are you going to be here?" Connors responded, "Well, sir, I mean Steve, I just got back from a WestPac cruise on the Kitty Hawk, stayed in San Diego for a couple of days, and got orders to be an instructor in VT-4. My assignment is for a year, but I also applied for Test Pilot School at Pax River. It doesn't begin until next year, so it could work out pretty well. My CO, Commander Phelan, seems to think I have a good shot at it and wrote a letter of recommendation." Pless replied, "That's great. I've met Phelan. He's a great pilot and a straight-shooting officer. If he recommended you for test pilot school, you deserve to get accepted. Your AOCS class was the last class I was assigned, so I remember you and a lot of your classmates. I also remember that you were first in the class, and I heard that you finished first in your VT-4 class. I'll tell you what, stop by my office and give my assistant the info about the class you've applied to, and I'll write you a letter of recommendation as well." Connors, a little embarrassed, thanked Pless and said, "I really appreciate your doing that for me, Steve. I was already going to go to your office tomorrow morning to see if you can make it to our class reunion. First Sergeant Wardlaw has been spearheading it, and he asked Ted Marx and me to call people. I know it is short notice, but it's not often that more than half the guys are close enough for a reunion. So, we're trying to set it up sometime in late July here at the O Club. Marx has the date, so I will call him tomorrow and find out when it is." Pless. "Just let me know when, and I'll be there. I'd love to see those guys again, especially Jack Wardlaw, who was a great Marine and a good friend. So, when you drop off the test pilot school info, leave the reunion date and place. I'm going to grab a quick beer and go. I have to be at an old squadron mate's house in less than an hour." Pless ordered a beer and was soon surrounded by admirers.

Riley walked in with a pretty girl. He saw Connors at the bar, and said, "Hi Connors, I want you to meet my friend Patty, she's a nurse at NAMI. There's a table over there. Do you want to join us?" Connors nodded yes and took his sandwich and beer to the table.

After they sat down, Riley excused himself and went to the head. Connors asked Patty, "How long have you been at NAMI?" She responded. "Almost three years, but I am being transferred to the OB/GYN Unit at Jacksonville. I have to report a week from today and will really miss this place." Connors then asked, "Do you know Lisa Thomas?" and Patty, smiling, said, "Sure. Lisa was my charge nurse. She is a super nurse and a great person, but her husband is a real asshole. He knocked up another NAMI nurse and then dumped Lisa. It broke her heart. She had to get away from there as soon as possible, so she volunteered to go to Subic Bay Navy Hospital. I haven't heard anything about Lisa since, but I think she's still there. Do you know where she is and how she's doing?" Connors answered, "I do. She is my ex-girlfriend's cousin. I met her when I was stationed here about a year and a half ago.

My ex and I had dinner with her and Tony a couple of times. I ran into her about two weeks ago when my ship stopped in Subic Bay to replenish. Of all things, we were both at the swimming pool, and she recognized me. She told me she had been accepted to a nurse practitioner training program at Bethesda Naval Hospital, starting in a month or two." Patty smiled, saying, "Good for her. She's such a nice person. I hope she finds someone else to love again." Connors replied, "I do too. She's a special lady." When Riley came back, Connors told him about the class reunion and that Pless would be there.

Chapter 24

Jane Carmody Finds an Apartment

Jane decided to drive over to the university to look for places that were not so close to campus. There were three available places listed, all of which appeared to be at least a mile or two from campus. Since traffic was heavy, she took a different route that went around Pensacola on the western shore of Escambia Bay, and then inland toward the university. The eighteen-mile drive took almost forty minutes, longer than going through town. There was a beautiful view of the bay along the way, and she decided to use this route more often. As she drove, she saw a few apartments and a lot of small homes. She found two apartments on her list, but she was not interested in either one. The third one, an apartment in a house, was closer to the water, so she decided to come back to it later.

As she drove closer to the bay, the houses got bigger, especially ones that were waterfront. She eventually ended up on a road called Mackey Cove Drive. She drove a little way down the street and saw a rent sign. There was a car in the driveway, so she pulled in and knocked on the door. A woman in her sixties came to the door and asked Jane what she wanted. Jane replied, "My name is Jane Carmody. I hope I didn't interrupt anything, but I saw the 'for rent' sign, and I thought I would ask about it. I'm at the university, and I need to find some place to live." The woman smiled and said, "Are you a student?" Jane responded. "No, actually, I was just appointed to an Assistant Professor's position at the university. I start work on the 16th. I'm twenty-six years old, single, and staying with my sister in Gulf Breeze. I'm trying to find a place close to the university, but not in the middle of a bunch of student apartments. I can provide references if you want." The lady smiled and invited her in, and then the woman said, "I'm Rosemary O'Neil, and I have lived here for nearly fifteen years. My husband passed away almost five years ago. He was a retired Navy Captain who was last stationed at Pensacola NAS. This was supposed to be our retirement home. When he died, we had just finished renovating the room above the garage into a two-bedroom apartment. We were going to rent it to military families for additional income, but for the last few years, my son and his wife and daughter lived there while he made two cruises. My son is a Navy pilot, just like his dad. They were recently transferred to San Diego and bought a house there. I decided to rent the apartment, but I do not rent to students, so I didn't list it at the housing office. Three or four students still found the sign and wanted to rent it. I told them that the rent was three hundred dollars a month, plus utilities, just to scare them away. It has worked so far."

Mrs. O'Neill asked, "Would you like to see it? By the way, the apartment is furnished and even has a television." Jane said she would, and Mrs. O'Neil took her outside to a garage with a stairway that went up to the apartment. Jane followed her up the stairs. Mrs. O'Neil opened the door, and Jane saw that the apartment was huge. It took up the entire area above a three-car garage. It had two bedrooms and two and a half bathrooms, a formal dining room, a living room with a fireplace, and an eat-in kitchen with a bay window overlooking a cove. Both bedrooms had full baths, and the bedroom in the back had another bay window. There was also a deck across the back of the house, which had entrances from the kitchen and back bedroom. The apartment was totally furnished, including flatware, dishes, and pots and pans.

Jane, after taking a deep breath, said. "Wow, this is gorgeous, but I can't afford three hundred dollars a month on an assistant professor's salary. I wish I could. I'd give you a deposit check right now." Mrs. O'Neal responded. "Miss Carmody, I can make it one-fifty, including utilities for you. I require a month's rent as a deposit plus the first month's rent when you move in." Jane said, "I'll take it. When can I move in?" Mrs. O'Neil responded, "I'm having the apartment cleaned, so on June 6th, you can sign the lease and move in when you want. Oh, you can also park your car in any empty space in the garage."

Jane immediately wrote out a check, and Mrs. O'Neil said, "I'll sign the lease and give you the keys Saturday morning." Jane responded, "I'll be here about 10 with my stuff if that's OK." Mrs. O'Neil shook her head yes and thanked her.

As she drove away, Jane was overjoyed about the apartment and couldn't wait to tell Wendy. As she sang along with the Rolling Stones, said, "Looks like today I can get what I want, eat your heart out, Mick Jagger."

When she arrived at the apartment, Wendy and Leah had already been back and gone out again. Wendy left a note that they were going over to Mrs. Hopkin's Boarding House for lunch. She also wrote down the address, the time they left, and an invitation to join them. Jane went right back to her car, found the address on the map, and headed there.

As she was going up the front steps to the porch, she caught Wendy's eye, and Wendy waved for her to join them. As soon as they sat down, Jane told them she had found an incredible waterfront apartment about two and a half miles from campus, then described every detail she could remember. When she finished, Wendy told Jane that they had good news too. Both she and Leah had been referred to schools that had available full-time positions. Both had already made appointments the next week with the principals. If selected, they would begin full-time in mid-August. After they ate, they agreed they would go to the beach and then go out to celebrate.

Chapter 25

AOCS Ends

It was almost the last week of AOCS, and Class 569 now included 31 candidates; Striker and his roommates were still there, but three candidates had failed to meet a PT standard, and two failed the math final. As worried as they were about Bulldog and Hound, they easily finished the one-mile swim, doing the breaststroke for over an hour. When Bulldog finally climbed out of the pool, he ran around the pool and hooted loudly, all in a moment of exuberance. He had overcome his greatest fear. Since such outbreaks were not allowed in AOCS, the irritated swim instructor ordered Bulldog to do two hundred side straddle hops. Even after he just swam a mile in a flight suit, Bulldog completed them and barely broke a sweat.

The last day of AOCS training for Class 569 was June 29. Senior candidate week would begin the next morning. The day began as all Sundays did, with the candidates getting up at 0530, going for a four-mile run in formation, and then back to clean up for religious services at the chapel.

When everyone returned, First Sergeant Sullivan did not take them to the mess hall. He told them that they had fifteen minutes to prepare for an inspection with weapons in front of Battalion Three. Striker and his roommates made sure that their uniforms and shoes looked perfect and their weapons were flawless. With three minutes to go, they were on their way to the front of the building.

When all the candidates were in formation, Sullivan told them to form, in no particular order, a straight line across the front of the building. Striker was the last candidate on the right side of the line. He didn't realize that he was standing directly under some low-hanging tree limbs and a telephone line where a flock of blackbirds was resting. Sullivan, with a notebook in hand instead of his swagger stick, started the inspection on the left side of the line and went from candidate to candidate, ordering each one to recite the required memorization and drilling each one through the manual of arms. When they finished, he didn't say a word, but after each inspection, he wrote something in the notebook.

When Sullivan got to Striker, he began to inspect his uniform. He looked at Striker's feet and saw that bird droppings had almost covered the toe of his right shoe. Sullivan then looked up, saw birds flying overhead, and pointed at the shoe, "Mr. Striker, is that a mess hall omelet you dropped on your shoe? Look at it and tell me what that is." Striker looked down at his shoe, looked up, and said, "No sir, Drill Instructor Sullivan, the substance on this candidate's right shoe is not a mess hall omelet. The substance on this candidate's right shoe is bird shit." Many of the class began to laugh quietly. Sullivan replied. "Are you sure that is not an omelet on your shoe, Mr. Striker? Look at it again. It sure looks like a mess hall omelet to me." Striker looked down and said, "First Sergeant Sullivan, the substance on this candidate's right shoe does not look like an omelet served in the mess hall to this candidate. It looks more like bird shit, but it is difficult for this candidate to tell the difference between the two." Sullivan, now laughing along with the class, replied, "You are absolutely correct, Mr. Striker. It is very difficult to tell a mess hall omelet from bird shit. You finally learned something in AOCS, Mr. Striker, congratulations."

Then, without ordering Striker to do the manual of arms or anything else, Sullivan pivoted, and walked to the center of the line and ordered the class to stand at ease. Then he addressed them, "Gentlemen, almost sixteen weeks ago, I told you it was my job to determine which of you had the right stuff to be a Naval Aviator and which did not, and then mold you into leaders. I did it as best as I could. You now have only one more week in AOCS to show me and the other drill instructors whether or not we have made any mistakes. We have done everything we can to teach you leadership. It is now up to you to prove that you have learned." Then Sullivan ordered the class to get into formation and marched them to the mess hall. When they returned to the barn, Sullivan told them they would have on-base liberty from 1800 to 2200 to prepare for their last week of AOCS. Then he dismissed them.

The week of senior candidate duty was the final AOCS leadership test, as evaluated by the drill instructors. Every candidate's assignment had been posted. Striker was the commanding officer of INDOC, and Bulldog was his executive officer. Hound was the XO of Battalion Two, and Sticky was the XO of the First Battalion. But before it began, Striker was selected by First Sergeant Sullivan to be the last Class 569 Officer of the Day, beginning at 1800 and ending the next morning at 0430. That meant Striker would get very little or no sleep, but being chosen to be OD on the last day of training was a high honor. He was more than willing to lose sleep since he probably wouldn't be able to sleep anyway.

Chapter 26

Surprise at the BOQ

At the Ready Room, Connors filled Riley in on his plans for the next day, including going to the beach to look for Jane again. A few beers later, he left to get some sleep, and Riley wished him luck.

When he got to the BOQ, Connors saw a large group of guys around the swimming pool, cheering and applauding. Intrigued, he walked over and asked a nearby ensign what was happening. The ensign responded, "A couple of guys were walking towards their rooms when they saw some people in the pool and some others running towards the parking lot. As they got close to the pool area, they saw three naked girls in the water and yelled, 'Naked girls in the pool.' Soon, everybody in the BOQ came out to look. Apparently, the girls left their clothes on the grass and didn't have any towels. They either have to get out of the pool naked or stay in the water. They looked like they might be eighteen, maybe younger, and probably were drinking and got themselves into a difficult situation." Connors then told the ensign, "Obviously, the guys are cheering for the girls to get out of the water naked. I assume their boyfriends either panicked and left or went to get towels somewhere. I'm sure none of these guys are going to bring the girls any towels." A few minutes later, he said, "It's just another night in the world of the officers and gentlemen we know as Naval Aviators. "

Just then, two cars pulled up, and three guys with blankets and towels ran to the pool. As they went by Connors, he estimated that they were sixteen or seventeen years old. As the boys approached the pool, the guys around it began to boo loudly but made no effort to stop them. Now covered with towels. The girls got out of the pool and quickly walked to the parking lot. Once in the cars, they left with tires squealing. Connors. "I bet they're Navy dependents who live on base. I don't think they'll skinny dip again anytime soon."

The next morning Connors got up before 7 and went to Pless' office to drop off his Test Pilot School and squadron reunion information. Later, he came back to the BOQ, ate, and made some phone calls. First, he called Marx and got the tentative date of the reunion: July 20th. Then he called his parents, followed by a call to his sister. His family was thrilled to know that he was coming home. Before he left, he wrote a note to Riley and left it with the room clerk.

It was already crowded when he walked into the Tiki Bar. On weekends, people would get there really early to get the best spot. Connors sat at a small table, ordered a Bloody Mary, and looked around. From his table, he could see almost everyone who came into the bar or sat nearby. Over an hour and a half later, he was sure that Jane wasn't there, and he headed to his parents' home.

Chapter 27

Jane's Dissertation Review in Gainesville

The phone was ringing as Jane walked into Wendy's apartment. It was Dr. Sandler. As soon as Jane said hello, Dr. Sandler told her that the review committee had too many conflicts and wanted to reschedule the review for June 6 at 11 am. Since her dissertation was the only item on the agenda, it should be over in less than two hours. Jane immediately said she would be there. Then Dr. Sandler told her that if she wanted him to prep her, he would be available at any time the next day. They agreed to meet at the next morning.

Jane told Wendy what happened and that she would pack a bag, call her landlord, and drive to Gainesville. After she packed an overnight bag, she called Mrs. O'Neill to change their meeting to 3 pm on the 7th. Then Jane hugged Wendy and left. Jane stopped once for gas and was in Gainesville by 7:30. She checked into a hotel near campus, went to the hotel's restaurant for a sandwich, and then to her room. She called her parents' house and talked to her father. He said that her mother was in Kansas City visiting her sister but would be back in the morning. She told him about the apartment and that she was in Gainesville to defend her dissertation on Friday. Then her father told Jane that her mother had a message from one of her old boyfriends, but he didn't know who the caller was. Jane said she would ask her mother the next day.

Jane was asleep by 10 and up at 7 when she showered, dressed, and went downstairs for breakfast. She brought the final draft of her dissertation to review before she met with Dr. Sandler. She couldn't stop wondering if it was Connors who called.

She arrived at the Math Department promptly and went to Dr. Sandler's office. The door was open, and she saw him taking notes while he read her dissertation. Rather than disturb him, she waited for him to finish, but he saw her and called. "Jane, please come in. I was just finishing my notes." Jane went in and told him that she had spoken to Dr. Williamson and really appreciated the faith Sandler had in her. She told him about the apartment and how everything seemed to be falling into place. Dr. Sandler told her again that there was no need to thank him; she deserved the recommendation. Her dissertation was a brilliant piece of research, and he had no doubt the committee would approve it unanimously. Then he showed her his notes, it was two pages of comments. Normally, he would have at least ten pages. As Jane looked at his notes, he said, "As you see from what I have written, this will not take too long. Are you ready to begin?"

Dr. Sandler started with a synopsis of Jane's research, and then followed with specific questions about her hypothesis, research methods, bibliography, and conclusions. Jane was focused and to the point in her responses. She was also careful to validate everything in her conclusion. After almost three hours of give and take, Dr. Sandler said, "Jane, you're done. You absolutely nailed every question I asked. You're ready to face the committee. I'll see you tomorrow morning." Jane thanked him again and left.

Jane was starving, so she drove straight to her favorite Chinese restaurant. After she finished eating, she went to the hotel and called her mother. Jane told her about her apartment and that she was prepared to defend her dissertation. Then she said that her father had said someone called to speak to her, but he didn't know who it was. Her mother replied that she mislaid the message and would look for it. She did remember that his first name was Tim, and she would give Jane his phone number when she found the message. Jane didn't say anything for a few seconds, then asked her mother to call as soon as she found the message. After the call ended, Jane wondered why Connors had called and then went for a swim. After doing laps for about an hour, she went back to her room and took a nap.

At 5:30 pm, Jane ate a quick dinner at the hotel restaurant and returned to her room. She ordered a bottle of white wine and, for the next three hours, studied her dissertation. When she was done, she finished her glass of wine and went to bed. She didn't notice that the desk phone indicated she had a message.

Chapter 28

AOCS Senior Week

Striker's shift as Officer of the Day began at 1800 and ended at 0430. It was an unremarkable night until 2200. As the procedures required, Striker checked each room to see if everyone returned on time. Of the 31 candidates remaining in Class 569, Striker could only verify that 30 people were present. The one candidate missing was Sticky. Striker asked Bulldog and Hound if they had seen him at the AOCS club. Bulldog told him they bought Sticky a beer around 1900 but didn't see him again until about 2130. Hound saw Sticky taking bets that he could drink two "Hairy Buffalo" concoctions, the bar's specialty drink. There was a standing challenge that anyone who drank two of them without vomiting got the drinks for free, plus another one the next time they came to the bar. The drink was almost eight ounces of rum, Irish Whiskey, Grenadine, Grand Marnier, and pineapple juice blended into a mixture that looked like antifreeze and tasted like sweetened jet fuel. Striker thought it was incredible that any sane person would even drink one, much less two. Hound saw Sticky chugging one Hairy Buffalo, but it could have been the second. About fifteen minutes later, Hound saw Sticky stumbling out of the club in a hurry and assumed he went outside to vomit. It was the last time either one of them saw Sticky that night.

Striker, unsure what he should do, decided to check the heads. There were four heads in the building, two on each floor. The first-floor heads were empty, so he went to the one closest to their room. As he opened the door, Striker heard a shower running and went to look. Sticky was there, out cold on the floor, with the shower going full blast. His clothes were lying outside of the shower room. Striker sprayed cold water directly into Sticky's face for about five minutes. Striker opened his eyes, coughed, and tried to wipe the water off his face. Then he attempted to speak, but he could only slur, "Stop the damn shower, I'm drowning." Striker propped Sticky up against the shower wall and he managed to stay on his feet until Striker turned off the shower. Then he picked up Sticky's crumpled uniform from the other side of the room. Returning to Sticky, he said, "I'm going to try to get you to the room if you can stay on your feet and walk. You ready?" Sticky, eyes half closed and barely able to stand, slurred, "Sure can. Where are we going?" Striker replied. "Out the door and about twenty feet down the hall to the room." Sticky opened his eyes wide, tried to focus, and pointed at the door. Then he slurred, "Hell yeah, I can make it. Let go." Striker led Sticky by the arm slowly down the hall. As they got close to the room, Bulldog and Hound put him in bed. He was asleep as soon as his head hit the pillow. Striker hung Sticky's uniform in his locker, left the room, and looked at his watch. It was 2250. Sticky made it into his bed ten minutes before Taps was broadcast.

As he got back to the OD office, Striker thought to himself, "Hopefully, nothing else bad will happen during the next five hours, and my days in AOCS can end successfully." Striker was correct; the rest of the night was dull by comparison. The biggest problem he had was staying awake. The many weeks of little sleep had drained all the reserve energy out of him. After a couple of hours, he could not sit because he knew he would fall asleep. He even had a hard time staying awake while he was standing, just like First Sergeant Sullivan had predicted.

Striker simply refused to fall sleep. He made frequent patrols around the building and splashed cold water on his face.

He jogged in place and even assumed the sitting position against the office wall so the pain would keep him awake. He also checked Sticky several times to see if he was in bed. His snoring sounded like an F-4 afterburner.

Finally, it was 0400 and Striker patrolled the building for the last time. At Reveille, he signed out in the OD log and went to his room. Bulldog and Hound managed to get Sticky out of bed and into a shower. He didn't remember anything that happened after 2100, including chugging the Hairy Buffaloes. He did know that he got sick and his head hurt like a wrecking ball had hit it.

The shower seemed to help Sticky sober up to the point he could dress himself. As he did, he said, "It's a good thing we don't have any more inspections or PT because if we did, I'd be a dead man walking. I already feel like death warmed over. It's good that I puked most of that napalm out of my system. If I hadn't, I would be still on the lawn next to the AOCS club."

Striker and his roommates put senior candidate insignias on their shirt collars. Then they smiled as they looked at each other and got into formation in front of Battalion Three. Knowing that he was now a senior candidate gave Striker the energy he needed to make it through the day, now as the INDOC commanding officer.

Both Lt. Emmet and First Sergeant Sullivan came out of the building and stood next to each other. Sullivan, "Gentlemen, today you begin the final phase of AOCS training, Senior Candidate week. You all have come a long way and have endured all the long hours, difficult classroom work, and exhausting training. Only thirty-one out of the over a hundred people who walked into INDOC over fifteen weeks ago are still here. Congratulations on what you have accomplished. It is not over yet. You still have to complete this next phase. You now have your assignments, and you should know what your missions are. When you leave here this morning you are on your own. Good luck, Gents." Then Lt. Emmet spoke, "At ease, Gents. I also want to congratulate you for your success so far, but as the First Sergeant told you, do not let up; it's not over yet. I also have some very good news for you. Since Friday is the Fourth of July and many events will be taking place on base this weekend, the Training Command CO, Admiral Thorsen, has decided to cut AOCS training by two days. Commissioning will occur on Thursday, July 3, instead of Saturday. I also want to announce that there will be two honored guests at the ceremony: Major Stephen Pless, a Medal of Honor recipient will swear everyone in, and Captain Andrew Striker, a Mustang officer and the father of Class 569 Senior Candidate Striker. Captain Striker is the rare enlisted man who rose through the ranks and became a highly respected career Naval Aviator. Good luck, Gents. I hope to see you all on Thursday."

First Sergeant Sullivan then brought the class to attention, and marched them to the mess hall for breakfast. When they finished, they marched to Battalion Three and put fresh uniforms and toiletries into pillowcases, then went to their assignments. Striker, Bulldog, and nine other senior candidates went into INDOC and met in the quarterdeck to discuss their assignment. They expected 96 new poopies to arrive at any minute. Sullivan told Striker that the senior candidates had free reign with the poopies as each walked in the door. Harassment would last about two hours or until every new poopy had been confronted. First, Sergeant Sullivan and the other two drill instructors would then take over. Senior Candidates would stay at INDOC until Wednesday at 1800, when they would return to Battalion Three to prepare for the commissioning ceremony. Striker's duties included organizing the watches, making sure the poopies remained in their rooms, and keeping an accurate list of poopies as they DOR'd. One Senior Candidate had to be in the office at all times in case any poopy had questions or unforeseen emergencies. Striker and Bulldog chose to be in the office until 2000 that night.

The next morning, the soon-to-be-poopies cautiously walked past the welcoming signs into uncontrolled chaos. With Drill Instructor Sullivan watching, all ten Senior Candidates and two Drill Instructors pounced on the poopies, giving them the same harassment Class 569 received when they first walked in those doors. Most of the poopies didn't know whether to tap dance or set their hair on fire. The harassment went on for almost two hours. Finally, First Sergeant Sullivan signaled Striker and the other Senior Candidates to stop and let the Drill Instructors continue. As the poopies were assigned rooms, Striker and the other Senior Candidates began patrolling the building to insure all of them were doing what they were ordered to do.

Before three hours passed, ten poopies DOR'd. Striker recorded their names and room numbers, and Bulldog escorted them to a small barracks near the administration building. The next few hours INDOC replayed what Class 569 went through fifteen weeks earlier. Striker thought, "It sure is better watching this nightmare than being in it."

After dinner, Striker and Bulldog took turns patrolling the building to check the rooms and get a head count. When the nightly wake-ups began, Striker expected several poopies to DOR, and several did.

While Striker was on patrol, a poopy showed up at the Senior Candidate's office door. First Sergeant Sullivan told the class they had to "Pound the Pine" in order to enter the INDOC office. The poopy was braced up against the wall outside the office. Earlier, he clumsily attempted to enter but didn't come close to following the procedure, which was detailed on a plaque on the wall. The poopy was doing everything wrong and apparently didn't realize he could read the procedures in front of him. Bulldog wasn't sure what to do, so he went out to the hall and faced the 6'3" and 230-pound poopy. Bulldog yelled at him, "What the hell is wrong with you, poopy, can't you read? If you are trying to pound the pine, you are really screwing it up. The pound the pine procedure is behind you on the pine board that is the target of your pounding. Since you do not yet know how to do an about-face. I am going back into my office and forget you've been here while you turn around, read the procedure, and start again. You have thirty seconds. Then Bulldog went back into the office and waited. Thirty seconds later, Bulldog screamed, "Pound the pine, poopy." The big poopy suddenly appeared in the center of the entrance and pounded the pine. Bulldog went closer to the poopy and looked down at his feet, which were three inches from the toe marks painted on the floor. He faced the poopy and yelled, "You aren't even close to where you're supposed to be, poopy. Do it again at my command." Bulldog went back into the office and yelled, "Pound the pine, poopy." Again, the big poopy didn't do it correctly. Bulldog went to him, told him what he was doing wrong, and ordered him to do it again.

About half an hour later, Striker arrived back at the office, saw the poopy sweating, and braced against the wall. Bulldog told Striker that it was the poopy's eighth attempt to correctly pound the pine. Bulldog asked, "What do you think I should do? That poopy could be there all night trying to get in the damn door." Striker answered, "Go lay out the steps in numbers. Do it a couple of times and ask him to repeat it out loud." Bulldog went back out and numbered and repeated each

121

step and told the poopy to repeat it out loud. Bulldog said, "By the numbers, poopy, pound the pine. Begin." The poopy did it perfectly and came into the office.

The poopy was finally allowed to speak, "Senior Candidate Schnider, this candidate is asking permission to call this candidate's wife, who had a premature baby boy early this morning. This candidate was notified as the bus was leaving the hotel this morning. The message had a phone number and said that this candidate's wife and son are doing OK so far." Bulldog looked at Striker, who said, "Poopy, what's your name, your wife's name, and the name of the hospital?" The poopy replied. "This candidate's name is Ted Sherman; the wife's name is Mary Anne and the number of the hospital is on the message." Striker replied, "Sherman, give me the message, and I will call the hospital. If I can get your wife on the phone, Senior Candidate Schnider and I will leave you alone in the office for fifteen minutes." Sherman, now with tears in his eyes, handed the message to Striker, who picked up the office phone. After explaining the call to the operator, Striker eventually reached Sherman's wife, Mary Anne. Striker handed the phone to Sherman, and then he and Bulldog left Sherman alone in the office.

Fifteen minutes later, Striker and Bulldog went back into the office. Sherman was standing at attention in front of the desk. He had tears rolling down his cheeks, but he was smiling. Striker asked, "Everything OK, Sherman?" Sherman replied, "Yes sir, Senior Candidate Striker, this candidate's wife and son are fine but will be in the hospital for a couple of weeks. This candidate wants to thank the Senior Candidate for allowing this candidate to speak to their candidate's wife. This candidate was so worried about this candidate's wife and son, this candidate could not properly pound the pine and was ready to DOR." Striker looked at Bulldog and then said, "Congratulations, Sherman for your new baby son and for completing the pound the pine correctly. Now get your big poopy ass back to your room." Sherman smiled, did a clumsy about-face, and ran out of the office.

Bulldog then went on a patrol around the building, and everything looked in order. It was almost 2000 when Bulldog returned and updated the daily log, including the time spent with Sherman. When he returned, two other Senior Candidates, Langford and Collins, were in the office to begin an eight-hour shift. "Thank God you're here," Striker said. "I've been up for over forty hours and am beyond exhaustion." Collins responded, "We're ready to go, now you get some sleep. You look beat." Langford and Collins logged in as Bulldog said, "You guys have the Con." Striker and Bulldog went to the Senior Candidate quarters and got some sleep.

The next morning, Striker was out of bed before Reveille and was in the head, shaving. He put on a clean uniform and went to Bulldog's room to see if he was ready to go. Bulldog had just gotten out of bed and said he would be in the office in fifteen minutes. Striker told him he would see him there and left.

As he walked down the hall, he saw First Sergeant Sullivan come out of the office. Striker braced against the wall. Sullivan came over to him and said, "Stand at ease, Mister Striker. I just read yesterday's log and saw what you and Bulldog did about Sherman's wife and new baby. I want to tell you that you did the right thing. You handled it well. Leadership is not just ordering your people what to do and where to go. It's about taking care of them. Because of what you did for him, Sherman will now follow you and Bulldog into the gates of hell. You took care of him, a person under your command, not just another nameless poopy. The most important rules of leadership are to take care of your people and to leave no man behind. Last night you showed me you mastered the first. I have no doubt you will succeed at the second. Now get your ass back to work." Encouraged by Sullivan, Striker thought for the first time since he started AOCS, "Maybe I can get through this shit after all."

The remaining days of the INDOC assignment flew by without incident, largely fueled by Sullivan's encouraging words. On July 2nd, Sullivan ordered Class 569 to the meeting room, where they had to do their last peer review. Unlike the first peer review, Sullivan told them to rank only two candidates, the best and the worst. After the rankings were finished, Sullivan ordered them to fall in and marched them to their final mess hall dinner. The special of the day was Salisbury steak, which was the same as the first dinner they had in INDOC. As they ate, Sticky looked at Striker and said, "The first time we ate this, it tasted like shit; now that it's the last time we'll eat it in AOCS, it tastes great."

When they finished, the class marched back to the Battalion Three meeting room. After they lined up in the room, First Sergeant Sullivan told them to stand at ease while he counted the votes he had collected earlier. A few seconds later, he said, "This is going to be real easy, Gents. No one received three votes for being the worst. By far, the majority of votes for best are for one candidate. Mr. Striker, you were ranked first by 27 of 31 of your classmates. Since I already reviewed your Academic and PT Out Tests results last night, it is clear that you finished first overall in Class 569. Congratulations, Mr. Striker. Gents, you can now let him know how you feel." Striker's classmates then cheered and hooted, and many shook his hand or slapped his back.

Ten minutes later, Sullivan said, "As you were, Gents, now we have some official business to complete. We will fall in and march to the Main Administration Building." They formed a single line at the entrance and went into an office where four clerks were waiting. Striker and his classmates stood in silence for a few minutes and wondered what was going on. Each clerk then called out a candidate's name and motioned him to come to the workstation. Then, one by one, each candidate was given an Honorable Discharge as an enlisted man and then immediately given his commissioning documents to sign, as well as new dog tags and serial numbers. In effect, once Striker and the rest of Class 569 signed the documents, they were officially ensigns. They just had to go through the ceremony.

Chapter 29

Connors Visits Family and Looks for

Jane

For the next few days, Connors visited his family at Melbourne Beach. He had not seen his parents for over a year and the rest of the family for almost two years. While he was with the family, he told them about his efforts to find Jane, the girl he had reluctantly broken up with the previous year. He didn't know how they would react to his pursuing a seemingly hopeless dream. All of them, especially his sister Sheila, could tell that he really cared for Jane and encouraged him to try. She strongly believed that Jane still felt the same way about him.

The drive up the coast of Florida was, at times, beautiful, but he was slowed by red lights and heavy traffic most of the way. It took over five hours to get to Gainesville and another half hour to find a hotel close to the university. He checked in and put his bag in a room, then went downstairs to the business office and started looking up Jane's name in the local phone books. He found her number, but it was disconnected. There was also a university phone book in the office, and he again found her number, but when he called this time, a man answered. Connors asked him if he knew Jane Carmody or where she might be. The man said he didn't know her, but he had heard she had finished her dissertation and was looking for a job. He also said that Jane probably knew a lot of math faculty and was sure one of them could help him. He gave Connors the math department's office number and told him to ask for Dr. Sandler. Connors called Sandler's number, but he was gone for the day. It was after 6 pm, and Connors decided there was not much more he could do, so he went to his room to take a short nap before dinner.

Connors did not wake up until almost 8 pm; when he got up, he was groggy and very hungry. He decided that the hotel restaurant was the best place to eat at this time of the day. There were only ten people in the dining area and three at the bar when he arrived. Connors sat at the bar near the bartender. A chalkboard menu displayed the house special, a spicy fried chicken sandwich; he ordered one and a draft beer. The bartender, who had a noticeable limp, brought the beer and, after some small talk, asked Connors his story.

Connors told him he was originally from Melbourne Beach but lived in Gainesville while he was at the university. He was now in the Navy, stationed in Pensacola. The bartender, whose name was Paul Givens, said he was a senior at the university, majoring in mechanical engineering. He had been a Marine Recon and did two tours in Vietnam. In the sixth month of the second tour, shrapnel from a mortar hit him and almost took his right leg off below the knee. The doctors pieced it back together again, but the damage was extensive. He was med-boarded out of the Corps and granted a disability. After he finished rehab, he used the GI bill to go to the University of Florida. Connors told Paul that he got both his Bachelor's and Master's in Florida before he joined the Navy.

Paul asked Connors what brought him back to Gainesville. Connors said he was looking for a friend who was a grad student there. Her name was Jane Carmody. Paul, surprised, said, "She was my math professor's graduate assistant. She helped me get through the class. She was a great teacher who really knew math. I heard she recently got a job in Pensacola at the University of West Florida. She even got an assistant professor position. Believe it or not, I saw her here in the restaurant last night just as my shift was over. I was walking out of the restaurant, and I saw her sitting at a table across the room. I was in a hurry to get home, so I didn't say hello to her, but I'm positive it was her."

Connors was speechless for a couple of seconds. Then he asked if Paul knew if she was still at the hotel. He responded. "I didn't see her tonight, but my shift started at seven, so I don't know. My cousin is the front desk manager, and he might tell me. Please understand that it is the hotel's policy not to release the names or room numbers of registered guests. Since she is someone I know, he might tell me. I'll give him a call. In case I can't get him before you leave, give me your room number and I'll call you. Give me your name and phone number. I'll give it to my cousin. If I see Jane after you check out, I'll give it to her."

Connors thanked him, ate the sandwich, and waited to see if Jane might come back. Two hours and three beers later, Connors went to his room, showered, and went to bed. As soon as Connors turned off the desk lamp, Paul called and said that his cousin had confirmed that a person named Jane Carmody was a guest in the hotel, but he could not tell him anything else. Connors set the alarm clock for 5:45 am so he could be in the entrance lobby if she left early the next morning.

Chapter 30

AOCS Commissioning Day

Commissioning Day, July 3, began as every other day of AOCS, with Reveille at 0430. Striker and his classmates woke up knowing that all the harassment, inspections, drilling, PT, classwork, and mess hall food was over. Only breakfast remained, then the class would return to the barn, turn in their weapons to the armorer, put all of their khaki uniforms, shoes, and toiletries in a basket, and change into dress white choker uniforms, complete with white shoes and white gloves. Sullivan told them to march in formation to the mess hall, where they took their time enjoying their last breakfast in AOCS. Unlike every other meal at the mess hall, the candidates were not apprehensive about the coming day and were not cautious about talking about the daily rigors of AOCS. Instead, the mood was exuberant, and their comments were celebratory. No matter what they went through, good or bad, it was over. Thirty-one of them had made it through AOCS. Breakfast lasted almost forty-five minutes instead of the usual twenty. Even First Sergeant Sullivan was relaxed. When it was time to go, he just said, "It's time to go, Gents, get into formation, and we head back to Battalion Three for the last time." A cheer broke out in the mess hall.

When they arrived at the barn, Lt. Emmet was waiting for them and said, "Good morning, Gents. Stand at ease. I'm sure all of you think it's a really good morning, maybe the best in your life. You made it, you made it through AOCS, and seventy percent of the people who started with you did not, but you persevered. Congratulations. In about an hour and a half you will be ensigns and begin the greatest adventure anyone could have, learning how to be the best aviators in the world. It will mean more long hours of work, but as I'm sure First Sergeant Sullivan has told you, the training you just finished will provide you with what you need when things get tough. Getting through AOCS is probably the hardest thing you will ever do. Good luck with your Naval careers and your lives. Gentlemen, I want to announce one more thing before you go. Beginning next month, First Sergeant Sullivan will be Command Sergeant Major Sullivan, the highest-ranking NCO in the Training Command. It's a promotion he should have received years ago, so it is well deserved. His office will be directly next to the commanding admiral's office, which is truly a great honor. Gents, how about showing Command Sergeant Major your appreciation for what he has taught you during the last sixteen weeks?"

The class exploded with cheers. Even though Sullivan was tough, even ruthless at times, they all respected his incredible leadership and would follow him through the fires of hell. Sullivan, with tears in his eyes, thanked the class and told them he was proud to have been part of their journey to become officers. More importantly, he was proud that they came into AOCS as undisciplined kids and were going out as confident men. Finally, he said they all knew where his new assignment would be, and his door would always be open. Then he said, "OK, Gents, get up to your rooms, pack your shit, and get ready for your big day. Dismissed."

At 0815, Class 569 got into formation for the last time. First Sergeant Sullivan stepped in front of the class, looked around at them, smiled, and said, "OK, Gentlemen, anybody wants to change their minds before it's too late?" There was only dead silence from the class. "Are all you Gents ready for this?" A loud "Yes, sir." came from the class. Then, "Come on, Gents, didn't I teach you anything? I can't hear you." Then, a boisterous, loud unison of, "YES, SIR." Sullivan said, "Ok, Gents, let's get this done." He led them on a roundabout route, which took them past the Lex, the damaged aircraft, the obstacle course, and finally, INDOC. At each place, Sullivan stopped the formation, let the class take a last look, and moved on. When they got to INDOC, Sullivan stopped them for a few minutes longer and said, "Take a look at this place. Always remember what the signs out front say and what happened inside. Now, would you sign up for AOCS if you knew then what you know now, especially now that you are about to get your gold bars? I bet that every one of you would do it all over again. Am I right, Gents?" The class responded with a resounding. "Hell, no, First Sergeant." followed by raucous laughter. Sullivan, now laughing as well, led them onto the parade grounds and halted them directly in front of the reviewing stand, "Gentlemen, you have endured weeks of finding within yourselves what it takes to become a Naval Aviator, and you have done it. I'm proud to have been a part of your success. Now my job is done." Then he did an about-face and joined the other people on the reviewing stand.

Striker saw his father standing next to Major Pless. Both were in their dress white uniforms with an array of medals, and Pless had the Medal of Honor around his neck. Striker had hoped that his mother and sisters could be there, but none were able to get away. First Sergeant Sullivan was also on the stand, at the other end of the line of the officers. The Base Commanding Officer, Captain Jefferson, welcomed the AOCS graduates, soon-to-be Ensigns, and their families and friends. Lt. Emmet then gave a brief background of what Class 569 had accomplished and what happened next. Then, he introduced Admiral Mortenson, the Commanding Officer of the Naval Air

Training Command, who made a short speech about the history and mission of the Training Command. He finished by telling Class 569, "Gentlemen, as you begin your training as Naval Aviators, I want you to fully understand the commitment you are making. In your Commissioning Oath, you are promising that you will support and defend the Constitution of the United States. When you finish this training, understand that you will be the highest-trained professional killers on earth, nothing more, nothing less. If you are not ready for this commitment, you need to reconsider your future. Congratulations, Gentlemen."

Captain Jefferson returned to the podium and introduced Major Pless. "Ladies and Gentlemen, I'm sure that most of you have heard of our Guest of Honor, Major Steven Pless, but many may not know the reason why he was awarded the Medal of Honor. There are no better words than the official statement of his August 1967 mission than the official Marine Corps description of what happened that day. On this special day, I'm going to take a few minutes of your time to read directly from that official report."

At about 1600 hours, August 19, 1967, Pless and his VMO-6 crew, Captain Rupert Fairfield, Gunnery Sargent Leroy Poulson, and Lance Corporal John Phelps were on the way from Ky Ha to secure a remote landing zone where a wounded South Korean soldier was waiting for a Medevac helicopter. Capt. Pless had just refueled his UH1E gunship and replenished its pod of fourteen 2.75-inch rockets and 7.62 mm ammunition. On the way to the landing zone, Pless received multiple distress calls on the guard radio channel. An Army CH-47 Chinook helicopter with fifteen to twenty passengers aboard had been damaged by enemy fire, and the pilot made an emergency landing on a South China Sea beach near the

132

mouth of the Song Tra Khuc River. While Pless was on his way to the landing zone, the South Korean Medevac radioed that the landing zone had been cleared and the soldier was not seriously wounded, so the Marine escort was no longer needed. Pless immediately changed course to go to the aid of the stranded soldiers. The pilot of the downed CH-47 ordered the crew chief and three other soldiers to exit the aircraft to inspect the damage and establish a defensive perimeter. The Chinook was quickly attacked by Viet Cong (VC) soldiers who were hidden in a wooded area and a village about a hundred meters from the Americans. The VC fired automatic weapons and launched grenades at the downed helicopter and four crewmen. Before the Americans could climb back aboard the CH-47, it took off, stranding them on the beach. With no other alternative, the soldiers held off the attacking enemy with their weapons. But, after about ten minutes, their ammunition was spent, and they were easily overrun. A VC soldier sprayed the Americans with automatic gunfire, wounding three. A soldier who was hit in the shoulder played dead, but the other three were seriously wounded and, without assistance, would soon die. Once the Americans were disabled, approximately 30 to 40 VC joined their comrades who had surrounded the Americans. Instead of immediately shooting the four soldiers, the VC decided to take their time killing them by taking turns clubbing the Americans with their rifles and stabbing them with bayonets. When Pless approached the four captured Americans, he saw two or three attack aircraft circling about two thousand feet above the beach. There were also at least two helicopter gunships circling over the South China Sea about a half-mile away. Apparently, because of the close proximity of the VC to the Americans, none of the circling aircraft were attempting to stop the massacre or rescue the captured Americans. Pless received another radio

133

transmission stating that an extraction team would soon arrive to pick up the stranded soldiers. But Pless and his crew continued to fly towards the Americans. They could see what looked like mortar shells exploding and bullets striking near the soldiers. In order to get a better view, Pless took his Huey down to about fifty feet and flew directly over the Americans and their captors. The one conscious American saw the approaching Marine Huey, waved his arm, and was viciously clubbed by an enemy soldier. At the low altitude, Pless and his crew clearly saw the Americans being slaughtered and the waving soldier. Knowing that someone had to take action immediately, Pless instinctively yelled to his crew that he was going to attack. He asked them if they were with him, and all three crewmembers signaled their approval with a thumbs up. Pless, well aware that the Americans were in the target area, ordered Poulson to fire the door gun as close to the VC as possible without harming the Americans. Poulson fired the gun, leaving a track of bullets heading at the attacking VC. The VC broke ranks, left the Americans, and ran towards the tree line and village. Seeing the VC leave the Americans, Pless descended to a tree top level and turned his Huey toward the running VC. He centered his gun site on the back of the last VC in the crowd and fired the first of fourteen 2.75-inch rockets, and then he fired the remaining thirteen rockets through the rest of the group. The resultant explosions and Huey's rotor wash created an enormous cloud of mud and debris, which coated the windscreen. Pless flew his Huey directly through the cloudy mess, but the visibility was so bad and his altitude so low he expected to hit a tree at any moment. Without a second thought, he used the debris cloud as cover and repeatedly riddled the tree line and village with automatic gunfire. With most of his ordnance expended, Pless turned his Huey back toward the four American soldiers, about a hundred meters

134

away. On the way, he flew over as many as fifty wounded and dead VC soldiers scattered near the trees and on the beach. When he got within about thirty feet of the nearest soldier on the beach, Pless wrestled the nose of the Huey around to face the tree line and fired his guns towards enemy positions. He yelled to his crew that he was going to land and put the Huey on the muddy beach between the Americans and the VC as cover for the stranded soldiers. Intense automatic gunfire erupted from the tree line and village. VC soldiers began to advance across the sand toward the Huey, continually firing their weapons or launching explosives. Pless maneuvered the hovering Huey right and left while firing his automatic weapons. Pless then turned Huey around and ordered Poulson to go help the waving soldier get on board. Phelps took control of the door gun from Poulson and provided covering fire. After the first soldier, who could walk, got on board, Phelps then went to help Paulson get the other three. Fairfield also climbed from his co-pilot seat to go help when he saw three VCs near the rear of the Huey. He grabbed a door gun and fired at the VC, killing all of them. The soldier with a shoulder wound took the door gun and managed to hold it between his legs and fire it at the enemy, killing several. As Fairfield helped Phelps and Poulson get the second American, he saw three sappers within a few feet of the helicopter. He ordered Phelps to return to the Huey. On his way back, Phelps calmly drew his revolver and aimed it at the sappers, killing them. Fairfield and Poulson could not carry the second soldier, who was very heavy. So, they dragged him to the aircraft. Phelps rejoined Poulson and Fairfield, and the three of them then carried a third soldier to the helicopter, all the while firing their side arms at the closing enemy. Fairfield then ran to the fourth American, but he saw that his throat was cut, he had no dog tags, and he had been badly mutilated. After determining that the soldier had no

135

pulse, Fairfield returned to the Huey to tell Pless that the soldier was dead. Enemy gunfire intensified as Fairfield made his way back. Then, a South Vietnamese H-34 Medevac helicopter approached the area, and at least two Army gunships arrived and began firing their weapons at the VC. With this in mind, Pless decided to let the Medevac pick up the remaining (dead) American, and he and his crew would leave. But the Huey was overloaded. It was way too heavy to become airborne. Pless ordered the crew to jettison everything they could break loose. The crew began throwing out armor, spent shell casings, and any other equipment not bolted down or essential for flight. Pless torqued the engine to dangerous levels, but it didn't come apart. The Huey slowly began to drag itself through the wet sand and out over the water. As it became lighter and increased its airspeed, the Huey gradually gained altitude but still dropped and dipped its skids into the surf four or five times. Finally, after traveling over the water about a half-mile, Pless got the helicopter to a sufficient airspeed and altitude to set a course. Pless then flew directly to the field hospital at Chu Lai, about fifteen minutes away. On the way to the hospital, Phelps and Poulson frantically applied emergency first aid to the three rescued soldiers. Unfortunately, only the soldier with the shoulder wound survived. After the three soldiers were taken to Chu Lai, Pless, and his crewmates returned to their home base at Ky Ha.

Captain Jefferson paused for a moment and then continued. "Amazingly, in some of the most intense combat the VMO-6 Marines had ever seen; neither Pless nor any of his crew were wounded. The Huey was hit many times, including the vital rear rotor housing, which easily could have doomed the aircraft. Incredibly, the aircraft remained air worthy, and Pless and the men aboard made it to safety. The rescue mission that afternoon lasted only about fifteen minutes, and it was only one of several dangerous missions completed the same day by the Marines of VMO-6. But when the crew of the rescue mission was nominated for three Navy Crosses and a Medal of Honor, it became the most decorated Marine Corps Helicopter Crew in history. In September 1967, Pless was transferred to NAS, Pensacola, Florida, where he served as a flight instructor and class officer. In January 1969, he was awarded the Medal of Honor by President Lyndon Johnson. He was then promoted to Major and reassigned as the Officer in Charge of Aviation Officer Candidates School Physical Fitness here in Pensacola. Ladies and Gentlemen, Major Stephen Pless."

After a few minutes of thunderous applause, Major Pless thanked everyone, swore them in, and presented gold bars to each of the new ensigns. Jonathan Striker was the last new ensign to go up on the reviewing stand. When Major Pless saw him, he remembered him, and said, "Captain Striker, is this your son?" Captain Striker said, "Yes sir, he is, and I'm very proud of him." Pless replied, "I can see why. I met him about a month ago. He and a classmate talked to me about the Navy and AOCS for about a half an hour. I was impressed with him then, and now that I know he finished first in his class, I'm really impressed. Congratulations to both of you." Captain Striker then hugged his son and pinned on his gold bars.

As all the members of Class 569 had done before him, Striker went over to First Sergeant Sullivan to receive his first salute. As Striker returned the salute, Sullivan said, "Mr. Striker, you were the best of your class and I'm proud to have been a part of your success. I'm sure you will be a fine Naval Officer and Aviator. Good luck to you." Striker replied, "Command Sergeant Major Sullivan, thank you for teaching me how to do things I never thought were possible and then giving me the confidence to do them well. You are a great leader, and I hope to serve with you again." Then Striker shook Sullivan's hand and slipped him the traditional silver dollar, a symbol of gratitude.

Striker then joined the class formation for the last time. Sullivan stepped in front of them, called them to attention and said, "AOCS Class 569, dismissed." The class cheered, shook each other's hands, and proudly walked to be with their families and friends.

Before everyone left, Captain Jefferson announced that there would be a reception for the new ensigns, their families and friends at the small ballroom at the Mustin Beach Officers' Club. Striker and his dad found his roommates standing with their families. He introduced them using their birth names, Alan Stewart, Joshua Schnider, and Steve Hickey. As soon as he did, Striker told his dad to call them their official Drill Instructor Sullivan designated names, Hound, Bulldog and Sticky and they left for the reception.

When they arrived, Striker could see that most of the dignitaries were already in the buffet line. It was only 1100, a little early for lunch, but Striker could still eat when he saw the peeled Gulf shrimp, oysters on the half shell, prime rib, side dishes, and a variety of desserts. Plus, there was an open bar offering cocktails, wine and beer. Striker, "Dad, it looks like life is good as an officer. I think I'm going to like it a lot." He filled his plate and went to his seat between his dad and Major Pless.

Pless asked now Ensign Striker, "Who was with you at the Ready Room when we met?" Striker replied, "It was Sticky, Steve Hickey, one of my roommates. He's here somewhere." Pless said, "Did you say Sticky? I bet Sergeant Major Sullivan had fun with that." Striker, "He did, and Sticky paid a dear price." After lunch, Pless said, "Follow me, Gents, and let's go get a beer in the Ready Room. I've got some pull in there, and I'm pretty sure we can get some good seats,"

Pless had a reserved seat at the bar, and luckily, there were two vacant seats next to it. Pless went to his seat, grabbed the other two, and ordered beers for everyone. When the beers arrived, Pless picked his beer up and offered a toast, "Here's to Naval and Marine Aviators, the best in the world, and to those brave aviators we have lost. We have your six." After they finished another beer, Captain Striker, who had to take his son to the BOQ and catch a flight, tried to pay the bill, but Pless assured him that he had it covered, and they shook hands and left.

Striker's dad took him to the Third Battalion to get his uniforms and to INDOC for his civilian clothes and personal items. When they arrived at the BOQ, Striker signed in at the desk. Earlier, the four roommates decided to room together in the BOQ so Striker took #210, a second-story suite facing the swimming pool. After Striker and his dad carried everything into the suite, Captain Striker had to leave.

Striker was putting his clothes into a closet when Sticky came in the door, "Is this bed taken?" pointing to the one across the room. Striker, "Hi, welcome to paradise. Take any bed you want. This is much better than the dump we used to live in, isn't it?" Sticky. "Sure is, but just about anywhere could be better than the shit hole INDOC was." Sticky then started to put his clothes in the other closet, saying. "This one works for me. Have you seen Hound or Bulldog yet?" Striker shook his head and said he didn't know where they were.

When Striker finished putting his clothes away, Sticky asked, "Did you see the beer machine by the stairway? It looks

139

just like a soda machine, only it's beer. It's great! I haven't had a beer yet, so I'm going to go get one. You want one?" Striker said he didn't; he just had a couple with his dad. About five minutes later Striker could heard Sticky yelling, "Free beer, Free beer, come get em." Striker walked to the stairway to see what was happening. There Sticky was, standing in front of a dispensing machine, handing out cans of beer to anyone who came near. Sticky yelled, "Is this a great country or what? I put a quarter in the machine to buy a beer and the damn thing emptied all the beer down the chute. Must be forty or fifty of them. Grab all you want." Striker laughed as he took six back to the refrigerator in the suite. Sticky took ten that he also put in the refrigerator. A half an hour later Hound and Bulldog came in with their belongings and Sticky put a cold beer in their baskets and said, "Welcome to the BOQ and have a beer, courtesy of the US Navy." They put their baskets down and drank together for the first time as officers.

When it was near 1600 Sticky asked if anyone wanted to go to Tiki Bar. His brother brought his van to him before he moved into the BOQ. Striker said he didn't want to go to the beach, but Sticky could drop him off at a car dealership. Bulldog and Hound said they were going to visit with their families.

After changing into the uniform of the day, tropical short sleeve whites, Sticky and Striker went to town. As they drove, Striker noticed that the van was set up as a camper, complete with a bed, and asked Sticky, "Are you gonna keep this?" Sticky, smiling, "I was going to sell it when I finished AOCS but now I think I'll keep it a while. It might be useful out near a deserted beach; in case I get lucky."

A mile outside the front gate, Striker saw a Ford dealership that was open. He pointed to it and said, "That one will do, you can drop me off there." Sticky pulled over and said, "I'll drive by this place when I return. If you want a ride back, wait by the front door and look for me. I'll drive through this parking lot." Striker told him that sounded great, and he got out of the van and went into the showroom. As he did Striker thought, "I suspect I'll be driving something out of here long before Sticky gets back."

As soon as he walked in the door, a sharply dressed middle-aged man with a toothy smile walked over to him and said, "Let me guess. You just got commissioned and you're here so that I can help you buy the car of your dreams." He shook Striker's hand and said, "If I'm right, you got yourself the right guy. I sell more cars to new ensigns than anyone in this town and I've been doing it for over thirty years. My name is Tommy O'Shea and I sell cars. I also sing Irish ballads at McGuire's, but I make a living here. What's your name and what are you interested in?" Striker couldn't help but smile and said, "I was just commissioned this morning and I need to buy a car, hopefully a Mustang. My name is Jonathan Striker." Tommy smiling again said, "Jonathan, it's your lucky day. I have six new Mustangs that were delivered this morning and I have four more real clean used ones in the lot. This weekend is our biggest sale of the year, so I have a lot of room to give you a great deal. You ready to look at 'em?" Striker, chuckling said, "Let's go look, Tommy."

An hour later, they had looked at every Mustang except one that was in the back of the lot. Striker turned to Tommy and asked, "What about the dark blue one over there?" Tommy said, "It's sold, but the guy who bought it got emergency orders to go to sea and he brought it back and told us he would be gone for close to a year and he didn't want to pay for something he can't use. I agreed to see if I could find someone to take over the payments. Navy Federal Credit Union finances it. It's got less than 1000 miles on it. The first owner special ordered it to get the Navy-Blue paint. I'll show it to you if you're interested." Striker replied, "Sure. I'd like to see it."

As they walked toward the car, Tommy said that everything on the car except the paint was a standard feature. "It has one of the smaller V8s, is automatic, with a tape deck, air conditioning, black leather front buckets seats, and a sport roof. The MSRP was about $3,900. It's yours if you assume his $3200 loan and pay us a $200 fee. It's sitting back there because we don't have his release to transfer the title yet, but he's assured us that he mailed it last week and we should have it early next week. I tell you what, if you write us a check for $100 and agree to assume the loan from NFCU, you can drive it off the lot today. Then when I receive the release, I'll call you and we'll finish the title work here at my office. We can also take care of the NFCU loan assumption here, but you have to have an account with them and will need to get insurance".

Tommy continued as they walked back to the showroom, "Jonathan if you give me the additional $100, we're done." Striker, "I've had a NFCU account since I was born, and I'll join USAA today." Striker walked around the car, got in, and the two of them took a test drive around Pensacola. When they returned, Striker pulled into a parking space in front of the showroom and told Tommy. "You've got a deal; I'll write a check for $100 and sign the loan assumption application," Tommy said. "I told you it was your lucky day today. Come on into my office, and I'll draw up the paperwork." While he was waiting, Striker called USAA and opened an account. An hour later, Striker drove his new car back to the BOQ.

It was nearly 6 p.m. when he arrived at the BOQ. As he went up the steps, he went to the beer vending machine and saw that it had already been refilled. He put a quarter in to see if he would get the same result as Sticky did, but he only got one beer. He took the beer back to the suite, put it in the refrigerator, and thought, "Getting commissioned, a new car, and seventeen beers for fifty cents is a good day, any day of the year." Once in his room he read a note saying that his roommates had already gone to the open mess for dinner. Striker turned around and went to catch up with them. On the way, he decided to take a look around the BOQ.

As he went into the main entrance of the BOQ, he saw a large front desk with mail slots for each room. It was open 24 hours a day, every day, and was managed by Filipino stewards. Close by was a bank of phones and desks where residents could make free calls. Down the hall was a large television room that could seat about thirty people. After looking in the television room, Striker went back out the front door and towards the open mess, which was next door. On the right side of the open mess was a casual bar that was open from 1100 until one in the morning, seven days a week, and flight suits were allowed.

After he stopped at the casual bar, Striker went into the open mess to look around. He had never been in an officer's open mess before, and he could see that it was just a bigger, nicer enlisted mess. The main differences were the tablecloths, place settings, and Filipino stewards who both served meals and bussed the tables. There was also the option of a buffet that offered all-you-can-eat hot meals. Next to the buffet were drink dispensers that held water, iced tea, milk, and coffee. The cost to each officer living in the BOQ was $50 per month, which included all meals except on Wednesday nights when Filet Mignon was 75 cents.

Striker saw his roommates at a table near the buffet, and Bulldog waved for him to join them. As Striker sat down with his food, they were just finishing the first helping and were going back for more. The special that night was a choice between beef stroganoff and fried chicken, as well as soup, salads, vegetables, and dessert. As Striker was eating, Sticky said he assumed that he had luck getting a car, and Striker told him that he bought a 1969 Mustang, which was in the parking lot. The other two roommates said Striker could show them the car by taking them to the O Club after they ate, and Striker agreed. Later, they passed on dessert and headed to Striker's new car for a ride to the Ready Room. They wanted to get their first beer in the Ready Room, but mostly, they wanted to see if the stories about the girls who came there were true.

It was Thursday night, and a mixer was in progress in the large ballroom. Just as they had been told, there were at least five guys to every girl. Whatever the number, it was the most females that they had seen in one place in a long time. The four of them first surveyed the ballroom, and then Bulldog and Striker got in line to go into the Ready Room. It took about ten minutes to get in and another ten minutes to get a beer. At fifteen cents a beer, it was worth the wait.

From what Striker could see, there were about twenty girls in the bar, but every one of them was talking to a Navy or Marine officer. Then, he saw Major Pless sitting on the same stool as earlier that day. He must have gone home and changed because he was now wearing his summer khaki uniform. As always there were several people around him, most of them were girls.

The mixer ended at 9 pm, and the Ready Room quickly thinned out. As Bulldog and Striker started to leave, Sticky and Hound came into the bar, so they ordered beers and toasted their achievements and friendship. It was, after all, the day they received their commissions.

Chapter 31

Leah Meets Riley

After Jane left for Gainesville, Wendy and Leah decided to take practice runs to their new schools. Wendy's interview was at Pensacola High School, the oldest and largest high school in the system. It opened in 1905, had been renovated several times, and was centrally located in Pensacola, about nine miles from Gulf Breeze. Charles Soule Elementary, Leah's school, was near the Naval Air Station. It was named after the mayor who had championed its construction. After finding each school and confident they knew how to get there, they went back to Gulf Breeze, changed into bikinis and went to Tiki Beach.

It was Thursday afternoon, so the beach was almost empty, but the girls still had plenty of guys stopping by their blankets and trying to start a conversation. If either of them was interested in one of the guys, they would use their real names. If not, Leah was now Pepper, and Wendy was Salt. Most of the guys who met the girls that day only knew them as Salt and Pepper.

One guy who stopped by the blanket was a tall, thin guy who introduced himself as Clint Riley, but everyone called him Riley. With his short hair and lean build, they assumed he was in the military and probably an officer. His slow Texas drawl and dry sense of humor were very charming to Leah. She was immediately interested and introduced herself and Wendy with their real names. Riley told her he was a Navy Lieutenant who just finished his first tour in Vietnam as a F-4 RIO and had to report to Glynco NAS, Georgia, on the coming Monday. The girls had no idea what a RIO was and very little about F-4s. Riley explained what the mission of an F-4 was and what a RIO did. He and his pilot, Tim Connors, were roommates all the way through AOCS and knew each other's reaction to stress as well as anyone could, so they were a great team. Leah, startled, asked, "Did you say Tim Connors? Wendy, did you hear that? Riley flew with Connors, and he was his roommate in AOCS." Wendy, who was only partially paying attention to the conversation, sat up, "Connors is my sister Jane's ex-boyfriend. They dated for almost a year, but then they decided to break up."

Riley, amazed at the coincidence, said, "Connors told me all about Jane and how they broke up. He's still crazy about her and hasn't given up on seeing her again. He told me he was going to try to find her when we got back to Pensacola. She apparently loved coming here to the beach. In fact, two nights ago he left me a message that he left to visit his family in Melbourne Beach for a couple of days, then he was going to Gainesville to look for her at the university. He's probably there now."

Wendy, in disbelief, said, "Jane's also in Gainesville now. She's getting ready to defend her dissertation tomorrow. If everything goes OK, she'll be coming back here Friday night. She's supposed to move into her new apartment Saturday morning. I have got to try to find her. She should know Tim's there looking for her. I think we still have the phone message from her adviser. Leah, let's go back to the apartment. I have to call Jane. Riley, thank you so much. Can you try to get in touch with Connors to tell him that Jane is in Gainesville?" Riley agreed to call Connors' family in Melbourne to see if he had left for Gainesville yet.

Connor's father answered the phone but told Riley that Connors left about noon for Gainesville to look for Jane. Riley told him that he had met Jane's sister, Wendy, and Jane was in Gainesville. Connors dad didn't know where Connors was staying but he was familiar with the hotel where he and his wife always stayed, and he had told Riley the name of the hotel. Riley thanked him and relayed the information to Wendy. She called the hotel and asked to be connected to Jane Carmody's room. The clerk told her that he could not confirm that Jane was a guest at the hotel, but he would take Wendy's name and number and notify the person that she had a message. Wendy thanked him, and then relayed the information to Riley.

Chapter 32

Connors and Jane Reconnect

Jane had a difficult time sleeping that morning, so she got up at about 6:30 and took a shower. After she got dressed, she saw the red message light. She called the front desk, and the clerk told her that she had to show her ID at the main desk before she could get the message. Jane immediately grabbed her dissertation and purse and went down to the front desk.

Connors was sitting on a leather chair between the restaurant and the front door. He saw Jane leave the elevator and walk to the front desk. Connors left his chair and got within five feet of her. She was just getting Wendy's message when he said, "Jane. It's Connors." She turned around, saw him, and was stunned. A few seconds later, she whispered, "It is you." then she was silent. Connors replied, "Yes, it is, Jane. I've been looking for you." Jane slowly came towards him, then stopped a few feet away. Connors opened his arms, and she ran to him and jumped into his arms.

She was crying when she said, "It's really you. I've missed you so much. I thought about you every day since we broke up. I was so worried about you, and here you are. How did you find me…and why? Connors put her down, saying, "Let's get a table, and I'll answer your questions. Can you sit for a while?" She shook her head and said, "Of course, I can."

When they sat down, Connors began, "Jane, I made the worst mistake of my life when I broke up with you. Ever since that day, I've wanted to tell you that I was wrong. I want you in my life. The minute I got back to Pensacola, I started looking. I did everything I could think of, including finding your parents' phone number and leaving a message for you. I even went to the beach and searched for you. After I visited my parents, I came here to look for you at the university. I was going to the campus this morning, but last night, I asked the bartender, Paul, if he knew you. I was astonished when he told me he did. Incredibly, he was a student in your engineering math class. He even briefly saw you in this restaurant last night, but he was in a hurry and couldn't stop to say hello. He wanted to help me find you, so he asked his cousin, who is the front desk manager. His cousin couldn't give out information about you, but Paul called me and suggested that I come down here early this morning to wait for you, and here I am. I hope I haven't made a stupid mistake doing all this, but I had to try. I had to find out if you still cared." Jane looked at him and said, "Mistake? No way. I've loved you since the first time we met, and I always will. No, you didn't make a mistake. I've been hoping and praying I would see you again, and here you are." She reached across the table, pulled him to her, and kissed him. He said, "Jane, every day since I left, I've been thinking about this moment and what I was going to say. Ever since the day I left, I knew, without a doubt, that I wanted to spend the rest of my life with you." Then Connors got down on one knee, pulled the ring box out of his pocket, handed it to her, and said, "Jane Carmody, will you marry me?" Jane, with tears coming down her cheek, put the ring on her finger and replied, "Yes. I would have married you the first day I met you, Tim Connors."

For the next couple of hours, they caught up with each other's lives. Connors talked about his cruise to Vietnam, his present assignment as a flight instructor, and his application to test pilot school. Jane told him about her dissertation, her new job at the University of West Florida, and her apartment on the water. They ordered breakfast while they continued to talk. At about 9:45, she told him that she had to leave for her appointment and said, "Today, of all days, I have to defend my dissertation to the math department academic review committee. Normally, I would be nervous, but I am so happy that you came back to me. I'm not worried at all."

Connors told her that he would be waiting at the hotel for her return. As she got up to leave, she handed him the key to her room, kissed him, and said, "I'll see you in about three hours." Then she went to the front desk, got another key, and left.

Chapter 33

Jane Defends Her Dissertation

Jane was relaxed when she walked into the conference room, where the review committee would meet in about an hour. She was as prepared as she could possibly be, but she still paged through her dissertation, looking for anything she may have overlooked. Then, she reviewed Dr. Sandler's notes, which he had given to her the day before. When she finished, she closed her eyes and thought about her unbelievable engagement to Tim after their breakup so long ago.

Ten minutes into her reverie, the three senior math professors walked into the room. She knew all of them, having taken at least one class or seminar from each one. Without any introductions, the chairman of the committee began by questioning her about her hypothesis. The second went over her research methods, and the third examined her conclusions.

Jane remained relaxed and confident throughout the two-hour session. Nothing they asked came as a surprise, thanks to Dr. Sandler's preparations. Finally, the chairman smiled and told Jane that they were finished with their review and that the committee would now meet in private to discuss their findings. They hoped to let her know the results as soon as possible. Jane thanked them and left the room.

Before she returned to the hotel, Jane stopped by Dr. Sandler's office to thank him again. As she arrived, his assistant told her that he was on the phone, so she waited in his outer office. The door was open, and she could hear his booming voice. He mentioned her name a couple of times, saying that she was one of the best PhD candidates he ever advised. He said something about her already accepting a position at West Florida, and then he exchanged some pleasantries with the caller and hung up. He saw Jane and waved her into his office. He was smiling as he said, "Can you keep a secret?" Jane nodded, then he continued, "Don't tell anyone, but that was the chair of the review committee. He said the review went extremely well. In fact, he was calling to see if you had found a position yet. He was hoping that I could keep you here on staff, but I told him that you had already accepted a position over at West Florida. Congratulations Dr. Carmody. You have earned your PhD. You will receive the official approval in a week or so, so please don't tell anyone around here that you already know. I'm not supposed to tell you."

Jane thanked him for all his help and then told him that today was one of the best days of her life. Not only did her dissertation get approved, but she also got engaged that morning. Sandler congratulated her again and asked. "Who's the lucky guy? I didn't know you were even seeing anyone seriously." Jane told him that she wasn't. Then she told him their unlikely story and how Connors had found her this morning. "It's been an incredible day, and he's waiting for me at the hotel." Sandler then said. "Then get over there and share this day with him. I'd better get an invitation to the wedding. Good luck to both of you."

As she walked into the hotel lobby, she didn't see Connors, so she went up to her room. Connors' bag was on the floor, and she could hear the shower. She peeked into the bathroom and saw jogging shorts and shoes on the floor. She stripped off all her clothes and quietly got into the shower.

He was shampooing his hair and didn't know she was there. She tapped him on the shoulder and said, "Room service." He turned around, wiped the water from his eyes, and said, "Well, this beats service with a smile anytime. Come here."

At about 3 pm, they got up and showered again. They decided to stay another night, so they put on their bathing suits and went to the pool. When they got there, Jane said, "I almost forgot to tell you that my dissertation defense went very well this morning." Now smiling, "But, as you know, I was otherwise occupied upstairs." Then she began again, "I'm not supposed to know, but my adviser, Dr. Sandler, told me that it was easily approved. After all the work, I now have officially earned my PhD, today and got engaged too. It's been a great day."

Ten minutes later, they dove into the pool and swam laps until they tired. Back in their lounge chairs, Jane asked, "What do you think about getting married as soon as possible? Maybe in six weeks, or even less?" Connors replied, "The sooner, the better, as far as I'm concerned. I've already waited a long time to marry you. It's OK with me if we just went down to the courthouse and did it today." Jane responded, "We could, but I want to have my family and some friends come to a church ceremony, don't you?" Connors said, "Yeah, I'm very close to my sister and her twin daughters as well as my parents, and I'd like to have some squadron mates and old friends there as well." Then Jane added, "Plus, I have to meet with my landlord tomorrow at three to sign the lease for my new apartment. It's an incredible place with a spectacular water view. It's perfect for a couple." Then she grinned as she told him, "I'd sure love to have you move in with me if you want." Connors, "Sure, I want to. I'll get my clothes and gear from the BOQ tomorrow and meet you at your sister's place to move your furniture and clothes. If you want, I'll rent a truck." Jane, "That would be perfect. I'm staying at Wendy's apartment in Gulf Breeze. Tomorrow morning, you can follow me to my new apartment, then I'll lead you to Wendy's place, and you can see how much stuff I have before you get a truck." Connors responded, "Sounds great. If you want, when we get back tomorrow, I'll make some calls to see if the base chapel and O Club are available in the next few weeks." Jane replied, "Yes, that would probably be the best thing to do since I don't know the Pensacola area very well."

For the next two hours, they just relaxed and took naps by the pool. Then, at about 6 pm, they went back to the room and changed for dinner. As they were getting ready to go, Connors asked her if she wanted to go to one of the places they knew in town or just eat at the hotel restaurant. Jane responded, "I don't need to go anywhere else. It's quiet here; we can talk, and the food is decent. Let's just stay here if that's OK with you." Connors said, "I just want to be where you are, so the hotel restaurant is perfect."

After they sat down in the restaurant, Connors looked over at the bar and saw Paul pulling a beer. He asked Jane if she could remember him and, pointed towards the bar, and said, "That's Paul, the bartender who helped me find you. If he hadn't been here, I would probably have checked out of the hotel and still be looking for you somewhere else. Let me go see if he can stop by later. And Jane said. "No, let's walk over there now. I do recognize him."

As Connors walked up to the bar, Paul said, "Hey man, how'd it go? Did you find her?" Then he saw Jane standing behind Connors and said, "Well, you sure did. Remember me, Miss Carmody? I was in your Math 310 Class about a year and a half ago. My name is Paul Givens. Without your help, I would not have made it through the class, but I did. I actually got a B, thanks to you." Jane smiled and said, "Paul, I should be thanking you. If you didn't tell Connors that I was here, I would already be on my way back to Gulf Breeze. But now Connors and I are engaged. Thank you so much." Paul looked at Connors and said, "Man, you didn't waste any time, did you? Congrats to both of you. Let me get you a drink on the house." Connors thanked him and said, "It wasn't as quick as it appeared. I've wanted to ask Jane to marry me, but it took way too long to finally get it done." Paul said, "Like the old Bard once wrote, 'All's well that ends well.' Go sit down, and I'll bring your drinks over."

As Paul brought them each a beer, he said, "I'm not allowed to drink while I'm working. If I could, I would raise my glass to you guys and wish you the best of everything in your long lives together. Congratulations." Connors shook Paul's hand and thanked him again for his help, and then Jane added that without Paul, they might never have found each other.

While they ate their dinners, Jane said that she had some calls to make, beginning with her parents and then her sister. Connors also wanted to call his parents and sister to let them know he had found Jane and they were now engaged. Jane also thought she should probably call her landlord to tell her that Connors, now her fiancée, would be moving in with her. If the landlord wanted to increase the rent, it was fine. Then Connors added that all the expenses for the apartment should be his. With his flight and hazardous duty pay, plus his housing allowance, he would probably earn more than Jane did as a newly appointed Assistant Professor. He suggested that she bank her paychecks so that they could save for a house of their own. Jane thought it was a great idea, but once he saw the

155

apartment, he would probably not be in a hurry to move. Connors also remembered that there was an AOCS class reunion being planned, so he needed to call the BOQ to see if he had any messages. After they finished eating, Connors asked the waitress if she could send a bottle of champagne to the room.

Once they were back in the room, Jane called her parents. As soon as her mother answered the phone, Jane said, "Hi mom. I'm in Gainesville." Her mom replied, "Oh Jane, I'm so glad you called. I found the message from Tim Connors, who I remember now. He was in the Navy, wasn't he? He was a pilot getting ready to go to Vietnam. If I remember correctly, you were pretty serious about him, but it didn't work out. I'll give you his number." Jane quickly replied, "Mom, mom, I don't need the message. Connors is next to me. He came back from Vietnam and found me here in Gainesville on the day I had to defend my dissertation. I have some good news for you and dad." Her mother interrupted, "You passed your test, you got your PhD. Congratulations, Jane, that is wonderful." Jane responded, "Well I did get my PhD and that was great, but what I was going to tell you is that Connors and I are getting married. He asked me to marry him, and I said yes. I wish you could see the ring." There was silence on the phone for about ten seconds, then her mom said, "You're engaged? Did you say you're engaged?" and Jane answered, "Yes mom, you heard correctly, Connors and I are getting married." Jane's mother called her father over and said, "Jane is engaged, and she got her PhD. She's going to marry Tim Connors, the Navy Pilot who's been trying to find her." Then she said to Jane, "When and where are you getting married?" Jane answered. "Well, we both work. I am starting my new job a week from Monday. We'll have to find a place and date in Pensacola, probably at the base chapel with the reception in the Officers' Club.

Connors is going to start looking as soon as we get back to Pensacola. I'll keep you posted on what we decide."

Then her father took the phone and said he was thrilled for her. Then he wanted her to put Connors on the phone, and Jane handed it to him, saying, "It's my dad. He wants to talk to you." Connors said hello and her father congratulated him and said, "You must be quite a guy. Jane has had many young men interested in her, but she ignored almost all of them, even as far back as her freshman year of high school. I knew you two were dating for several months, but then you broke up when you got orders to deploy. She was really busy with her graduate work, so I assumed you both decided that your relationship just couldn't work. What changed since you last saw her?" Connors responded, "Well nothing happened, except I knew from the moment that I met her that I wanted to marry her someday, and that never changed. Every day I was overseas, I thought about finding her. As soon as I got back to Pensacola, I started looking for her. I had to know if she still felt the same way about me. Incredibly, I found her through a hotel bartender, who said she was a guest at the hotel. He had been in her class over a year ago. This morning, I found her at the front desk of the hotel, asked her to marry me, and she said yes. So, Mr. Carmody, nothing changed, even after more than a year."

Jane left a message for Wendy and then called Mrs. O'Neil, her landlord. When she answered, Jane told her that she had just gotten engaged that morning and wanted her to know that he wanted to move in with her. She added that she would willingly pay more rent if necessary. Mrs. O'Neil asked her who the lucky guy was, and Jane told her who he was and the story of their courtship.

Mrs. O'Neil said that it was one of the most romantic things she ever heard. She was thrilled Jane was marrying a Naval

Aviator, just like she had done. She appreciated Jane's honesty, so she only increased the rent by twenty-five dollars a month. Jane thanked her and said that they would be at the apartment by 3 pm the next day.

Connors then called his parents and told them he had found Jane. His dad said that Riley tried to get in touch with him. Connors then told them the unlikely events that led to finding Jane. Finally, he told them he asked Jane to marry him, and she said yes. Both of his parents asked the same questions that Jane's parents did and were just as elated about the engagement.

Connors then called his sister Sheila. Annie, his four-year-old niece, answered the phone. After she told him what she and Erin did that day and what they ate for dinner, she went to get her mommy. Sheila began the conversation by asking Connors if he had any luck finding Jane. He told her the same amazing story he had shared with Jane's dad. Sheila was beside herself when Connors told her that he and Jane were engaged. She asked to talk to Jane, and Connors handed her the phone.

Jane was near tears as Sheila told her that Connors confided in her that he had to find this girl named Jane that he had fallen in love with the moment he met her. He had said that if he did find Jane, he was going to ask her to marry him. It all happened right out of a fairy tale. Then Annie interrupted her mother and wanted to talk to Jane. "Hi, is this Annie? I'm Jane." Annie, "Yes, I'm Annie, and I'm a twin. My sister's name is Erin. She's pretending to read a book. Are you going to marry Uncle Tim? Will you be my Aunt Jane when you marry him? Will you play with my sister and me in the pool when you are my Aunt Jane? Erin will want you to read books to her all the time. Will you read books to me too? I'm going to get my doll now. Bye."

Jane was chuckling as Sheila got back on the phone. "Jane, do you see what you're in for when you marry Tim? The girls will be all over you just like they are all over my brother." Jane, "She is absolutely adorable. I cannot wait to meet you, your husband, and those little girls. Maybe Connors and I can get away to Melbourne in the next few weeks so I can get to know you and your wonderful family. Take care. Here's Connors. He wants to talk to the girls if he can."

When Connors was back on the phone, Sheila got Erin, who immediately said, "Uncle Tim, when are you getting married? Can I come, and Mommy and Daddy, and Annie? Will you come to see us when you are married? Jane said she would read to me. Does she like to play in the pool?" Connors attempted to answer all of Erin's questions, but before he could, she said bye and hung up the phone. He quickly called his sister back; they both laughed as he said he would let her know when they had some specific wedding plans.

Almost as soon as Connors hung up the phone it started to ring again. Jane answered, hoping it was Wendy, and it was. Jane was the first to speak, "Hi, little sis. I'm surprised to hear from you so soon. I thought you would be out with one of the many young officers who are tripping over themselves to meet you." Wendy responded, "Sort of. Leah and I went to happy hour at the O Club as we usually do, and there were so many guys asking me out that I almost fainted. I had to leave to get some air." Then she laughed as she said, "Actually, we left the Ready Room early because we wanted to go to the Pier Lounge, but there was a power outage, and they had to shut the place and we just came home. I heard your message. What's up? What's the big surprise? Did your dissertation get approved?"

Jane, "Well, it is part of it, but even more important is that Connors found me." Jane told her about the seemingly impossible string of connections that occurred in the last twenty-four hours. Wendy, almost breathless, said, "You can't make up a story like that. It's the stuff of dreams." Jane quickly added, "That's not the whole story. Connors and I are engaged. He asked me, and I said yes. It was about 7:30 this morning, and neither of us had even eaten breakfast yet."

Wendy, almost whispering, said, "Jane, I'm so happy for you. I know how much you loved and missed him. What an incredible surprise, especially on such an important day for you. It's just wonderful. Congratulations, big sis,"

Jane continued, "Wendy, I want you to be my maid of honor and Leah to be a bridesmaid. Is she there?" Wendy gave the phone to Leah and Jane said, "Leah, Wendy can tell you the complicated way this happened, but I'm engaged to Tim Connors, the Naval Officer I've talked about so much. I asked Wendy to be my maid of honor and I want you to be a bridesmaid. Will you?" Leah replied, "Yes, of course I will. From Wendy's reactions to what you were telling her, it must be an incredible story. I can't wait to ask her." Leah gave the phone back to Wendy, who asked, "Do you have any idea when and where you're getting married? If you need help, I'll do anything I can."

Jane replied, "We're just beginning to think about it. As soon as we know something, I'll get back to you. Connors has to make another call, so I'll talk to you later."

It was after 9 pm when Connors called the BOQ front desk. The clerk had a message from Marx. The day-old message was that twelve classmates and their wives/girlfriends would be able to come on July 20 and they asked Connors to see if the small ballroom was available.

No one answered when he called Marx, so he left a message that he would check with the O Club the next day. While he was on the phone, room service brought Jane a bottle of champagne on ice, two flutes, and strawberries dipped in dark chocolate. There was also a note congratulating them on their engagement, and the wine and chocolates were on the house. As soon as Connors finished his call to Marx, he saw that Jane was sitting on the bed, wearing only a slip and holding the bottle of champagne. He dimmed the lights and locked the door.

Chapter 34

Connors and Jane Return to

Pensacola

Connors and Jane made love until after midnight, then fell asleep in each other's arms. He was awakened at 8 am by the loud conversation of other guests in the hallway, but Jane remained asleep. Now wide awake, he watched her sleep. He was still in disbelief that after all the time and distance, he was finally with her.

They checked out of the hotel, made one stop for gas, and were in Pensacola by 2:30 pm. When they arrived at the apartment, Mrs. O'Neil opened the door almost immediately, explaining that she heard them in the driveway. She was smiling broadly as Jane introduced Connors, and she said, "Welcome. You are a very lucky young man to have such a lovely and intelligent girl as your bride-to-be. Jane, you have hit the jackpot with this handsome young Naval Aviator as your fiancée. I'm thrilled for both of you. Please come in and sit down." As they sat, she brought in the lease as well as a tray of cookies and then said, "Here's the lease. As you will see, I have made the change we discussed. If you want, both of you can sign it, but only Jane's signature is required. Please help yourself to the cookies, they're hot out of the oven." Jane looked at Connors and asked, "Do you want to sign?" He shook his head and replied, "Of course I do. We're in this together." As soon as she signed, he did the same.

Connors then wrote a check for the first month's rent. Mrs. O'Neil congratulated them and handed them two sets of keys.

Then she told Jane to take the cookies and leave the plate in the apartment. The couple thanked her and went to the stairs leading to the apartment. When they reached the top of the stairs. Connors picked up Jane and carried her through the doorway, and asked, "Where's the bedroom?" Jane, half laughing and half pleading, said, "It's four in the afternoon. She's going to know what's going on." Connors replied, "Of course, she knows what's going on. Her husband was a Naval Aviator. She wouldn't expect anything less." Jane, now giggling, closed the door behind them.

Later, Connors asked Jane, "Are you ready to show me the other bedroom? Jane, "Throttle back, Mr. Flyboy. There's plenty of time for you to put your tail hook down. We have to go to Wendy's apartment and rent a truck."

They found a truck rental office that was open, and they hurried to Wendy's apartment. Jane quickly introduced Connors to Wendy and Leah and showed him the storage room. Knowing what he needed, Connors apologized to Wendy for having to leave so soon, then explained that he and Jane had to rent a truck before the rental place closed. As they left, Jane asked Wendy, "If you guys don't have any plans this evening, we'd like to take both of you to dinner." Wendy, "Sounds great. We'll be ready whenever you are." An hour and a half later, they finished putting Jane's belongings in the rental van. After it was loaded, Jane told Wendy they were taking it to their apartment and then would meet the girls at Al's Castle Bar.

Wendy and Leah were there when Jane and Connors arrived, and then Wendy toasted the engaged couple, wishing them nothing but happiness. Just as the waitress came to take their order, Gina Martinez walked into the restaurant with a young man Wendy did not recognize. As the couple got closer, Connors recognized Gina, the Ready Room waitress, and Jake

163

Zimmerman, his AOCS and VT 4 classmate. He waved for them to sit at their table. As he did, Zimmerman introduced Connors to Gina, who said she already knew the girls. Connors, "I remember Gina from the Ready Room." Then Wendy added that they also met Gina at the Ready Room, and she had been very helpful to them.

Connors had not seen Zimmerman in over a year when both were in the RAG. Like Connors, Zimmerman was an F-4 pilot, but on the Aircraft Carrier Coral Sea. He was now also a flight instructor stationed at VT-7 in Meridian, Mississippi. Zimmerman and Connors briefly talked about their deployments, and then Connors asked Zimmerman if he was coming to the AOCS class reunion. Zimmerman confirmed that he was, saying, "I look forward to it. I hear Major Pless will be there." Everyone stayed at the Castle Bar and talked until the last call.

Chapter 35

Jane and Connors Make Plans, and

Connors Starts Flying Again

The next morning, Jane and Connors moved all her furniture to the apartment garage and then returned the moving van. Then Jane took Connors back to their apartment and left to meet Wendy at a bridal shop. They agreed to meet at Mrs. Hopkins for lunch.

Connors checked out of the BOQ and began the process of scheduling the wedding and reception. The small chapel, which held about 150 people, was available almost every Saturday through August. Jane estimated that they would invite about 125 people, so the small chapel would work. Next, the O Club manager told Connors that the small ballroom was available most Saturdays from May through July, except the fourth and most of August. Satisfied that there were plenty of convenient open dates for the wedding and reception, Connors left for Mrs. Hopkin's Boarding House.

A half-hour later, Jane, Wendy, and Leah joined him. Jane was excited; she put a deposit on a dress she liked and was down to a choice of two bridesmaid dresses. Since she was still unsure of the number of bridesmaids she would have, she intended to wait before she decided which dress to purchase. In addition to Leah, she was going to ask Connors' sister Sheila, her college roommate JoAnne, and her cousin Lisa. Connors, "Have you thought about flower girls? I know two little twin girls who would be perfect," Jane said, "Of course,

Annie and Erin, your nieces. That's a great idea. I'll ask Sheila this week.'

That night, Jane prepared their first home-cooked meal: roast beef with baked potatoes, green beans, and a salad. Connors set the table and opened the blinds so they could enjoy the view. When everything was done, Jane said, "I hope it's OK. I haven't cooked a full meal in over a year." Connors, "I'm sure it'll be great," Then he raised his glass of wine, "Here's to you and to us. I am so thankful that we found each other again. Miraculously, in a few weeks, I'll be married to the girl of my dreams."

After they finished dinner, Connors volunteered to wash the dishes. As he began, Jane kissed his ear and whispered, "Nothing turns me on more than a good-looking man who washes dishes. I'll show you what it does to me later." Then she winked at him and left to take a shower.

Later, after she returned to the kitchen, Connors suggested they take a bottle of wine out on the deck and enjoy the evening. When the bottle was empty, Jane took his hand and led him to the bedroom.

At 0745 the next morning, Connors joined about a dozen other pilots in the VT-4 ready room. When the XO, Lt. Commander Stanley, walked in, someone yelled. "Attention on deck." and Stanley answered with a friendly, "At ease, Gents, this is going to be very informal. Please ask any questions without coming to your attention. Most of you guys finished VT-4 within the last two or three years, so you already know what we do here. We begin the training cycle on June 16, and we're still flying the T-2 C, plus a couple of other birds that you'll be familiar with. Until then, you will each have between six and ten hops in each aircraft. Basically, we want you to do everything you will teach the student pilots to do, including unusual attitude flight, gunnery, FCLP, and traps on the Lexington. You will also refresh yourselves with all the outlying fields, radio procedures, and training zones. The next two weeks will probably be the most relaxed flying you have done in the Navy, in as much as no one will be telling you what to do from day to day. It's up to you to file flight plans indicating what you will be doing and where you will be going. I will be reviewing them to ensure you have covered all the bases. Today, each of you will be assigned lockers, new flight suits, helmets, and pressure suits. Everyone will schedule a recce flight later today. Once you have completed the flight, you will be finished for the day. I'll see you tomorrow at 0800. As you were."

After Connors completed his flight and scheduled several more, he went into the pilots' lounge and called his mother. He asked her if there were any upcoming weekends that they would not be able to attend the wedding. She said any weekend through August was fine. Connors then called his sister, Sheila, who also told him they would be there whenever he wanted. She added that she hoped that he and Jane could visit and suggested the July Fourth weekend. Connors thought the Fourth of July would work but would confirm it with Jane.

Connors called Jane to see if she would like to go to the Oyster Bar for lunch. She wasn't crazy about oysters, but Connors assured her that the restaurant also made the best red snapper sandwich in town. Jane agreed, and Connors picked her up a half hour later,

When they arrived, Jane began, "I think we're ready to finalize dates and times. Everyone agrees that August 2nd at 3 pm is best. Wendy and I will order the flowers and the cake, and all the dresses should be ready by July 15. It will also make

167

sense to have a military wedding since you won't have to rent tuxes, and everyone can stay at the BOQ." Connors said, "August 2nd is fine with Riley and the groomsmen, and Riley will find volunteer sword bearers. Tomorrow, I'll call the chaplain to confirm the date, and I'll book the O Club for the rehearsal dinner on August 1st and the reception for the next afternoon."

"When I talk to the chaplain, who is Catholic, I'll tell him that we want a mass. Is that OK with you?" Jane, "Yes. Even though I haven't been a very good Catholic for the last few years, I do want to get married in the church." Connors, "Same with me. I am sure that the chaplain will want to have a pre-marriage counseling session with us, so I'll make an appointment for that, too."

The next day after work, Connors met with the Catholic Chaplain, Father O'Reilly, in his office. He was an older man who smiled broadly as he greeted Connors, "Have a seat. I'm Sean O'Reilly. What can I do for you?" Connors then told the Chaplain that he and Jane were hoping that he would be available to marry them on August 2nd. "We're both Catholics, but I haven't been active since I got my wings and went to sea. She's in pretty much the same boat, with studying for her PhD the last two years, but we both want to get married in the church." O'Reilly replied, "I understand. I was a Naval Aviator myself, a Commander. I did over two hundred combat missions in WWII and the Korean War. I hadn't gone to Mass for years, either. When I retired, I decided to go into the seminary. My friends were shocked, to say the least. I was a hard-partying flyboy. So, I know what your life has been like." Then he looked at his calendar and said, "It's all clear August 2nd, so three pm is open. I'll schedule it, but I need to meet with you and your fiancée for a couple of hours to talk about what you're getting yourself into. That, OK?" Connors, "No problem, Padre, I'll call you to set it up in the next couple of days" Then he thanked the chaplain and left for the O Club, where he was meeting Jane.

When Jane arrived at the Ready Room, they went to the small ballroom to make sure it would be sufficient for both the rehearsal dinner and reception. Unless they invited over 150 people, it would be fine for both events. As they went back to the bar, Jane said, "I forgot to tell you. My cousin Lisa won't be able to be a bridesmaid. She'll be at Bethesda Naval Hospital in clinical training for the Pediatric Nurse Practitioner program. She hopes to get away for the wedding but will have to return to Bethesda the next day."

As soon as the waitress took their order, Connors felt someone tap on his shoulder. It was Major Pless. "Connors, how are you? I just got here from reception and have a couple of minutes before I meet some old squadron mates at Trader Jon's. I heard through the grapevine that you're engaged. Hell, half the girls at the beach are talking about it. I presume this is the lucky lady." Connors, "Yes, sir, you're right about my engagement, but the other part is far from the truth. There must be some other Connors around here, someone who is a lot better looking and smarter than me, because this lady has been the sole object of my affection for a long time. Jane, this is Major Steve Pless, who was my class officer in AOCS and my mentor through VT-4. And Major, this is Jane Carmody, who has, for some unexplainable reason, agreed to be my wife. Pless, "It's a pleasure to meet you, Jane. No matter what this guy says, he has an outstanding record. I bet if he decides to make the Navy his career, he'll be a flag officer before he's forty-five."

Connors, "Thanks for the kind words, Major, coming from you, it's a high honor. Before you leave, I know it's short notice, but I'd like to invite you to our wedding on August 2nd at 3 pm, here at the base chapel. You'll be getting an invitation in a week or so." Pless, "It would be an honor to be there. I'll put it on my calendar in the morning. Barring some 'must attend' function already scheduled; I'll be there. I have to go now. Congratulations to both of you."

Chapter 36

Striker Meets Wendy

On the 4th of July, Striker was up early and running on the same path he ran in AOCS. It felt strange to be by himself, especially when he saw a class of candidates running about a quarter mile in front of him. Knowing that he wasn't in the class and would never have to be in another one made his run seem easy. When he finished, he showered, put on the uniform of the day, and looked for his suitemates. They were gone, so he went to the Open Mess to see if any other classmates were there. It was the first full day of being a Naval Officer, and he wanted to share it with them. Once he was there, he saw his roommates in the buffet line and got behind them. He couldn't stop smiling as he loaded his plate and got a large glass of OJ and a cup of steaming coffee. He wasn't holding back; it was the best breakfast of his life.

After they ate, they went to the bulletin board to check for available recreation and special events. Striker saw that there would be fireworks from barges moored in the harbor. Free tickets to watch the display from the deck of the Lexington were available at the front desk on a first-come, first-served basis.

As each of them picked up two tickets, Striker said to Sticky, "All I need now is to find a girl to take with me." Sticky replied, "I know. Let's tape tickets to our foreheads and go to the beach. Any girl who can read them gets a chance to go. If even they can't read and weren't ugly enough to scare a seagull away from a french fry, I'd read it to 'em." All of them howled with laughter, but Striker knew that Sticky wasn't kidding.

There weren't many unattached women in Pensacola and those who were almost always surrounded by other guys. With few options, Striker decided to go to the beach after he went to the car dealer.

Striker went back to his room and put on his bathing suit while Sticky called some friends. Hound was meeting family members in town, and Bulldog wanted to work out for a couple of hours. Fifteen minutes later, Striker parked his Mustang in the car dealer parking lot and went inside. Tommy O'Shea greeted him like a long-lost cousin, "Jonathan, my boy. Your timing is perfect. You must have paid attention to the good Marines in AOCS and learned to be prompt at all times. Are you ready to get this paperwork done? Did you bring your check with you?" Striker took it out of his pocket and handed it to Tommy, who said, "Great. Come on in and sit down, and we'll take care of this." Striker went in, and Tommy handed him papers to sign. A half-hour later, Striker finished signing, and Tommy gave him copies. Then Tommy handed Striker a twenty-dollar gift certificate for McGuires, "This will buy a lot of pints at McGuires, but don't forget that it's on me when I finish an Irish ballad and pass my hat around."

Then he shook Striker's hand and, walked him to the door and said, "Now, don't hesitate to send your buddies to me when they want to get a great deal on a new Ford. You know old Tommy will take care of them, and I'll make it worth your while." He winked at Striker and went back to his office. Striker got in his Mustang and drove to Pensacola Beach to find a date.

By midmorning, the Tiki Bar parking lot was almost full, and since it was the Fourth of July, it would only get more crowded. After grabbing a blanket and a towel, Striker walked to the beach in front of the bar and got as close to the Gulf as possible. He looked around and saw that he was almost surrounded by Naval Officers. Striker resigned himself to the reality of being outnumbered at least ten to one. He decided he would spend the day in the water rather than wasting time trying to outdo ten other guys. If it happened that he came across a girl who showed some interest in him, he would try to meet her. Otherwise, he would have a good day on the most beautiful beach he ever saw.

Having lived on the banks of the Patuxent River and spending many hours in the water virtually every summer day, swimming in the Gulf was a special treat. Pax River was relatively clear, but the Gulf that day was as clear as a swimming pool. Even without goggles, he was able to see reasonably well underwater, especially as he went further out from shore. There were large schools of mullet and tropical fish above a sandbar about two hundred yards out. Striker loved being there and continued to swim and body surf for almost two hours. Then he began to tire, and was getting hungry, so he swam towards the beach. As he got closer, he saw two-to-three-foot waves breaking about a hundred feet from shore, so his body surfed back to shore on the biggest one.

Suddenly he ran into someone he did not see in the breaking wave. It was a girl, and he had accidentally knocked her off her feet into the churning water. She appeared to be having a difficult time, so Striker quickly grabbed her arm as she struggled to stand up. He easily got her on her feet and helped her to the beach. She was obviously upset and was wiping her long hair off her face and water out of her eyes. Striker apologized, saying, "I'm so sorry. I couldn't see you in the wave. I was body surfing and didn't know you were in front of me. Let me help you to your blanket." She continued to wipe her eyes as they walked to a blanket where another girl was sitting. Striker helped her sit down and said, "Are you OK? I hope I didn't hurt you." She smiled at him and said, "Thanks for helping me. I'm fine. You barely touched me, and it was just as much my fault as yours. I'm not used to being hit by waves. You don't see a lot of them in Kansas. I was more spooked than hurt, and I panicked. You were in the right place at the right time and really helped me. Thanks again."

Striker smiled and said, "I'm glad you're OK." and he started to walk away. Then she said, "Wait, don't go. Sit and talk for a while. What you did was really nice," Striker came back and sat on the edge of her blanket, saying, "I'm Jonathan Striker, but most people call me Striker." She introduced herself as Wendy and her friend Leah. They were both from Kansas and had just graduated from college. They moved to Pensacola for teaching jobs and the beach. Then, for the next hour and a half, they talked about their backgrounds and interests. Striker asked Wendy if she would like to take a walk on the beach, and she quickly agreed. For the next two hours, they walked on the beach, talking and getting to know each other. On the way back to her blanket, Striker asked Wendy if she would like to go to dinner and then to the Lexington to watch the fireworks that evening. Wendy said she would love to go. It was now close to 4 pm, so he said he would go to the BOQ, clean up, and then pick her up at about 6:15 pm. She gave her address and number to him, and he said he would see her soon.

When Striker arrived at the BOQ, he found a note from his father. His dad wanted him to call as soon as possible and left a number. Then striker went to a house phone and dialed the number. It was the flight operations officer's number at Andrews Air Force Base. An Air Force Lt. Col. Stedman answered the call, and Striker identified himself. Lt. Col.

Stedman quickly connected him to his father, who told Striker that his mother had been in a bad car accident and was now in surgery at a hospital near Pax River, NAS. At this point, his dad only knew that she was in critical but stable condition with multiple fractures and a concussion. Striker's sisters were now on the way to the hospital. His dad was at Andrews to see if there were any Military Transport Service (MATS) flights coming from Pensacola or Eglin Air Force Base that evening or the next day. The flight ops officer found an 8 pm flight out of Eglin and a 5:45 pm flight out of Pensacola NAS that evening. There were no other flights until 6 pm, July 6.

His dad had booked him on the Pensacola flight, assuming he was coming. Striker said he would pack a bag and go to the terminal as soon as he could. His dad agreed to pick him up at the airport and make arrangements for them to stay at the Pax River BOQ for two to three days.

Striker then called Wendy, apologized, and told her about his mother's accident. Since he was leaving for Maryland, he had to cancel their date. He also told her that if everything went OK with his mom, he should be back by Monday or Tuesday and would call her. Wendy understood and hoped Striker's mom would be OK. She told him that she and Leah were driving to Kansas on Monday and would be gone for about three weeks. They wished each other safe travels and ended the call. Striker left a note to Sticky describing what happened and where he was going. Finally, he notified the OD about his unexpected trip. He then quickly put some clothes in a bag, put on his uniform, and went to the Flight Operations Office.

The flight to Andrews was a VIP Navy passenger aircraft that was returning to Andrews after bringing senior officers and guests to Pensacola for the Fourth of July. It was scheduled to be the same aircraft that would bring them back to Andrews on

Sunday evening. Striker arrived at the terminal a half hour before takeoff, signed in, and got on board. He was one of only ten passengers on the plane, which had seats for sixty. Unlike any Naval aircraft he had been in, it was as plush as a commercial airliner, complete with a small galley. It even had two bunks for flight crews to use during long flights and a steward who handed everyone a box lunch as they boarded the plane.

Chapter 37

Striker Makes an Emergency Trip to Maryland

When Striker arrived at Andrews at 11, he saw his father and hugged him. The two of them got into his father's car and headed towards Lexington Park, about fifty miles away. Along the way, his dad updated him on his mom's condition. She was out of surgery and heavily sedated. She had suffered a fractured femur in her right leg and broke several ribs. She also had a skull fracture that did not require surgery but might require her to wear a protective cap for several weeks until it healed. So far, there was no indication of brain injury or bleeding, but in the next day or two, that could change. In the absence of serious complications and after considerable rehab, they hoped she would make a full recovery. She would be in a lot of pain for weeks and probably confined to a wheelchair until her leg healed. With some luck she could be on her feet and active in about six months.

Striker's sisters, Lizzy and Anne Marie had been staying at their mother's house about 15 miles from the hospital. Striker chose to be with his father in the BOQ, not only because it was closer but because his father would not stay at his mother's house. Striker never spoke to his father about the divorce, but he knew his father didn't want the divorce and believed they could somehow rescue their marriage. His mother had insisted on the divorce and his dad finally agreed. He was generous to her in the settlement. He gave her the house, which was mortgage-free, all their savings, kept her as the beneficiary of his Navy retirement, and had paid child support.

His father did tell Striker that he still cared for his mother and felt it was his duty to make sure she was well taken care of during her time in the hospital and rehab. He knew all the sacrifices she made for him during their marriage and appreciated her dedication to the family and his career.

It was after 1 am when they arrived at the hospital. They were allowed to briefly visit her since she was no longer in Intensive Care. When Striker saw her, she was unrecognizable. She had a huge cast on her right leg, which was propped up, and a bandage that covered her entire head. She was heavily sedated and only partially aware that they were in the room. The nurse told Striker that she was doing better, but the next day or two would be crucial. She also said that Striker's sisters were there most of the evening and left about an hour before they arrived. They stayed about an hour, then left for the BOQ.

The next morning, Striker met his dad for breakfast. When they finished eating, his dad told Striker that he had to take care of some business and dropped him off at the hospital while he went to the Naval Air Station. Lizzy and Anne Marie were in the hallway outside his mother's room, waiting for the nurse to take some vital measurements. He was in his uniform when they saw them. Lizzy, "Look at you, little brother. You look so handsome in your uniform. I bet you must chase the girls away, or else they would be all over you." Anne Marie added, "If I weren't already married, I would move to Pensacola just to meet some of your Navy buddies. I hear there's a gazillion of them down there looking for a woman." Striker laughed and said, "Lizzy, you're wrong about my having to chase the girls away. Anne Marie is right about so many other young officers

178

there. I bet there were 10 or 15 guys for every girl at any place I've been, especially the Officers' Club."

Just then, the doctor came in and told them that their mother was still sedated, but so far, there was no sign of brain damage or infection. If all went well, they would start to reduce her sedation in the morning. The doctor also asked the family to talk normally to their mother because it would stimulate her brain and help her acquire her full cognitive abilities as she regained consciousness.

After they went into the room and told their mother, who was with her, they reminisced about growing up in a Navy family. They began with their favorite places where they lived. Anne Marie liked the North Island Naval Air Station on Coronado Island. Even though she was only six when they lived there, she could remember the beautiful Pacific beach they used to picnic on and the incredible sunsets every evening. She always wanted to move there but understood it had become prohibitively expensive. Lizzy preferred Corpus Christi, Texas, with the azure blue waters of the Gulf and fishing with her dad. She also liked the horned toads that were so ugly they were cute. Striker loved living in Lexington Park and his days crabbing and fishing at his Grandma Nonna's house in Solomons. He missed the many hours he, his dad, and his sisters fished on the Pax River and the Chesapeake Bay. As they talked, their mother smiled, raising their hopes that she would be OK.

A few minutes later, their dad arrived, hugged his daughters, and asked how Fran was doing. Striker briefed him on what the doctor said and told him that Fran smiled a couple of times. He replied, "That's great news. I'm sure she'll continue to improve and be home soon. I've arranged for a caterer to provide her with two meals a day as soon as she goes home. Whenever she needs transportation, I hire a driver who will take her anywhere she needs to go." Anne Marie hugged her dad and thanked him for his kindness. They remained with Fran, talking about old times, for several hours.

Later, a nurse came in and asked the family to leave while she changed some of their mother's bandages and gave her a sponge bath. Striker suggested that they go to the Officers' Club for dinner. He hadn't been there for years, but he remembered its spectacular view of the Patuxent River, where it joined the Chesapeake Bay.

Since it was early on a Saturday evening, there was only a brief wait at the O Club. As they waited Striker went to get everyone a drink. When he returned, his dad was talking to a man he recognized but couldn't recall his name. As he handed the drinks to his father and sisters, his dad asked him if he remembered Captain Stevenson, the flight operations officer he called about flights from Pensacola to Pax River. After Striker thanked him for his help, Stevenson congratulated him, and said, "I'm told you finished first in your class, that's really an outstanding achievement." Striker replied, "Thank you sir, I was just hoping to finish AOCS and had no idea I would be first in the class. It was a complete surprise."

Stevenson asked Striker what he was going to do next. He told Stevenson that because of an eye problem, he was in the Naval Flight Officer RIO pipeline. Stevenson replied, "The same thing happened to me almost twenty years ago. I know your disappointment, but I can assure you it's not a bad way to go. I've enjoyed every minute of it, even flying with your father years ago." He laughed and slapped Striker's father on the back.

Becoming more serious, he asked Striker how his mom was doing. Striker told him that she was showing signs of improvement. If she does better by Sunday, he would try to get a flight back to Pensacola later in the day. Stevenson handed Striker his card and said, "There's a squadron of F-4s that came in from Pensacola for the weekend to do some flyovers. I think they're scheduled to go back tomorrow evening. The Blue Angels have been here a couple of days and are also scheduled to leave sometime tomorrow. Have you had your 'OMIAS' ejection seat training yet? If not, there's no problem. We have some guys who can train you in about an hour. Maybe there's a back seat spot on one of them. Would you like a ride on the 'Flying Anvil'? Give me a call in the morning and I'll let you know." Striker immediately said, "Yes, Sir."

At that point, their party was called to a table and Striker's dad asked Stevenson if he would like to join them for dinner, but Stevenson declined, saying he was meeting his wife in the bar. Their table had a great view of dozens of sailboats and powerboats on the river and bay. Striker, pointing at the water, said, "Dad, I remember when you and I did some bottom fishing about two hundred feet offshore right out there. We were catching flounder, Norfolk spot and perch; we must have caught fifty fish." His dad replied, "I do remember that day. It took us about three hours to fillet the fish so that we could freeze them when we got home. It was a great day on the water."

When they finished dinner, they went back to the hospital. Fran was sound asleep when they got to her room. Rather than wake her, they sat by her bed and talked quietly. About an hour later, Lizzy and Anne Marie left for Fran's house and Striker and his dad went back to the BOQ.

When they pulled into the BOQ parking lot, Striker's dad said, "They have a nice casual bar near the open mess. Want to go in and grab a couple of beers?" They went in, sat at the bar and ordered draft beers. For the next two hours they talked about life in the Navy, then went to their rooms.

The next morning Striker was up early and ready to go. He called the Flight Operations Office, but Captain Stevenson wasn't there. The duty officer gave him a message from Captain Stevenson that one of the Blue Angel pilots, Lt. Rick Millson, would love to give a fledgling NFO a ride back to Pensacola. His flight was leaving at 1800 but Striker had to be there by 1630 to get a flight suit, G-suit, helmet, as well as OMIAS training. He thanked the duty officer and went to meet his father.

While Striker and his dad were eating breakfast, his dad said he was going to Mass at the base and asked him if he wanted to join him; Striker said he did. After Mass, Striker and his dad went to see Fran. The girls were already there and smiling. As soon as Striker walked in, he saw that his mother was awake and alert. She tried to reach out to him, but he took her hand and gently squeezed it, "Hi mom, you've had a rough time but you're getting better. You've been sedated for a day or two, but you came around before the doctors thought you would. With a little luck you might be out of here in a week or two."

Fran tried to shake her head in agreement but was obviously in a lot of pain. Striker told her to take it easy and asked her if she liked him in his Naval Officer's uniform. She smiled and attempted to nod her head. Then his father said, "I came to help you, Fran. You will always have a special place in my heart for being both mom and dad, all the years I was gone. The least I can do is to help you when you are in need. I'll be around to help any way I can."

Tears rolled down Fran's cheeks and Anne Marie went to wipe them off. Anne Marie added, "Lizzy and I will take turns being here until you get better. I'll be here for weekdays and Lizzy will be coming weekends. There's something I've been waiting to tell you and everyone else, I'm six-weeks pregnant. I'm going to have a baby. Jerry and I have wanted a baby ever since we married, almost four years ago. I'm so glad I got to tell you while we are all together."

Lizzy came to her sister and cried as she hugged her. Then her dad hugged her, followed by Striker, who said he was thrilled. Anne Marie, now crying, went to her mother and gently hugged her.

Soon the attending physician came into the room and introduced himself as Dr. Goldman. He briefed the family on Fran's condition and the prognosis for recovery. He explained, "Her fractured femur was the most serious injury. It was repaired with two metal rods and several surgical screws. Barring complications, her leg should be 90% back to normal in about six months. Initially she will need to be in a wheelchair, but with rehab, she should be walking in about a month. She'll start with a walker or crutches, then a cane until she is totally healed. I want to emphasize that her recovery rests largely on her willingness to do what the physical therapists tell her to do. She will be receiving limited rehab while she is here, but most of it will be as an outpatient. Her skull fracture was not as bad as we initially thought and there are no signs of permanent damage. It should be totally healed in about a month. Her broken ribs, while painful, will heal without any more treatment. The rest of her injuries are bruises and minor lacerations that will be gone in less than two weeks. Again, barring an infection or other complication, she should be out of here in about two or three weeks and will begin rehab. Any questions folks?"

After a few seconds of silence, Anne Marie thanked the doctor and said he covered it all extremely well. Doctor Goldman gave Anne Marie his card, told her to call if she had any questions. As soon as he was out of the room, Lizzy looked at her mom and said, "Mom, it looks like you are doing a lot better than anyone expected, but you have a lot of rehab coming. Knowing you as we do, I'll bet you'll be up and around a lot sooner than expected, too."

The family remained in the room until the nurse came to bathe her. Once in the hall, they decided to go to the O Club for lunch. Their mood was upbeat as they all ordered the lunch special; Maryland crab soup and a crab cake sandwich. Even though the food was delicious, it tasted even better with the news that Fran was recovering quicker than expected.

When they finished lunch, their dad took everyone back to the hospital. Fran seemed to be improving by the hour as she came out of sedation. At 1:30, when the nurse came to change Fran's bandages, Striker and his dad decided it was time to leave. Striker told his mom he had to get ready to fly back to Pensacola. He promised that he would check with his sisters to see how she was progressing. He then hugged her and said goodbye. His dad gave Fran the phone numbers of the caterer and driver and he told her to call him if she needed anything else. Then, the two of them left for the BOQ.

Striker had about two hours before his dad would take him to the Flight Operations Office, so he went for a four-mile run, showered and prepared to leave. After a quick bite together at the BOQ, his father dropped Striker off at the terminal, and drove home.

Striker went directly to the Flight Operations Office. A Chief Petty Officer logged him in and took him to a locker room, brought him a flight suit, boots, and helmet. Once Striker was dressed, the CPO brought him a G-suit, told him how to put it on and how it worked. Then he took Striker to the hangar where there was another CPO who took him to an ejection seat facsimile that was bolted to the floor. It was attached to a vertical track that went about fifteen feet up the hangar wall. The seat was the same as the one in an F-4 but the explosive charge under the seat was much smaller. The CPO strapped Striker in and showed him how to disconnect the straps in an emergency. Then he explained how Striker would eject. There were several ways to deploy the seat, which varied from aircraft to aircraft, but usually a lever or button on the right side of the seat, one underneath the seat and one above his head. There was also a fourth one, which on the facsimile was on the left side of the seat. The first three would eject the back seat and the fourth would eject the pilot, if needed. The CPO then said he would count down from five. At one, he would deploy the seat. Then he began the countdown and on "one" there was a loud explosion under his seat. Striker was immediately jerked up about ten feet to a gradual stop at the top of the track, and then slowly came down to its base on the floor. The CPO said, "All OK Mr. Striker?" and Striker said, "Hell yes, can we do that again?" The CPO laughed and said, "I wish I could, but my ass would be in a sling if you injured your back, which has happened before. The next time you do it you'll be in an aircraft." Then the CPO told Striker, "Now I'm going to teach you the proper way to land on your feet after you do eject." He led Striker to a six-foot high platform next to a thick 10 x 10-foot pad. The CPO went up the steps to the platform, walked to the edge and said, "When I jump, I will go into a forward roll to absorb the force of landing. If I were using a parachute, I would be hitting the ground at 15 to 20 miles per hour, which could easily injure my ankle or legs. Then he jumped. When he hit the pad, he rolled forward, got to his feet and said, "Now it's your turn. I want you to do it three times. When Striker got on the edge of the platform, the CPO said, "On my command, now. Jump." Striker almost did it correctly, but by the third try he did it well. The CPO said, "That's it, Mr. Striker. You are now a certified member of the OMIAS club, which is one of the most exclusive clubs in the U S Navy." Then he thanked the CPO and followed him to see Commander Wheat, the Blue Angels Team Leader.

After Commander Wheat talked briefly about what Striker would experience, he introduced him to the pilot, Lt. Millson. Millson led Striker out to the flight line. Striker had not seen an F-4 since the day he and Sticky were on the Lexington. Up close it was the most impressive aircraft Striker had ever seen. It looked like a flying blue beast that could outperform any aircraft in the world. Striker was in awe as Millson took him around the aircraft and pointed out its airframe features and massive engines. After Striker climbed into the cockpit, a crewman strapped him in so tight it was hard to breathe. The crewman told him he was sorry it had to be so tight, but that Striker would appreciate it later.

Striker looked around at the instruments and was amazed at the number and complexity of the gauges. He thought to himself, "No wonder it takes nearly two years to learn how to fly one of these bad boys." Then Millson spoke to Striker on the intercom, saying they were cleared to take off in ten minutes, so he briefed him on the capabilities of the F-4. First, he told Striker that, except for ordnance, this was exactly the same aircraft that was now with the fleet in Vietnam. No other aircraft could even stay close to an F-4 when it engaged its afterburners.

A few minutes later, the tower cleared him for a high-performance takeoff, which meant they would take off with full afterburner and fly up to their cruising altitude of 27,000 feet. A minute later the tower cleared them for the roll up to the numbers at the end of the runway. Millson started the two engines and they slowly left. At the numbers, the tower cleared them for takeoff and Millson went to full power. As soon as the wheels left the ground, he kicked in the afterburner and the aircraft lurched forward and went straight up. Striker felt the G-forces crush him into his seat. His pressure suit inflated, forcing blood from his legs and lower chest upwards toward his head. Less than thirty seconds later they were at 27,000 feet and Millson put the aircraft into a high-speed turn to get the first heading. Then he shut down the afterburners and slowed the aircraft to the cruising speed of 550 knots. Millson called Striker on the intercom and asked, "How was it? Did you enjoy the takeoff?" All that Striker said was, "Holy shit, sir. It was incredible." Millson chuckled as he clicked off.

Striker had flown many times, but only in large passenger aircraft that didn't approach what he was experiencing in the F-4. First, he was amazed how quiet it was. Even at full afterburner power, it was quieter than most of the older four-engine prop aircraft. He was so tightly strapped in he had no sense of gravity, except when he felt the G-forces of the vertical takeoff. He was most impressed with the panoramic view that he had in the canopied cockpit. During most of the flight he was mesmerized by everything around the aircraft as it made its way to Pensacola. It was then that he knew he made the right choice to remain in AOCS even though he could not be a pilot.

They arrived in the Pensacola area a little early, about 2015 and Millson had to circle the area for about ten minutes. He pointed out two of the other Blue Angels who were in the same pattern several miles away. They had taken off five minutes apart from each other and would land in the same sequence. Finally, they were cleared for final approach and landing, and were on the ground ten minutes later. Millson rolled the aircraft to its designated parking spot near the terminal and shut the engines down. With assistance of the ground crew, they climbed out of the cockpit and walked to the Blue Angels Flight Operations Office.

Millson completed the flight log and led Striker into the pilot's lounge. He introduced Striker to the two Blues they saw in the approach pattern, telling them that Striker was just commissioned and was following in his father's footsteps to become a Naval Aviator. Both of the other Blues congratulated him, wished him well and left. Striker again thanked Millson for letting him fly to Pensacola in the F-4, and told him it was the chance of a lifetime. Millson told him he was welcome to fly with him any time he wanted.

Fifteen minutes later, Striker changed his clothes and went to the Ready Room to tell somebody he had just flown with a Blue Angel.

Chapter 38

Striker Meets Terry

Because there were so many people on base for the July 4th celebrations, the Ready Room was crowded at 9 pm on a Sunday. Striker still found three empty bar stools, and he took the one at the end of the bar. As he sat down, he saw Pless in his regular place, several seats away. He was having a discussion with a Marine Captain that he seemed to know well. Striker ordered a beer and waited until the Captain left before he approached Pless.

Soon after he got the beer, two Navy Nurses sat down on the vacant stools next to him. After they ordered drinks, they began to discuss their day at work. From what Striker could tell, they were surgical nurses who were involved in a lengthy procedure to repair multiple fractures of a car crash victim. The patient, a Navy wife with two kids, was T-boned by a drunk driver while she was bringing her children back from Orlando. The children were not seriously hurt, but the mother had serious damage to her leg that would take months to heal.

In a quiet moment, Striker told the nurse closest to him that he couldn't help but overhear their conversation. He wanted to tell them that he had just returned from visiting his mother who had very similar injuries. Then he said that he felt bad that he didn't have time to thank the nurses and medical staff who helped to save his mother's leg. He offered to buy the two nurses drinks because so often their efforts went unnoticed.

The nurse next to him replied, "Thank you so much. Believe it or not, very few people have thanked me for helping

189

a patient. Surgical nurses are pretty much invisible since we only see patients in the operating room. Once the procedure is done, we turn their care over to post-op services. Our job is done, and their job begins." The other nurse said, "What is really hard to take is that most of the time we have no idea what happened to the patient after the procedure is complete. Many times, we don't even know their names or how they were injured. It's just another patient in surgery, and our training kicks in. In today's case, we've worked with the surgeon before, and he told us the patient's background. So, thank you for the drink and kind words, they're really appreciated. By the way, I'm Linda Mahoney, and my friend is Terry Gunther." Striker followed with "You're more than welcome. I'm Jonathan Striker, but most people just call me Striker."

Terry responded, "I'll call you Striker as well, if that's OK. Are you in flight school like most of the guys around here?" Striker answered, "Yeah, just got commissioned on Thursday and I'll start NFO training next Monday." Terry said, "I know all about it. My ex is an NFO in a P-3. He was stationed in Norfolk and I'm not, so we broke up about six months ago. We met here, at the Ready Room, about a month after I arrived from Madison, Wisconsin. That was about two years ago, and he was about halfway through VT-10. A year later he was sent to Norfolk and was assigned to a P-3 squadron. As much as I cared for him, we broke up. I had a long-distance relationship before, and it didn't work, I absolutely love the area, especially the beach. If I have my way, I'll stay here for my entire tour in the Navy. How about you, Striker?" He told her about his growing up in a Navy family and his dad being a career Naval Aviator. He also said, "The Navy is the only life I know. Right now, I want to make it a career, but things change, as you know. Since my parents are divorced, I also know that long-term relationships are hard to sustain, especially in the Navy. It's a reality that I'm willing to accept, so I'm single, but that hasn't stopped me from looking." Then Linda said, "That seems to be the case with so many of the aviators here. They want to meet a girl, but they don't want anything long-term. Some girls can live with that, but a few, like me, can't. There are a lot of local brokenhearted young girls who think they can change the inevitable. When their true love gets orders to leave, he'll be gone for at least a year, especially if it's his first tour. As far as I know, there is no room on an aircraft carrier to bring along a girlfriend or wife. That starry-eyed girl will probably never see her man again. After living here for about two years, I understand the real world of Naval Aviation, and now the guys I go out with are more senior officers who have done at least one tour and may be considering leaving the Navy. I don't often come here to the Ready Room, where there are so many brand-new ensigns. I learned the hard way that many are only looking for a one-night stand, and I'm not."

Linda got up to go to the bathroom and Terry smiled at Striker and said, "I'm not as concerned about it as my friend is. While I'm not looking for one-night stands, I'm also not interested in long-term relationships. Here's my number. Call me if you'd like to go out for a drink sometime. I live over in Gulf Breeze, in a house the two of us share." Striker said he would love to and put her number in his pocket.

Just then Major Pless tapped him on his shoulder saying, "I saw you here as I was getting ready to leave. I wanted to tell you I really enjoyed talking to you and your dad the other day. I've not met many Navy mustang officers who have been as successful as he has. Coming up through the ranks and making Captain is quite an achievement. You should be very proud of him." Striker responded, "Thank you sir. I am very proud of him, and I hope my Navy career is half as successful as his. I'll probably be talking to him in a day or two about my mother, who is recovering from injuries in a car accident. I'll tell him what you said." Pless said he hoped Striker's mother recovered soon and wished him good luck.

Terry then said, "Now that's impressive. Major Pless is a superstar around here. Most of the time people, especially girls, surround him. Then he just walks over to you and greets you like a member of the family." Striker then said, "Believe me, knowing him is entirely circumstantial, but I have to admit that he has been one of my heroes ever since he won the Medal of Honor." The girls finished their drinks and got ready to leave. As Linda got up, Terry whispered to Striker, "Don't forget to give me a call." Then she caught up with her friend. Ten minutes later, Striker was back in the BOQ.

Striker woke up to the sound of Sticky dropping a can of shaving cream in the bathroom. It was only 6:30, but he decided to get up and take a run. Just as he was leaving, Sticky asked Striker how his mother was doing. Striker responded, "She's a lot better than they first thought. But she does have multiple injuries and the doctors repaired them as best they could. With no complications, she should begin rehab this week. My sisters are staying with her, and even though my parents are divorced, my dad is helping her too. Thanks for asking."

"Oh, I almost forgot the big news. I flew back from Pax River in a Blue Angel F-4. It turned out that the Pax River Flight Ops officer is an old friend of my father's. Dad called him to see if he could get me on a flight home last night. He told Dad that the Blues were at Pax for a couple of shows, and they were scheduled to fly here last night. My dad's friend arranged for me to get a seat on one of them. I couldn't wait. The pilot, a great guy, even got clearance for a high-

192

performance take off. It was unbelievable. I can't wait to climb into one of those bad boys."

Striker continued, "Just to put some icing on the cake, I met a girl when I got back. As soon as I left the Flight Ops Terminal, I went to get a beer at the Ready Room. There were two nurses sitting next to me and I overheard them say they had a really rugged day. I offered to buy them beers to thank them for all that nurses do to help their patients. They really appreciated it. To my surprise, when they left an hour later, one of them slipped me her number and said she'd like to go out sometime. I'm going to call her later this week."

Sticky was silent for a second, and then said, "Striker, you're unbelievable. I've never been within 20 feet of an F-4 and have only seen the Blue Angels in a show. I'm batting zero trying to get a date with any girl who is over seventeen and can spell Pensacola. You've already ridden with a Blue Angel and out of the blue, a girl hands you her phone number without you even asking. Holy Shit." Striker laughed and said, "It was just a stroke of luck, Sticky. I was in the right place at the right time. Then as he headed for the door, "I'm going to order some uniforms and then go to the beach. Maybe I'll catch up with you there."

After he ate breakfast, Striker called his sister. Anne Marie told him that their mother slept most of the time, but the doctors would gradually reduce the pain meds and get her out of bed. Then he called Terry, left a message for her to call him at the BOQ, and left. Before he arrived at the beach, he stopped at Abbott's Military Tailors, where he bought additional uniforms and changed into his bathing suit.

When Striker arrived at Tiki Beach, he grabbed a blanket and looked for Sticky. It didn't take long to find him. Sticky

193

was near the front of the bar, sitting on a blanket with two girls. Striker put his blanket next to them, and Sticky introduced him to Lee Ann and Julie. It was clear to Striker that Sticky was focused on Lee Ann. After speaking with Julie for a few minutes, he was certain that she was only sixteen or seventeen. He lost any interest in her and went for a swim.

After about an hour of body surfing, Striker came back to his blanket. Julie was still there but Sticky and Lee Ann were gone. When Julie said she didn't know where they went, Striker looked around and scanned the water, but didn't see them anywhere. Striker, "Do you live around here, Julie?" Julie, "Sort of, I live about thirty miles from here, in Foley, Alabama. Lee Ann and I are cousins. She lives in Gulf Breeze; I stay with her a lot when school is out. When I graduate, I'm going to move here too." Striker then asked, "Where do you go to school, Julie?" and she replied, "Foley High School. I'll graduate next June; I can't wait to move here. There's nothing to do in Foley, it's not much more than a gas station and a fire hall. But here, there's always something going on and a bunch of guys to choose from." Striker, "Where does Lee Ann go to school?" Julie responded, "She just graduated from Tate High School about a month ago and will start at Pensacola Junior College in August. She's a waitress at a Maria's Mexican restaurant near the Navy Base. She shares an apartment with a friend. That's where I stay when I come to the beach." Striker, "How old are you, Julie?" Julie. "I just turned seventeen. Lee Ann is almost a year older than me." Striker said, "You're really a pretty girl Julie, don't you have a boyfriend?" Julie, "Thank you. I used to have a boyfriend. We split up because he deployed to Vietnam. He's a Marine helicopter pilot. We met at a mixer at the Officers' Club about six months ago. Have you been there?" Striker, "Yes, I've been there a couple of times." Julie, "Are you a pilot?" Striker, "No, but I'm training

194

to be a Naval Flight Officer. It's kinda like a pilot." Julie, "I like you; I'll give you my phone number." As she reached for her purse, Striker stopped her. "I have a girlfriend Julie, and I don't go out with anyone else." Julie, "OK, Thanks for telling me. I've met too many guys who lie about not having a girlfriend, even a wife or fiancée." Striker, "Yeah, I know guys who are like that."

Just as he finished talking, Sticky and Lee Ann came back. Sticky, "All that swimming made me thirsty; I'm gonna get a beer. Anyone else want one?" All three said yes and Striker said he'd help Sticky. Once they got inside, Striker said, "Sticky, Julie was really hitting on me. She just turned seventeen and she's asking me out." Sticky, "Lee Ann's just going to be eighteen in a few weeks, but I'm not concerned about her age. She told me her ex was a twenty-four-year-old NFO. They broke up when he went to Glynco a couple of months ago." Striker, "Man, things are sure different here, especially when it comes to dating. It's going to take a while for me to get used to it." Sticky, with a sly smile, "I'm just a quicker learner than you are, Striker. You've got to go with the flow. If she's giving, I'm taking."

An hour later, Striker finished his beer and went to a pay phone to check for messages. There was one from Terry, who said she would be getting off at 4, and to call her then. It was only 2, so he decided to swim again, and then return to the BOQ and call her.

Chapter 39

Striker and Terry Date

As soon as Striker got to the BOQ, he called Terry and asked if she wanted to go to dinner that evening. She did, but she suggested that it might be nice to go to the beach for an hour or two, then to a nearby place for dinner. Striker agreed and went to take a shower and put on a dry bathing suit. As he left, he thought, "I never thought I would leave the beach, go home, take a shower then go back to the beach. Women can really do strange things to your mind."

Terry lived in a small house that backed onto Pensacola Bay. Her directions were precise, so it was easy to find. As soon as he walked in, he saw the view of the bay from the living room and said, "I can see why you wanted to live here, the view is spectacular." Terry, "Yeah it is. I originally didn't want to have another roommate since my last one suddenly married and moved, but I couldn't afford this place on my own. I asked Linda if she wanted to share it. We really didn't know each other very well; but both of us had just broken up with boyfriends, and she thought this place was great. She moved in about three months ago. Ironically, even though we work in the same unit, I normally don't see her until Friday morning, when we are both off."

"I see her a lot more than my last roommate, who spent most of the time with her married boyfriend, a thoracic surgeon at the hospital. She got pregnant; he divorced his wife and married her. It was a big scandal at the hospital. I suspect that if he wasn't such a highly regarded doctor, he would have been transferred somewhere else. His ex-wife was my charge nurse

196

and a good person. After her husband left her, she volunteered for duty just about anywhere, and volunteered for a tour in the Philippines; that's where she went."

Striker, "Wow. If that happened anywhere but the Medical Corps, he would have faced a court martial for fraternizing with a female officer under his command." Terry, "Well it goes on all the time, in every hospital. In my opinion, my ex-roommate went after that good-looking surgeon the first time she saw him, and her getting pregnant was no accident. As you aviators say, 'She had target fixation,' but in her case she completed the mission with a lot of collateral damage." Terry then took Striker by the arm, "Enough hospital gossip, let's go to the beach."

Striker asked Terry if there was any place wanted to go. Terry responded, "Anywhere is fine, but my favorite is the Tiki Bar. Striker, "That's where we are heading," Ten minutes later they found a deserted spot about a hundred feet from the Gulf. It was still hot, but a cool breeze made it a beautiful evening.

Terry asked Striker how he ended up in the Navy. He gave her a thumbnail description of his life as a Navy brat, his decision to become a Naval Aviator, and his trip to visit his mother in the hospital. Terry asked him if he had a girlfriend back home or a love interest here in Pensacola. Striker, "I was so busy finishing college, followed by AOCS, I haven't had a date in over a year. So, to answer your question, I'm about as single as you can get."

Terry, "Whoa, I better watch out for you. You've got a lot of catching up to do. Either I'm a very lucky girl to have met you or I'm the only choice you have." Striker, "Well, I am fascinated by your dedication to nursing and your patients. Maybe you can tell me a little about yourself and we can start from there. Before you do, can I get you something to drink?" Terry, "I'd love a beer."

When Striker returned with the drinks, Terry began, "I'm from Madison, and I went to the University of Wisconsin, where I received my RN. I have a married sister and a brother who was a Marine. He was badly wounded in Nam. He told me the main reason he survived his injuries was the care he received from a dedicated nurse named Callahan. She wouldn't let him die. She stayed by his side long past her shifts, doing whatever she could, simply because she wanted to save his life. She succeeded, but my brother never saw her again and wanted to thank her. When he told me that, I decided I wanted to be like her. I decided to become a Navy nurse. Four years and three months later, I was one and was stationed here, and I love it here. If the Navy lets me, I'll stay here as long as I can. As far as boyfriends are concerned, I've had my share. There was one in high school and through the first year of college, but most have been since I moved here. All of those were Navy or Marine Aviators, but only one was serious. His name was Paul, and as you know, we split up because he's now in Norfolk, and neither of us was ready to get married. Since then, I've gone out with a few guys, but no more than two or three casual dates."

Striker, "I'm not even close to be looking for a wife. I've been an officer for less than a week. I have a long way to go before I'm able to be a decent husband. You're an attractive girl and I think I'd really enjoy spending time with you. Only time will tell, but I will always be honest with you. If you're willing to see me after tonight, knowing where I'm coming from, I want to see you." Terry, "Here's to the beginning of a beautiful friendship."

They remained at the Tiki Bar until about 6:30 pm, when Striker asked her if there was someplace, she would like to go to for dinner. Terry said, "There's a place on the bay, the Sandbar, that has decent food and a spectacular sunset view. I've only been there a couple of times, but if you're game, I am too. It's only down the road about a mile, on the bay." Striker said it sounded great.

The Sandbar was not much bigger than an average double car garage, but it had a huge deck overlooking the bay. They were early enough to get a table on the bay side of the deck and ordered drinks. Terry wanted more details about his growing up in a Navy family. After he did, Terry said, "I lived in the same house my entire life. My father worked at the same company for over thirty years and my mom took care of my brother, sister and me. She died about a year ago. When I went to college, I knew exactly what I was going to do, and I finished a semester early. As I told you, after I graduated, I joined the Navy. It's been a straight line from Madison to Pensacola for me. You bounced all over the place and ended up here, in Pensacola, a place with a long history of bringing different nations and cultures together. We met when neither of us was even trying to meet someone. Life is sometimes hard to explain."

Striker thought about all the moves and said, "Even though I've lived in a lot of places, Pensacola will always be a special place for me. It is where I completed AOCS, and where years ago, my dad was stationed. He went to the same beaches and partied at the same places I go to now. It's a big part of our lives."

As the sun began its slow descent over Pensacola Bay, Striker signaled to the waiter that they were ready to order. Having lived for years near the Chesapeake Bay, he preferred a fish sandwich rather than a burger at any time. He ordered a cup of gumbo and a spicy red snapper sandwich, and Terry got a Caesar salad topped with steamed shrimp and crabmeat. They took their time eating and enjoyed a spectacular sunset. After they finished eating, they went back to the Tiki Bar, where they watched the moon rise over the Gulf and talked some more.

Terry looked at her watch, "Whoa, it's almost midnight. I hate to break this up, but I've got to get some sleep. I'm sorry, but we must go." Striker, "Yeah, I didn't realize that it was that late. I'll pay the tab and take you home."

When they arrived at her house, he walked her to her door. She turned to him and said, "I'd love to invite you in, but it's too late, I have to be at work at 6 am, so I need to sleep. I really enjoyed being with you and hope to see you again soon. Maybe next time, I'll cook for you, and you can bring a bottle of wine." Then she embraced him and kissed him goodnight. Before she left, Striker said he would call her in a day or two. He drove back to the BOQ and went directly to bed. Before he fell asleep, he noticed that Sticky was not there.

Striker was up a little after 7:00 and went for a run. When he returned, Sticky was still gone. Then he checked the other bedroom, and Bulldog and Hound were also somewhere else. Striker cleaned up, put on civilian clothes and went to breakfast at the open mess. It was still too early to go to the beach so he went to the base exchange to buy a sword, belt, and additional khaki shirts and pants.

Even though he wasn't planning to call Terry again before the end of the week, he changed his mind. It occurred to him that if he didn't call her, she probably would make other plans. After all, Terry was attractive and available, and there was so much competition for her attention. If he didn't ask her out, someone else certainly would. When he left the base exchange, he went back to the BOQ and called Terry at the hospital. She was unavailable, so, he left a message saying that he would be at her place at 6 pm.

Striker called Anne Marie to again check on his mother's condition. Anne Marie, "If mom still doesn't have complications, she might be sent to the rehab unit in the hospital this afternoon or tomorrow. When I find out, I'll call you and maybe you can talk to her. She is still on heavy-duty painkillers and sleeps a lot, but Dr. Goldman is very optimistic that she could resume all her normal activities in about six months, assuming she plays by the rules. I gotta run, I'll call you later."

It was after 10 am, so Striker decided to head to the beach. When he got back to his suite, Sticky was putting some things in a bag. Striker, "Hey man, I haven't seen you in a couple of days. Have you been with the girl we met at the beach the other day? Sticky, "Yeah, after you left, we hung around at the beach, and had a couple of drinks. Then her friend, Julie, wanted to leave so I told Lee Ann I'd take her home later. We ate dinner and had a couple more drinks, and then I asked if she wanted to stay overnight with me, and she agreed. It was that easy, no sweet talk, and no bullshit. We checked into a motel about a block from the Tiki Bar. All I had was the bathing suit that I was wearing, so I came here to get some clothes and my shaving kit. Lee Ann is waiting for me back at the beach. I'll take her back to her apartment tomorrow. Oh, how's your mom doing?" Striker, "She's progressing well, and may be moved to the hospital rehab unit later today or tomorrow." Sticky, "How's it going with your new lady friend?" Striker, "Good so far. I'm going to her place and she's cooking dinner." Sticky, almost serious, "Holy shit, Striker. A girl making dinner is a sure sign that she wants to play house with you, like permanently. Food beats sex in the long run every time. Ask any guy who has been with the same woman more than a couple of months. The sweet young thing might attract you with sex, but she'll keep you around by feeding you. It's the natural nesting thing with them. You better watch out and hope that what she makes tastes like Alpo, or else she's set a trap for you. I wish you luck, man." Then he chuckled and slapped Striker on the back as he left.

Striker changed into his bathing suit, grabbed a blanket and a towel, and then threw some toiletries into a bag. As he left the BOQ, he checked the front desk for messages; there was one from Terry. She had to work until 6 pm so it would be too late to make dinner. Instead, she wanted to meet him about 6:30 at the Ready Room to get a sandwich and a beer. Striker called the hospital and left a message that he'd be there. Then he headed to Tiki Beach.

On the way he stopped at a K-Mart and bought some flippers, a snorkel, and a diving mask. It was a warm but overcast day so there was plenty of room on the beach. Striker chose a spot in front of the bar, about fifty feet from the Gulf. As soon as he put his blanket and towel down, he picked up his snorkeling gear and waded into the water. The Gulf was as calm as a lake, so the water was almost crystal clear. He put on the mask and flippers and swam to the sand bar about two hundred yards from shore. He spent most of the time below the surface, diving near the sandy bottom and then up and through schools of fish. The natural beauty of the multicolored fish surrounded by the azure blue of the Gulf was mesmerizing, a spectacular underwater kaleidoscope. Even though the salty water made it easy to stay afloat and keep moving, he eventually tired and returned to shore. As he left, he checked the time; he had been in the water for almost three hours.

When Striker returned to his blanket, he propped his head up with his towel and quickly fell asleep. About an hour later the clouds were gone and the combination of nearby voices and bright sun woke him up. When he sat up, he saw that there were more people at the beach, most of them were guys his age, but there were a few girls as well. As usual, the girls looked to be very young; some of them were probably high school girls on their summer vacation. Virtually all of the girls had older guys close by.

He observed the Tiki Beach mating rituals until after 4 pm, and then he gathered his belongings and went back to the BOQ. As he always did, Striker checked for messages at the front desk before he went to his suite. There was one from his sister Anne Marie, who said that their mother had been moved to the hospital rehab unit and left a phone number. She added that he should wait to call until the next day since their mother was sleeping a lot.

When he got back to his suite, no one was there, so he left a note that if anybody wanted to get together with him, he would be in the Ready Room. It was after five, so he changed and went to the bar before it was too crowded to get a table. The Ready Room was already three quarters full when he arrived. He sat at a table close to the door so he could see people coming in, and then he ordered a beer.

Soon. Bulldog and Hound walked in, and Striker motioned for them to sit down and asked, "What have you guys been up to the last couple of days?" Bulldog "I've been with my family at the beach. They rented a big house about a mile away from the Tiki Bar. It was great seeing my brothers and sisters. I'm the oldest of six kids, ranging down to my ten-year-old kid sister. It was the first time most of them had seen any place to swim as big as the Gulf, and they loved it; we had a ball." Hound, "I've been at my sister Peggy's house in Pensacola. Her husband is a JAG officer here at the base and they live in a restored Victorian house in town. What've you been up to?"

Striker told them about his visiting his mother in the hospital, then how he got a ride back in a Blue Angel F-4. Then he said, "Believe it or not, as soon as I got back, I met a nurse here, at the bar. She gave me her number and whispered in my ear that she wanted me to call. I took her out last night and she's supposed to meet me here in a few minutes." Then the waitress stopped by and he ordered three beers.

Bulldog, "Are you kidding me? In less than a week since you were commissioned, you've ridden in a Blue Angel F-4 and had a date with a girl who basically asked you out, and now you're going to see her again?" As the beers arrived, Striker replied, "You got it right, Sherlock, and I didn't mention that I met another really pretty girl, a local schoolteacher, at the beach. Or I should say, I knocked her down when I was body surfing, helped her back to her blanket, and she gave me her number. I would've taken her out on the Fourth, but I had to cancel because I went to Maryland to visit my mother. Life is good, baby." Hound, "Hell, First Sergeant Sullivan should've named you hound, 'cause you're a walking-talking dog. What do you have that we don't?" Striker, "Other than my sheer animal magnetism, sexy body, and amazing charm, I can't think of a single thing."

The other two both laughed and yelled, "Bullshit!" and Bulldog added, "That's exactly what you got, a lot of bullshit and a baby-face they can't help but believe, 'cause you look like a damn altar boy and boy scout rolled into one. They don't know you're really an angel with a crooked halo, you devil." Striker just smiled without saying a word and then winked. All three of them laughed and sipped their beers.

Terry came into the bar just as his roommates were finishing their beers. She looked great in her Summer Navy white uniform, which was obviously custom-made for her impressive figure. Striker saw her walk in and waved to her. As she got to the table, he stood up and introduced his friends, "Terry, this is Josh Schnider, better known as Bulldog, and Al Stewart, AKA Hound. We were roommates in AOCS, and now in the BOQ.

Terry smiled as she said, "Nice to meet you guys. If I had known you were going to be here, I would've asked some of my friends if they wanted to join us." Quickly followed by Striker, "Oh, they just stopped by to have a beer and were getting ready to leave. Right, fellas?" Bulldog said, "Of course, but I'll tell Striker to let us know when you are coming here again so that you might be able to bring some friends with you." Terry, still smiling, "Just let him know a day in advance and I'll do my best, guys. I know a lot of young nurses who would like to meet such good-looking young Naval Officers." Bulldog and Hound both gave her a thumbs-up and joined the crowd at the bar.

Terry sat next to Striker, sighed, and said, "I'm sorry I backed out of cooking dinner, but it was another rough day in the OR. We had a lot of procedures because of the long Fourth of July weekend. None were that complicated but it was constant. One orthopedic doctor had four procedures in a row and must've been in the OR for ten hours straight. I assisted in one of them, which took over two hours. I am sure ready for a drink. Instead of waiting for a waitress, Striker went to the bar and brought back two mugs of beer. Terry thanked him and asked, "Have you been here long?" Striker responded with, "Not that long. I came in about five so I could beat some of the happy hour crowd. Right after I got here, my roomies came in. I hadn't seen either of them for a couple of days, so we sat and talked until you arrived."

When the waitress came to the table, Striker ordered his usual bowl of gumbo, and a spicy grouper sandwich and Terry got a Caesar salad with gulf shrimp. As they finished their beers, Striker described his day at the beach, in particular how young the girls were and how much older the guys were. He said, "Maybe I'm old-fashioned, but before I came here, I never would have considered dating a seventeen- or eighteen-year-old girl, at least not since I was nineteen or twenty. I'm learning that things are different here. It seems to be perfectly OK that a high school girl would be going out with a twenty-five-year-old pilot. Terry smiled and said, "I agree, when I was in high school, my mother would never let me go out with someone who was more than a year older than me."

When they finished their dinners, the bar had become crowded and loud. Terry looked at her watch and said, "It's only seven-thirty, want to head to the beach? Ever been to Dirty Joe's Saloon? It's always a hoot there, but it's my kind of place. I play a mean game of foosball if you're willing." Striker, smiling, "You're on. I haven't played foosball since I was a kid, but I was pretty good at it. You better bring big money cause I'm going to whip your butt."

Striker followed Terry to her apartment where she changed into shorts and a tee shirt. It was only a short drive over the Santa Rosa Sound Bridge then across Via De Luna to the strip mall where Dirty Joe's was located. Once they were out of the car, they heard cheering and applause coming from inside. As they walked in, Striker immediately thought he was walking into the Rendezvous (Vous) Bar, which was a raucous college bar just off campus at the University of Maryland. But Dirty Joe's didn't look like the Vous at all; Dirty Joe's was festooned with pictures of Navy and Marine aircraft, the Blue Angels and scantily clad girls on the beach, while the Vous was decorated mostly with pictures of Maryland football and basketball players, game balls, and game pictures. The Vous was always crowded with coeds, while Dirty Joe's was clearly a Naval Aviators' watering hole, a testosterone-laden place for high-spirited aviators. The only similarity was the smell: stale beer, peanuts, and urine.

Luckily, the place was not crowded, but several people were gathered around the foosball tables. Apparently, there was a tournament and Striker could see someone taking bets. Since so many people were near the foosball tables, there were plenty of seats at the bar. Striker and Terry took two of them near the tables and ordered drinks.

Striker asked the barkeep what was going on, he responded, "It's guys against girls' tournament. There are two teams, four men and four women, three rounds of four games, one at each table. The team that first wins eight games is the overall winner. The players rotate after each game so that their opponents change. Each of the eight games is one hundred dollars, put up by the players, and its winner take all. The house puts up two hundred bucks, so the winners get a total of a thousand dollars. The manager keeps score and holds the cash. It's now the second round and the girls are ahead. I'm willing to bet that the girls will win the match because 'Foosball Franny' is heading up their team. She's been playing foosball since she was a kid and is the best player I've ever seen. I think she's now about nineteen and goes to UWF. She's the small blonde in white shorts and a gold Marine Corps tee shirt. Her

207

boyfriend is a Marine helo pilot in Nam. Oh, by the way, my name is Joe and I own this place."

Striker and Terry then introduced themselves, and Terry said, "I've seen Franny in here before. She has the fastest reactions I have ever seen. She can see and hit the ball even when it's been slammed back at her. When we get our drinks, let's take them over and watch her for a while." Striker, "I'd love to see her in action."

As soon as their drinks came, they got as close as they could to the table where Franny was playing. Terry was in front of Striker as she squeezed next to another girl opposite Franny. Striker couldn't help but notice the ceiling directly above the table. It was an anatomically correct 6' x 6' painting depicting all the positions of the Kama Sutra. Striker had never seen anything like this painting and was totally distracted until Franny yelled loudly after scoring a point. Then he looked at the foosball being smacked back and forth at lightning speed. Franny's hands were pulling and pushing the steel rods back and forth to control the ball as if they were an extension of her arms. Franny could stop the ball, maneuver it back and forth, and then suddenly slam it past her opponent's players into the goal. As Franny scored, she let out an ear-piercing screech, then immediately refocused on the game. Her opponent, a guy about twenty-five, was no match for her, and just did the best he could until Franny shut him out. The girls were ahead two to nothing and needed one more victory. Franny easily defeated her opponent and the girls won two rounds to none. After they hugged each other, the four girls on the team collected their winnings from the manager and went to the bar.

Terry, who was cheering loudly for Franny, turned to Striker, "Franny was unbelievable. Joe is right, she is the best." Then most of the people who were watching Franny left. Terry grabbed Striker by the hand, "Now it's our turn. Let's see what you got, Mr. Flyboy." She waved him to the other side of the table and dropped the ball into the slot. They played three games; Terry won the first two while Striker rallied to win the third. When the last game was finished, he asked Terry, "Want to go for three out of five?" and she responded, "No way, Flyboy, I'm quitting while I'm ahead. I'm thirsty, let's get a beer." Striker laughed and replied, "A beer sounds good, but it's obvious that you wanted to play at this table because you knew the painting on the ceiling would keep me from focusing on the game, I would've crushed you at a different table." Terry said, "All's fair in love and foosball, Flyboy."

About an hour later, they had finished their beers and Terry turned to Striker, "It's almost 9. Any place you want to go? The good news is I don't have to be at work until 10 am tomorrow. The bad news is that I won't get off until 10 pm. We could go to my place or even better, go for a walk on the beach? There's full moon and I haven't seen it over the Gulf in a long time." Striker, "That's sounds great. I have a blanket in my car, as well as a couple of towels. If you want, I'll grab a carryout bottle of wine and some cups here at the bar." Terry was up for it, so Striker got a bottle of wine and they left.

Striker headed east, toward Navarre Beach, then they walked on the empty beach along the Gulf. After about a half-mile they got to a place where no one was in sight. Striker, "How's this look? Want to park our stuff here?" Terry, "This is perfect, it's just beautiful."

They sat on the blanket and Striker opened the bottle of wine and poured a cupful for both of them. Striker raised his cup and said, "Here's to a gorgeous girl and a beautiful evening." Then he touched her cup and sipped his wine. Terry sipped her wine, smiled, and then reached over to hold his hand. They sat and drank as they watched the moon slowly move up and over the Gulf. As their eyes became accustomed to the dark, they could see the phosphorescence of the surf as the waves gently broke on the shore.

As she was finishing her second cup of wine Terry stood up, clearly tipsy, and said, "Let's go skinny dipping. I haven't done that since my junior year in college. Are you game, Flyboy?" Without waiting for an answer, she began to take off her clothes. Striker, a little stunned, waited until she was only wearing her bra and panties, then he started to take off his clothes. Just as he started to pull off his shorts, Terry was already naked and running towards the water. After she dove into a wave, she stood in waist deep water, waved at him with her breasts exposed, and yelled. "What's the matter? You need some help getting your clothes off?" Striker yelled, "Hold on, I'm on my way." Then he yanked off his skivvies and ran as fast as he could into the water and dove into a breaking wave. He swam underwater the last ten feet to her, grabbed her by the waist, picked her up on his shoulders and spun her around two or three times before he gently threw her into the water. Terry was shrieking with laughter as she hit the surf, then stood up and splashed Striker as much as she could. Striker dove again, circled around and came up behind her. Then he again grabbed her by the waist and raised her up as high as he could and dropped her into the water. This time she came up in front of him, and slowly slid up his body, caressing him gently as she rose. When she was stood up, she wrapped her arms around his neck and whispered in his ear, "Let's go back to the blanket."

Chapter 40

Striker Finds a Girl in the BOQ

Striker and Terry made love on the beach and then watched the stars for about an hour. Terry reluctantly whispered, "I hate to go, but I have to get up and be at work by 10 am, and I will probably be in the OR for four or five consecutive procedures. It'll be a long hard day." They put on their clothes and walked back to the car. When they got out at her house, Terry smiled and said, "I know we've agreed that there would be no strings, but I still want to see you again. I really enjoyed myself tonight, it was the best time I've had in months, especially the time on the beach." Striker replied, "It was the same for me. By the way, tomorrow I have a lot to do, and I start training again the next day. I have no idea when I'll even be able to call you, but I promise, I'll call when I can." They held hands while walking to the door. Terry kissed him and said good night.

Striker drove back to the BOQ, and walked up to his room. When he opened the door, he was shocked to see Sticky kneeling on the floor next to his bed as if he was praying. Next to him was a girl who was doing the same thing. Both were completely naked. Striker left the room as quietly as he could and went to the couch in the living area. He sat down, "Now I think I've seen everything. Sticky has outdone himself. I thought that getting plastered the last night of AOCS was insane, but this is even crazier. I can't wait to hear his explanation of what was going on." Even though he was a little irritated with having to sleep on the couch, he chuckled at Sticky's most recent escapade, and soon fell asleep. About two hours later, Sticky woke Striker up and told him that they were leaving. Striker mumbled something, then stumbled into the bedroom and got into bed.

Striker woke up a little after 7, looked at Sticky's empty bed, and went for a run. When he returned, Sticky was still not there. After he dressed and went out to the living area, Bulldog and Hound were just coming out of their bedroom. Striker, "You guys going to get some breakfast? That's where I'm heading." Bulldog, "Yeah, come on with us." As they were walking to the open mess, Hound asked Striker if he had seen Sticky recently. Striker, "Yeah, a couple of times. I believe it was Sunday that I was with him at the beach. We were there less than a half hour and he picked up a seventeen-year-old girl who is going to Pensacola Junior College in September. After I left, I didn't see him again until a day or two later. He was getting some clothes at the BOQ and taking the girl to a motel on the beach. Then, last night about midnight, I saw him again when I was getting back from a date. Believe it or not, he and a girl were kneeling next to his bed, stark naked. I don't know if it was the same girl he was shacked up with or not. I slept most of the night on the couch." Hound, "That sounds like something Sticky would do; he is a piece of work. I'm amazed he made it through AOCS; he can really find ways to screw things up. He's a great guy, but he's also an accident waiting to happen." Bulldog, smiling said, "I wonder if his new main squeeze has any friends, she could fix me up with. I'm not proud; I'd take out a seventeen-year-old. Do as the natives do. If it's OK with her parents and it's not illegal, I'm all for it." Striker, "She does. I met her on the beach with the girl Sticky picked up. Sticky's girl was really pretty, but the younger one, Julie, was a movie star. She had just turned seventeen and was going to be a senior in high school. She actually asked me out, even volunteered to give me her phone number, but I said no; and told her I had a girlfriend. Right after that I left. The next time you see Sticky, ask him about her. I'm sure he could get his lady friend to set you two up. I bet that she would be all over you like a cheap suit." Bulldog grinned and said, "That's my kind of girl, young and dumb."

Since the next round of training did not begin until the next day, Striker went into town to try on the new uniforms he had ordered. The tailor needed to make a few alterations and said they would be ready in a couple of days. Striker returned to the BOQ to call his mom at the rehab unit. His mother answered the phone after one ring, and said "Jonathan, it's so good to hear from you. I'm doing great, but it's not easy. I'm still in a lot of pain but I've stopped taking the heavy-duty meds and trying to put up with it. The PT every day makes it worse, so I'm not able to get a lot of sleep. I'm not going to rely on the drugs to keep me going. My doctor says that I'm healing very well, especially for my age, probably because I've played tennis for so many years. Your sisters and father have been a great help. I couldn't have made it without them. Now tell me how you're doing, and how you like the Navy." Striker, "I'm doing great, Mom, and the last six days have been the best days of my life. Back when I was first accepted into AOCS, I was confident that I would make it through. I had no idea that it was going to be so difficult. Even though I was in pretty good shape when I started, I still lost fifteen pounds, just from the sheer amount of physical training, because I sure didn't eat any less. The hardest part was the lack of sleep everyone had to endure all those weeks. Fatigue wears you down and drains your motivation to keep going, but I made it, even though more than half of the class didn't. Dad pinned on my gold bars, so that was really a special day. I start survival training tomorrow, so I'll be really busy for the next few weeks. I'm really excited about finally getting strapped into an airplane, but first I have to go through a lot of preliminary stuff."

When he returned to his room, Sticky was there, talking to Bulldog and Hound. He was smiling as he told them about his new girlfriend, Lee Ann, who he had just taken home. It turned out that Sticky was the third or fourth Naval Officer that she had dated; she was even engaged to one of them.

Bulldog jumped in, "That settles it, Striker told us that Lee Ann has a friend who is gorgeous. You must ask her to fix me up with the girl, even if she just turned seventeen. There is no doubt that some other Naval Officer will be all over her soon, especially if she is that good looking." Striker responded, "You're right; I bet she won't be alone very long. By the way, what in hell was going on last night, Sticky? Were both of you actually naked and kneeling against your bed? Or was that some kind of weird dream I had?" Sticky, "It was no dream. I came here to get some clothes because we decided to stay at the motel another night, Lee Ann insisted on coming in the suite with me. She'd never been in the BOQ before and wanted to see what it was like. So, I brought her up here. One thing led to another and all of a sudden, she said she wanted to pray before we got in the rack. Right then you walked in. Amazingly, she didn't know, or care, that you came in, because she finished praying and got right into bed. I thought it was really weird, but you do what you must do; that's the Navy way. Later I woke you up as we were leaving. I didn't think there was any chance we would get caught, but the security guard saw us. He took my name and told me if he saw me doing it again, he'd turn me in, and I would probably be booted out of the BOQ. I gotta be really careful from now on." Bulldog, laughing at what Sticky said. "Sticky, buddy, I gotta be honest, I don't think there's a 'careful bone' in your body. You better start looking for a place off base real quick, 'cause it won't be too long before you sweet talk some other young thing into sneaking in here again, just to prove to yourself you can get away with it." Sticky, "You're probably right, Bulldog. Deep inside I know that I'll try again, if nothing else, just for the challenge. Hell, even if the girl can scare away crows, I'd still try to get her into the room." They all laughed and went to the beach.

Chapter 41
Water Survival Training Begins

Striker reported to Survival Training with his roommates, ten AOCS classmates, and several Marine Second Lieutenants. After everyone was accounted for, they were transported to the Water Survival Building, where they all had completed Dilbert Dunker training. After, they changed into flight suits and removed their boots. Lieutenant Ed Olsen introduced himself as their water survival instructor.

Olsen told them to remain at ease, and for the rest of the day, he would teach them how to inflate a Mae West, inflate, climb into a one-man raft, and use their flight suits as emergency flotation devices. Olsen also displayed all the items in the survival kits that were attached to parachute harnesses. Each kit included a water condensation bubble, mirror, fishing line, hooks, flare gun, survival gun, slingshot, ball bearings, flint, compass, and an emergency radio. He also showed them a survival knife, which each of them would be issued later that day.

Then, he demonstrated how to inflate the condensation bubble and told them to familiarize themselves with the rest of the equipment. Then he said, "Gents. What I will teach you today may someday save your life, but first, let me tell you a little about myself. I was a 1500-meter distance swimmer all through high school and college. Every summer, I worked as a water safety instructor and a lifeguard. I am very comfortable in the water. After college, I completed AOCS, became an A-4 pilot, did two tours in WestPac, and I hope to do a third. About a year ago, as I was returning to the boat from a sortie over

North Vietnam, I was hit by AAA fire. My main fuel tank was ruptured, and a piece of shrapnel ripped open my lower leg." Then he pulled up his right pants leg and showed a seven-inch scar where half of his calf had been blown off. Then he continued, "About ten minutes after I was hit, I was out of fuel over the South China Sea, about twenty miles from the carrier. I couldn't see any friendlies in the area, so I reported my position and ejected as I was descending straight down at 300 knots. The next few minutes were a blur as I tumbled away from the aircraft, separated from the seat, and the chute opened. Five minutes later, I hit the water, bleeding heavily and getting weak. Adrenaline kicked in, and I managed to inflate my Mae West and the raft. As soon as I was in the raft, I pulled my survival knife from its sheath, luckily on my left leg; otherwise, it probably would have been gone. I cut off part of my flight suit and made a tourniquet to stop the bleeding, and it worked. Even though I was really tired, I forced myself to assess what gear had survived the ejection. I had the knife, a condensation bubble, fishing line and hooks, a flare gun, three flares, and a signal mirror, that's it. I looked around and couldn't see anything but water, so I inflated the condensation bubble, tethered it to the back of the raft, and fell asleep. I floated in that raft for six days without seeing anything except occasional aircraft at about 10,000 feet. I flashed the mirror at all of them but with no response. I had eaten nothing for six days, was severely sunburned, and very weak. I made just enough fresh water to stay alive but was still very thirsty. The bleeding stopped, but the wound was infected. I almost passed out when I floated into a field of kelp. I rallied to pull large pieces on board. I looked for any crabs or shrimp that might be there but found nothing. I began to eat some kelp when a seagull, either exhausted or sick, suddenly landed on the front of the raft. As fast as I could, I grabbed the bird and wrung its neck. Then I plucked its feathers and cut it up with my knife. Without any hesitation, I ate its breast raw. It tasted horrible and smelled worse. Then, I wrapped smaller pieces in kelp and put them under some of the gear. I floated on the raft for two more days without seeing anyone. I was so hungry I ate more seagull, which was by then rancid. I puked most of the seventh night, but the next morning, a Sea Knight chopper was about two miles away at about 2500 feet. I got the mirror and flashed it at the chopper about twenty times. It turned and came directly at me, so I fired a flare. The chopper stopped about thirty feet above me and lowered a rescue basket. I used what little strength I had to climb into the basket. When I got up to the chopper, the crew pulled me in, threw a blanket around me, and gave me some water. Later, when I could speak coherently, they asked for my name. I could barely speak, but I managed to tell them. Then I passed out."

"We arrived at the Oriskany about twenty minutes later. I was carried to the infirmary, mostly sleeping for the next two days. Then, COD transported me to the hospital at Subic Bay and three days later to Honolulu. The docs repaired my leg as best they could, enough for me to remain in flight status. I was on a drip antibiotic for two weeks before I was put on sick leave."

"I was in rehab for about six months and then was detailed to Pensacola and VT-7 for two months of A-4 proficiency training. I returned to my squadron, where I completed the last thirty days of a nine-month WestPac tour on the Oriskany. About ten months ago, we returned to San Diego, and I was reassigned to Pensacola. Since then, I have been teaching water survival, as well as doing flight duty as a squadron pilot."

"Gentlemen, I told you my story so that you will know that if I could survive eight days floating in a one-man raft, so can you. Even though I'm a guy who won't normally eat anything but meat and potatoes, I ate a stinking seagull. I stayed alive using the gear I just showed you. Now, Gents, take an hour to get some lunch. When you return at 1300, we'll get started."

Striker and his roommates walked to the gedunk to get a sandwich. Unlike most shipboard gedunks, this one on base served a variety of prepared sandwiches, burgers, and daily specials. When they arrived, the place was almost fully occupied, but they still found a table for four. Hound, looking at the menu, said, "I'm not real hungry after listening to Olsen's story about eating a raw seagull. Every bite I eat will make me think I just bit into a stinking bird and make me want to puke. I think I'll just get some chips and a coke." Bulldog replied, "You wuss, I'm so hungry I could eat a dead seagull with an order of maggots and wash it down with warm seawater. Remember, in jungle survival, we'll be eating whatever we can find and drinking swamp water. We'll probably have to eat squirrels, snakes, maybe even bugs the whole time we're there. Hound, laughing, "Stop, Bulldog, I'm gonna get sick just thinking about it, and if I do, you're gonna be my target when I let loose." Bulldog said, "Man, you're just making me hungrier. I'm gonna get the special, a chili dog and a bowl of split pea soup just because I like their colors." Striker, still laughing, joined Sticky and Bulldog in line. Hound got a coke and potato chips. While he ate, Bulldog occasionally made grunting noises and loudly slurped his soup. Hound, staring at him doing it, "Bulldog, First Sergeant Sullivan was right. You are part dog. You'd probably wolf down a can of Alpo if I opened it." Bulldog, eyes wide, looked around, "They got Alpo here? You get it, and I'll eat it. Next to pickled pig's feet, it's my favorite." Hound quickly replied, "I hope you're kidding, but I know better than to challenge you. Let's get back to the tank before I do lose my lunch." They walked back, joking with each other like schoolboys.

They got back and joined the other students by the tank. At 1300, Lt. Olsen came out of his office and began, "OK, Gents, each of you grab a deflated raft and a Mae West from the pile over there then. Strap the Mae West on and hold the raft in front of you, up against your chest. Then, on my command, one by one, you will jump into the pool holding the raft and then inflate the Mae West. The Mae West will be inflated before the raft is. When the raft is fully inflated, you will climb onto the raft and remain there until I tell you to get out. Later, when you take the raft and Mae West out of the pool, deflate them by pulling the plugs on the sides and putting them back in the indicated bin. Now line up, single file."

The students began jumping into the pool, inflating the rafts and Mae Wests, and climbing into the rafts. Three or four bigger students had a difficult time getting into the rafts, attempting it several times, but everyone finally got in. When everyone was floating in rafts, Olsen told them to get out of the rafts and get in again. After they all were in the rafts a second time, he ordered them to do it again. Altogether, they got in and out of the rafts five times. They were exhausted, and Olsen allowed them to rest in their rafts for ten minutes. Then the Instructor told them to deflate the rafts, throw them onto the deck, and remain in the pool.

The instructor jumped into the pool and began to tread water. He told the students to deflate their Mae Wests and tread water while they took them off and threw them on the deck. Once all the vests were on the deck, he took off his flight suit and directed them to do the same. While he was treading water, he showed them how to use the top part of the flight suit as a flotation device by capturing air, holding the two arms

220

together, and making a cloth air pocket. He explained that the bubble would only last for a few minutes, so the process had to be repeated. The students stayed in the water for almost twenty minutes while they repeatedly inflated the flight suit air pockets. Finally, Olsen told them to get out of the pool and put on their flight suits.

Once everyone was dressed, Olsen told the class to form a line across the long side of the pool, face him, and count off. Then he said, "Gents, I'm now going to show you how to save someone who is drowning, while not drowning yourself. If you are wearing a Mae West, you will be able to hold another person above the water. If you have survived a sinking boat, there is almost always floating debris that you can give to the victim. If it is only two of you and the other person is drowning, then you can attempt lifesaving techniques. Just understand, drowning people will panic and grab you any way they can. I will show you a way of breaking loose from them if they do." Olsen then told the first student in line to be a drowning victim. He showed the class how to approach a drowning person, how to turn the victim around", grasp the victim by the shoulder and push his back so that he was floating close to the surface. Then he told the student victim to grab Olsen from the front. Olsen quickly squatted down while pushing the victim away. Then the student grabbed Olsen by his back, and again Olsen squatted down, and pushed him away. Olsen, standing up, "Gents, notice that in both instances I pushed myself down and away from the victim. I did it because drowning people will not go down with you. They want to stay on the surface as long as they can; underwater is not where they want to be. I have saved dozens of people, all ages and sizes. Not one of them held on to me when I went underwater. It works. The victims immediately let go."

The instructor continued, "Now, all the even numbers get with the person to your right and get in the pool. When I blow the whistle, even numbers will be the victims, odd the rescuer. You will repeat the technique just shown to you until you hear the whistle a second time. Then you will reverse roles until the whistle again." For the next half hour, the twenty-six students practiced what Olsen had taught them. When they were at the point of total exhaustion, Olsen blew the whistle a third time and everyone slowly climbed out of the water. Olsen, "Hit the showers, Gents. We'll see you here tomorrow in flight suits and boots promptly at 0700." All twenty-six students walked to the locker room.

Chapter 42

Connors and Jane Visit Melbourne

On July 2, Connors and Jane left their apartment about 2 pm and were in Gainesville a little before 7. Jane had made a reservation at the hotel where Connors had proposed to her three weeks earlier. They checked into a room and went to the hotel restaurant. Unfortunately, Paul the bartender was not on duty, so Jane left him a message in an envelope at the front desk. Jane included a wedding invitation for him and a note about Pensacola hotels. While they ate dinner, they went over the unfinished details for the wedding and the guest list. Since they were tired from travelling, they went back to their room and were quickly asleep.

Connors woke Jane up at 6:30 the next morning to get ready to leave. A half hour later they grabbed a quick breakfast at the restaurant and checked out. He put their bags in the car, and they headed south to Melbourne Beach. It was normally about a three-hour drive, but it took almost four hours, since it was the Fourth of July weekend. As they got out the car and approached the front door, Connors could hear squeals of delight coming from the backyard. He immediately knew the screams were from his nieces, who were probably in the pool. "Come on Jane, let's go around back. Everyone's probably back there."

When they got to the backyard, they could see Connors' sister Sheila pulling Annie around on a raft in the shallow end of the pool while Erin was playing with a large ball with her grandmother. As soon they approached the pool, Annie waved at him, saying, "Look at me Uncle Tim, I can swim." She paddled a few feet towards the steps, climbed out of the pool and ran to Connors. He reached down to greet her, and she jumped into his arms and soaked him with a wet bear hug. Erin, seeing that Connors was getting wet, ran to him giggling, and gave him a wet hug as well. Sheila, laughing as she came to him, said, "Now it's my turn to get you wet." and hugged him. Connors, laughing said, "If I had known I was coming to a splash party, I would have worn my bathing suit."

Annie then asked Jane, "Are you Jane? When you marry Uncle Tim will you be my Aunt Jane? Do you fly airplanes up in the sky like Uncle Tim does? I am a twin. My sister's name is Erin. She is right there next to my mommy." Jane smiling, "I sure will, sweetheart. I'll play with you and Erin as much as I can. I don't fly airplanes. I'm a teacher." Then Sheila smiled and said, "I'm Sheila Cavanaugh, Tim's sister, and I'm thrilled to meet you. He talks about you all the time and looked all over God's creation for you. Welcome to our family." Connor's mother gave Jane a hug, saying, "I'm Anne Connors, Tim's mom. What an extraordinary story you two have. It's just a miracle that Tim found you. I believe it was meant to be. Welcome to our family." Then Erin looked up at Jane and asked, "Will you and Uncle Tim still come see me after you are married?" Jane picked Erin up and said, "Sweetie, we'll be back here as often as we can. Neither of us could stand being away from you and your wonderful family for very long." Connors' mother suggested that they all gather on the patio while she set up lunch.

When Connors sat down, Annie came over and climbed into his lap and showed him her new doll, Lolly. "I named her Lolly because I like lollipops." Erin, who was next to her mother, then came to Jane holding her doll, Butterfly. She said, "My mommy said I can almost swim. I'll show you when you get in the pool. Pretty soon I can go into the deep water, over there." Then Erin ran to the lounge chair and picked up a book and brought it to Jane. "Will you read this to me? It's my favorite book; it's about green eggs. It's funny. I've never eaten green eggs, have you?" Jane said, "No, I've never eaten green eggs, but I'd love to read to you." Erin got into Jane's lap and listened to her read as though it was the first time it was read to her. Then, about halfway through the book, Annie curled up to Jane's other side, listening to every word.

When Jane was finished, Erin and Annie ran into the house to get another book. While they were gone, Sheila congratulated Jane for getting an assistant professor's position and said, "I'd ask you about your dissertation, but I know it's abstract theoretical math. Even though I have a Master's degree in math, theoretical math involves subjects that are way above my ability to comprehend. I won't embarrass myself by asking you." Jane, smiling as she answered, "Sheila, there's no embarrassment in not understanding the theories in my dissertation. I even suspect that a couple of the professors who reviewed it didn't have a clue what it's all about. It's the nature of theoretical math, but whatever it is, it impressed them enough to convince UWF to hire me."

Anne then came out to the patio and told everyone to come get something to eat. The twins were already at a sideboard that had been set up as a buffet. Erin immediately waved at Jane to sit next to her. Then Annie said she wanted to sit next to Jane as well. Jane smiled as she fixed her lunch and sat between them. Connors said, "I think you have made two little friends. They'll both come back in a few minutes with books to read or more dolls to show you." Jane, "That's OK with me. The girls are just adorable. It would be my pleasure to read or play with them as long as they want. I love children but haven't had much opportunity to be around them for years. So being with them is just wonderful. Connors said, "One of these days we'll have kids, and you will be just as good a mother as Sheila."

Fifteen minutes later Annie came out carrying her doll. "Aunt Jane, are you going to the pool now?" Jane. "In a few minutes, but first your mom and I need to ask you and your sister something. Could you tell Erin to come here for a minute?" Annie, "OK, I'll get her." About ten minutes later both girls came into the room and stood shoulder to shoulder between Jane and their mom. Sheila, "Girls, when Uncle Tim marries Aunt Jane, they want you two to be flower girls." Annie immediately asked, "What's a flower girl? Does she pick flowers like we do when we hike in the park and put them in a vase when we get home?" Jane, "No, Annie, a flower girl in a wedding carries flowers in the church as part of the wedding procession. Both you and Erin will wear pretty dresses, have flowers in your hair, and carry baskets of flowers. Your daddy will be in the wedding too, but he will be standing with Uncle Tim and meet us as we get to the front of the church." Erin, "Is it like being in a parade?" Sheila, "A little bit, honey but it's just a few people inside a church. There will be music, but no marching bands or anything like that." After getting her purse out, Jane pulled a couple of pictures of flowers girls she had cut out of wedding magazines and showed them to the twins. She held the pictures up while Erin pointed to one little girl carrying a basket of roses in front of a bride walking down the aisle. "Is she a flower girl, the one with the basket?" Sheila, "Yes, and you two will be carrying baskets of flowers just like this girl is doing." Annie, "Yep, I wanna be a flower girl just like the girl in the picture." Erin said, "Me too, Aunt Jane, I want to carry roses, too. Can I?" Jane, "You bet, both of you can." Then both of the girls clapped their hands and yelled, "Yeah, we're going to be flower girls."

Once they were finished looking at the pictures of flower girls, Connors returned to the kitchen. Annie asked him if he would go swimming with them. Connors, "That's up to your mommy, Annie. If she says OK, then I'd love to go swimming with you." Sheila nodded her approval and said, "You sure can, and it's a beautiful day so you should enjoy it." Connors, "OK, as soon as we change clothes, Jane and I will meet you guys at the pool." Ten minutes later they were all in the pool.

Later, Connors' father and brother-in-law walked out the back door. As soon as the twins saw them, Annie yelled, "Look, I'm going to swim." followed by Erin, "Me, too." The two of them dog paddled across the pool, and then they climbed out and ran to their daddy and grandpa as Jane and Connors got out of the pool. Jim walked over to Jane and said, "You must be Jane. I'm Jim, Tim's dad, and this is Pat, Sheila's husband." Jane smiling, "I'm so glad I've been able to finally meet you and your beautiful family."

For the next couple of hours, they talked about everything from Jane's new job to Tim's duties as a flight instructor. Then Jim said, "I made a 6:30 reservation for us at the country club to celebrate Jane and Tim's engagement. We all better get ready to go. We'll be sitting at the bar and grill out by the golf course, so it is very informal there." Connors said it sounded great, and everyone got ready to go.

They had reservations in the Beach House Bar and Grill, which was much more elegant than the name implied. It was about a quarter mile away from the main country club and had a huge bay front deck on two levels. The hostess welcomed Connors' dad by name and led the family to their upper deck table. After ordering drinks for everyone, Connors' father ordered several appetizers. After forty-five minutes of conversation, they ordered dinner. While they waited, Jim raised his glass to toast his son and future daughter-in-law and wished them only the best, and said to Jane, "I couldn't ask for a better choice for a new daughter in our family, I'm overjoyed that Tim found you after being apart for so long. Welcome to our family." Just as the sun was setting, they finished eating and headed home.

As soon as they were in the house, Erin ran into her bedroom and brought three books out for Jane to read. When Jane began to read, Annie immediately cuddled next to Jane's other side. When she finished all the books, Erin was asleep on her shoulder and Annie was stretched out next to her. Sheila gently took Erin and Jane picked up Annie and they took them to their bedroom, and then rejoined the adults.

Jane asked Sheila how she and Pat met and married. A year and a half older than her brother, Sheila was an attractive brunette with shoulder length hair. Like Connors, Sheila had been a good athlete in high school, and she went to the University of Florida on a swimming scholarship. Her husband Pat was also a swimmer at Florida. They didn't start dating until he was in his second year of law school and she was beginning graduate school. A year later, after he had passed the bar and she was teaching, they got married. Pat was in Air Force ROTC and was commissioned. He was assigned to the Judge Advocate Corps after he attended law school. For a few years, Pat was a JAG Officer stationed at Eglin Air Force Base, and Sheila taught high school math. After Pat finished his military obligation, they moved to Melbourne where he opened a law practice and she transferred to a different school. Pat remained in the Air Force Reserve and had recently been promoted to Lt. Colonel. Two years later, their twin daughters were born.

When she finished telling their story, Sheila said, "Pat and I had a very ordinary courtship compared to you guys. Your story is right out of a movie, it's the most romantic one I've ever heard." Jane, "It was romantic, but during the time we were apart, it didn't feel that way. I was miserable most of the time, wondering if we had done the right thing, and I couldn't stop thinking about him. I just buried myself in my work. I had to defend my dissertation the day he found me in Gainesville. Then there he was at the hotel, and he asked me to marry him, all within about five minutes. It was unreal, but it is all really happening, and we'll be married in about a month." Sheila responded, "It's an incredible story, but it's one with a happy ending."

They sat around telling stories about Connors when he was a kid. He laughed and denied that the stories were true, but his family knew they were. Finally, at about midnight, and after a few more glasses of wine, they all went to bed.

Once they were in their room. Jane hugged Connors and said, "Your family has been so gracious and welcoming to me, but the twins are really special. I just love them both and can't wait to spend more time with them. Sheila is a lucky woman." Jane suddenly had tears in her eyes and said, "I had a wonderful time with your family today. You said one of these days we will have kids, I'm afraid it might be happening sooner than we want. I think I might be pregnant. I missed my last period, and that's never happened before. I've been nauseous almost every morning the last few days. I know it is early to tell, but since we have not been using any form of birth control, it's very possible that I am pregnant. I'm going to make an appointment with an OB/GYN, but I'm pretty sure we're going to have a baby. I hope you're not angry." Connors took her in his arms, "Angry, why should I be angry? I'm thrilled. I think it's great."

He held on to her until she began to speak again, "We shouldn't tell anyone yet. I want to wait until I see the doctor, and until after the wedding. It's only a month away. Is that OK?" Connors said, "It sure is, we'll just keep it to ourselves until we definitely know, and are married." Connors reassured her that he was happy about the pregnancy and held her throughout the night.

Connors woke up early and went for a run while Jane slept. While he ran, he wondered about the coming birth of his child. He hoped he could do as good a job as his father had done. Being a Naval Aviator was not an ideal occupation for fostering a stable family life. He would be an absentee father during much of the child's developing years. Did he want to raise his children in that environment? Then he wondered how Jane would deal with having to abandon her academic career, which she had worked so hard to achieve; it was a lot to ask of her. As he came to the end of his run, the only conclusion he reached was that the baby was almost nine months away. He had time to adjust.

Connors greeted his mother, "Good morning, I think I'll go in there and get myself and Jane some of that fresh coffee." Jane met him in the hallway and said, "I'm going to see the girls for a few minutes." Connors watched as Jane sat on the floor next to the twins, who were playing with a book of animal stickers. Annie looked at Jane and said, "Want to help us Aunt Jane?" Jane, "I'd love to Annie." Soon Erin came over and Jane helped both of them.

Connors' mother stood beside him, and quietly said. "Tim, I can see why you fell for Jane. She is gorgeous, very smart and she obviously loves children. She is just a treasure. I'm so happy that you found each other. She's really special and will be a great mother someday." Connors hesitated, "She sure will.

I didn't really know how much she meant to me until we went our separate ways. I would be a real mess if I hadn't found her again."

After they finished breakfast, Connors took Jane on a tour of Melbourne and Melbourne Beach. He showed her where he went to high school and his favorite places on the beach. They also drove north to Cocoa Beach to see the Apollo 11 spacecraft as it waited for launch to the moon. They stopped for lunch at a waterfront restaurant and then returned to Connors' home.

That evening, the family found a spot on the shore of the bay where they could have a picnic and watch fireworks. Connors stood with Pat near the edge of the water as Jane and Sheila waded into the gentle surf holding hands with the twins. Both girls squealed with joy as the two women splashed them and swung them through the small waves. About an hour and half later, Connors' mom called for everyone to come and eat. Led by the ravenous twins, the food was almost gone within twenty minutes. Sheila put a platter of brownies on the blanket and told the girls to limit themselves to only two brownies each. The girls quickly ate them as if they were the best things they ever had. Connors took two bottles of wine from a cooler his father brought, opened them and poured everyone a glass. They sat there, sipping wine and enjoying the evening until the fireworks display began. As the sun went down, Connors gently patted Jane's abdomen.

When the fireworks ended, they packed everything up and left. Halfway home, Erin and Annie were sound asleep. Once they pulled into the driveway, Jane and Sheila carried the girls to their beds. When she returned to the living room, Jane told Connors she was tired, so they said goodnight to everyone.

The next morning, Jane and Connors were up early. Connors asked Jane if it was okay to leave early for Pensacola to avoid traffic and break the trip into two days. Jane agreed and suggested that they tell his parents right away in case they had something special planned. Connors went to the kitchen to get some coffee and to ask what his mom's plans were. She was already preparing breakfast and said, "Good morning, I hope you slept well. Sit down, I'll bring you some coffee." Connors, "Thanks Mom, I'm concerned about the traffic tomorrow. Jane and I are leaving earlier than we planned. We'll stay overnight in Gainesville, and then go to Pensacola tomorrow. It'll be a lot easier than fighting traffic for six or eight hours." Anne, "We were just planning to have a cookout this evening, maybe burgers and dogs, so you won't miss anything special. But we were planning to go to noon Mass at St Theresa's. Maybe you could go to Mass with us before you leave? Does that sound OK?"

Connors hadn't been to Mass in a couple of years. Jane, who was also raised a Catholic, hadn't been to Mass since she was an undergraduate student. She thought for a minute, then responded, "I think we should. I really haven't been very religious for a long time, and it's probably a good time to start again, especially since we're having a Catholic ceremony." Connors said that they would be ready when everyone else was.

Jane remembered the prayers and responses fairly well. When they left the church, Jane said to Connors, "That was beautiful. That baritone singing Ave Maria brought back memories of being in church with my family. I'm glad we went, and I want to start attending Mass regularly when we get home. Connors, "I agree, I had forgotten the feeling of peace it gave me."

232

After they said goodbye, Jane and Connors were on the road; Jane was asleep almost as soon as they left. When she woke up, she said. "You have a wonderful family. Your parents are gracious hosts, Sheila and Pat are super people, and their twins are just precious. They had me charmed the minute I met them; it was hard to leave them." Connors held her hand and replied, "Jane, in a few months, we'll have our own little one you'll never have to leave." She leaned over and kissed his cheek.

It was almost 6:00 when they arrived at the same hotel as before, and after they dropped their bags in their room they went to get some dinner. After they ate they were tired and went to their room. When Connors woke up, Jane was in the bathroom. Ten minutes later she came out, looking pale, "Morning sickness, one of the unfortunate side effects of pregnancy. But after being around the twins, I'll gladly throw up every morning to have children like them. It'll be a while before I can eat anything, though." An hour and a half later, Jane was feeling better, so they stopped for breakfast. Traffic was moderate the rest of the way and they were at their apartment by early afternoon.

Chapter 43

Survival Training Continues

Striker took Terry out again but was back in the BOQ before 1100 pm. The next morning at 0600, he and Sticky were ready to go to breakfast, but his other two suitemates were not. He told them he would save them seats in the Open Mess. Just as Striker and Sticky got their meals, Bulldog and Hound joined them. Sticky, "Did you have a date last night, Striker?" Striker, "Yeah, with Terry, the Navy nurse I met the night I got back from Maryland. We went to a nice bar and grill on the Bay, then we went to her place for a little while. We both had to get up early for work so I came back to the BOQ. Spending most of the day in the water yesterday was a bear. I was beat. What were you guys up to last night?" Bulldog, "We just went to the beach and fell asleep on our blankets. Then we came back here, cleaned up and went to the O Club to eat and have a couple beers. Major Pless was there, in his usual spot at the bar, holding court. The guy must really like being the center of attention, because he always seems to enjoy talking to a lot of people." Sticky asked, "Was he drinking heavily? I've heard he's been drinking a lot and had to be taken home a few times recently." Bulldog, "I've heard the same thing." They finished breakfast, went back to the suite and left in separate cars for the training facility.

They walked into the water survival building at about 0645 and gathered around Lt. Olson. At 0700, Olson called out their names, assigned each a number, and then began, "Good morning, Gents, I hope all of you slept well last night. I know it was a strenuous day in the water yesterday but what you learned might get you out of a tight spot someday. Today's training will not take as long but it is just as important. We're going to take you out in the Gulf in a specially equipped launch and teach you how to properly remove your parachute harness, inflate the Mae West and one-man raft, and get into the raft after you have ejected and landed in open water. You will be doing all this while you are being dragged behind the launch by parachute risers at about thirty knots. You'll be wearing a flight suit, a helmet, and a parachute harness. A deflated Mae West and a raft will be attached to your harness. You will be on top of a fifteen-foot tower on the back of the boat. One-by-one you will climb to a platform on the top of the tower, and an instructor will attach the risers to your harness and show you where to stand. At his command you will jump off the tower, hit the water, release the risers, and deploy the Mae West and raft. Then you will climb into the raft and remain there for at least two hours. Before we leave, you will practice getting into rafts while you are wearing harnesses." Before they left on the launch, they practiced in the tank. They each put the harness on, each of them jumped in the tank and climbed into one of two rafts already in the water. Since they had to do it three times, it took about two hours before Olson gave them a break.

The launch was modified exactly as Olson had described, with a fifteen-foot tower on the stern. When everyone was aboard, they headed to the open waters of the Gulf. On the way, everyone took a turn at the helm, so, the trip took an hour and a half. When they arrived, Olson told them to again line up in single file and wait for their number to be called. After the launch was cruising at 30 knots, the first candidate jumped into the Gulf. Three Zodiac boats with rescue divers were in position on both sides and behind the trainee being dragged through the water.

Later, Striker watched Bulldog as he climbed the ladder. He looked nervous when he got on the platform, but he jumped when he was told. Thirty seconds later, he popped up, climbed onto the raft, and gave the divers a thumbs-up. A few minutes later, Hound looked confident when he got on the platform. When he was ordered to jump, he gave everyone a thumbs-up. A few seconds later, the entire class cheered as Hound climbed into his raft and raised a clenched fist in a moment of exultation. Striker was one of the last to get onto his raft. Two hours later, he was asleep when he was the last to be picked up.

As soon as the launch was secured in harbor, the bus took them back to the Water Survival Building. When they got out, Olson addressed them, "At ease, Gents, that completes your water survival training. Congratulations, you all made it without anyone being pulled out of the water. That doesn't happen with every class. I hope all of you learned something, and I hope you are never in a position that you have to use what you learned."

"Tomorrow, you will begin jungle survival. You will report at 0700 to the classroom building where your instructor, probably Chief Anderson, will teach you how to survive if you eject and land in the thick jungles of Vietnam. The next day you will be transported to Eglin Air Force Base where you will be taken to a remote section of the base that is also a primitive jungle. The base is huge, about 350,000 acres. You will probably hear explosions from bombs being dropped by training Air Force pilots. You will be left in groups of three or four to fend for yourselves for three nights, using what you learn in the classroom tomorrow. You will complete jungle training on July 17, and on the following Monday you will begin flight training, your goal. Have fun, and good luck Gents. Dismissed."

Striker had not eaten anything since that morning. Along with his roommates, he went to the BOQ to shower and then get something to eat. On the way, Striker picked up a message from Terry, "Last night was fabulous. Call me if you can do it again this evening. Can meet you at the RR at 6:15, T." He called her work number and left a message, "Can do. See you at the club."

Half an hour later Sticky was cleaned up and talking to Sticky, who said, "Man, I needed that shower. Spending the day in the Gulf really made me sticky, no pun intended. I'm meeting Lee Ann at the Tiki Bar at 6 pm, what are you up to?" Striker, "I'm meeting Terry at the Ready Room. I hope to be back by 10:30." Sticky, "Ok, I'll see you later."

Chapter 44

Jungle Survival Training Preparations

Terry was already at a table and waved at him. "I got here early and grabbed this table, how was your day?" Striker, "The first couple of hours in the training tank were grueling but the training on the Gulf was almost fun and even relaxing. I fell asleep in a one-man raft. But after being in the water all day, I need a beer, what'll you have? A Rum and Coke?" She agreed, and then Striker got the drinks and menus. When he returned, he said. "Next, I'll be in Jungle Survival training at Eglin for a few days. If I don't get bitten by a snake, or get food poisoning, I'll be home in four days."

Terry, feigning a sad face, "So unless you somehow hide me in the jungle near you, I won't see you later this weekend." Striker, "Yeah, it looks that way, but it's what I signed up for. It's only three nights, it'll go by quickly." When they finished eating, Terry said, "Let's go to my place. My roomie is at the hospital again tonight and I promise I'll get you out of there by 10:30." Striker, "I'll follow you whenever you're ready."

Striker was back in the BOQ by 11 and was quickly asleep. The alarm went off at 0530 and Striker was up and ready to go just as Sticky finished shaving. Striker, "How'd it go last night, how was the Tiki Bar?" Sticky, "It was pretty empty. After we ate, we went over to Dirty Joe's, which was as crazy as usual. We had a few drinks and played a couple of foosball games, then we left and did the horizontal polka at her place for about an hour, then I left. How about you? Were you with the nurse again? Striker, "Yeah, it went about the same, we ate, had a couple of drinks at the Ready Room, then went to her place for about an hour and a half. I was back here and asleep by 11. Are you getting some breakfast?" Sticky laughed and said, "You bet, for the next three nights we're gonna be eating snakes and lizards in the stinking jungle. Ain't the Navy great? Let's get some food while we can."

They checked to see if Bulldog and Hound were going to breakfast, but they had already left. As they walked over to the mess, Sticky asked, "Did I tell you that I found a great little house just off base? It's a two-bedroom, two-bath bungalow that rents for $150 a month, plus utilities. If you're interested in splitting the cost, I'll show you the place." Striker, "To be honest, I don't really need another place. In fact, I like living here in the BOQ, but I'll let you know in a day or so." Sticky, "No hurry, the house won't even be ready until the first of August."

They joined Hound, Bulldog, and Striker asked what they did the night before. Bulldog answered. "Me and Hound hit a couple of bars, starting with Trader's, then the Pier Lounge, and ended up at the Tiki Bar. We both struck out at all three places. It was five guys to a girl at Trader's, about the same at the Pier, and the Tiki Bar was almost empty. I'm gonna follow you guys around to see what I'm doing wrong." Sticky, "It's easy, man. You just act like you're not interested, and they'll be all over you. Just ask Striker; he's the man. Like I've said before, if you don't mind taking out a seventeen-year-old, I'll ask Lee Ann to fix you up with Julie." Hound jumped in, "Hell, if Bulldog isn't interested, I sure am." Bulldog, "I'm way past being interested. When we finish Jungle Training, I'll take you up on your offer." Sticky, "And, Hound, I'll ask Lee Ann if she can fix you up too."

Later, they were seated in the classroom; Lt. Olson entered and told them to remain seated. He introduced Chief Petty

Officer Anderson, who was an expert on jungle survival. Anderson grew up near a hunting and fishing camp in the Everglades. Before he joined the Navy, he was a guide who took hunters and fishermen through the Everglades, often camping for several days. Most of this time they lived off the land, eating what they killed or caught and local vegetation. Then Anderson described the items that they brought in their survival kits: a slingshot, flint, water bags, iodine pills, and a survival gun. They did not bring fresh water, but he showed them how to purify swamp water so that it was safe enough to drink. He showed them how to use the compass to navigate and told them that each team would have a shortwave radio that could only be used in an emergency.

After showing them how to use a flint, he picked up the gun and unfolded its barrel and stock. It was an "over and under" with one barrel for a .22 round and the other for a 410-shotgun shell. Then he held up the slingshot in one hand and the rifle in the other, he said, "Gentlemen, the slingshot is used to kill animals for food. It works very well; I expect each team to use it to kill at least one animal that they will eat. The survival gun is a last resort weapon. It is not meant to kill animals. It is only for use against the enemy, and only if you have no other choice. Most of you will be issued a .38-caliber revolver, but don't count on having it after you eject. I've heard that some pilots squeezed an M-16 into their cockpit only to find out that it was lost when they ejected. That is why there are no pistols and only one survival kit for each team.

The next few hours, Chief Anderson and Lt. Olson brought examples of edible vegetation found at Eglin Air Force Base. They also showed photographs of vegetation that was not safe to eat, as well as those that were poisonous to touch. Anderson, "Watch what the birds and squirrels eat. Generally, the berries and seeds they eat are safe for you. Many insects, especially crickets, worms and snails, are good sources of protein, even raw. Obviously, you should stay away from spiders, wasps and bees, some of which can be eaten if prepared properly. Gents, while the thought of eating bugs may disgust you, later you will listen to debriefing tapes of former POWs describing how they survived. They were willing to eat or drink just about anything. Those who weren't willing to do it usually didn't survive. If you don't believe me, just ask Mr. Olson about the seagull."

Lt. Olson then told them to take some time to familiarize themselves with the photographs; he and Chief Anderson would be there to answer any questions. After that they would have an hour to get lunch. When the class resumed, Lt. Olson played recorded debriefings of former Vietnam POWs. For almost three hours, everyone in the room was totally focused as man after man described the constant beatings, lack of medical care, and long solitary confinements in 4x4x4 wooden boxes with only spoiled food and filthy water. All of them had chronic diarrhea, and some had dysentery or malaria. They were constantly dehydrated, and often near death from starvation. A few said they even ate their own vomit to stay alive. Some wept as they described fellow prisoners who died simply because they would not do it anymore; they lost the desire to survive. But many did survive, and as the last tape ended, Lt. Olson told the class, "The people you just heard survived because they had the toughness developed in AOCS and survival training. Think about it gentlemen." With that sobering thought, Lt. Olson reminded them, "We will see you tomorrow at 0600. The uniform of the day will be flight suits, boots and survival knives. Good luck the next four days, Gents. Dismissed."

It was almost 1600 when they walked to their cars. Sticky, "You want to see the house I told you about, Striker? It's only about two miles off base." Striker, "Sure, let me make a quick call, and I'll follow you there." Sticky gave Striker a thumbs-up, and they went to the BOQ. Striker called Terry and left the message, "I have to be up at 4:30 tomorrow, so I'm going to take it easy this evening. I'll call you when I get back. Striker." He caught up with Sticky, who said, "I'm going to the beach after I show you the house. You want to ride together?" Striker, "No. I'll follow you. I want to take a run and make a couple of calls."

Fifteen minutes later Striker parked behind Sticky in the driveway of a well-kept little brick bungalow in a tree-lined neighborhood of older homes. Sticky, "The tenant left, and the owner said he would have the place cleaned and painted by the end of the month."

The bedrooms reeked of tobacco and the kitchen was tiny, and the house had window air-conditioners. Striker was not convinced. Sticky, "What do you think, want to share the cost? We would split the rent and utilities, and we could shut the AC off when we aren't here, so figure maybe 90-95 bucks a month." Striker, "Once it's cleaned up and painted, it might be OK. It would be nice to have a place to take Terry, but I'm not sure how long I'll be seeing her. As it is now, I'd have to say no." Sticky, "No problem. You still have a month to change your mind."

After Striker finished running, he cleaned up and checked his messages. Terry had left one, "Understand, will miss you. Call when you are finished. T." He smiled, and then wondered if Terry had forgotten their "no strings" relationship.

Chapter 45

In The Jungle

Lt. Olson and CPO Anderson were waiting for them on the bus. Before the students got on, they counted off and were separated into eight teams of three people and one with two. An hour and half later they had driven through the main base and were following a dirt road which wandered through the massive primitive section.

The bus stopped at a small clearing and CPO Anderson distributed two parachutes and a survival kit to each of the three-man teams and one parachute and survival kit to the two-man team. Because of a shortage of the canteens which they normally would be issued, Anderson gave each team two canvas water bags. Teams one through five followed Olson and six through nine followed Anderson in opposite directions into the jungle.

As Olson led his teams through the thick vegetation, he told them to note their compass headings. Then he stopped them, "Gents, the morning we leave you will disassemble any structures you built, spread out any trees or vegetation that you used, and bury the parachutes. When that is done you will use your compasses to find your way back to the clearing." After they walked about a mile, Olson told team one to stop, then changed course and walked another mile, where team two stopped. He repeated the same process until all the teams were situated.

Striker was in team four with Sticky and Jim Gaither, a member of their AOCS class. Gaither grew up hunting and fishing in the south and worked as a guide in college. As soon as Olson left, Gaither told the others that since he was used to being in primitive areas, he volunteered to be the team leader. Sticky and Striker immediately agreed. Gaither, "OK, let's find a dry place to build a lean-to. It'll need about thirty small trees or large limbs, and lots of leaf fronds and ferns. We'll lash the limbs together on the top and sides of the lean-to. Then we'll cover the lean-to with the fronds of banana leaves. Once we have it covered, we'll cut risers and lay the chute over the frame, tie it to stakes and cover it with more vegetation. Once the lean-to is done, we'll put as many ferns as we can on the interior ground. Finally, we'll fold half of the other chute over the greenery and secure it to the ground."

The team completed the lean-to in less than four hours. It was obviously not perfect, but they hoped it would be good enough to keep them dry during the frequent Florida rain squalls. Gaither told Striker to fill the water bags, add iodine pills, and shake them until the pills were dissolved. He told Sticky to search for the kind of edible berries and succulents that Anderson had displayed. Then said he was going to use the slingshot to hunt wild game. He then reminded the other two to break off tree limbs every 10 feet wherever they went.

Striker remembered crossing a small creek about a quarter mile from their campsite. Before he started walking towards it, he cut off a four-foot tree limb and trimmed the forked end to four inches. He would use it as a walking stick and to push away potentially poisonous plants. Then he cut two-foot-long pieces of riser, tied the water bags together, and hung them over his shoulder.

After making sure his survival knife was easy to reach, he grabbed the walking stick and headed towards the creek. Marking the path as he went, he walked for about fifteen minutes before he saw a narrow creek. The surrounding area became more and more swampy as he looked for a pool of water that was not very murky. As he went further, he came to a large pool that was relatively clear, yet still moving. He decided it was the best he was going to find, so he dipped a bag into the water. As it started to fill, he was startled to see a large water moccasin lying on a mound of dirt about two feet from his right boot. It was coiled and hissing, but he hadn't heard it because of the gurgling of the creek. He quickly pinned the snake to the mushy ground with his walking stick and easily cut its head off with his survival knife. He picked up the dead snake, washed the blood away in the creek, and laid it around his neck like a necklace. He finished filling the bags, laid them over his shoulder, and began his trek back to the campsite.

Sticky went the opposite direction from Striker. Before he left, he cut off a three-foot triangular piece of chute, and using part of a riser, made a bag to carry whatever he found. He walked about a quarter mile as he looked for edible vegetation. He knew from CPO Anderson that several species of edible plants were in the area. He eventually found several palmetto trees that he cut down to the hearts and put them in the bag. About twenty minutes later, he came to a clearing near a small pond. Large blackberry bushes heavy with fruit were on the edge of the pond. Being careful not to jab his hands with the plant's thorns, he picked enough berries to nearly fill the bag. He decided that he would get more berries later if he didn't find anything else. After another half hour of searching, he saw several plants that he was unsure of, and he walked back to get more blackberries.

Thirty minutes later, as he approached the lean-to, Sticky smelled a fire. Then as he got closer, he saw that Gaither was standing about six feet from the lean-to, near a small fire.

Sticky saw that he was cutting up game. "What'd you get? What is that?" Gaither, "A raccoon. I saw a nest in a tree about a half-mile from here. I didn't know if anything was in it, so I fired three ball bearings into the center of the nest and this big boy fell down in front of me, unconscious. I cut its throat and brought it back to camp. I skinned and gutted it, and now I'm carving up the meat. I'm guessing it'll taste gamey, because it smells pretty bad. But it's protein, and if we cook it well done, it might get us through the next three days."

Sticky walked to where Gaither was standing and saw a pile of raw meat on some large leaves. Next to it was the rest of the butchered animal. Gaither, "I got a fire started. As soon as it's just hot coals we'll cook the meat on some sticks. I'm also going to cut up some of the guts to use as bait in that creek we passed. The rest I'm taking a couple hundred feet from here and dump it, 'cause it's going to stink really bad soon. What's in the bag?" Sticky, "Blackberries and six big palmetto hearts. I found a bunch of berries by a pond about a mile away and palmettos are scattered everywhere around here." Just then Striker walked into camp and saw the cut-up game. "Based on what's laying over there, I'd guess you got a raccoon. It should be an interesting meal, tonight. Look at this." Then he held up the big water moccasin in front of him." Gaither, smiling, "Good job, Striker, snake meat is good eating, and that's a big ass snake. It'll make at least two meals. It's easy to prepare. Just skin and gut it, cut it up into small sections, put them on sticks and cook them over an open fire. It's really lean meat, so fifteen minutes over the fire, max, and they're well done. While I'm doing this, why don't you guys go over to that pond Sticky found and fish with some cut up raccoon guts? There's a couple of hooks and about a hundred feet of line in the survival kit. I bet that pond has got some big catfish, and they love organ meat. While one of you watches the fishing lines, the other can use the bag to bring back four or five large stones that I'll use in the fire." Sticky, "Let's go. I'll lead the way."

Twenty minutes later, they got to the pond that Sticky had found. Striker, who fished a lot growing up, tied the hooks on the lines, attached bags of pebbles above the hooks, and put liver pieces on one of the hooks. He cut off two twelve-foot tree limbs, sharpened the bigger ends and tied the line to the narrow ends. After finding a sandy area near the pond's edge, Striker threw each bag of pebbles and bait as far as he could into the water and jammed the pointed end of the limbs into the soft sand.

About an hour later, Sticky was back at the pond, now carrying a water bag. "I was thirsty so I figured you would be, too. The water wouldn't taste so bad if I didn't have to put so many iodine tablets in it, but it's safer to put 'em in, I guess." Then he handed the water to Striker who took a swig and said, "It's bad, but I've tasted worse when I was camping with my dad. Thanks for bringing the bag."

Suddenly a line was jerking one of the limbs. "Striker, something's on a line." Striker quickly started bringing in the line and pulled out a large fish. As Gaither predicted, it was a big catfish. Striker cut the line and put it in the empty rock bag, and said, "Holy shit, this thing's about three pounds. It swallowed the hook, but I'll take it out when I clean it." Then he tied the line to the limb, and said, "I'll leave the other line in the water while we're gone, but I'm gonna shove the limb deeper in the ground. I'll come back and check it later." Meanwhile, Sticky put more stones with the others he already had, and said, "You ready to go? Let's take this stuff back to the lean-to and get into some shade. It's hotter than hell out here."

It was nearly 4:30 when they got back to the lean-to, and they were getting hungry. Gaither had wrapped the palmettos hearts in large green leaves. Then he skewered the raccoon and snake meat on the thin branches. He enlarged the fire and put flat rocks on the hot coals. When he saw Striker carrying the fish, he said. "You hit the jackpot, Striker. Clean it and we'll wrap in it some more leaves and bake it on hot rocks when we cook the skewered meat over the fire. While we're waiting for the rocks to heat up, let's go get more firewood. There's a felled live oak about a quarter mile away.

Thirty minutes later everyone was back, and the wood was stacked next to the lean-to. Gaither spit on a flat stone, and it sizzled, so he put the wrapped fish and palmetto hearts on them. He told Sticky and Striker to hold some of the skewered meat over the fire and turn them to keep the meat from burning.

Fifteen minutes later, he opened one of the fish wraps and could see that it was flaky, a good sign it was cooked. The palmetto was not tender, so he put it back on the fire. He piled the fish wraps up and covered them with an empty chute bag. Striker then said that the meat looked like it was done. Gaither took a piece of coon off a skewer and cut it in half with his knife. It was still pink, so he told Striker to keep turning it over the fire. He removed the snake pieces and put them with the fish. After another ten minutes, he told Striker to put the coon and palmetto with everything else. Gaither then piled some blackberries on a large leaf and opened the bag containing the rest of the food. "Come get it, boys. No guarantee that it tastes like your momma's pot-roast, but it's all we got."

Sticky was the first to try the coon. As soon as he put some in his mouth, he made a face like his fingernails were being pulled out, but he ate the entire piece. "Well, there's good news, it tastes like rancid meat, but it's not as bad as dog shit smells.

He tried another piece with some blackberries. "The berries help, even though most of them are sour, but they still make the meat almost edible." Striker then ate some snake and catfish and said, "The fish and snake are really bland, but they are edible. Everything could use salt and pepper, but it's adequate food, especially if you are hungry." Gaither, chewing on some palmetto hearts, "Same with the palmetto; it's a little slimy, kinda like okra, but it's not bad."

After they ate as much as that wanted, Gaither wrapped everything in leaves and put it in the back of the lean-to. Then he stoked the fire and added more wood. Striker got up and said, "Before it gets dark, I'm going to get some more bait and go check the fishing line. Anyone want to join me?" Both said they did, and they headed back to the pond.

When they arrived, Striker checked the line; it was cut and the bait and hook were gone, but not the pebbles. "Look at that, I bet it was a turtle, probably a snapping turtle. Those bad boys can almost cut a two-by-four in half with their powerful jaws. Unless you guys are ready to head back, I'm going to bait the other hook and try to catch something else." Sticky and Gaither both gave him a thumbs-up.

Ten minutes later, the second line was in the water, and the three of them were sitting in a shady spot overlooking the pond. An hour later Sticky said, "This jungle survival training shit isn't as bad as I thought it was going to be. Except for the constant attack of mosquitos and the heat, this is almost fun. I sure wish we could have snuck in a couple of cases of beer, though. Three or four cold Jax could almost make that rotten coon taste decent. Beer would certainly taste better than the pond water we're drinking. The last swig I took, I almost puked." Gaither, "It could be a lot worse, and probably will be." Then he pointed to the southwestern sky where black

249

clouds were closing in like a shutting eyelid. "We better hustle back to the lean-to and get ready for a bad-ass storm. It'll be here in about thirty minutes." Striker left the fishing line in the water and the three of them left.

There were strong winds and nearby lightning strikes when they got back to the lean-to. Before they could get in, a torrential downpour soaked them. They looked over the lean-to to see if everything was secure. Gaither found a way to direct rainwater off the front of the lean-to, so he dumped out the iodine water, and filled both bags with fresh water. When he finished, he said, "I've done everything I can, so we might as well get inside and wait the storm out," Striker replied, "First I think I'll take a shower, INDOC style." Then he took off his boots and tossed them into the lean-to and stripped to his skivvies. He stood in the chilly rain while he squeezed the water out of his flight suit and socks. Soon the other two followed suit, with Sticky doing his version of *Singing in the Rain.*

Striker was the first to get under the lean-to. "That shower was really refreshing." He said as he dressed and sat down on one side of the lean-to, "That rain sure took the stench of fish guts off me. I feel and smell a hell of a lot better." "Ditto that," Gaither added as he got dressed and sat next to Striker. "Let's just hope this shelter can stay together in this wind." Sticky, now dressed and sitting next to Gaither, said, "Well so far it has, and I'm betting that it will all night."

Sticky was right. Except for rain that was blown in by the wind, the lean-to remained intact and dry. More importantly, they all managed to sleep through most of the night. Early the next day, the winds eased but the showers continued into mid-morning. Except to go out to relieve themselves, the team either slept or sat quietly and watched the rain.

As it approached noon, the skies became partly cloudy, and the summer heat reemerged. Not only was it hot, the humidity made it very uncomfortable. As soon as it began to dry, the mosquitoes and flies again made life in the jungle even more miserable. Gaither suggested that they rub mud on their hands, faces and necks to prevent the pests from biting them. They soon looked like they were participants in some sort of tribal ritual, but the application of mud kept the bugs away.

Just after noon, Striker told his teammates that he needed to check the fishing line. Before he left, he took a big drink of the rainwater, grabbed some of the meat that was cut for bait and another hook. As he left, Sticky said that he was going to help Gaither repair any damage caused by the storm, then go with him to hunt for more game.

As soon as he got to the pond, Striker saw that the fishing line was taut and moving erratically. He started to pull the line in, and whatever was on it, fought hard. As soon as it broke the surface, Striker knew it was a snapping turtle, and like the catfish, it had swallowed the hook. Striker dragged the turtle onto the sandy bank, put a thick stick in front of it, and the turtle immediately bit it. Then he held up the stick with the turtle hanging from it and cut its head off. As he looked at the headless turtle, he thought, "This turtle is going to really test Gaither's survival skills. I hope he knows how to clean one, 'cause I don't. I know that they are good to eat, at least as a soup. I'm sure that if it is properly prepared, it must taste better than coon meat." He estimated that the turtle weighed at least ten pounds. With any luck, Gaither could harvest three or four pounds of edible meat, easily enough for the duration of the training. He put the turtle in a shady area and covered it with leaves to keep it moist and away from the flies. Then he dropped another line with coon meat on it into the pond and stayed for another hour. Nothing took the bait, and it was getting hot, so he picked up the turtle and walked back to the lean-to.

Gaither and Sticky were slogging their way through the swamp, and they hadn't seen any sign of animals except for nests built high in the trees. When he saw them, Sticky said, "Gaither, we have plenty of stinking coon to eat, certainly enough for two more days and probably enough for a lifetime. I can eat only so much of that dog shit, and squirrels are just miniature coons that are a pain in the ass to clean. Let's look for snakes and palmettos." Gaither, "I agree, there's got to be more snakes here, so keep looking, especially in low-hanging tree limbs and on the edge of the water. We already know where we can find palmettos." As soon as they began looking again, there were several loud thunderclaps coming from the west. They immediately turned and headed back to the lean-to. By the time Sticky and Gaither arrived at the lean-to, the wind picked up and the rain began. As they got inside, they could see that Striker was holding something in his lap. It was the headless snapping turtle.

Striker, "It looks like you guys got back just in time. From the looks of things, we're in for another stormy night. Did you get anything?" Sticky replied, "Nope, the storm stopped us in our tracks, so we didn't get a thing. What's in your lap?" Striker, "A snapping turtle; it took the hook, so I killed it and brought it back, but it doesn't look like we're gonna be able to clean and cook it any time soon." Gaither, "Yeah, I'll wait a couple of hours to see if it clears up. If it's more than three or four hours, we'll have to toss the turtle and do with what we have until it clears up."

After checking the back of the lean-to, Gaither counted three pieces of snake, two palmetto hearts, several pieces of

252

catfish, and a lot of coon meat which smelled rancid. They also had blackberries and plenty of fresh water. When he finished, Gaither said, "We can hold our noses and eat the fish, but the coon is just too rancid to eat. I'm gonna put it outside and use it for bait. We'll split up the palmetto, snake and berries. Eat what you want. It's up to you 'cause it might bounce, but there might not be any more food until they come to get us in about thirty-six hours."

Sticky responded, "Hell, this is a piece of cake. I've eaten two-day old anchovy pizza after a couple of days of hard partying. I have an iron gut, so I figure that if I eat some fish and snake now before they get too rotten, I'll make it to the end. I won't need a thing to eat until we get back on base. Just think, in about forty hours we'll be back in the Ready Room loading up on shrimp and washing it down with ice-cold beer. Just the thought of that will get me through a few hours. I'm ready, baby." Sticky held his nose and ate fish and snake and followed each bite with large gulps of water.

Less than four hours later, Sticky ran out of the lean-to to vomit. He continued to get sick the rest of the night and into the early morning. Gaither and Striker, who had only eaten berries and drank water, didn't get sick; they took the turtle, fish and snake out to bury it.

The storm brought heavy rain, but less wind than the previous one, and it lasted until after dawn. Sticky had stripped to his skivvies and lay across the front of the lean-to so that he could easily get outside when he needed. After refilling the bags with rainwater, Striker and Gaither slept perpendicular to Sticky, on either side of the lean-to so that Sticky did not disturb them. Except for a few errant drips near the entrance, the lean-to kept them dry on their second night.

Early the next morning, the rain ended, and the sun was starting to break through the clouds. Striker stepped over a snoring Sticky and went outside. The usual stagnant smell of the swamp was displaced by the cleansing effect of the storm. The normally ever-present insects were dormant, unable to fly with wet wings. For a brief period, the jungle's beauty, rather than its flaws, was dominant. "But" Striker thought, "Soon, the jungle will return to its natural state, and the challenges to survive will begin again."

Gaither came out to the sunshine and spent a moment surveying the lean-to. Except for a few displaced leaf fronds, it had more than proven its sturdiness. Gaither easily replaced the fronds, and then said to Striker, "Unless there is a really bad ass storm tonight, I think this place will make it until tomorrow. I don't know what made Sticky so sick, but I'm not taking any more chances with the game. We can make it with just berries and palmetto hearts until they come get us in the morning."

Sticky finally staggered out of the lean-to and took a long drink from a water bag. As he finished, he held his stomach and said, "This is the worst hangover I ever had, and I didn't have a single beer. Something I ate sure kicked the shit outta me. I thought I was gonna die, but I made it. You guys get sick, too?" Gaither, "Nope, neither one of us, but we only ate berries and palmetto. After you got sick, I threw out all that shit, some of which must have kicked you in the butt. We've decided to just eat berries and palmetto until this little vacation ends tomorrow. Striker and I are going to get some more this morning but were waiting to see if you were getting better. How do you feel?" Sticky, "I'll let you know if I keep the water down. I'm weak and need some fluids in me. Everything else that was in me is gone, so I am dehydrated. I'm just gonna take it easy here and drink as much water as I can hold. Go ahead."

Chapter 46

Jungle Training Ends

Striker and his team were up at dawn, eager to get back to the BOQ and a hot shower. Sticky seemed to be feeling better and had made it through the night without getting sick. As he was stretching his legs outside the lean-to, Sticky even said he was looking forward to a cheeseburger and a cold beer, a sure sign he was getting back to normal. Gaither then told the team that they needed to get ready to leave. As they were ordered, they took their intrepid lean-to apart and spread its limbs and leaf fronds in the surrounding jungle. They buried the remnants of the two parachutes in the soft soil of a marshy area and covered it all with some of the fronds they had used in the lean-to. Their cleanup was completed by 0730, Gaither easily led them back, and 20 minutes later they were waiting in a shaded area for everyone else to arrive.

Gradually, all the teams made it to the clearing by 0900. When Bulldog and Hound finally got there, Striker asked them how it went. Bulldog gave him a thumbs-down, saying, "Boy, I'm glad to leave that shit hole. We ate nothing but sour berries and a few boney fish and drank water that tasted like diesel fuel. Even worse, the parachute tent we built was destroyed by the first storm, leaving us out in the open. We had to wrap ourselves in what remained of the parachutes and sit on the ground in torrential rain. We got soaked to the skin. The next tent we built was sturdier and made it through the second storm. But it leaked like hell, and we got soaked again. Luckily last night there were no storms. Then when we headed back, we got lost and wandered around the swamp for about 45 minutes before we finally found the clearing. I can't wait to get back to base. The last three days just sucked. I'm thirsty, starving and ready to sleep for about a week." Sticky, smiling, told them he spent one night vomiting and with raging diarrhea. Bulldog slapped him on the back and said "Thanks, Sticky, you always find a way to make me feel better."

As soon as everyone was in their seats, Lt. Olson addressed the class. "Welcome back, Gents. I hope you all learned something these last few days. You may need it in the future. From what I heard, some groups had a rough time. If you did get sick and don't feel a lot better in a day or two, go to the infirmary and get checked out. There are probably some organisms in the water that can cause long-term problems, and you need to be careful. Gents, your water and jungle training are now complete. As soon as we get back to base, you will be off until you begin the next phase of the flight program, whatever it is, at 0700, July 21. Good luck, Gents, and have a great weekend."

Virtually everyone in the class fell asleep as soon as the bus was on the road to Pensacola. About an hour and a half later, they woke up as the bus came to a stop at the Water Survival building. When the door opened, Striker and his roommates walked to their cars and drove straight to the BOQ.

Once they were in their room, Striker and Sticky flipped a coin for the first shower. Striker won and went to the bathroom; Sticky flopped down on the bed. When he finished cleaning up, Striker saw that Sticky was sound asleep. Rather than letting him sleep all day smelling like a dead goat, Striker woke him up. Still half asleep, Sticky got up and stumbled into the bathroom, where he stayed in the shower for almost a half hour. Now clean and dressed in civilian clothes, he came out and got back on his bed, saying, "I'm starving but I'm too damn tired to eat. Don't let me sleep too much past two; I'm supposed to get hooked up with Lee Ann later." Striker said he would, and then he went to eat.

There was a message from Terry at the desk. It was dated the day before and said that she had gone to Madison for two weeks to help her sister who had a premature baby. She ended the message by saying she missed him a lot and would give him a call when she got back. As he walked over to the open mess, he thought, "Well, it looks like I'm batching it for a couple weeks. I wonder when Wendy's getting back in town. I'll give her a call later today." When he got inside the mess, he looked around for his other two suite mates, but didn't see either of them. He did see a couple of guys who had just been through training with him. Striker joined Tony DeMaio and Greg Sensibaugh, who were NROTC grads and a Marine second lieutenant, Jack Peters. Like Striker, all three of them were training to be NFOs. Striker asked Peters how the jungle survival training went. Peters "Except for the stench, the putrid water, the mosquitoes, the torrential rain, the terrible humidity, the heat, the shitty things we ate, and sleeping on the ground in a leaky lean-to, it was great. I'm an ex-college football player, who, I admit, lived a pretty pampered life for five years. I didn't mind the practices and I loved playing. I ate only the best food at the training table, had the best dorms on campus, and had about a dozen cheerleaders to chase around. I'm not used to sleeping on dirt or eating a squirrel or boney little fish. I wouldn't touch the snake Sensibaugh killed and cooked. Now when I was at Quantico, I did have to train in the jungle, but at least we ate K-rations, which, as bad as they are, are a thousand times better than a gamey squirrel. I guess the OCS jungle training seemed to be better because we were so busy figuring out how to get to our objectives and setting up ambushes. Even with that, it was not even close to being as bad as the last three

258

days. The main reason I applied for flight training was so I wouldn't have to live in a jungle for weeks at a time. I'd rather fight the enemy anywhere but in a stinking swamp." Now pointing at the other two at the table, "These two guys were my teammates, they can tell you that this tough-ass Marine was a wussy in jungle survival. I only ate and drank enough to say I did what I was supposed to do, but I complained continually and openly hated every minute of it. Am I right guys?" DeMaio "Hell, it was even worse than that. Peters took up most of the tent, snored like a tractor-trailer revving up, and farted like a sewage treatment plant exploding, all three nights. Several times I had to get out of the tent and into the rain to keep from puking my brains out. I'm telling you; the Geneva Convention should outlaw this guy's farts. They're deadly." Everyone laughed and Peters just smiled and proudly gave two thumbs-up.

When they finished eating, Striker told them that he would see them at VT-10 and went back to his room to wake up Sticky. As he walked into the living room, he could already hear Sticky snoring in their bedroom. It was only 1100, so he decided to go make some calls and let Sticky sleep for another hour.

He first talked to Lizzy to see how their mother was doing. She told him that their mom's recovery had far exceeded the doctor's prognosis. She was using a walker and was working from home. She even canceled the delivery of food but still used the driving service. The best thing that happened was that their mom and dad were now friendly again. While there was little chance they would get back together, Lizzy was optimistic that they could now celebrate birthdays and holidays together as a family.

259

Striker then called his mom at home, but she didn't answer. He did reach his father at his office in the Pentagon. His dad had only a few minutes to talk because he had to go to a meeting. Striker briefly told him how his training was going. His father told him that the worst part was over, and now the fun begins. He said that some of his best days in Pensacola were during basic flight training. Hopefully Striker wouldn't get a screamer or a cowboy who just wants to hot dog instead of trying to teach. He said, "Unfortunately, the Navy often reassigns a returning combat aviator to duty as a flight instructor as a reward, not because of his ability or intent to teach. I know that is still going on, so you probably will get a bad instructor; almost everyone does." Striker told his dad that he had heard that there were some terrible instructors, but he was ready to deal with them. He thanked his dad for his advice and said he would keep in touch.

Sticky was leaving just as Striker walked into the room. As he had told Striker earlier, Sticky was planning to hook up with Lee Ann that afternoon and would probably be gone until late that night. As he left, Sticky said, "We'll probably go to Tiki Beach and maybe to her place, but it's up to her. If you and Terry get together at the beach, look for us at the Tiki Bar." Striker, "I just found out that Terry will be out of town for two weeks. After I go for a run, I'm going to Tiki beach and take it easy. I'll look for you guys there." As soon as Sticky left, Striker went for a run. Forty-five minutes later, he returned to his room and peeked into Bulldog's side of the suite. Both were gone, presumably to get something to eat. He cleaned up and went back to the desk to try to reach Wendy and his mother.

Wendy's message service was full, and he had to leave his mother a message. He again looked for Bulldog and Hound in the open mess but didn't see them. He returned to his room, changed into his bathing suit, and left for the beach.

Striker arrived at Tiki Beach and found a place to park. It had become cloudy, and he wondered if rain or storms were forecast, causing the normal crowd to stay away. It really didn't matter since he intended to just lie on the beach and catch up on the sleep, he missed the last few days. If it started to storm or rain, he'd leave and do something else. Ten minutes later, he was sound asleep on his blanket.

A few hours later, he was awakened by the sound of children playing. He stretched, got up, and looked around. The sky was now partially cloudy, but there was an offshore breeze that kept it cool. He decided to take a walk towards Fort Pickens to loosen up his legs, which were still tight from his run.

About a mile down the beach, he heard a girl calling to him. As he walked toward her, he saw that it was Julie, Lee Ann's seventeen-year-old friend, sitting alone on a blanket. She was wearing a tiny yellow polka-dot bikini, and she was gorgeous. "Hi, Striker. Come over and sit down." Reluctantly, he walked to her. As he sat down, he asked her how she was doing. Julie replied, "I'm great. I have just been hanging out with my friends, but they just left to get something to eat. Where've you been? I haven't seen you here at the beach in weeks" Striker, "Been in training, mostly. I just finished water and jungle survival training this morning. I'm going to be off for a few days, so I decided to relax on the beach until I begin flight training on Monday. I was looking for Sticky. I think he's with Lee Ann. Have you seen them recently?" Julie, "Not today, but I've been staying in Lee Ann's apartment this summer. I help pay her rent, but on weekends, when Sticky comes over, I stay

261

somewhere else. I think she's starting to get serious about him."

Then, she looked at him with a shy smile and said, "Striker, I know you've been seeing someone, but I was still hoping you'd give me a call; here's my number. I'd sure like to go out with you sometime." Striker, "Julie. I have been seeing someone else. We're not exclusive, so I see other girls as well. You're a beautiful girl, but I don't date high school girls. No matter how innocent it would be, I'd still feel like I was taking advantage of you." Julie. "I understand, but I've been dating guys your age for almost two years. I might be young, but I'm not naive. I know most of you Navy guys are just looking for a one-night stand, but I'm not that type. I assure you that I know how to handle myself with guys your age." Striker, "I believe you, Julie, but that doesn't change how I feel. I can be your friend, but nothing else. I'm supposed to meet up with Sticky at the Tiki Bar in a little while, so I'll see you later." He waved to her and walked away.

As Striker drove back to base, he saw a large roadside billboard advertising Fort Walton Beach and wondered what it was like.

Chapter 47

Connors and Jane are Together in Pensacola

Connors' training flights were becoming routine, but they were not without mishaps. During one flight, a T-2C lost an engine while engaged in gunnery practice, but the student managed to safely return to base. On another flight, the aircraft was low on fuel just as a severe thunderstorm shut down Sherman Field. The flight had to be redirected to Whiting Field, where it landed safely. Otherwise, Connors was home by 4 pm almost every day.

Recently Jane was always tired, often asleep by 9 pm. She had other side effects of pregnancy; her breasts were larger and more sensitive, and her libido was stronger than ever. Even though she wanted to make love with Connors more often, her constant fatigue prevented it. She believed that the clash of hormonal drives was nature's way of rewarding her for bearing a child. In spite of everything, one Saturday morning, Jane made up for her celibacy.

Later, as they were eating breakfast, Jane told Connors that she wanted to tell her parents about the baby before the wedding. "I'm starting to gain weight. Mom will certainly notice it when they bring the girls' furniture here," Connors said, "That's OK with me. You can tell them when they get here."

They decided to relax at Tiki Beach for the day, and they found a quiet spot near the bar. A half-hour later, Jane was asleep, and Connors went for a swim. An hour later, he was out of the water and walking to their blanket. As he did, he heard a familiar voice yell at him, "Connors, Tim Connors, over here. At the Tiki bar." Connors saw Major Pless sitting with a couple of people at a table just outside of the bar. While he walked toward them, a band began playing, and he could barely hear Pless ask, "Connors, how are you? Sit down. I'll buy you a beer." Connors, "I'm doing great Major, but I've been really busy during the day and getting ready for my wedding in the evenings. Jane and I came to the beach to relax a bit; she's over by the Gulf, sleeping on a blanket." Pless, almost yelling, introduced Connors to his friends, then asked, "Aren't you getting married around the first weekend of August? I think it's on my calendar, and unless hell freezes over, I'll be there." After the waitress brought Connors a beer, Pless said, "I remember that day at the Ready Room when you told me about wanting to be an astronaut. Do you still feel that way now that you're getting married? I thought about you earlier when we were talking about the Apollo astronauts. Did you know that they did a lot of training here at the base?"

Connors, "Major. I've been following the space program since I was a kid. Long before I thought about joining the Navy, I saw pictures of the astronauts in the base water survival tank. I still dream about going to test pilot school and becoming an astronaut." Pless, "Connors, from what I know about you, you've got a great chance of reaching that goal, especially if my recommendation has any weight. Then, he invited Connors to join him and his friends at the Pier Lounge. Connors declined, saying he wanted to get back to Jane and left.

When he got back to Jane, Connors said, "Since I was gone for about an hour and a half, I was concerned that you would be worried about me. Did you sleep the whole time I was gone?" Jane, "Almost, I just woke up. I was out cold. You really wore me out this morning, but it was wonderful. We have to find time to do that more often. Were you in the water the whole time I was asleep?" Connors, "No, when I got out of the water, I ran into Major Pless. He insisted on buying me a beer, and he introduced me to his friends. He told me they were meeting some people at the Pier and invited us to go. I declined, telling him that we were busy preparing for the wedding."

Chapter 48

Wendy and Leah Return from Kansas

Leah, Wendy and her father, Jeff, arrived in Jackson, Mississippi on the evening of July 18th. After they checked into a motel, they met in the lobby to look for a place to eat. They had only eaten sandwiches and snacks that they brought, and now wanted to eat a real meal somewhere. The desk clerk recommended Bubba's, a local favorite bar and grill, about a mile away. Bubba's reminded Wendy of Mrs. Hopkins Boarding House, especially the house specialties, chicken fried steak, fried okra and fried green tomatoes, all served family style. Large pitchers of sweet tea were on every table. When they were done, they couldn't resist the house dessert, freshly baked peach cobbler with homemade vanilla ice cream. Leah ate every bite, and said, "After all that, I'll never fit in my bikini, but it was worth it."

Exhausted by eleven hours of driving a lumbering moving van, they decided to go back to the motel and take it easy. Before they left the restaurant, Wendy's dad bought a six-pack of beer at the bar, and Wendy took a bottle of wine from the cooler. They sat on their beds, drank and talked about their trip to Kansas. Wendy, "It was great to see my family, friends, and the places I used to go, but being there also brought back sad memories, especially about the night Roger died. Kansas will never be the same for me. Now as I look back at what happened, I believe that our marriage was not meant to be. Starting a new life and meeting new people somewhere else is what I'm supposed to do, and so far, it has been a great experience. I'm glad I did it." Leah, "I feel the same way, but my breakup with Larry was the best thing I ever did. I was crazy to put up with his cheating all those years. He was charming and good-looking, but he had no moral compass. I can't believe that I just ignored his constant lying. Somehow, I finally realized I was being foolish, and I knew that if we got married, he wouldn't stop. Finally, I broke it off. When we got back to Overland Park, I was worried that he would find out I was in town and try to contact me. Thankfully, he didn't. Now, after a few months in paradise, surrounded by young Naval officers, there's no way Larry could ever be in my life. I'm totally over him and can't wait to get back to Pensacola. Life is good again."

Wendy realized it was nearly midnight and told Leah they had better get some sleep. Her father wanted to be on the road by eight and they were supposed to be at Bubba's for breakfast by 7. The next morning, Jeff had his bag in the car and was waiting for them in the lobby. It was Wendy's turn to drive the car, so Leah joined Jeff in the truck.

It was obvious that breakfast at Bubba's was the thing to do in Jackson, Mississippi. It was packed, so they waited for a table. As soon as they were seated, a waitress brought menus and asked what everyone wanted to drink. Just as they finished reading the menu, she brought them coffee and orange juice, and took their order. While they waited, Jeff estimated it would take almost five hours to get to Pensacola and another 45 minutes to get to Jane's apartment. They decided to first unload some furniture at Jane's place, and then take the rest to Wendy's apartment. They needed to return the truck to the rental company by noon the next day.

Breakfast arrived quickly, and it was obvious why the place was so popular. The portions were huge and as good as dinner had been. Neither girl could eat even half of their meals and

Jeff struggled to eat most of his. As they were finishing, Jeff said, "I'm gonna put this place on my list of great places to eat, but, as good as it is, we'd better hit the road."

After getting past Mobile, it was an open road to Pensacola. They were in town by about 1:30 and stopped to call Jane for directions. Flight operations shut down at noon that day, so Connors was home and answered the phone. He told them that Jane was running some errands but that he would be at the apartment the rest of the afternoon. He also told them the quickest way to the apartment, and they easily found it. Connors was in the garage, moving things around when they arrived. Wendy honked her horn and waved as Leah and Jeff got out of the truck. Connors walked towards them, saying. "Welcome to Pensacola. Come in and relax for a while." Then he hugged Wendy and Leah then shook Jeff's hand, "Mr. Carmody, I'm Tim Connors. Good to see you again. We met about a year ago when you were visiting Jane in Gainesville." Jeff, "I remember you were hard to forget since Jane constantly talked about you. The way you two got back together is something out of a novel, but it really happened, and we're thrilled. Please call me Jeff."

They went to the apartment and Connors led them to the deck. Jeff, "This place is great; the view is amazing." Connors responded, "It's all Jane's doing, she found it. It has everything we need, including dishes and flatware, and it's a short drive to the University. Since I'm usually on the road before 7, there's no traffic; let me get you something to drink. What'll you have?" Wendy wanted iced tea; Leah and Jeff wanted a beer.

After they finished their drinks and talked for a few minutes, Jeff said, "We'd better start taking the furniture off the truck." Connors replied, "I made room in the garage so we can begin there." Wendy and Leah decided to use the beds and

268

other furniture in the apartment, so most of what they were leaving were the bed frames, mattresses, and small furniture. They were done in less than an hour.

Jeff closed up the truck and followed Wendy to her apartment, where they quickly unloaded everything. After they agreed to meet for dinner later, the girls began to sort out their belongings. Connors followed Jeff to return the truck, then took him to his apartment. As they walked in, Jane rushed to her dad, hugged him, and said, "Daddy, it's been too long. I'm so glad to see you. Thank you so much for helping Wendy; have you seen our apartment?" Jeff, "I sure did, Connors gave us a tour when we first arrived. We came back here to get you and pick up your mom at 6:30." Jane said, "Sounds great. After we get her, we'll take you out to eat.

When her mother arrived, Jane greeted her, "I'm so happy you're here, Mom, come meet Connors." Jane led her mother by the hand to Connors, and said, "This is my mom, Marianne" Connors, "I'm Tim Connors, remember me?" Marianne, "Of course, we met when you were just finishing flight training and were getting ready to move to San Diego. It was sad that you two broke up, but now that you have found each other again; I couldn't be happier for both of you. Welcome to our family." Connors, "Thank you so much. There was a time when I thought I would never see Jane again, but I promised myself I would do everything possible to see if she still cared about me. I found her, she did, and I asked her to marry me. Unbelievable as it seems, she said yes." Just as he finished talking, Jeff said, "The luggage is here."

After Connors picked everyone up at the terminal, he said, "How about we meet Wendy and Leah at the O Club for dinner? We can eat in the main dining room, or if you guys want something more casual, we'll go to the Ready Room.

269

Take your pick." Jeff immediately replied, "The Ready Room sounds great to me. I've heard a lot about that place and I'm a pub kind of guy." Marianne, "If it's not too crowded, the Ready Room sounds like fun." Jane said, "Then it's agreed, I'll call Wendy and set it up."

When they arrived at the Ready Room, Connors pushed two tables together. A few seconds later, a waitress brought menus and asked what everyone wanted to drink. Then she remarked, "You really lucked out. Normally this place is packed at this time of day. You'd never find two empty tables close to each other." True to her words, fifteen minutes later the place was standing room only. Striker was one of them; he had no idea that Wendy was fifteen feet away.

Chapter 49

Striker Goes to Fort Walton Beach

Sticky was with Lee Ann and his two other suitemates had made plans, so Striker decided to try out the closed casual bar. As he walked in, he could see two people sitting at the bar playing bar dice. Both were Marines in flight suits, a Major and a Captain.

Striker sat several seats away from the Marines and ordered a draft beer. Apparently, they had been drinking for a while because they were cursing loudly when the dice didn't fall their way. As Striker watched them, they gradually got louder and angrier, and eventually threatening. Then without warning, the Major hit the Captain in the face. They started trading punches, knocking each other off the barstools, and rolling on the floor. Then the part time bartender, a Marine Lance Corporal asked Striker, "Sir, are you gonna break it up? They might hurt each other," Striker shook his head and said, "Hell no. As soon as I grab one of them, the other's going to come to the aid of a fellow Marine and both of them will kick my ass. They'll soon get tired and stop fighting. They're probably old friends who just got back from Nam and are still combat crazy. They're just letting off some steam."

Two or three minutes later, the Major stopped fighting and asked, "Had enough?" The Captain replied, "No, I got more, but I don't want to hurt a senior officer too badly." Both laughed, wiped the blood off their faces and got back on their barstools. The Major looked at Striker and the bartender and said, "You guys didn't see anything, did you?" The bartender smiled, and said, "Not a thing, sir. It's been as quiet as a tomb

271

in here all night." Striker shook his head, "No sir, it was so boring in here, I almost fell asleep." The Major smiled, gave them both a thumbs-up, "That's what I thought, your next drink is on me." The two Marines began playing bar dice again as if nothing had happened. Striker finished the first beer, drank the one the Major bought him, and left. As he walked to his room, he chuckled as he thought, "If I had never been around Marines, I would not believe that happened." He was still chuckling as he got into his bed.

The next morning, he got up early and went for a run around the base. When he was done, he showered, put on civilian clothes and went to see if either Bulldog or Hound was there. No one was, so he went to get some breakfast. As Striker walked into the mess hall, he saw them in the buffet line, and got behind them.

As he sat down, Hound asked Striker where Sticky was, and how he was feeling. He replied, "He seems to be feeling fine. I saw him last night at the Ready Room. He was with Lee Ann, his girlfriend. After we ate, he left with her and said they were going to be at the beach for a couple of days. He didn't say where they would be, but I suspect it's a beachfront motel. On weekends when Lee Ann is gone, she lets her cousin Julie stay at her apartment. I saw Julie at the beach yesterday, and she didn't say anything about them being at the apartment." Bulldog, "Is Julie the really cute girl we were talking about?" Striker, "You mean the under-eighteen, almost a senior in high school girl I met on the beach?" Bulldog, "Yup, that's the one. Was she by herself when you saw her?" Striker, "She sure was, and she looked twenty-five in a tiny yellow polka dot bikini." Bulldog, smiling, "Seventeen is just my speed. You don't have her phone number, do you?" Striker, "Sorry, man, I don't, but when Sticky gets back, I'm sure he can get it."

Then Striker said, "I almost forgot to tell you guys what happened last night at the casual bar." Then he described the fight between two Marine officers. Hound, "The other night at the Tiki Bar, I saw one of the guys in our survival class, a big Marine, taking bets that he could break a glass beer mug with his teeth. I think his name is Peters. Sure enough, after the bets were on the table, he took out some of his teeth, put the mug in the gaps, and broke off the top of the mug. I had to turn away; I thought for certain he was going to cut himself. He didn't, I think he won a couple hundred dollars."

They soon finished their meals and went back to their suite. Fifteen minutes later, Bulldog went to the beach to see if he could find Julie, and Hound went to visit his sister and her family. Now by himself for the weekend, Striker decided to leave for Fort Walton Beach. He put on his bathing suit, threw some clean clothes and toiletries into his bag, and checked for messages.

There were no messages, but there was a notice on the bulletin board that asked for junior officers to be volunteer sword bearers at a wedding on Wednesday, July 23. The ceremony was moved from its original date because the entire wedding party, except for the groom and best man had to report for an emergency deployment. Even though Striker didn't recognize their names, Gina Martinez and Lt. Jake Zimmerman, USN, he thought, "What a deal, single girls, free booze and food; it's a win-win proposition. I'm there, and I bet Sticky will be too," Then he added both their names to the list of volunteers.

He estimated it would take about an hour to go to Fort Walton Beach on Okaloosa Island. His route took him through Gulf Breeze and along the inland side of the Santa Rosa Sound. Once he was out of town, he opened up his Mustang and soon was cruising at over 100 MPH. He was in Okaloosa Island in less than forty minutes.

Fort Walton Beach was more developed than Pensacola Beach, with many motels and restaurants. Striker drove east for about fifteen minutes, but didn't see anything that interested him. He turned around and drove west for about a half hour and. began to see less crowded beach parking lots. At one of them he saw a waterfront motel, the Gulf View Lodge, and a sign advertising Grumpy's Bar and Grill.

Intrigued by the sign, he parked his car and went inside. The bar was dark, but he could see that it was about half-filled with young people. Most of the light in the room came from large windows and a glass door on the beach side of the bar. He walked across the room and out the door. There he saw a pavilion and tiki bar with a view of the beach. He was hungry so he sat down, asked for a menu and a beer. He ordered a fried oyster poor boy and turned around to take a closer look. He saw a few couples sitting at nearby tables and nine young women, in bikinis, sitting at large table at the far side of the pavilion. They were apparently having a bachelorette party. The bride-to-be was wearing a red-sequined tiara and was sipping what looked like a gigantic pina colada; the other girls had a variety of drinks. It was not yet noon and all nine girls sounded like they were already buzzed. Striker thought, "This place is looking better and better. I think I'll stick around awhile."

A stool at the end of the bar became vacant, so he moved there to get a better view of the girls. Striker was not very good at estimating girls' ages, but he suspected that they were all either college girls or recent graduates. He finished his beer and ordered another, then asked the barkeep if he knew who the girls were. Jimmy, the barkeep said, "I don't know all their names but the one on the right of the bride is Donna, the maid of honor. She told me to let her know when the bill hits $100. They haven't hit 25 bucks yet, so it's going to be a long day for them. She did tell me that the girls were members of the Florida State volleyball team. Donna and the bride, whose name I think is Jillian, just graduated in June. I heard them talking about the groom. I think he just finished Air Force pilot training and is here on leave before getting some advanced training in Texas. I believe the wedding is on base next weekend." Then as Jimmy brought Striker his second beer, he said, "By the way, Donna reserved the beach volleyball court for two hours, beginning at 1. If I were you, I'd put my blanket down as close to the court as possible. Those are good-looking girls and they want to party." Striker gave Jimmy a thumbs-up and said, "I think I'll follow your advice."

Twenty minutes later, Striker was asleep on a beach blanket next to the volleyball court. It wasn't long before a stray volleyball hit his head. Slightly stunned, he reached for the ball at the same time as one of the girls from the bar bent over to get it. Looking worried, she said, "I'm so sorry, are you OK?" Then she smiled as Striker tossed the ball to her. Striker, "I'm fine, thanks. Sorry my head got in the way of your ball." As she walked away, she said, "Normally I'm a much better shot. I'll try to do better."

A few minutes later, Striker retrieved two more errant balls that missed him by only a few inches, and another one that hit him. When the same girl came to him a third time, he noted that she was blonde, over six feet tall, with an athletic body and striking blue eyes, Striker, "Since it appears I've become one of your teammates, if only a ball boy, I should know your name, don't you think? I'm Jonathan Striker, but now that I'm in the Navy, most people just call me Striker." She grinned and

275

said, "I'm Ingrid Carlson. What do you do in the Navy?" Striker responded, "I'm training to become a Naval Flight Officer, hopefully in the back seat of an F-4." Ingrid, "That's cool. My dad is a reserve Air Intelligence officer in the Air Force. Oops, I have to go back to the game."

After the game began again, Ingrid yelled at Striker to join in the game. "We're getting our butts whipped. They have five on their side and we only have four. Have you ever played volleyball?" Striker, "Sure, I've played a lot, but I don't play as good as you guys." Ingrid, "That's OK. We practiced against a men's intramural team almost every day. You'll do just fine." Striker gave her a thumbs-up and ran onto the sand court. As he did, Ingrid yelled at her teammates, "This is Striker, he's agreed to help even things up a bit." Then she pointed to each of the other players who waved and yelled their names.

The score was tied at one set each and it was Ingrid's team turn to serve. Her serve made it over the net and an opposing hitter spiked it hard into Striker's face, knocking him down. Ingrid quickly came to him to see if he was OK. Striker, red faced, said, "Yeah, I'm OK, just a little embarrassed." He got up, gave her a high five and the game continued. With the score tied in the last set, Striker fed Ingrid a high pass, and after a fake spike, she gently lobbed the ball into an empty space on the other side of the net. Their team won the match 3 sets to 2. Before Striker could say a word, Ingrid gave him two high fives, saying, "For a Navy guy you can play pretty good."

Then Allison from the other team yelled, "Ingrid, Striker's a ringer. He turned the game around and we want a rematch." Ingrid, laughing, "Sorry, our court time is up, we can't. We might as well go for a swim." She quickly turned to Striker, "Want to join us?" Striker, "Sure, let's go."

When they were in chest deep water, Ingrid yelled at Striker, "There's a sandbar about a hundred yards out, let's go body surf." Striker followed her. When they got to the sandbar, Ingrid caught the first wave before it peaked and rode it halfway to shore. Striker waited for a bigger wave, and then rode it to where Ingrid was standing. As the day progressed, they surfed until Ingrid was tired and headed to shore. Striker was close behind.

On the way, Ingrid stopped in waist deep water with her back to the incoming surf. Striker saw a rogue wave coming directly behind her and yelled, "Look out!" but it was too late. The big wave hit her, tumbling her into the surf. When she got up, she was screeching with laughter. The wave knocked off her bikini top. In an effort to be modest, she squatted down and searched in the water around her, but the surf kept moving the top. Frustrated, she stood up, "The hell with modesty. This is ridiculous. I'll never find it doing this." Now topless, she continued to look for her top.

Striker saw the bikini top floating nearby and retrieved it, "Here it is." and threw it to her. As he feigned covering his eyes, "You better put it on before the beach patrol locks you up for public nudity. You can trust me, I won't testify against you 'cause I didn't see a thing." As she put her top back on, Striker made a weak attempt to look away and walked to shore.

As he sat down, Ingrid came next to him and said, "Now that you've seen me half naked, we're well acquainted. Why don't you move closer to me? We can't talk thirty feet apart." Striker, "I was hoping you'd ask, but I didn't want to interfere with your party." Ingrid, "You're not interfering, you're now part of the group, you might as well join us. This is Jillian's bachelorette party; it'll be a great time, come on." Striker, "I'd have to turn in my man card if I refused to party with you guys." Ingrid winked as Striker grabbed his blanket and followed her.

As soon he spread out his blanket, he asked Ingrid where she was from and what her plans were. Ingrid, "I'm twenty-two years old, just graduated from FSU, Majored in Kinesiology and am going to the University of Florida's School of Physical Therapy in the spring. After the wedding next weekend, a bunch of us are going on an eight-week tour of Europe. When I get back, I'll work in my uncle's law office until I start grad school. I was on the FSU volleyball team for three years and I worked in my uncle's office every summer. I have two sisters, Elsa and Sylvia. Now, what's your story, Striker?"

Striker, "I'm 24, a Navy brat, lived all over the place, went to several elementary schools, one high school. My home of record is Lexington Park, Maryland, a Navy town located near the Chesapeake Bay and the Patuxent River. I graduated from the University of Maryland in College Park. Last year I got accepted to AOCS in Pensacola. I was commissioned three weeks ago, and I start flight training in about a week. When I'm off, I normally spend most of my time at Pensacola Beach, but I came here just to see what it's like."

Ingrid, "I've been to Pensacola Beach several times; it's a meat market there. I bet I was hit on by a half dozen guys a day, even when I was sitting with my boyfriend. We broke up about six months ago." Striker, "Yeah, with all the Navy and Marine people there, it's pretty much that way all the time, but I'm surprised only six guys hit on you. Your boyfriend must have been a big guy who scared the others away." Ingrid, "He is. He was the starting middle linebacker on the FSU football team until he tore up his knee. He's got a new girlfriend now, a cheerleader, of course. Do you have a girlfriend?" Striker,

"Nope, I'm unattached. Naval Aviators are away a lot, so I decided to stay single until I complete my first tour and life becomes more predictable." Ingrid, "How long are you staying here?" Striker, "A day or two, and you?" Ingrid, "Well, we've been here all week and plan to leave tomorrow, but I don't have any plans until I have to be at work on Monday." Then with a wink, "I might come back here tomorrow, if you're still gonna be here." Then she looked at her watch and said, "I have to go now. We're going shopping, but we're coming back here to party. Donna reserved a private room at Grumpy's. Why don't you join us after we eat, about 8." Striker replied, "I'll be there, and I'll be here tomorrow." Ingrid smiled and left to join her friends.

Soon after Ingrid left, Striker got his bag from his car and went to book a room. The clerk said, "You're in luck, there was just a cancellation, and a second-floor oceanfront suite is available. It has a two-night minimum, but since we kept the deposit, I can book it for half price and give you the military discount." Striker, "What the hell. I'll take it." Striker got a key, paid the first night's bill and went to the suite.

After sitting on the balcony for about thirty minutes, Striker called the BOQ and left a message that he was at Fort Walton Beach, gave the motel's phone number, and that he would be back Saturday or Sunday afternoon. He had no messages, so he changed his clothes and went for a run.

It was approaching 90 degrees outside, but a breeze kept it fairly comfortable. After he put down his blanket and towel, Striker ran west towards Pensacola Beach. Two miles down the beach, he saw aircraft on their final approach into Eglin, most of which were A-10 Warthogs. They were probably returning from live bombing practice over the jungle where he had just spent three miserable nights. He decided to head back to his

279

blanket and waded into the Gulf to cool off. He swam out to the sandbar where he had body surfed, but the waves were small. After a half hour of trying to catch a wave, he went back to his blanket and took a nap. Nearly an hour and a half later, he was awakened by nearby cheering and momentarily forgot where he was. When he saw several girls playing volleyball, his memory cleared, and he went to take a shower.

At 7:30 pm, he went into Grumpy's, sat at the bar, and ordered a beer. Just as he ordered a second one, Jillian, in a red veil, led the other girls in black dresses. It was obvious from their laughter that they were ready to have a good time. Ingrid waved for Striker to follow; he paid his bill and caught up to them. Ingrid, "I see you stuck around. It must have been those hits to the head you took from the errant balls. They surely damaged your better judgment." Striker, "Not a chance. If anything, they knocked some sense into me. If they hadn't hit me, I probably wouldn't have had the courage to talk to you."

After they sat down, the waitress announced, "Happy hour closes in 10 minutes. if you want to order more drinks, do it now." Striker, "I'm OK but the ladies might want something." Donna wrote down what they wanted, gave the list to the waitress, "This should be enough for an hour or so."

Striker, "I hit the jackpot. I booked a late cancellation for an oceanfront suite for half price. If you guys want, we can move the party there." Ingrid, "That's sounds great. We only have this private room reserved for two hours. I'll check with the girls."

Donna pulled a large box out of a closet and yelled. "It's party time." She opened a trash bag and pulled out a well-endowed male love doll, put it on Jillian's lap, and introduced it as "Dick." Jillian closed her eyes and shook her head in disbelief. Donna then handed Jillian her presents, including a leather baby doll camisole, a pair of velvet-lined handcuffs, and a see-through bra and panty set. It got worse; Jillian got three "toys," which were immediately passed around the table. When the last one got to Striker, he just shook his head and quickly gave them to Donna. She strung the toys together with a red ribbon, put it around Jillian's neck, and placed the love doll in front of her. Jillian, now totally mortified, begged her friends not to take any pictures, but they ignored her and lit up the room with camera flashes.

When Jillian finished opening the presents, Ingrid told Donna about Striker's invitation to continue the party in his suite. There was a spontaneous cheer, and Donna told everyone to follow Striker to the suite while she bought more beer and wine.

The girls partied while watching the sunset. Allison, "Anyone up for a swim? It's perfect outside, and hardly anyone is on the beach." Jillian, who would do anything to get rid of the sex toy necklace, immediately said yes. Ingrid asked Striker, "Are you up for it?" He immediately agreed, and she left to change.

Striker waved at Ingrid as she walked out of the motel. He dove in the water and swam until he was in about five feet of water, then stopped as she swam toward him. When she got closer, she stood up and began to splash him. Striker noticed that she was tipsy, and now he saw she was unstable on her feet. Concerned for her safety, he led her to shallower water. Donna was attempting to ride the doll in the surf, cowgirl style. After she failed, all the other girls, except Jillian, tried to do it. Ingrid pushed the doll to her, who shook her head and repeatedly yelled "No way." The rest of the girls began to chant, "Ride 'em cowgirl." Finally, Jillian reluctantly attempted to get on the doll, but accidentally opened the doll's air valve, causing it to deflate. Jillian gave the doll Donna who yelled, "You wore him out." She put it across Jillian's outstretched arms as she walked back to the motel. It looked like a primitive funeral procession as everyone followed Jillian to the stairs. When they got to the suite, Jillian, eager to get rid of the doll, dropped it on the bathroom floor.

The games ended about midnight and a few girls left, and others fell asleep on the floor. Ingrid was half asleep in a chair next to Striker. Slurring her words, "I gotta get some sleep. Can you help me lay down somewhere?" Striker tried to help her get up, but she collapsed. Donna helped him take her to the bedroom. After they got her in bed, Donna, nearly as drunk as Ingrid, said, "I don't think I can make it to my room. OK if I lay down for a while?" Without waiting for an answer, she fell on the bed. Striker went to the living room, saw that no one was on the couch, and thought, "I guess this is my place to sleep tonight." He turned out the lights and was quickly asleep.

Striker woke up, and forgetting that the girls were in his bed, went to his bathroom. The noise of the toilet flushing woke Ingrid up. Half drunk, she whispered, "Get in bed." As he tried to gently get on the bed, Donna raised her head and said, "I think it's time for me to head to my room."

A little after sunrise, Ingrid went to the bathroom. When she returned, she took off her bikini and edged close to Striker. She rubbed his back until he stirred, then whispered, "Take off your bathing suit." He felt her naked body, removed his bathing suit and threw it on the floor. Ingrid "Did you bring any protection?" Striker, "I did. I'll be right back." After hour of lovemaking, they both went back to sleep.

Later, after they dressed, Ingrid told Striker that she was going to Jillian's house for the bridal shower. "If you want, I could be back here by five." Striker, "You bet I do." After Ingrid left, Striker cleaned up the suite and went to the beach. He found a spot, swam for about an hour, then fell asleep on his blanket.

That afternoon, Ingrid found Striker asleep on the beach, and she gently rubbed his back. When he woke up, she said, "I'd say your nap was the sleep of the innocent, but we both know that's not even close to the truth. Whatever it was, you were in a coma." Striker, obviously groggy, "Ingrid, you really caught me out cold." Twenty minutes later they went to Grumpy's. After ordering draft beers, Striker asked Ingrid how the party went. "Very well, I had a great time. Jillian's mother and grandmother were there, so she got rid of the presents somewhere; she couldn't wait for the bachelorette party to be over last night."

After taking a long walk, they cooled off in the Gulf, then slept for about an hour. When they woke, Ingrid said she wanted to take a shower. Striker gathered their belongings and followed Ingrid to the suite. Before he dropped the bag and blanket, Ingrid was in the shower; a few seconds later, he stripped and joined her, Ingrid, "We better get out of here before we get too revved up. You need to save your energy." She got out, wrapped herself in a towel and began to walk away. Striker grabbed her towel, stripping her. Ingrid giggled and led him to bed.

When they got to Grumpy's, they talked while a quartet played soft jazz. Ingrid told Striker that she hoped to see him the next weekend and Striker replied that he would be there. Soon, when people starting dancing on the beach, Ingrid said, "Let's dance." He took her hand and joined them on the sand.

In between sets they ate and had more drinks, then about 10, Ingrid said, "Unless you want this girl to fall asleep as soon as I get upstairs, we'd better leave." Striker paid the bill and led her to the suite; she kept him awake for nearly two hours.

Chapter 50

Connors, Jane, and the Moon Landing

After they ate at the Ready Room, Jane invited everyone to watch the Apollo 11 moon landing the next day. Wendy and Leah said that sounded like a lot of fun and left. Connors and Jane also left to take her parents to their motel. On the way Jane told them that she thought she was pregnant but wouldn't know for certain until she went to see her OB/GYN. Marianne began to cry, and Jeff was overjoyed. When they got out of the car, Marianne hugged her, said that she was thrilled, then hugged Connors and said he would be a great father. Jeff echoed his wife's sentiments, shook Connors hand, and said he couldn't wait to be a grandfather.

As they left her parents at the motel, Jane held Connors' hand, "I sure hope I'm right. Maybe I should've waited until after the OB/GYN appointment, but I wanted to tell them. Mom wants to be a grandma so badly, and I want to be a mother even more." Connors squeezed her hand and said, "Don't worry, you did the right thing. Your parents are almost as excited as we are."

When they got back to their apartment, Jane was tired and went to bed. Connors called Riley to see if he was set for the wedding. Riley confirmed that he was and told Connors that he would be in Pensacola Saturday until Tuesday for a training session. Connors invited him to the party, and then added that Leah was coming. Riley quickly said he would be there.

Connors went to bed but forgot to close the drapes. At dawn, the rising sun woke up Jane. She gently kissed his neck until he woke up. After making love for the better part of an hour she fell back asleep. Connors got up and went to make breakfast. Thirty minutes later he set up a spread of coffee, scrambled eggs, sausage, fruit and toast. Happy with himself, he went to check on Jane. As he walked into the bedroom he heard her in the shower, so he poked his head in and whistled. When she turned, he said, "Silly me. Instead of joining this gorgeous lady in the shower, I went and made breakfast." She laughed and replied, "You had your chance, but you chose food, silly boy." Then she playfully tossed a handful of water at him. Connors dodged the water and went back to the kitchen.

Jane came into the kitchen glowing with the radiance of an expectant mother. Connors got up from the table, hugged her and told her she was more beautiful than the day they met. Jane kissed him and said, "Flattery will get you whatever you want, Mr. Hotshot Jet Jockey, but right now this pregnant lady has to eat. You're gonna have to circle the field for a while." Connors laughed and replied, "Yes, ma'am, I read you five by five."

After breakfast, Connors went to the commissary to buy everything they needed for the cookout. When he got home, he helped Jane prepare the food, then she made a peach-blueberry cobbler that could be warmed up for dessert.

As they worked, they talked about Jake Zimmerman's emergency orders, losing his wedding party, and rescheduled wedding. Jane hoped that they would still be able to go. Connors, "Of course we will. It's terrible that it happened, but it's not unusual. A Navy life is not a normal life; they are two very different paths that rarely coincide. We will probably face a similar situation, maybe even several times. If the time comes that I have to choose between the two, there is no doubt in my mind that I'll take the path that I share with you." Jane didn't say a word as she hugged Connors.

Later, after Jane went down for a nap, Connors received a call from the Officer of the Day, who asked Connors to identify himself. Connors did, but before saying anything more, the OD told Connors that what he was about to tell him was confidential information, and he could not repeat it to anyone, including his wife. Then he distinctly stated, "This information is being relayed to you because you are known to be a personal friend of Major Stephen Pless. About 1000 today, we received a report that Major Pless was killed in a motorcycle accident early this morning. No further information is known, and nothing more will be released until a preliminary investigation has been completed. It may be sometime tonight before anything else is available. Again, until then, you will not discuss this with anyone else." He paused for a moment and ended the call. Connors said a silent prayer and went back to the kitchen,

Riley arrived about noon, followed by Wendy and Leah. After getting drinks, they all sat down to watch the Apollo 11 lander as it approached the moon. Right before it touched down, Jane's parents arrived. Her father apologized for being late and explained that he had taken a wrong turn and were briefly lost. Then he laughed and said that her mother showed him the right way to go, just as she had done for the last thirty years. Connors winked at Jane as he brought drinks for everyone. At about 3 pm they heard Armstrong announce, "The Eagle has landed"; the lunar module had safely landed on the surface of the moon.

Since the astronauts had a lot to do before they could walk on the moon, Connors grilled the steaks, and everyone ate. After everyone finished, Jane went to the kitchen to warm up the cobbler. As she did, Riley asked Connors to step out on the deck.

When they got outside, they talked about briefly about the wedding preparations, and then Riley changed the subject, "Have you seen Major Pless recently?" Connors, knowing he could not discuss what he was told, replied, "Yeah, I saw him on the beach about a week ago. He was at the Tiki Bar with people I'd never met. We spoke for a few minutes, but the band started playing, so I couldn't hear much of what he said. He did ask Jane and me to join them. I told him we had other plans, and he said that he would see us at the wedding."

Riley responded, "This morning at the Open Mess; I talked to some Marine Aviators who used to party with Pless in Nam. One of them, a RIO Instructor, told me that Pless was drinking heavily last weekend at the Pier Lounge. He was also taking bets that he could jump over the open span of the Santa Rosa Sound drawbridge on his motorcycle. Even worse, I've been told by other people that Pless has been doing some other crazy things recently, including trying to surf with his Medal of Honor around his neck and attempting to jump off a second-story balcony into a pool."

Connors, as if nothing had happened to Pless, replied, "I've heard some of the same stories. It seems like he really needs some help, but that is not part of his game plan." Connors then ended the conversation by saying, "I don't think he would listen to any advice from us. Let's go back in and watch man walk on the moon."

When Connors and Riley came back into the apartment, Jane was serving the warm peach-blueberry cobbler with ice cream. Everyone gobbled up the dessert and went back to the living room to watch more of the moon landing. Jane's mother commented about the wonderful dinner and how thankful they were that they were able to share this memorable day with everyone. Then she said that they were tired and were going back to the motel to watch the moon walk.

After her parents left, Wendy, knowing that she and Leah had a lot to drink, asked if they could crash there. Connors said it was a good idea, and the girls got their overnight bags. Shortly before 10 pm, Neil Armstrong stepped out of the lunar lander and took his first steps on the moon. After they celebrated for a few minutes, Riley decided it was a good time to leave. He knew then that he wanted to spend a lot more time with Leah.

Chapter 51

Steve Pless Dies

Early on July 20, 1969, while most of the world was watching the Apollo 11 Lunar Module flight coverage, a group of Naval aviators, including Steve Pless, were drinking heavily at the Pier Lounge. When the bar closed at 2 am, one of the aviators saw that Pless was too drunk to drive his motorcycle and offered to take him home. Pless agreed to go, but insisted on stopping at a friend's house first. While there, he convinced two of his friends to take him back to the Pier Lounge to get his motorcycle.

When they arrived at the Pier Lounge, Pless stumbled to his motorcycle, eventually started it and sped off towards the drawbridge. His two friends tried to follow him, but Pless was going too fast. As he approached the drawbridge, the warning lights came on, the alarm went off and the barricade started to come down. As Pless went under the barricade it grazed his bike and caused it to wobble. Pless continued up the rising span, went over the gap, hit the opposite span, and fell into the water. His friends rushed to the bridge, yelled at the attendant to call for help, and looked for Pless in the water. He was nowhere to be found. Emergency personnel found the body of Stephen Pless in the Sound at 10:45 CST that morning.

Connors answered the phone at 7 am the next morning. It was the VT-4 Officer of the Day, Jim Tansey, who called Connors to confirm that news of Pless' death had been released. He added that all that was known was that at approximately 3 am CST, Pless was killed in a motorcycle accident on the Santa Rosa Sound drawbridge. Immediately after the call, Connors received more calls from former classmates, squadron mates, and friends, including Riley. Connors then received a call from Marx, who said that he would notify everyone that the AOCS reunion was cancelled, but he that he hoped to see everyone at the funeral. Most of the callers were surprised that Pless was dead but not how he died; he often drove his motorcycle after a night of hard drinking.

In between calls, Connors told Jane, "Steve Pless is dead. He somehow drove his motorcycle off the Santa Rosa drawbridge early this morning. Not much else is known. I'm going to stick around here for a while to find out more. Since all the TV channels are focused on the Apollo 11 landing, I expect very little news about Pless will be reported." Jane replied, almost in a whisper, "It's sad that Pless never got the help he clearly needed. His death was totally unnecessary. All it took was for someone to intercede and maybe it wouldn't have happened. I hope it is not as bad as it looks, but I suspect he had been drinking again. Whatever happened, I hope his brilliant Marine career and his incredible courage will overshadow the self-destructive way he lived his last few months."

Then she said, "I'm going to run a few errands and have lunch with Wendy and Leah, but I'll be back so that we can go to my OB/GYN appointment." Connors, "I almost forgot, but I'll be ready to go." Jane kissed him and left.

As Jane drove away, Connors got another call from Jim Tansey. "I just got a notice from the admin office that Pless' funeral is scheduled for this Wednesday the 23rd at 1330 and there will be a viewing at the funeral home Tuesday from 1000 to 2000. Admin is asking for volunteers from our AOCS class to stand watch at his coffin. They want two guys at a time to stand watch for two hours each. I hope you don't mind, but I put your name on the list, with a note that you finished first in his last AOCS class. Admin also wants volunteers to provide an honor guard from the hearse to the chapel before and after the funeral and at the gravesite." Connors quickly responded, "Put my name on both lists, I've gotten to know Steve Pless pretty well in the last few months. If you haven't already done it, please give Riley a call. He's assigned to RIO school in Glenco, but he is here at the BOQ until Tuesday."

In Fort Walton Beach, Striker was awakened by a call from Sticky. It was 8:30 and he was asleep after a second night with Ingrid. Even though he was half asleep, it didn't take long for him to comprehend what Sticky was saying: Major Pless died in a motorcycle accident. Sticky also shared that Bulldog had called to tell him the news and check to see if he wanted to volunteer to assist at the funeral. Assuming they would want to volunteer, Bulldog said he had already put all four roommates' names on the list, but if someone couldn't do it, he would remove their names.

As Striker hung up the phone, Ingrid asked him if anything was wrong. Striker nodded and said, "It was very sad news. A legendary Marine Aviator, a Medal of Honor winner named Major Steve Pless, was killed in a motorcycle accident. At this point that's all anyone knows. My roommate called to tell me about it and to let me know that the Navy is looking for volunteers to assist at the viewing and funeral on Tuesday and Wednesday. I knew Major Pless fairly well so I'm volunteering for both." Then Striker smiled and said, "Hopefully the ceremonies will be over by Wednesday evening, so it won't affect seeing you next weekend. I need to get back to the base as soon as possible." Ingrid expressed her condolences and said she understood. As soon as they were showered and dressed, the two of them grabbed their bags and went downstairs for breakfast.

As they finished eating, Ingrid said, "I had a great time, and I can't wait until next weekend when can I see you again." Then she handed him her phone number, and asked him to call. They embraced and went their separate ways.

Striker went back to the BOQ and checked for messages. The clerk handed him two. The first was from Sergeant Major Sullivan, which said that Striker was selected to be an honor guard at both the viewing and funeral. The second message was from the base chaplain's office. He and Sticky had been selected to be sword bearers at the rescheduled Martinez/Zimmerman wedding.

No one was in the suite when Striker arrived. He took a minute to see if his choker was clean enough to wear for three formal ceremonies in two days. It wasn't. He put the choker and matching white trousers into the overnight laundry bin. After thinking about it, he decided that the safe thing to do was to buy another choker. One would not be enough for three consecutive events on hot days in July. On his way out to the Base Exchange, he left his suitemates a message that explained what he was doing.

When he got back, Sticky, Hound, and Bulldog were sitting in the suite living area discussing Pless' death and funeral. As Striker walked in, Sticky asked him if he had been selected for any of the funeral duties, adding, "We just found out that the three of us were selected." Striker, "Same here. I just got back from buying another choker at the Base Exchange. Sticky, did you get the message about the wedding being moved up?" Sticky, "Yeah, I already had my choker cleaned, but in a couple of minutes, I'm also going to buy another one, just in case."

Bulldog, "Mine's clean. I think I'll be OK with just one for the two days." Hound followed with, "Same here, I'll stay with one choker."

Before he left for the Base Exchange, Sticky asked, "Striker, have you heard anything about how Pless died? We have only heard what the news has already reported." Striker, "Not a word. I've been at Fort Walton Beach all weekend and only know what you guys know. I'm sure we'll hear a lot of rumors before the facts come out."

After Sticky left, Striker and Bulldog went to the open mess to see if they could find anyone who might have more information but had no luck, so they ate a quick breakfast. Then they went into the TV lounge to see if there was anything on the news. The lounge was full of people who were watching one of two TV's. One was a muted broadcast of the moon landing, while the other was tuned to a local station that occasionally provided updates on Pless' death. The only new thing reported was that the Sheriff's Department confirmed that Pless did go off the open bridge and into the Santa Rosa Sound and that alcohol was believed to be involved. The sheriff's spokesman then ended the update by stating that no other information would be released until the accident investigation was complete.

As they were leaving the open mess, Striker saw that he had another message. It was from Sullivan's office. All volunteers for the July 22 Special Detail must report, in dress whites without swords or sabers, to Sergeant Major Sullivan in the Admin Building Auditorium by 0700. Secondly, it ordered that all volunteers for the July 23 Special Detail must report in Class A summer whites to Sergeant Major Sullivan in the Admin Building auditorium by 0800.

At about the same time, Connors was notified by his XO that his leave was cancelled in order to report to the Special Assignments. The XO also told Connors that in addition to his orders, he and Jane would receive an invitation for the funeral, internment, and reception at the Officers' Club.

Jane got home and found Connors taking a shower. As he dressed, Jane asked if he had heard anything else about Pless' death or the funeral arrangements. Connors told her about his orders and their invitation to attend the CO's reception Connors added, "I won't be able to attend Gina's wedding. An invitation to a CO's reception is virtually the same as orders, but you can go to the wedding if you want." Jane shook her head and said, "You'll be my husband in a few days. I'll be with you at the funeral and reception and everywhere you go. I'll call Gina to let her know we won't be at the wedding." Thirty minutes later they left for her appointment.

The OB/GYN examined Jane then reviewed the results of her blood work. With a smile on his face, "Congratulations, Jane, you're going to be a mother. You're about six weeks pregnant. It looks like your due date is about mid-March. I'll give you a guide to a healthy prenatal diet and a list of the changes your body will experience over the next few months. Unless you have any bleeding, severe nausea, or other unusual symptoms, I'll see you once a month until the last couple of weeks." As soon as the doctor left the room, Jane began to cry as Connors hugged her. Then she said "You're gonna be a great daddy, I'm so happy. I can't wait to be a mother." They left the examination room, scheduled the next appointment, and left.

It was almost 6 pm and Jane had made plans to meet her parents, Wendy and Leah at Mrs. Hopkins' Boarding House. Everyone was already seated when Jane and Connors arrived. Jane was smiling as she walked towards them, but before she said a word, her mother knew the doctor had confirmed that Jane was pregnant. Wendy and Leah were trying to figure out why her mother was crying but seemed happy at the same time. Jane then said, "I'm going to have a baby." Wendy and Leah hugged Jane. Her father, now certain he was going to be a grandpa, hugged Connors, told him he couldn't be any happier, and went to hug his daughter. The rest of the evening was a time of joyful anticipation of the birth of a child. Pless' death was not mentioned.

Chapter 52

Public Viewing for Major Pless

Connors, Riley, Striker, Sticky, Bulldog and Hound and about forty other volunteers were sitting in the Administration auditorium at 06:45, July 22. At exactly 07:00, Sergeant Major Sullivan walked to the center of the stage. He was wearing his Marine Corps dress uniform with a full display of medals and awards. "Good morning gentlemen. On behalf of the Naval Aviation Training Command and the Pless family I want to thank you for volunteering for these assignments. Most of you were chosen because you have some connection to Major Pless, but all of you are here because you chose to pay your respects to one of the Marine Corps and Naval Aviation's most highly decorated combat veterans."

Sullivan spent the next half hour briefing the volunteers on the protocols that they would follow. Then he provided all of them with a written timeline that detailed their individual duties. He finished the briefing by advising the first watch team that the viewing was reserved for Mrs. Pless and her children, immediate family, and VIPs.

Later, as Sergeant Major Sullivan went into the Chapel vestibule, he saw Connors and the three Marine Captains. Sullivan, "I understand Mrs. Pless is in bad shape, so you'll need to watch her carefully. She'll be escorted by one of Pless' close friends, a Marine Major named Hughes, but may need additional assistance. The hearse should be here soon, so you need to go to your positions. I'll be in the back corner of the church."

The hearse arrived, accompanied by several black limousines carrying Mrs. Pless, her children, and members of the family. Following behind them were limousines which held the VIPs and close friends. An honor guard of enlisted Marine pallbearers slowly carried the coffin into the Chapel; Mrs. Pless and her children followed behind.

Connors watched Mrs. Pless touch the casket and weep. Suddenly she began to shake, and Hughes kept her from collapsing. Her mother took the children out of the Chapel while Mrs. Pless placed a rose on the casket and whispered a few private words to her dead husband. As she turned away from the casket, Mrs. Pless started to collapse again. Connors rushed to hold her arm as she walked to a pew. He remained with her while she spoke to her mother, then escorted her to the limousine.

As he stood watch, Striker was intimidated by the extraordinary gathering of people that passed by him; they controlled the lives of everyone in the Navy and Marine Corps. They were also the same people who sent Pless into harm's way and were now mourning his death.

When the viewing was over, the four roommates went to the Ready Room. As they waited to be served, Hound said he heard a report that the Escambia County Sherriff's Department had statements that described Pless drinking heavily the night he died; but the report also stressed that the Sheriff's Department was waiting on the County Medical Examiner to provide a final report.

Hound voiced what they were all thinking, "It looks like Major Pless thought he was invincible. After all, he walked away from a suicidal rescue mission without a scratch. His incredible bravery made him seem superhuman, but he wasn't. What a sad end to such a great Marine's life."

Chapter 53

Pless' Funeral and Interment

The evening before the funeral, Connors cooked burgers on the grill and Jane made a salad. He didn't discuss the sad events of the day; he focused on good news that they were going to be parents. Eventually Jane asked him how the viewing went. Without going into detail, Connors said, "It was tough. Mrs. Pless was overcome with emotion. I felt helpless, but I still tried to comfort her as best I could." Then pausing a few moments, "I hope I don't have to face such a gut-wrenching event anytime soon."

At 07:45 the next morning, Connors reported to Sergeant Major Sullivan who said, "Mr. Connors, as soon as everyone gets here, I'll begin the briefing." It was rough yesterday, but you handled it well and Mrs. Pless appreciated your help." Connors, "Thank you, but I only did what any other person would do in the same situation." Sullivan shared, "there's more, she remembered that you were first in her husband's last AOCS class. She requested that you be an usher instead in the honor guard. You and the other usher, Mr. Striker, will assist guests to their assigned pews. Striker finished first in my last AOCS class. I'll introduce you to him."

Striker was talking to some classmates. Sullivan, "Excuse me Mr. Striker, I want to introduce you to Mr. Connors, the other usher. When I finish the briefing, I'll explain what you'll be doing, and give you a list of invited guests and their assigned pews. Now excuse me, I'm going to start the briefing." Connors and Striker only had time to shake hands before Sullivan was asking for everyone's attention.

Less than an hour later the volunteers took the shuttle to the Chapel where Sullivan explained their duties. When that was complete, the shuttle took them to Barrancas National Cemetery where Sullivan did the same. Then they were transported to the Admin Building and given an hour to eat lunch. Before he joined his roommates Striker mentioned to Connors, "It's gonna be a long day. I'm also in a wedding tonight." Connors, "Is it the Martinez/Zimmerman wedding? How do you know Gina or Jake?" Striker, "Never met either one of them. My roommate and I volunteered to be sword bearers." Connors, "I heard about Jake's emergency orders; it sure screwed up their plans. We were supposed to go to the wedding, but we can't because we're attending the Pless reception. Maybe you know my future sister-in-law, her name is…" Before he finished, Sullivan yelled, "OK, Gents let's get on the shuttle."

Later, when Striker was in the vestibule, Connors introduced Jane to him; he noticed that she had an amazing resemblance to Wendy and wondered if they were related. He dismissed the thought when the funeral procession approached the Chapel.

Mrs. Pless and her children followed the casket into the chapel. It was a brief service after which the minister introduced the Commandant of the Marine Corps, who gave the eulogy. He began by saying, "Major Pless was the epitome of what a Marine should be, from the day he enlisted as a private to the day he received the Medal of Honor." Then he described Pless' assignments and the citations for his many awards, including the Medal of Honor. He finished by saying, "For his unending courage and service to his country, Major Pless will always be remembered as one of the greatest Marines in history." He then saluted the casket and loudly

301

stated," Semper Fi, Major Pless," Everyone in the church stood as the organist played the Marine Corps Hymn, and the pallbearers carried the casket to the hearse.

Connors and Striker assisted Mrs. Pless and her children as they walked behind the casket. The Marine escorts relieved Connors and Striker at the front door and escorted them to the limousines. At the gravesite, the Chaplain said a last few words, and the flag was removed, and handed to the Commandant of the Marine Corps. After saying a few words to her, he handed her the flag. A bugler played Taps, and a Marine rifle detail fired three volleys. Mrs. Pless dropped a rose on the casket as it was lowered into the ground. She and her children were then taken to a VIP house where they remained until the reception.

Chapter 54

Pless Funeral Reception and Striker Finds Wendy

When Connors arrived back at the Chapel, Jane was waiting on the front lawn. He kissed her and said, "I know you must be hungry; we might as well go to the Ready Room and wait." They left, found a small table in the bar and ordered appetizers.

Striker and Sticky went back to the BOQ, where they showered and changed into clean chokers. Fifteen minutes later, they went to the casual bar to get a sandwich. Five Marines in flight suits were at the bar. Sticky sat next to a Captain who was discussing Pless' death. "He was one hell of a rotor pilot, and he was willing to take on any mission, no matter how dangerous." A Major added. "I got to know Pless pretty well, even though he liked to be around his jet jockey friends more than his own squadron mates. I think he didn't want to get too close to any of us because the casualty rate for rotor heads is so damn high. That also might explain why he was a heavy drinker. After he got the MOH, he got worse; he couldn't buy a drink. It was obvious that he was in bad shape and getting worse. Knowing the chances he liked to take, I wasn't surprised how he died. No matter how his life ended, I'm proud to have served with him."

Striker, who had been listening intently to the Major, realized it was time to get to the Chapel. "Let's go, Sticky. We have to be at the Chapel in fifteen minutes." He nodded to the Major, paid the bill and left.

303

Ten minutes later, they joined the other volunteers. A Navy Lieutenant greeted them. "Hello, gents, I'm Ted Coleman, the best man. Thank you for volunteering to be here today. As you may know, everyone in the original wedding party except the groom, Jake Zimmerman, and myself, were ordered to report for an emergency deployment. We had to make a lot of substitutions in a hurry. With the assistance of the Training Command, we got everything done, including finding all of you to be sword bearers and ushers. Now, do any of you Gents know either the bride or groom?" Hearing no one respond, he continued, "In that case, I want everyone to form two lines of people across from each other with the tallest close to the front door."

Once everyone was in formation, he asked for the name of the tallest person; it was Striker. Coleman, "Mr. Striker, you will give the commands. The first two in each line will be ushers and the rest will be honor guards. The family will be seated in the first two rows of pews, and the next two rows are reserved for senior officers. The bride's family will be on the left and the groom's family on the right. When the organist begins playing, the bridesmaids and maid of honor, followed by the bride and her father will walk through the formation and into the church."

Once the honor guard was in place and guests started to go into the Chapel, Striker and the other ushers began escorting people to their pews. As he returned to greet more people, he was shocked to see Wendy waiting to be escorted. Her hair was now shoulder length, and she was prettier than he remembered.

Leah saw Striker first. "Wendy, there's the guy you met on the beach before we went to Kansas. He's coming towards us. Look at him, he looks fantastic, suntanned and in uniform. I'll tell you what, if you don't go after him, I will, he looks like a keeper." Wendy, looking at Striker, "Well, I'm sure not going to tackle him, but I hope to talk to him if he's at the reception." Striker, approaching them, said, "Wendy, what a surprise. How are you? May I escort you to a pew?" Wendy, smiling, "You sure can. Remember Leah, my roommate?" Then after hesitating for a minute, she said, "I can't believe you're here. There's got to be an explanation. Will you be at the reception?" Striker, "I will. I hope to see you there and I'll explain everything." Striker took Wendy's arm and led the two girls to a pew near the middle of the Chapel. Wendy, smiling, "Thank you, Mr. Striker, I hope to see you later." As he walked to the back of the church, Striker thought, "I'll be damned, she remembered me."

After a brief ceremony, the priest gave his blessing and introduced the newly married couple. The *Wedding March* began, and the couple walked down the aisle. As they approached the doors of the Chapel, Striker gave the order "present arms", and a canopy was formed as the tips of their swords touched. Gina cried and clutched Zimmerman's hand as they walked through the canopy.

As the wedding party and guests gathered outside the Chapel, Striker strained to see Wendy. As she got closer to him, she smiled; Striker smiled back. After the Chapel emptied, Coleman addressed the formation. He thanked them for volunteering, then reminded them that they were invited to the reception. When Coleman finished, Striker gave the command "Formation dismissed" and the sword bearers went their separate ways.

As Striker walked to his car, Sticky asked, "I saw that girl smile at you. She's a movie star. Who is she?" Striker. "Her name is Wendy. I met her on the beach right before my mother's accident. She moved here from Kansas a couple months ago and found a teaching job. We were supposed to go out the night I left to visit my mother, so I had to break the date. She left the next day to get her furniture and was gone about three weeks. I tried to call her last week but her answering service didn't work. I was going to call her this week but got involved in the funeral and wedding. I had no idea she would be here."

Sticky, "During that time, you've also been busy with a couple of other girls. You really hit the jackpot with the ladies lately. Now you've got another one in your black book. How are you going to work all of them into your schedule? Let me guess what she teaches. I know, Sex Education." Striker, "Close, Wendy's a science teacher, but I don't even know if she wants to go out with me. As far as the other girls are concerned, I'm not serious with any of them, and they know it." Sticky. "Shit, I bet the girls you're dating are all googly-eyed about you and are sitting by their phones waiting for you to call. Now, you're gonna break all their little hearts." Striker, "No way, they're big girls. They know I'm not interested in any long-term relationship. It will be the same with Wendy if she even goes out with me."

Connors and Jane were at the Pless reception. After offering their condolences to Mrs. Pless, they joined other volunteers at a reserved table. As they sat down, Jane whispered to Connors, "Mrs. Pless is amazing. I'm only in my first trimester and I'm exhausted just watching her. She's in her last trimester, due in about six weeks, with three other small children, and she was recently widowed. She's been standing there for over an hour, graciously thanking total strangers for coming. All the while, she must bear the terrible memory of her husband's awful death. She's a saint."

Connors, "She is, and on top of everything else, she's probably heard all the stories about Pless' antics, and there are a bunch of them. You must wonder how they managed to keep their marriage together. Until yesterday, I'd never met the woman, but I've been told that she adored Pless. She was a senior in high school when they met, and they got married about a month after she graduated. She was probably only eighteen and Pless was a combat hardened First Lieutenant. Now she's a widow with three kids, another on the way, and no job. She's had a lot handed to her at such a young age."

A few minutes later, the food was served, and the lights were dimmed for a film about Pless. It was almost thirty minutes long and was produced for a White House reception when Pless was awarded the Medal of Honor. It included pictures of him in military school, as an enlisted man, in AOCS, a beginning pilot, his duty stations, and his many awards. It ended with a moving segment that detailed the mission that earned him the Medal of Honor. When it was over, and the lights came on, the room erupted with applause. Mrs. Pless, obviously crying, stood and waved, then quietly sat down.

Connors and Jane mingled among the guests for another hour. At one point, Connors introduced Jane to Sergeant Major Sullivan, calling him "One of the men responsible for forging hundreds of young college graduates into Naval Officers and Aviators." Sullivan shrugged off Connors' praise by responding, "If I, or any Marine Drill Instructor, did anything, it was to make those men confident enough to accomplish anything they wanted. I'm proud to say that it worked most of the time; those guys are now fine Naval Officers. Now, before I have to go, I'll introduce Jane to Mrs. Pless."

Mrs. Pless smiled as Sullivan approached and said, "Sergeant Major Sullivan, I was looking for you. I wanted to thank you for the great job you did setting all this up. It took a huge burden off me, and I will always appreciate it." Sullivan, "It was my honor, Mrs. Pless. You have met Mr. Connors, but I'd like to introduce you to his fiancée Jane." Mrs. Pless said, "Good to meet you, Jane. Steve told me about you and Mr. Connors. I wanted to congratulate you on your upcoming wedding. Steve and I were planning to attend, but I'm not going to make it now." Jane responded. "I understand completely, Mrs. Pless. Please know that we both want to help with anything you need. Let me give you our phone number." Jane then handed Mrs. Pless one of her cards with her home number written on the back. Now, with tears welling up in her eyes, Mrs. Pless thanked Connors for his help and explained that it had been a very difficult time for her. Then she excused herself to talk to other guests.

Connors and Jane returned to their table and spoke briefly to other guests. About twenty minutes later, Mrs. Pless and her family left, so they decided it was time to leave. As they walked out, Jane asked if he thought it would be inappropriate for them to go to Gina and Jake's reception. Connors, "I think it's a great idea. We've done everything that we're supposed to do. I'm sure Mrs. Pless would insist on it."

The bride and groom had not yet arrived, so Connors scanned the ballroom to see if he saw Wendy or Leah. He didn't, but he saw Striker talking to other volunteers near the bar. He told Jane there was someone he wanted her to meet, and he led her to Striker. "I see you finished your sword bearer duty. With the viewing, funeral, and the wedding, you've had a really full schedule the last couple of days." They shook hands, and Connors introduced Jane. "This is my fiancée, Jane.

308

I may have introduced you already; it's been so busy I can't remember. Anyway, we're getting married next week. If you can make it, we'd love to have you there." Striker said he would love to come to the wedding. Again, it occurred to him that she really looked a lot like Wendy."

Jane saw Wendy and Leah talking to people on the other side of the ballroom. "There's Wendy." She said as she waved for her to join them. Seeing Wendy, Striker said to Jane, "Do you know her?" Jane said, "Sure do, she's my younger sister." Striker, "This is crazy."

Wendy hugged her sister and future brother-in-law. Then she turned to Striker and said, "This is an amazing coincidence. How do you know my family? What about Gina and Jake? Are they friends of yours?" Striker shrugged his shoulders and said, "I didn't know any of your family until the other day, and I've never met either Gina or Jake. I met Connors when we both reported for our volunteer duties. About a week ago, I saw a bulletin asking for volunteer sword bearers. I signed up, and here I am."

Wendy, "Incredibly, so am I." She smiled and said, "I'm sorry, this is my best friend and roommate, Leah. I'm sure you remember Striker?" Leah, "I sure do. You're the guy at Tiki Beach who knocked Wendy down in the surf." Striker, "Guilty, but I assure you it was a total accident. I'll admit, I'm glad it happened since I got to meet you guys." Then he remembered that Sticky was next to him and said, "I'm sorry, this is my roommate, Sticky. We went through AOCS and now are beginning flight training together." Sticky, "Happy to meet you. In case you're wondering about my nickname, Sticky is short for Steve Hickey. Some friends started calling me Sticky in college, and once I was in AOCS, Drill Instructor Sullivan found out, and no pun intended; the name stuck." Connors,

"You guys have to excuse us. I see Riley across the room. I haven't seen him for a few days, and we need to talk about the wedding. We'll see you later."

Wendy, "How is your mother? If I remember correctly, she was in a serious car accident, and you were going to Maryland to see her." Striker, "She was, her car was totaled, and, among other things, she had a compound fracture of her femur. She had a great surgeon who says she'll regain most of her mobility, but it'll take a lot of therapy. Thanks for asking. How was your trip to Kansas?"

Wendy, "It was great seeing old friends, but rough emotionally. I don't know if I told you, but my fiancé was killed in a car accident a year ago in May. We had been dating since high school and were supposed to get married in June after he graduated. After he died, I continued in school, and when I graduated, I decided to start a new life somewhere else. By coincidence, Leah had just broken up with her long-term boyfriend, so she also wanted to get away, anyplace far from Lawrence, Kansas. During college, I visited Jane in Gainesville and local beach towns several times. Leah and I decided to check out different places in Florida, loved Pensacola Beach, and decided to move here."

Wendy then described how Connors and Jane dated, broke up, and a year later asked her to marry him. She ended with, "Isn't that an amazing story?" Striker, "That is out of a fairy tale, but so is how I met you at the beach."

Sticky interrupted and asked Leah to go to the bar. As they left, Striker continued, "I tried to call you last week to apologize for stiffing you. Now that I've found you, I'd sure like to start over." Wendy, "There's no way you stiffed me, and certainly no need to apologize. I understood your

310

circumstance; you did the right thing. You belonged with your family at a time like that, not with me. We'd just met. But to answer your question, I would like to start over again, but for the next few days, I'm going to be booked." Now coyly, "I might be able to slip out for a little while one evening." Striker, "Any day this week or next is OK with me. Flight training is the only thing I can't cancel." Wendy, "I'll check with Jane, but since we're together, why not make this our first date?" Then, smiling impishly, "It would be a terrible shame for you to be all dressed up in a formal uniform and be by yourself." Striker, returning her smile, "That's the best idea I've heard all week. I'd love to be your date tonight. To make it official, I'll get us some drinks."

As Striker brought the drinks back, the band began playing *Here Comes the Bride*. Then the frontman announced, "Ladies and gentlemen. Allow me to introduce the wedding party." As they came into the ballroom, he called out their names as the groomsmen and bridesmaids. As soon as they were all in the room, he went on, "Now, let's give a hearty welcome to the newlyweds, Jake and Gina Zimmerman." Everyone stood and applauded.

When the couple reached the dance floor, the frontman announced. "Now, ladies and gentlemen, Jake and Gina will enjoy their first dance as husband and wife." Then he began to sing *Unchained Melody* almost as well the popular recording. When the song was finished, the band kept playing a set of other romantic ballads. The bride and groom danced with their parents and were soon followed by the wedding party.

Finally, the frontman announced, "Jake and Gina would now like to invite everyone to join them on the dance floor." Striker asked Wendy if she would like to dance. She quickly replied, "I sure would." He took her hand as they joined everyone on the floor. The band played *I Can't Take My Eyes Off You*, followed by several Motown and Rolling Stones hits before taking a break.

Wendy was glowing as she walked off the dance floor, "I love to dance. Thank you." Striker apologetically, "Well, I admit I'm not the best dancer in the world, but I managed to avoid stepping on your feet or knocking you down. Would you like another drink?" Wendy, "That sounds great."

When Striker returned, Wendy and Leah were with Sticky, who said. "Striker, I saw you out there shaking your tail feathers. You looked like Mr.Bojangles." Striker, "I'll take that as a compliment. Most of the time, I'm compared to Frankenstein when he got the electric shock." Sticky. "Come to think of it, there is a strong resemblance," Leah said, "You shouldn't talk, Sticky, you're not exactly Fred Astaire. You looked like a three-legged cat on ice." Sticky, "Ouch, you really know how to hurt a guy."

Just then, the music began again. "Let's go," Wendy said as she grabbed Striker's hand and led him to the dance floor. The band began a set that included more Rolling Stones, Blood Sweat and Tears, and Credence Clearwater Revival. At the end of *You Put a Spell on Me*, the lead singer announced "Ladies and Gentlemen, thank you for being here tonight; we hope you enjoyed our music. This next song will be our last, but Gina and Jake want to remind you that the bar will remain open until 11, and you are welcome to stay and enjoy the rest of the evening." Then, the band ended with a prolonged version of Percy Sledge's *When a Man Loves a Woman*. Wendy put her arms around Striker's neck, and he wrapped his arms around her waist. As he did, he thought, "I may have to rethink not having any long-term relationships. This girl is special." The music stopped, and Wendy said, "Let's go find Jane."

312

Chapter 55

Striker Begins Flight Training

Jane signaled Wendy to join her, since Connors found an empty table. As Jane sat down, Striker asked if anyone wanted a drink and went to the bar. As soon as he left, Wendy asked Jane about her schedule for the next few days. Jane, smiling, "Let me guess, you want to go out with Striker. It's obvious; you have a glow on your face that I haven't seen in a long time. I don't blame you. Striker is very charming, and I've noticed a lot of girls looking at him. To answer your question, there are only a few things that need to get done, most of which I can do except for the bridal shower on Thursday and the rehearsal dinner on Friday. The evenings are all open, so don't worry about me. Go for it, have a good time."

When Gina and Jake came by to thank everyone for coming, Connors introduced Striker and Wendy. Gina, "I know, Wendy. I met Leah and her at the Ready Room a couple of months ago. I showed them around town and warned them about the predatory habits of the sex-starved new ensigns and second lieutenants who would surround them everywhere." Striker, laughing, said, "I resemble that remark, but, in my case, meeting Wendy was the result of a totally unplanned accident. I didn't see her and knocked her down when I was bodysurfing." Gina, "Yeah, yeah, yeah, I believe you, but I never underestimate the extremes young Naval Officers will go to meet girls, especially those as pretty as Wendy." Then Wendy added, "Well, there is always the possibility that I saw him bodysurfing, so I purposely got in his way and took the hit so that I could meet him." Connors jumped in, "On behalf of

313

all Naval and Marine officers, I have to say that most of us have honorable intentions, but some may be overcome by primal instincts that are the natural result of being subjected to long periods of celibacy. After all, we are only human." Jake added, "Well said; I believe the honor of being an officer has been kept intact. Striker, it's confirmed; you behaved as an officer and a gentleman the day you met Wendy. Your behavior was again apparent when you volunteered to help at our wedding. You and the others saved the day for Gina and me. Thank you." Gina added, "Yes, Striker, thank you so much." Now giggling, "By the way, if I hadn't known Jake, I would've made sure that you knocked me down at the beach that day." Everyone at the table exploded in laughter as Striker turned red. When the laughter ended, Jake and Gina thanked everyone for coming and excused themselves so they could visit other guests. A few minutes later, Jane said she was tired and left with Connors.

Now alone with Striker, Wendy told him what Jane said, but she would feel better if she didn't plan anything until Friday. She added, "Jane was being way too nice." Then she continued, "One of Connors' friends is having a party on the beach after the rehearsal dinner. I was planning to go with Leah, but maybe you could be my date. The dinner is in the small ballroom, but it'll be over by 8. Does that sound OK?" Striker, "That's sounds great. I start flight training tomorrow and I'll have a boatload of reading to do every night, not including the two days I've already missed. Friday evening is perfect. I'll eat here, then look for you. If there are changes, here's the number of the BOQ." He wrote the number down on a napkin and handed it to her.

Wendy, "It's a date. By the way, I hope to have my phone working by tomorrow. If it isn't, call the resident manager's office and she'll get me the message; Here's the number." After she handed it to him, Striker looked at his watch, "Wendy, as much as I'd like to stay longer, I have to get back to the BOQ and get some sleep. It's been really busy the last couple of days." Wendy said she was also ready to leave but needed to find Leah. She scanned the room and saw her talking to Riley near the bar. "There she is." She led Striker by the hand across the room. As they approached, Leah said, "I was just going to come get you, Wendy. Are you ready to go?" Leah said she was, then Striker asked Wendy, "Can I walk you to your car?" Wendy, "You sure can," Striker waved at Sticky to meet him at the car.

On the way to her car, Wendy stopped and faced Striker. "I had a wonderful time, easily the best time that I've had in many months. Thank you." Before Striker could say a word, she kissed him on the cheek and quickly turned toward her car. As she walked away, she said, "I'll see you here, Friday at 8, don't forget." Striker waving, "Not even a small chance of that happening."

As Wendy got into her car, Striker got into his. Sticky, already in the passenger seat, blurted out, "You hit another home run tonight, my man. The rich just get richer," Striker, "You might be right; I have to make some decisions here pretty quick."

Halfway home Leah broke the silence, "Wendy, it's obvious Striker made a big impression on you tonight. I haven't seen you pay so much attention to a guy since we were in college. "Wendy, "That's because I haven't met any guy who really interested me since Roger died. Striker does have a way about him. He brought out emotions I haven't felt in a long time. We did seem to be on the same wavelength, but it might not last long." Leah, "I'm willing to bet a month of cleaning the apartment that it does. He couldn't keep his eyes off of you.

Believe me, Wendy, if you want him, Striker will be around for a long time."

Striker was out of bed and in the shower by 0445 the next morning. While he was putting on his uniform, Sticky was up and in the shower. At 0500 both of them were eating breakfast, and then left for VT-10. As Sticky drove, Striker tried to remember what the 16 weeks of NFO training would include. If he was correct, the first half of the program was basically the same as pilot training. Then the next eight weeks shifted to at least 50 hours of in-flight training, including navigation, radio communication, unusual attitude flight, gunnery, and field carrier landing practice. According to the VT-10 handbook, the aircraft they would be flying included the C45 Navigator, also known as the SNB "Secret Navy Bomber", T-2C Buckeye, T33B Shooting Star, and T39 Sabreliner.

The VT-10 Executive Officer gave each of them a student manual and curriculum. Then he pointed out the sections of the curriculum they had missed and told them to review it in their time off. When he finished, he showed them around the building and took them to the classroom where their squadron mates were already seated. Striker sat near the front of the room, while Sticky headed to the rear.

Soon, a Navy Lieutenant named Flanagan, entered the room, "At ease, Gents, please take your seats." After a brief introduction, he began a lengthy slide show of US and foreign aircraft. As each aircraft was shown, he pointed out the aircraft's specifications and capabilities. He emphasized that the primary mission of an NFO is to find and destroy bogeys. Then he said, "Remember Gents, two sets of eyes are always better than one, so always be scanning around your aircraft, especially here in the training command where there are hundreds of launches every hour. Think about this; more Naval

Aviators are killed in training than in combat. It is a dangerous job, so be alert at all times."

After nearly three hours of lecturing, Flanagan announced, "Gents. We're stopping a little early this morning, and instead of classroom instruction this afternoon, you will be flying. It'll be an introduction to Point-to-Point navigation, also called Dead Reckoning. You will be in groups of three students in C-45s, sometimes called the Bug Smasher or Secret Navy Bomber. In the ready room is a list of this afternoon's flights, showing the time of your flight and the assigned aircraft. In addition to students, each flight will have an instructor, a pilot and a copilot. As soon as this class is dismissed, each of you will be issued flight suits and helmets at the equipment shop. Once you get your gear, you're free to eat lunch. Report back to the ready room, in flight suits, by 1200. Dismissed."

After changing into flight suits and eating at the casual bar, they returned to the VT-10 ready room. The schedule indicated that Striker was flying with Sticky and 2nd Lieutenant Greg Manning. Fifteen minutes later, Lt. Flanagan handed out instruction manuals, dead reckoning calculators and charts. Then he explained that the instructor would describe how to identify landmarks, determine airspeed, ground speed, heading, and chart a course.

At 1300, a Navy Lieutenant came into the room and directed Striker, Sticky, and Manning to follow him. He led them to a C-45 and told them to climb in and strap themselves into any seat except the one in front. As soon as they did, he stood facing them and introduced himself. "I'm Lieutenant Cliff Starling. I'm an F-4 RIO. I've made two tours in WestPac and am in line for a third. I'll be your flight instructor when we begin regular flights later in the program. Today is about familiarizing you with the aircraft you're going to be flying in.

Your pilot is Lt. Hank Donaldson, an F-4 pilot and the guy I flew with during both tours in Nam. After next week he'll be rotating to primary jet training for a few weeks, and before we both go back to the fleet, he'll be teaching people how to fly the F-4 Phantom. The copilot today is Lt. Tony Rosado, another old friend and an A-6 Intruder pilot. When Donaldson leaves, Rosado will become the pilot and another copilot will be assigned. Gents, today's flight will be educational as well as fun. Hopefully what you learn today will be helpful when the serious business starts. So, welcome aboard."

The pilot and copilot climbed into the aircraft, introduced themselves and welcomed the students aboard. Then the copilot detailed the flight plan, "Gents, after we launch, we'll head northwest through Alabama, climb to 5500 feet, then change course toward southern Georgia. On the final leg we'll fly down the coast into northern Florida, then northwest over central Florida and back to Sherman Field. Today we'll be following Visual Flight Rules, so you Gents need to be vigilant about scanning the area around us for other aircraft. You can see an array of instruments on the console in front of each seat. During the flight, Mr. Starling will explain each instrument. As soon as I finish, plug your helmet earphones into the indicated jack near your seat, and listen carefully to the radio transmissions. When we reach altitude, Mr. Starling will tell you to switch to channel four, and will begin his instruction. The weather today looks great, so I expect a smooth flight, but unless told otherwise, remain strapped in. If everything goes as planned, we will be in the air about three hours. Enjoy the flight, Gents."

As he waited for the engines to start, Striker realized how hot it was in the aircraft. The outside temperature was almost ninety, but in the close quarters of the cabin, it had to be above a hundred degrees. He knew that the Nomex flight suit was a safety requirement, but gloves and steel-toed flight boots made it extremely uncomfortable. Knowing that the vintage aircraft did not have air conditioning, he expected the flight to be almost unbearable.

Once the pilot was in his seat, the copilot fired up the engines. Striker was startled by the explosive sounds the engine made, beginning with a smoky sputter, interrupted by what sounded like cannon fire, then gradually turned into a noise louder than a train engine. Then the left engine started with the same sequence of smoky misfires and gradually joined the right engine in an ear-splitting roar that made yelling the only discernable voice communication. Striker, thinking to himself, "What a joke, the 'Secret Navy Bomber.' A blind man would recognize the roar of this old bird from fifty miles away."

As soon as the engines warmed up, the tower cleared the flight for takeoff and the aircraft began its roll to the assigned runway. At the numbers, the pilot stopped and revved the engines up to full power and headed down the runway. Less than 45 seconds later the aircraft was airborne and on a heading toward northwest Alabama. As they turned and climbed, Striker scanned the sky around him for other aircraft. Seeing nothing close, he spent a few minutes watching the beautiful Gulf of Mexico slowly disappear from sight. He couldn't wait to begin flying over the azure blue water, especially along the glistening white shoreline.

His thoughts were interrupted as he felt the cabin temperature quickly drop. Then he remembered that since the aircraft was staying below 10,000 feet, the vents could be open, allowing outside cold air into the cabin. So now it was getting chilly, and he appreciated wearing the flight suit and gloves. It was also apparent that the open vents increased the engine noise significantly, making normal voice communication impossible.

As they approached 5000 ft. and leveled off into smooth flight, Starling unbuckled his harness and stood in the gap behind the cockpit and the front seats. "Gents, welcome to Naval Aviation. I'm going to spend about two hours familiarizing you with this aircraft and the navigation aids you will be using during your training." Then without warning, the copilot, followed by the pilot, came out of the cockpit and stood next to Starling. "First lesson, Gents, what are you going to do?" Then the aircraft turned slightly to the right and started to dive. Sticky, who was sitting in front of Starling, unbuckled his harness, stood up and screamed, "Holy Shit." As he started to move toward the cockpit, the aircraft bounced, and Sticky suddenly stopped and vomited on the floor.

Striker, who was sitting on the other side of the aisle, unbuckled and rushed into the cockpit as fast as he could. He got into the copilot's seat and, not knowing exactly what to do, gently pulled back on the yoke until the aircraft resumed straight and level flight. After what seemed to be an hour, the copilot tapped Striker on the shoulder and said, "OK Mister Striker, I'll take the con. You did well." Striker, feeling an enormous sense of relief, returned to his seat. As he did, the pilot said, "Good job, Mr. Striker," and returned to his seat.

Starling found some rags and tossed them to Sticky, who began to clean up his mess. While Sticky worked, Starling said, "Gents, being a Naval Aviator is all about making the right decision, all the time, no matter the circumstance. As you've just experienced, things happen quickly in an aircraft. Most of the time you will have less than ten seconds to make the right decision. Gents, the wrong decision is almost always fatal. As today's exercise just demonstrated, there is no predicting when the shit will hit the fan, especially in combat. When you are in a high-performance aircraft on a dangerous mission, things happen even faster. Time becomes your enemy. So, as you have been told a thousand times, pay attention to details, it will save your life."

Starling paused while Sticky finished cleaning, then began again, "Gents, during the rest of the flight I'm going to teach you the basics of Dead Reckoning navigation. Pay close attention, you will begin navigation exercises next week. By the way, we were never in any real danger today. This old bird would have eventually righted itself and kept flying until it ran out of fuel."

For the next two hours, Starling taught the rudiments of Dead Reckoning. Then he walked them through several point-to-point navigation problems, including the last leg of their flight. As they got closer to Sherman Field, Starling completed his instruction and told everyone to switch back to channel one and listen to the communication between the flight crew and tower as the aircraft landed.

Once parked on the tarmac, Starling told the students to take a break in the ready room. Before Sticky got to its entrance, Starling told him to get a mop and bucket from the crew chief, saying. "You made the mess in the aircraft cabin, now go clean it up. The crew chief will show you how to do it properly." Sticky, looking slightly embarrassed, quickly responded, "Yes, Sir." and walked quickly to the crew chief's shop. Striker, overhearing the conversation, said quietly to Manning, "I have to watch this. Sticky's got latrine duty. I haven't seen him clean anything since AOCS ended. He's basically a slob." Then the two of them hooted and whistled as Sticky got back in the Bugsmasher and did what he was told.

When he finished, Striker, Manning and Starling whistled and applauded. Sticky came to attention, took a bow and saluted. Then in perfect AOCS style, he marched back to the crew chief shop carrying the mop on his shoulder like a rifle, placed it a closet, made an about face and saluted again.

Chapter 56

Connors and Jane's Rehearsal Dinner

It was Thursday, July 31, two days before the wedding. Jane went to her bridal shower hosted by Wendy at her apartment. At the same time, Riley, the best man, took Connors and several other friends to Trader Jon's Strip Club for a bachelor party. The strippers were part of an old-fashioned Burlesque show, complete with a 10-piece jazz band. They were listed on the program as the fourth act, which included a comedian who told bawdy jokes, a Can-Can line up of scantily clad dancing girls, and a female magician who made her clothes disappear.

The marquee stripper that night was Marie, the Flame of Florida. Marie was popular with Naval Aviators, including John McCain when he was stationed in Pensacola. McCain was shot down in October 1967 and had been a POW ever since. Connors knew about McCain's affair with Marie. When she strutted on stage, it was obvious why McCain had been attracted to her; she was gorgeous.

While Connors and his friends were watching Marie strip, so were Striker and his roommates in another part of the theater. Sticky convinced everyone that they had to see Marie take her clothes off. Unfortunately, Sticky, feeling his beer, was unhappy with how Marie was stripping. He repeatedly yelled. "Come on, Marie, speed it up, I didn't pay to see you shake your ass." When she ignored him, he started yelling louder and more often. Then he screamed, "McCain must have been drunk when he first saw you, you can't strip worth shit." Unfortunately for Sticky, the manager heard him and was not happy; Marie brought the customers in. When Sticky continued to heckle her, the manager told the security staff, an off-duty Pensacola police officer, to escort Sticky out.

As Marie continued her act, the police officer tapped Sticky on the shoulder, told him he had to leave and pointed to a nearby exit. Sticky was sober enough to know he didn't want to get into an argument with the cop, so he reluctantly complied and walked toward the door. When he looked closer at the diminutive cop, he realized he was only about 5 feet 6 inches tall, and Sticky said, "Hey Officer. When did Pensacola start hiring midgets?" The cop, not amused, said "You a smart ass, son?" Sticky, not sober enough to keep quiet, replied, "No sir, but I gotta know. Are you related to Barney Fife? You look just like him." The cop, now angry, radioed for backup. Almost immediately, a much larger cop was there and the two of them grabbed Sticky and rushed him out the door. Seeing what was happening, Striker yelled, "Come on guys, let's get Sticky home before he ends up in jail."

Striker followed behind the police as they escorted Sticky out of the building, and noticed Connors was there. As soon as Striker got outside, he saw that his roommates went into the alley to pee, so he followed them. Then he heard the cop yell, "I got 'em now." As the roommates left the alley, the smaller cop drew his gun and yelled, "Stop, put your hands above your heads, turn around and get up against the wall. Don't move a muscle. You're all under arrest for Indecent Exposure, Urinating in Public."

Surprised, the four roommates followed the cop's orders as if he were a Drill Instructor. The cops frisked them, ordered them to put their hands behind their backs and handcuffed them. A paddy wagon soon arrived, and the arresting cops began to put Sticky and his roommates in it. Connors, suspecting trouble, had followed them out and yelled, "Officer, where are you taking my friends?" The smaller cop answered, "Get back in the theater sir or you'll be going with them." Connors, unconcerned said, "I have a perfect right to stand here and ask where you are taking them. I intend to assist them get a lawyer, which is their absolute right. If you wait a few seconds, I will introduce you to him, he's on his way out of the building." A few seconds later a tall man with a handlebar mustache walked out of Trader Jon's. He looked directly at the small cop and said, "Officer, my name is Jerry Fishman, I'm an attorney who represents a lot of clients who allege the police have overstepped their authority. Now before you go any further with this arrest, I want to remind you that simple urination in public is only a misdemeanor in Escambia County. More importantly, the courts have consistently ruled that arresting people for a simple misdemeanor with drawn weapons or using handcuffs is grounds for a civil liability action against you personally. I'm sure you know, without aggravating circumstances, the proper procedure is for you to issue each of these gentlemen a misdemeanor civil citation, which carries a fine of twenty-five dollars. My friend here witnessed the entire incident and assures me that these gentlemen may have urinated in public, but there is no evidence that they, in any way, resisted arrest or created a situation which required you to draw your weapons, to handcuff them, or to lock them up. If you proceed with this arrest, I will be in court tomorrow filing a civil suit for an undisclosed amount from each arresting officer. You have a decision to make. Either issue them civil citations, as your procedures require, or I'll see you in court."

The larger cop looked at the smaller one, and said, "He's right Billy. I'm not going to risk my pension by perjuring myself testifying that these guys resisted arrest or some other shit. Let it go, just give them the citations and we'll get the hell out of here. It's over." Billy, now looking defeated, shook his head, then turned towards the paddy wagon and yelled, "I've decided to give them a break, let 'em out." As Striker and the others got out, the two cops unlocked their handcuffs and told them to wait by the paddy wagon. Then, in an effort to save face, Billy told them, "OK, I've decided to give you all a break and issue you civil citations. You each have a twenty-five dollar fine, which must be paid to Escambia County within thirty days. If you have not made payment within thirty days, the court will issue a warrant for your arrest." Then the two police officers filled out the citations and gave them to Striker and his friends. Without saying another word, the two officers went back to Trader Jon's.

Striker and his roommates thanked Connors and Fishman, and Striker asked Connors why he helped. Connors responded, "I've been around this town long enough to know that Naval personnel are often caught up in phony police scams, especially coming out of bars. Jerry was my college roommate and is here with other friends for my bachelor party. Earlier we actually were talking about some of the scams that have happened in town, and this is one of them. A guy gets drunk, is thrown out of a bar, then a rent-a-cop follows him out, looking for him to do something illegal, like peeing in an alley. If the guy does pee, the cop locks him up, gives him the name of a lawyer who handles these cases. After he's released, the guy goes to the lawyer who tells him that if he is convicted, he could face a court martial. For a fee, usually at least $500, he'll get the charges reduced or dropped. The guy pays the lawyer, who goes to the prosecuting attorney knowing that 95% of these cases are reduced to a civil citation or dropped. Either way the lawyer gets paid and, under the table, he gives the cop a kickback for referring the guy to him. Unless there are other things involved, the Navy never pursues the case any further, even if the guy is found guilty." Fishman added, "Connors is right, but don't be embarrassed. These kinds of cases happen in every military town in the country, and Pensacola is definitely no different." Striker again thanked them, asked Fishman if they owed him anything, and he said no, he was glad he could help. Striker told Connors he'd see him at the wedding and left with his roommates.

As they walked to the car, Striker said, "Sticky, it was fun for a while, but next time Connors and his buddy won't be there to save our asses." Sticky followed with, "Yeah I'm sorry I got you guys caught up in all that." He hesitated for a few seconds then said, but you must admit, McCain can really pick his women." Striker could only shake his head as he got into the car.

The next day Striker spent most of the morning catching up on what he had missed at VT-10 during the ceremonies for Pless. At about 2 pm, he decided to take the last training manual with him to Tiki Beach. As he lay in the warm sun attempting to read, he fell asleep and didn't wake up until after 4 pm. "So much for that idea. I might as well head back to the BOQ. I have to call Ingrid to let her know that I won't be seeing her this weekend. I don't know what to say but I don't want to lie to her. Ingrid just isn't someone that I want to get serious with, especially since I'm getting to know Wendy." As soon as he got to the BOQ he went to use a phone. Before he dialed her number, he rehearsed what he would say, "Ingrid, I won't be able to make it this weekend. A good friend of mine is getting married the same day as Jillian. I wasn't going to go, but recently he's done a lot for me, so I feel that I should go. I hope you are not too upset, and I apologize for not letting you know earlier. If I don't talk to you before your trip to Europe, have a great time. Take care, Striker."

He then took a deep breath and dialed her number. To his relief, no one answered, and he left the message he rehearsed. As he hung up the phone, he said to himself. "That's one down. Now, if things go the way I hope with Wendy, I'll call Terry in a week or so." Feeling better, he took a forty-five-minute run. When he finished, he cleaned up and headed to the Ready Room.

As he drove, Striker saw large storm clouds forming in the southwestern sky. He noted to himself that if the storm turns out to be as bad as it looks, there wouldn't be any beach party that night. An hour later, the storm hit Pensacola with wind gusts exceeding 50 mph and torrential rain. As he watched the storm, he said to himself, "Well, it looks we're not going anywhere."

Later, as he was finishing a beer, Wendy and the entire wedding party entered the bar. Striker waved and Wendy made her way through the crowd to him. As she sat down, she said, "Well, I'm here, but as you can see, I'm not alone. When the storm broke, everyone decided to wait it out here. Most of them were supposed to go to the same party, but I'm sure it was cancelled." Striker replied, "Yeah, I watched the storm as it covered the sky. It looked like it was going to be a bad one, and it is. I'm just happy we didn't plan to meet at the beach. By the way, I see Jane standing with Connors over by the bar. I'd like to give our table to them. They shouldn't have to stand the night before their wedding. OK with you?" Wendy, "Absolutely, what a nice thing to do."

As he approached Connors, Striker said, "First of all, thanks again for your help last night. Can I offer you my table?

You can see Wendy sitting there by the window. I'm sure you guys are tired, so please take it." Connors looking at Jane, responded, "Normally, I would say there's no need, but I know Jane is tired, so we'll take it." Wendy gave her seat to Jane, who said, "Thank you, I really needed to sit down. I've been standing up almost all day and my legs are killing me. If you can possibly find a couple of chairs, please join us." Connors said, "Before I sit down, can I buy you guys a drink?" Striker said he'd love a beer and Wendy wanted a Rum and Coke.

When Connors left, Striker searched around the bar and found two more chairs. When he got back, Connors had returned with the drinks. Striker gave a chair to Wendy, then sat down and asked her if she had heard about the night before at Trader Jon's. Wendy looking at him with a smile, "You mean at the strip club? I did hear that four Naval Officers were too rowdy, got thrown out and almost locked up for indecent exposure. Yes, I sure did hear about it. Were you one of them?"

Striker, sheepishly, "Well, yes, but it was Sticky's idea. He wanted to see Marie, the Flame of Florida, John McCain's ex-girlfriend. She's the star of the show." Wendy, seeing him starting to squirm, "I'm sure you went there kicking and screaming, right?" Striker, knowing he was trapped, "Uh, not exactly, I did agree to go, but only if I was driving everyone home." Wendy, obviously enjoying his suffering, "But you certainly covered your eyes while Marie, the Flame took her clothes off, didn't you?" Striker, now desperately looking for an out, "Uh, no. I was too busy applauding her performance." Wendy, "I'm sure that was because you thought she was a good dancer, right?" Striker, shaking his head enthusiastically said, "Yes, absolutely, she could be in the Bolshoi Ballet. She's really graceful." Wendy just laughed, and Striker, knowing he was busted, didn't say another word.

Wendy continued, "Striker, I have to tell you, Connors told me all about what happened last night. He said he witnessed the whole thing. I just had to tease you about it. I'm not mad; after all, Connors, my soon to be brother-in-law, was there too. From what he said, it looks to me like the whole thing was a set-up. I'm glad his friend the lawyer, recognized what was happening and was able to stop it."

Striker, looking at Connors, added, "Yeah, Jerry Fishman saved our butts. Be sure to thank him again for me if I don't see him tomorrow. The bottom line is Sticky was clearly out of line, but the cop was worse by taking advantage of the situation. Thanks." Connors, "No problem. That kind of thing happens all the time. It's inevitable that some local cops, and lawyers, will take advantage of them."

Wendy laughed and said, "I have a confession to make. Leah and I went to Trader Jon's when we first moved here. It was a big mistake. Gina told us that next to the Ready Room, it was the most popular place in town to meet young officers, but she meant the bar. We didn't know there was a strip show there too. We went in thinking it was something like Rosie O'Grady's. We walked in late, between acts. When the next act started, a magician, we thought it was a regular magic act. Well, it wasn't. Her act was to make her clothes disappear, all of them. She got totally naked; we were mortified. We left, even though Gina was right, the place was packed with guys, but they weren't there to meet girls, that's for certain." Striker laughed as he replied, "You should have stayed to see Marie. She could really dance." Wendy playfully hit his shoulder and said, "I'm sure you never even noticed that she had legs, much less notice her dancing. You were focused on her other moving parts." Striker shook his head and said, "Oh, no, I sit here an innocent man."

As the storm was subsiding, Leah, who had been talking to other bridesmaids, came over to Wendy and asked, "The storm is almost over and I'm ready to leave. Are you coming with me, or is Striker bringing you back?" Striker, "I was hoping to take you home but if you want to go with Leah, I understand. Wendy, "I was planning to stay, and Striker would take me home." Striker, "That's what I hoped."

Twenty minutes later Jane was tired, and she and Connors left. Alone with Striker, Wendy said, "OK Jonathan Striker, tell me all about yourself." He thought for a minute then began, "I may have told you some of this before, so I apologize if I repeat anything. My name is Jonathan Emmett Striker, named after my father's brother Jonathan, who was killed in WW2, and Emmett, which is an old family name. I was born into a Navy family in 1947, in Lexington Park Maryland, which is still my home of record. We moved a lot when I was a little kid, all around the US and Europe, including Corpus Christi, San Diego, Virginia Beach, Mississippi, Rota, Spain and back to Pax River Naval Air Station in Lexington Park. I went to five elementary schools but only one high school, St. Charles, a Catholic school in Lexington Park. In high school I ran track all four years and was in the marching band a couple of years. Even though I had partial scholarships to two or three small colleges, I went to the University of Maryland in College Park. I had visited one school and planned to go there, but after staying a weekend at Maryland, I fell in love with the place." He stopped to smile, "Some say it was because it had 15,000 coeds." He continued, "I was a late admission, so I didn't get many classes I wanted, including Physical Education. Then until the second semester of my junior year, every registration was alphabetical, and I never got all the classes I needed. I ended up taking a lot of classes I liked, mainly English and Political Science. To make it worse, not one of the PE classes

I was assigned interested me, so I never went to any of them, four semesters in a row. As a result, when I reached senior status, I had enough credits to graduate but not enough for a double Major. When I talked to my advisor, he told me if I wanted to have a double Major, I needed twenty-one more Major credits. Since I did want a double major, I would probably take five years to graduate. I told him that I was in no hurry to graduate, but when my advisor realized I had four flags in PE, he asked if I had a problem with exercise. I said I didn't; I ran four or five miles several times a week. At that point he told me that I had to complete a PE class in order to graduate. As it happened, at the next registration, I finally got a class I was very interested in, Track and Field."

"At the same time all this was going on, the University changed the class attendance rules to allow unlimited class cuts, or so I thought. I took advantage of it; I cut a lot of classes that semester, but I still maintained about a 3.3 GPA. One of the classes I cut was PE, but only four times. About two weeks before final exams began that semester, my PE instructor called me to his office. He told me that I had four cuts, more than the maximum three cuts PE allowed. I told him that I knew that, but since the University eliminated the cut limit, I was OK. The instructor was quiet for a moment and then said I should have read the entire new rule. PE was exempted from the change and the limit was still three cuts. Since I had four, I failed the class. Then he dropped a bomb on me when he said since I now had five failures in PE, I would be automatically expelled from the University. It was an academic requirement; there was nothing he could do. If I wanted to try to appeal, I should talk to the Department Chair."

"I didn't say a word and went straight to the PE office to see the Chair of the Department. Both he and the Dean of Men told me the same thing. The decision would stand. I was out. I immediately left the campus, went to a local Navy Recruitment Office and enlisted. Then to make a long story short, because there were so many enlistments, boot camp was delayed for up to a year. After I passed all the tests and the physical, I was sworn in and issued uniforms, and then was sent home to await orders."

"Then, about three weeks after I enlisted, I got a letter from the Chancellor of the University. To my horror, the letter said my expulsion was overruled, along with a dozen other students who were expelled for the same reason. It turns out that someone appealed on the basis that the regulation had not been properly explained and advertised, and the Chancellor agreed. I was immediately readmitted. Now to my surprise, I had a C in PE, but needed to repeat the other four classes I failed."

"Even though I was in the Navy, I repeated those twelve credits in summer school and got a 4.0. Then I registered for twenty-one credits in the fall semester. In early October of that year, I got orders to report to Andrews' Naval Wing on November 15. When I reported, my CO reviewed my record, including my transcript, and asked me what I wanted to do in the Navy. Before I answered, he noticed my grades and that I was close to graduation and asked me if I wanted to be a Naval Aviator. Without any hesitation I said yes and asked what I had to do. He detailed the application process, then handed me a contract and an application, and I signed them both. He cancelled my orders to report for duty and told me to go back to school. As I was leaving, he said I would hear the result in a few weeks. In December, I graduated with a double Major and was accepted to AOCS. Almost a year since coming to Pensacola, I was commissioned, began flight training, and I'm here with you. Now it's your turn."

333

She smiled and said, "Compared to yours, my life has been pretty dull, but here it is: My full name is Marianne Elizabeth Gwendolyn Carmody. I was named after my two grandmothers, but since my mother uses Marianne, my parents called me Gwen. When I was a little kid, I was fascinated by the story of Peter Pan, and I wanted it read to me over and over. I soon could tell the whole story and loved everything to do with Wendy Darling, the girl in the story. After a while, it drove my mother nuts, and she even started calling me Wendy. I loved it, and never answered to Gwen again."

"Now back to the beginning, I was born and raised in Kansas, lived in the same house in Overland Park, where my parents still live. My first move was to Lawrence, Kansas for college. Other than those two places I have never lived anywhere else other than here in Pensacola. In fact, I had never been out of Kansas until I first visited Jane in Gainesville two years ago. Now, let me tell you more about my late fiancé, Roger. We met in my junior year in high school and became friends on the track team. I already had a boyfriend at the time, and Roger was very popular; he dated a lot of girls I knew. We didn't date until over a year later when I broke up with my boyfriend. I was shocked when he asked me to the Senior Prom. After that, we dated straight through college. He went to Kansas on a track scholarship, and the next year, I followed him there. Four years after we met, we got engaged. A month before he was supposed to graduate and almost two months before we were supposed to get married, a drunk driver killed him when he was coming back to school. I was totally devastated, but with the help of my family and friends, especially Leah, I stayed in school. I graduated a year later and in June I moved here. I got a job teaching school and I start in about two weeks, so here I am."

Then she continued, "I have to tell you that it has been a really rough year; I was a mess. When I went back to Kansas, one of the things I did was go to his grave and tell him I was going on with my life. I even gave my engagement ring and some of his things back to his mother. I left Kansas with the intent of never going back. Now I'm almost totally healed, but I need a little more time. Please don't be frightened away, Striker. You're the first guy that I've been really interested in since Roger died, but I need to take it slow. I hope you understand, but I really want to continue seeing you."

Striker, still holding her hand, "Wendy, if time is what you need, I'm willing to wait as long as it takes. I knew from that day on the beach that you could be someone special, and you are. I'll be with you as long as you want." They stayed at the Ready Room and talked for another hour, then Wendy said, "I could talk to you all night, but I have to go home and get some sleep, tomorrow will be a long day." Striker paid the bill then took her hand as they walked to his car.

It was a twenty-minute drive to Wendy's apartment. When they got to her door she kissed him, smiled and said she would see him the next day. On his way to his car, it occurred to him that it was the first time Wendy had ever kissed him on the lips. When he got back to his car, he realized that Wendy's apartment was just a block away from Terry's. As he drove away, he thought, "Now I know what to tell Terry: the truth. I found a keeper."

Chapter 57

Connors' Wedding and Reception

The next morning, Striker got up early to take a run. Before he left, he noticed that Sticky had not slept in his bed and assumed that he had stayed with his girlfriend the previous night. When he got back, he saw a note that said Sticky was at the house they had looked at the previous month. The owner had called Sticky to tell him that if he wanted to rent it on a month-to-month basis, the rent and utilities would only be $125 a month. Then if anyone offered to lease it for a year, Sticky would have to be out of the house by the end of that month. Sticky agreed, picked up his girlfriend, and moved in for the weekend. The note also said that Striker could stay at the place on weekends for $25 per month. Striker thought about it, and then said to himself, "What the hell, I'll try it for a month and see how it goes." Then he wrote Sticky a check and put it on his dresser. As it turned out, he never stayed there.

After Striker cleaned up, he went to the other side of the suite to see his other suitemates, but no one was there. He then looked for them at the open mess and didn't see them. He ate breakfast and went back to the suite and no one was there. It was not yet 9 am, and the wedding wasn't until three. After debating whether or not to go to the beach, he grabbed his snorkeling gear and left.

Tiki Beach was virtually deserted and almost no one was walking or jogging near the water. Striker was there to swim, so after putting his blanket on the beach, he put on his goggles and snorkel and swam out to the sand bar. The Gulf was again alive with tropical fish, red snapper, mullet and an adult sea turtle. He remained there snorkeling for almost two hours and was continually in awe of the beautiful Gulf and its apparent unlimited bounty of sea creatures. Finally, he tired and returned to his blanket where he quickly fell asleep.

An hour later he woke up to the sound of people playing football. As he sat up and looked around, he was surprised to see a girl that looked like Terry sitting on a blanket with a guy he didn't know. He waited until she stood up and looked around to be sure it was Terry. When the guy with her waded into the Gulf, Striker observed that with shoulder-length hair and a ponytail, he didn't look like he was in the military. Then Striker saw that he had an obvious limp and a Marine Corps tattoo on his left arm.

Terry glanced at Striker, quickly turned around, and then looked back at him. She hesitated for a few seconds, then waved for him to come to her. As he did, he thought, "Well, this might change things." When he sat down, she was obviously embarrassed, but still managed to say "Hi, Striker. I've been meaning to call you, and I am embarrassed that I didn't. Obviously, I got back from my sister's earlier than I thought." Then, after a pause to collect her thoughts, "While I was there, I reunited with my high school boyfriend, Glenn. We broke up during my sophomore year in college. I didn't know until I was home for Christmas that year that he dropped out of school and joined the Marine Corps. He did almost two tours in Nam, got seriously wounded and was medically discharged. After he got out, he moved back home, finished college and is now in law school. To make a long story short, I ran into him at a bar where we used to hang out. We started dating again, the old feelings were rekindled, and I asked him to visit me. Now he's moved in with me and is transferring to Florida to finish law school." Then she paused again, "I should

337

have told you, I feel really bad, and I apologize." Striker. "Don't feel bad, I have no hard feelings. When we first met, we agreed on a no strings attached relationship. While you were gone, I've been seeing other girls. I only wish the best for you, and I hope we can stay friends, you're a great girl." Terry, tearing up, kissed him on the cheek, thanked him, and Striker left.

On the way back to the BOQ, Striker thought to himself. "It's beginning to look more and more that meeting Wendy was supposed to happen." When he walked into the suite, Sticky left a note saying he took the check and would make a key for Striker. Then he reiterated that he was staying at the house until Sunday afternoon. Striker cleaned up and put some civilian clothes in his flight bag. Although he didn't have to, Striker wore a choker to the wedding; Wendy thought he looked great in it.

Striker arrived at the Chapel and joined several people who were waiting outside. He didn't know any of them, but soon the best man, Clint Riley, the groomsmen, and the sword bearers arrived and got into place for the ceremony. When the Chapel started to fill, Striker went in and took an aisle seat, and realized that he had been in this Chapel three times in the last week, more than he had been to church in months. Then he focused on the wall next to the altar that was almost covered with Gold Wings. His dad told him that the wings were placed there in honor of Naval Aviators after they passed away. They were left there as a testament to the complete devotion to duty that being a Naval Aviator meant. It was a solemn reminder that the Navy came first; wives, girlfriends, and family were all controlled by the needs of the Navy. He thought about his father, whose wings would certainly be there someday, and if he earned his wings, they would be placed there as well. Striker silently prayed that his decision to be a Naval Aviator, with all its demands, was the right one.

The organist playing the entrance march interrupted his thoughts. A few minutes later the groomsmen, then the best man and the groom walked in. Connors, not one to show much emotion, was smiling broadly. As the bridesmaids came in, Wendy looked at Striker with tears in her eyes, then wiped them away and smiled. It was then that he knew that she was the one.

As the twin girls gleefully dropped rose petals in front of them, Jane's father escorted her to the front of the church. She was beautiful and was smiling even though tears were rolling down her cheek. At the altar, Connors took Jane's hand from her father, who wept as he returned to his wife.

Once the Catholic ceremony began, Striker could not take his eyes off Wendy. The Mass ended with a final blessing and the priest introduced the new Mr. and Mrs. Tim Connors. They kissed, the congregation applauded, and the couple led the wedding party to the exit. Striker was one of the last people to leave the Chapel. He waited outside the door, but the wedding party was taken to a side room for pictures. Half an hour later they returned and were quickly surrounded by well-wishers, making it impossible for Striker to see Wendy. As the bride and groom made their way through the crowd, Wendy saw Striker, went to him and asked him to sit at the head table with her. He agreed, and Wendy hurried to join the other bridesmaids in a limo taking them to the reception.

Striker waited outside of the O Club for the limousine to arrive. It soon did, but the wedding party waited for the guests to enter the building. One of the people who walked in was

Jane's cousin, Lisa, who had just arrived from Bethesda, Maryland.

A few minutes later Wendy got out of the limo and waved for Striker to join her. "I want to introduce you to my parents before we go in." Then she led him to them, "Mom and Dad, this is Jonathan Striker, the guy I told you about. Most people just call him Striker. As you know, that's a Navy thing." Striker greeted her mother and shook her father's hand, who said, "You're the guy who knocked my daughter down at the beach, aren't you?" Striker looked stunned, but managed to mumble, "Well, sort of, but it was an accident." Then her dad laughed and said, "I'm kidding, Wendy told me all about it. She said that it was just as much her fault, and that you were a perfect gentleman." Then Wendy added with a giggle, "He was, but the next time I saw him was the morning after he got kicked out of a strip club and was almost arrested." Before Striker could say a word, her father laughed again and added, "Hold on, I know it isn't as bad as it sounds. Connors told me what happened, and since he was also in the strip club, I can't be mad at you. By the way, I was in the Marine Corps during the war and am well aware of what goes on during liberty." Then as he smiled, "Most of it I can't talk about in mixed company." Just then, Riley interrupted him, telling everyone to line up for the grand entrance. The Master of Ceremonies then introduced the wedding party as they entered. When they were in the ballroom, the band started playing the *Wedding March* and Lt. and Mrs. Timothy Connors came to the center of the dance floor. Then the band began playing *Unchained Melody* and the MC announced that the newly married couple would have their first dance as husband and wife.

Connors and his bride danced, totally oblivious to anyone else in the room. It was the moment that they both longed for.

340

When it ended, the band played *Moon River* and the couple broke up and danced with their parents. A few minutes later, Connors danced with his sister, and his twin nieces gleefully joined them. Soon Wendy joined Striker and they danced until the music ended and they sat down. The MC announced that the food was ready, called the head table to the buffet, followed by everyone else.

When most of the guests were finished eating, the MC introduced Clint Riley, who would offer a toast to the bride and groom. Riley stood up, slowly looked around the room and began, "Good evening, folks. My name is Clint Riley. If you can't tell, I'm from Texas, Lubbock, Texas, to be exact. My parents taught me to follow these basic rules in life: Be loyal to your faith, your country, your family, and your friends, and trust that the good Lord will take care of everything else. Even though neither of them are Texans, the incredible story of Tim Connors and Jane Carmody proves that those rules work. I've known Tim Connors since we began AOCS over two years ago. We were roommates during many weeks of the most challenging training I have ever experienced. As anyone who has made it through AOCS will say, 'Once you've finished AOCS, everything else in life will be easy.' You sure wouldn't be able to convince me otherwise during the first ten days of the hell called INDOC. I was always screwing up, out of step or forgetting something I was supposed to memorize. The Marine Drill Instructor didn't miss a thing I did wrong. I must have done thousands of pushups, squat thrusts, and side straddle hops and was often near collapse. I almost DOR'd several times, but Tim Connors wouldn't let me quit. When I thought I was at the end of my rope, his never-ending belief that I could make it kept me going. Later, after I completed RIO training and earned my wings, he found me and asked me to fly with him. There is no doubt that his confidence in me

341

made me a better RIO. As a team and with the help of the Good Lord, we made it through nine months of fierce combat and dozens of carrier landings. I know, probably better than anyone, what Tim Connors is made of."

"One of the things so special about him is his absolute belief that he would somehow find the love of his life, Jane Carmody. He simply would not give up. He knew that she believed the same as he did. His mission in life became finding Jane. She was the girl he broke up with because they felt their lives were going in very different directions. He knew he had made a terrible mistake, and he was going to fix it. He believed that the two different directions they were going would somehow merge. As they sit here tonight as husband and wife, you know he was right, this is what the Good Lord planned for them. Now it is my honor to be his best man at their wedding. So, I ask everyone to stand and join me as I offer this toast to Jane and Connors: That the Good Lord will continue to look over them and lead them to love and honor each other for the rest of their days." Everyone in the room applauded and raised their glasses.

Before the rest of the traditional toasts began, Lisa came to the head table and spoke to her aunt and uncle. She told Jane that she was beautiful and that it was wonderful that she and Connors had found each other. Jane told Lisa that she was saddened to hear that Lisa had broken up with her husband and hoped that she would find someone soon. Lisa teared up, thanked her, and then moved to Connors. She hugged him, wished him nothing but happiness, then turned away and walked toward her table. Before she got there, she stopped in the ladies' room, went into a stall, and quietly wept. As she came out of the bathroom, she decided to leave before Jane tossed her bouquet.

Chapter 58

VT-10 Training Continues

The reception ended after the band played a long version of *Baby, I Love You*, immediately followed by the *Love Theme from Romeo and Juliet*. Striker and Wendy danced with their arms wrapped around each other. When the music ended, Wendy kissed Striker on the cheek and whispered to him that she had hoped the evening would never end. But it did, so he asked her what she wanted to do. As they walked to the head table, Wendy replied, "My dad booked a party room at his hotel and is hosting an after-reception party. I really want to go. Will you?" Striker, "You bet I will. Can I take you or are you going with Leah or your family?" Wendy, "With you. But first, I want to stop at my apartment to change clothes. My parents brought Leah and me to the wedding, so I don't have a car. Could you take me and Leah?" Striker, "Sure, and if you don't mind, I'll change into some civilian clothes I brought." Wendy, "No problem, I'll ask Leah if she wants to ride with us."

Leah was near the head table talking with someone. As Wendy and Striker walked close to her, Leah asked. "You ready to go to your dad's party?" Wendy replied, "I am, but first Striker is taking me to the apartment to change clothes. Want to go with us?" Leah, "I sure do. I love this dress but it's not very comfortable, especially when I'm dancing." While Striker drove, Wendy scooted close to him.

When they arrived at her apartment, Striker changed in the powder room. Once he was ready, he looked around the apartment. It was nicely furnished, apparently with items her parents had given her, and a few things she had in college.

There was a cabinet in the dining room that held several photographs of friends and relatives and a few of her as a child and in a high school track uniform. Near the back of the top shelf Striker saw a picture of Wendy in a light blue formal dress next to a good-looking boy in a tuxedo that matched her dress. Striker assumed it was Roger when they went to a prom. He chuckled as he wondered if Roger wore that light blue tux because he wanted to or because she wanted him to. It occurred to him that if Wendy wanted him to wear it, or anything else, he'd do it in a heartbeat.

Wendy came out of her bedroom dressed in a light green summer dress that fit her perfectly. Striker was stunned; he had never dated a girl as beautiful as she was. He hoped that he wouldn't screw up their budding relationship. Just as Wendy was asking Striker if he liked her dress, Leah came out of her bedroom and interrupted, "Of course he does, he'd have to be blind and stupid to say he doesn't. It's gorgeous, and so are you." Striker could only say, "It sure is. I'm glad I'm not blind or stupid, because you look really great." Wendy, slightly embarrassed, responded, "Thank you. I wasn't sure if you would like it, but I took a chance that you would." Striker, "Oh, I like it all right, but you could be wearing baggy jeans and a sweatshirt and look great." Wendy, "You're too sweet, but I'm happy you like it."

Leah interrupted again, "Ok, that's enough flirtation. This room is starting to heat up. We better get to the party before you guys decide to do something else." Wendy, feigning irritation, "Leah, I don't know what you're referring to. I'm ready to go." Striker thought, "Leah read my mind. If I had my way, Wendy and I wouldn't make it to the party."

There were about 75 people at the party, most of them were family and friends of the bride and groom. Wendy saw Jane sitting by herself while Connors was talking to some old friends. When Striker went to get drinks, she sat next to her, "Jane, this has to be the happiest day of your life." Jane, "It is. I still can't believe that Connors and I are together, much less married." Then she whispered in Wendy's ear, "And expecting a baby." Then she continued, "On top of everything else, I start work this week as an assistant professor, which I never dreamed would happen so soon after grad school. I'm the luckiest woman in the world."

Just as Wendy finished talking, Striker handed her a glass of wine, then asked Jane if she wanted anything. Jane said she'd love a glass of iced tea, and he went to get it. As he walked away, Jane took Wendy's hand and said, "Wendy, I know Roger's sudden death was really hard on you. He was the only guy in your life for almost six years, but like I told you the other night, I think Striker is someone special. What happened to Roger was terrible, but it's over, there's nothing you can do to change it, and life goes on. Don't let your past tragedy prevent your future happiness. Don't make the same mistake Connors and I made when we broke up. If you care deeply about Striker, and I bet he does about you, don't push him away because it's too soon. Let it happen, and if it works out, stay with him." As she finished, Striker returned, handed Jane the iced tea and sat next to Wendy. Without saying a word, she took his hand and gently squeezed it.

Leah saw Riley on the other side of the room. After talking to him at Jane and Connors' cookout, she was interested in learning more about him. His Texas drawl and dry sense of humor made him different from any guy she knew, and he was nothing like her ex-boyfriend in Kansas. She appreciated that he wasn't like the new ensigns who swarmed around her and Wendy wherever they went. There was no leer in his eyes when they talked, and she didn't get the feeling he was disrobing her whenever he looked at her. She understood that he certainly had his share of women, but he seemed to be low-key about his approach to them. He appeared to be one of those people who said, "This is who I am, take it or leave it." Plus, when they previously spoke, he seemed to want to get to know her before asking her out. After his moving toast earlier at the reception, she now wanted to get to know him better.

Riley had just finished talking to Ted Marx when Leah tapped him on the shoulder. She began by telling him that his toast to Jane and Connors was beautiful. Riley responded, "I just told the truth, and made it from my heart. Connors and Jane are very special to me. I'll always be there for them, as he was for me." Then Leah asked, "How long will you be here in Pensacola?" Riley, "Until Tuesday, but I just found out that I'm going to be stationed back here in a week. I'm replacing an instructor who was called to duty with Jake's squadron. They asked for volunteers, and I immediately said I would. I liked what I was doing in Glynco, but I love living in Pensacola. While I'm here I'm signing up for a room at the BOQ and I'm gonna buy a car." Leah, "I thought you were strictly a motorcycle guy." Riley, "I still am, but it's hard to move a lot of stuff when you only have a Harley. I need to get another vehicle, probably a pickup or a Bronco; something that I can carry my Harley and everything else I need whenever I move. While we're here talking, can I get you a drink?" Leah smiled sweetly and asked for a Pina Colada.

When he returned, he handed Leah her drink and then, almost shyly, asked. "You know, I'd sure like to spend more time with you. When the party is over, would you like to go to the Tiki Bar for a while? I can take you home. I promise I won't keep you out too late." Leah, without hesitating, said she'd love to and told Wendy she didn't need a ride.

Striker and Wendy remained at the party until after 10. As people began to leave, Wendy asked Striker if he'd like a walk on the beach. The party room backed onto the beach, so they just had to go out the door. It was a relatively cool evening for early August in Pensacola, and the normally ever-present mosquitoes were kept inland by a strong breeze. As they walked along the edge of the water both eventually took off their shoes and waded into the incoming tide. They held hands and talked about the wedding and the miracle that brought Jane and Connors together again.

Wendy asked him why the wings were attached to the wall in the Chapel. Striker, "They were put there at the request of Naval Aviators or their families. As I understand it, they are an acknowledgment of the commitment each of them made to the Navy. Naval Aviation was their calling in life, but the Good Lord controlled their fates. It's a reminder of what every Naval Aviator contemplates when he is strapped into an aircraft. They are the most highly trained professional killers on earth. If the Navy wanted them to have a wife, the Navy would have issued them one. That's why I wasn't interested in having a long-term relationship; then, I accidentally knocked a pretty girl down in the surf."

Wendy looked at Striker for a few seconds before she said anything. Then she smiled, "That's an amazing coincidence. I was not looking for any lasting relationship either, but then, one day, while I was standing in the surf, a handsome Naval Officer suddenly knocked me off my feet. He was very gracious as he helped me to my feet and escorted me to the shore. I was charmed by him. It was then that I began to believe I could find another someone special." Then she put her arms around Striker, kissed him, and said, "I hope you care enough to be patient with me. I don't want to lose you." Striker squeezed her hand and said, "Wendy, you know by now that I'm not going anywhere, not until you tell me to or you go with me."

The room was nearly empty when Wendy and Striker returned. Leah saw her come in, "I thought you guys might've snuck out. I've been waiting to tell you that Riley and I are going to the Tiki Bar for a while, and then he's taking me home on his Harley. I can't wait. I've never been on a motorcycle before. You guys want to join us?" Wendy glanced at Striker, "I'm with you." Wendy said it sounded like fun, said good night to her parents, and left with Striker.

They stayed at the Tiki Bar until after midnight, when Wendy said she was ready to go home. Almost as soon as they left the parking lot, Wendy fell asleep on Striker's shoulder. When they got to her apartment, she apologized. "I'm so sorry. I hope I didn't hurt your feelings; I was just so tired." Striker. "No reason to apologize. I should have taken you home earlier." Wendy, "I didn't want you to. I wanted to stay with you as long as I could. I hope you don't mind that I'm not going to invite you in. I'm just not ready yet, but I want to see you again, tomorrow actually. My father is hosting a small family dinner in the O Club; Jane and Connors will be leaving for their honeymoon when it's over. I want you to be with me if you can." Striker, "Sure I can, but I hope I'm not intruding in a family event." Wendy, "Striker, every member of my family who has seen me with you would be surprised if I didn't bring you." Striker, "Then, of course, I'll be there." Wendy kissed him goodnight and went into her apartment.

The next evening, Wendy met Striker at the Officers' Club, and took him around the room and introduced him to everyone in her family. Many asked him if he was scared when he landed on an aircraft carrier. He explained to them that he was still a student and had not yet landed on an aircraft carrier but hoped to do so in the next few months.

An hour later, the dinner buffet was opened, and Wendy's dad invited her and Striker to sit with them. While they ate, he took the opportunity to ask Striker about his childhood, family, education, and his goals in the Navy. After about an hour of questions, Wendy jokingly told her dad to give Striker a break, or he might just leave. Striker, "It's OK. If I had a daughter as pretty as you are, I'd be even worse." Wendy's dad immediately gave Striker two thumbs up and told Wendy, "You hit the jackpot. This guy is OK with me." Now embarrassed, Wendy said, "Striker is just being sweet, Dad, but before he changes his mind, we're going to go see Jane and Connors before they leave." On the way there, she said, "You must excuse my dad. He has always done that to guys I introduce to him, all the way back to high school. He's a police Captain, and he sometimes doesn't leave his police manual at work. He means no harm; he's just being overly protective of me, especially since Roger died." Striker, "I understand, and I meant it when I told him I'd be the same way, maybe worse if you were my daughter." Wendy smiled and then took his hand as they sat and talked with her sister and Connors.

After Jane and Connors left, Striker and Wendy went out by the pool and sat on a large rocking chair. As they looked at the moon reflecting on the bay, Wendy said, "You made a big impression on everyone we met, especially my parents. My dad even gave me another thumbs-up as we left to see Jane and Connors. I'm impressed, too. I was a little nervous about inviting you tonight. I knew everyone would compare you to Roger, but you handled it well. You are so sweet."

She kissed him and said, "I'm sure you know that you're very special to me, and I want to see you again as soon as I can, but I need to go home early tonight and get some sleep; the last week or so has really been hectic." Striker, "I understand. It's been a very busy time for me, too, the last couple of weeks. I'll call you tomorrow if that's OK. She smiled, "You know it is." Striker walked her to the car, and kissed her good night.

Chapter 59

Tragedy Occurs

On the last day left in Ground School, the class met in the classroom for a briefing before their final exam. Lt. Starling, the instructor, walked into the classroom carrying a stack of documents that he distributed to the class. When he was finished, he addressed everyone, "Good morning, Gents. As you know, part of VT-10 training is ensuring that you are knowledgeable in basic aircraft avionics, airframes, and engine functions. This morning, we're going to review everything you need to know before you take the final exam. I've handed out a sample test, which we are going to go over question by question, so pay close attention." For the next two hours, Starling read each question and then asked a student what the answer was. If he was wrong, Starling told everyone the correct answer until all the questions were answered. Then, he told them to take a ten-minute break and return to the classroom.

When they returned, Starling handed out the tests and told them they had an hour to complete them. Striker soon realized that it was the same test the class had just reviewed, and he knew all the answers. When he was done, he went to the ready room to prepare for a flight. As he did, Hound walked in, "Ain't the Navy great? This is the first time in my life that I'm positive I aced an exam. Fly Navy, Baby."

The next day, Striker and his squadron mates completed VT-10; unfortunately, it wasn't without some terrifying moments, and sadly, it ended in tragedy. The first of Striker's last two flights launched at 07:30. It was supposed to be the final navigation and radio communication training flight. The instructor, Marine Captain Joseph Crandall, turned it into a test of Striker's mettle. They were in a T-2C about ten miles off the coast of Pensacola Beach, in a flight zone normally used for unusual attitude flight. Crandall was well known; he completed two tours in Vietnam as a helicopter pilot before transitioning to jets. He was shot down five times and received two distinguished flying crosses, a silver star, and two purple hearts. When he returned to Pensacola to be an instructor, he was allowed to do whatever he wanted, and that day, he wanted to test Striker. While they cruised at about 10,000 feet and 300 knots, Crandall announced, "Watch this, Mr. Striker." Then he suddenly went full throttle, took the aircraft, nearly vertical, to over 40,000 feet, and did a modified wingover into a steep dive.

Instead of leveling off in the opposite direction, Crandall continued to dive straight down. Striker, thinking Crandall might have passed out, started calling out their altitude and airspeed as they streaked down toward the Gulf. When they reached 5000 feet and over 500 knots, Striker thought for certain they were going to crash. He decided that if they got below 2000 feet, he was going to ask Crandall if he was OK. Regardless of what Crandall did, if the aircraft got below 1500 feet, Striker was going to eject. Just as they reached 2500 feet, Crandall pulled the aircraft out of the dive. Almost immediately, the G-forces caused Striker, and presumably Crandall, to totally blackout. Striker had experienced over 2Gs during unusual attitude flight and gunnery training, but this flight was vastly different. He greyed out before, but this time, he was out cold. When he woke up, he didn't know how long he had been out, but he was alert enough to realize that they had leveled off. He called Crandall, who only said, "How'd you like that, Mr. Striker?" as if it was just a routine training flight. Striker, not amused, responded, "It scared the shit out of

352

me. I thought we were going down." Crandall laughed and said, "I did that maneuver to see what you would do, and you did what you were supposed to do." Without any further conversation, he set a course for Sherman Airfield and returned to base.

Later that day, Striker was flying with Crandall again, but in a T-33B. They were returning to Sherman Field after completing a Field Carrier Landing Practice (FCLP) flight when a thunderstorm suddenly developed in the Pensacola area. Just as they were about to enter the landing pattern, they flew into thick black clouds with zero visibility. At last look, Striker noted that the aircraft was at 5000 feet, 250 knots. They were bouncing all over the sky in unstable air when they were struck by lightning. The analog gauges jumped around, some spinning with the surge of power. Then the radio static became so bad communication with air traffic control became impossible. When the instruments began to function again, Striker didn't know whether or not to trust them and he asked Crandall what to do. Crandall replied, "Continue on the last known heading and airspeed, and look for blue sky." Even before the lightning struck, the fuel gauge indicated they were at bingo fuel, and now Striker wasn't sure of their altitude, heading, or airspeed. He tried to remain calm; Crandall was an outstanding aviator, even if he took unnecessary chances.

Five minutes passed with no change in visibility, so Striker decided he would prepare to eject if there was no improvement in another two minutes. Fortunately, they regained communication with air traffic control, which directed them to change their course and altitude. Thirty seconds later, a patch of blue sky appeared on the horizon, and they made a safe landing. When he exited the aircraft, Striker promised himself that he would never fly with Crandall again.

VT-10 students often flew FCLP flights with VT-4 student pilots who were in their final phase of training before Carrier Qualifications. It was the most dangerous part of VT-10 training, with trainees flying with trainees. Often, the student pilot had completed a solo FCLP only a day or so before, which was the case for Striker's last FLCP flight. The student pilot, Brian Harrigan, told Striker that he had just soloed the previous Friday, making Striker the first non-instructor to fly with him. Striker, without hesitation, told Harrigan that it didn't concern him; he had full confidence in Harrigan's ability. When they were making their first final approach into Saufley Field, Striker was not so sure. During the last fifteen seconds, when they were rapidly descending at about 160 miles per hour, Striker was terrified. He fixed his eyes on the 'Meatball' on the left side of the landing strip. The LSO gave them the OK, and they made the hardest landing that Striker had ever experienced and then immediately accelerated and took off. After they repeated the process several times, Striker became more relaxed, and toward the end of the day, he began to enjoy the flights.

The worst possible outcome occurred on September 29 at 09:30. Hound was flying an FCLP with another student pilot who had just soloed the previous week. It was his last FLCP flight, and the same storm that was battering Sherman Field also struck Saufley. Fred Spiros, the student pilot, checked with the LSO to see if they should continue to attempt a landing. They were given the go-ahead. Just as they were beginning their final approach, a severe wind shear developed over Saufley Field. Spiros kept the T-2C on the meatball as best he could, but when they were about to land, a blast of wind drove the aircraft down. In an effort to stabilize the aircraft, Spiros over-corrected, and the right wingtip hit the ground. The T-2C cartwheeled on the runway, broke apart, and caught fire. Hound and Spiros were instantly killed.

As Striker walked into the ready room at Sherman Field, he heard the tower announce that an aircraft was down at Saufley. Striker immediately went to the flight schedule and saw that Hound was assigned to an FCLP at that time. He said a silent prayer that both aviators were OK. Soon there was another announcement: firefighting had begun, rescue teams were on site, and Saufley Field would be closed indefinitely. Striker knew that one or both aviators were injured, maybe killed. He didn't know what to do, so he said another prayer, and waited for more information.

The ready room quickly filled with Striker's squadron-mates, including Bulldog and Sticky, who sat silently next to him. Soon the CO, Lt. Cdr. Eric Magnuson came into the room and addressed the waiting students. "At ease, Gentlemen. As I'm sure you know, there was a serious accident at Saufley Field about an hour ago. Since an inquiry has just begun, I only know that there were two fatalities. I cannot officially release the aviators' names until their families are notified, but both of them are listed on the flight schedule. All Training Command flight operations here at Sherman and the outlying fields are cancelled until further notice. You are welcome to stay here as long as you want; we'll post more information as it is released. Gents, today two of our fellow aviators died in the service of their country. It makes no difference if it happened during training in Pensacola or in combat over North Vietnam. They were doing their duty, what they dreamed of doing. I ask that each of you offer a prayer for your fellow aviators and their loved ones in a moment of silence." A minute later he broke the silence saying, "Mr. Striker, Mr. Hickey and Mr. Schnider, please come to my office. As you were, Gentlemen."

355

Striker, Sticky and Bulldog followed the CO into his office and were told to have a seat. "At ease, Gentlemen. I'm sure you've figured it out, but I still regret to tell you that Mr. Stewart was killed today, as well as Mr. Fred Spiros, the student pilot. I know you were roommates with Stewart in AOCS and shared a suite in the BOQ. I also know firsthand that AOCS roommates build a strong bond during those many weeks of hell. I did too. You learn to rely on each other to survive; you become brothers. One of the missions of AOCS is to train future aviators to trust their wingmen. I know the empty feeling in your gut that you're now experiencing. Last year, I lost a roommate, the best man at my wedding, so I know it will take a while, but you will get better." Then he paused for a moment as he gathered his thoughts and continued. "I will give your names to the Chaplain and tell him that the three of you will be available to provide any assistance to the Stewart family. For the rest of the day, you need to stay close to the BOQ. Until then, the XO will advise you of any additional assistance. Each of you will be scheduled to accompany me when I greet the families at the airport. Gents, the next few days will be rough; you will be dealing with Stewart's grieving family. Since you were close to him during the last few months of training, they will find comfort in talking to you. I am excusing all of you from your remaining VT-10 training so that you can be available to them. You have to report back here at 0800 Friday, for graduation, the awarding of your VT-10 wings and receiving your next assignments. Before you leave today, submit your wish list of the top three aircraft you want. By the way, it looks like RIO training will be delayed, maybe for several weeks. The pipeline is apparently backed up, but we'll know more Friday. Finally, the XO will let you know when we meet the families and friends at the airport. Good luck, Gents. Dismissed."

Striker and his roommates left the CO's office and stopped in the ready room to see if there were any new reports. There weren't, but they sat down for a few minutes to talk. Bulldog began, "I don't know where to begin. When I brought Hound here this morning, he was excited that we were almost finished VT-10, just one day to go. He still wasn't sure what aircraft he wanted, but he was leaning towards picking the A-6. He figured he had a better chance at getting the Intruder than the F-4, since almost everyone, me included, wants the F-4." Then, in a rare display of emotion, Bulldog covered his eyes. A few seconds later he resumed, "He had only one more flight, and this happened. I remember the time when Sullivan PT'd him so badly. Hound said only way he would quit was when he died. Now he is gone. Bulldog took a minute to get composed, then continued, "He was a good man and a great friend. I'd trust him with my life. Rest in peace, Hound."

They remained silent in their seats for a few minutes, and then they were called into the XO's office. Once there, the XO said, "Gents, I've heard from the Chaplain, who talked to Stewart's dad this morning. As you may know, Stewart's sister Peggy, who lives in Pensacola, is married to a Navy JAG Officer. His name is Commander Gene Mason, and he will be the family's representative during the coming days. I called him and gave him all of your names because I didn't know who Hound's roommate in the suite was. He said he would meet you at the BOQ office at 1400 to review Stewart's belongings and take what he can to his home. Before you leave, I'll give you Cdr. Mason's home and office numbers and issue each of you a pager so that we can reach you anywhere." Then Bulldog stood and said, "Sir, I'm Stewart's roommate in the suite. I know where he parked his car, where his spare keys are and a lot of other things, including a letter he showed me in case something happened to him." The XO replied, "Cdr. Mason told me he would be busy until he left for the BOQ, so you can tell him when you meet him. Unless you have any questions, that's all I have, Gents."

Once they picked up the pagers, Bulldog said, "I know it's not a good time, but Hound would want us to carry on, even if he couldn't. After we change, let's go to the Ready Room, offer a toast to our friend and eat lunch. The XO has our pager number." Striker quickly replied, "I agree. Hound would be the first to join us if he could." They got into their cars and drove to the BOQ to change clothes.

They quickly changed, but before they left, Bulldog checked out Hound's dresser and closet. As far as he could tell, they only contained his uniforms and a few civilian clothes. Then he opened his desk drawer and took out the sealed envelope with "For my family in the event of my death." written on the front. He held it for a few seconds, put it on the desk, then turned away and left the suite.

When they walked into the Ready Room, they saw that Lt Cdr. Magnuson had arranged for Hound's picture to be placed on the bar. It had a black cloth draped across it and a card with his name and a VT-10 patch in front of it. Striker and his roommates looked at it for a few seconds before they found a table. When they finished eating, Bulldog asked everyone to raise their glasses to Hound, their classmate and fellow aviator, then he and his roommates quietly left.

Later, Cdr. Mason met Bulldog Striker and Sticky at their suite. After he showed Hound's belongings to him, Bulldog handed Mason the envelope. Without opening it, Mason helped the roommates take everything to his car and led them to his house.

Hound's sister, Peggy, was inconsolable when Striker and his roommates arrived. After Mason helped her to the couch, Peggy began to calm down. But when the roommates carried in Hound's clothes, she began to cry uncontrollably again. Mason then told Bulldog that the family needed some time alone and would not need anything the rest of the evening.

After he was back at the BOQ, Striker called Wendy. She told him she panicked when she heard about the death of two student pilots, but she calmed down when she got his message. Then she asked, "How are you doing? I know it must have been a terrible day." Striker, "I'm fine, but it was a rough day. We're all stunned and now things are happening fast. Hound's sister, Peggy, was a mess; we couldn't calm her down. After only being there a few minutes, we came back to the BOQ to wait for more instructions. We're planning to eat here. If you want, I'll tell Sticky and Bulldog to go ahead and I'll wait for you." Wendy, "I'll be there in thirty minutes." As soon as he ended the call, he got a message from his XO. The Stewart family would arrive at Pensacola Airport at 0930 the next day.

Twenty minutes later Wendy walked in, saw Striker and ran to him, "I was so worried about you. I thought you were one of the students who died." Then they sat on a couch and held hands for about ten minutes. Striker, "Do you feel like you could eat something?" She nodded that she could, and they walked to the open mess.

Chapter 60

Hound's Family Arrives

It was Filet Mignon night at the open mess, the only time wine was served with meals. Striker avoided discussing Hound's death and Wendy relaxed after having a glass of wine. When she told him that Jane was pregnant, Striker was happy to hear good news after dealing with two deaths in less than three months. After they ate, Striker said he had to get back to the BOQ and took Wendy to her car. Before she left, she held Striker and told him that Hound's accident made her realize how much she cared for him.

At breakfast the next morning, Bulldog said, "Man, I am not looking forward to this day. I'll probably be just as upset as Hound's family is. What could I possibly tell them that would make them feel better?" Sticky, "Probably nothing. But I know that you, Striker and I can offer them some good things to remember about him. We can share things that may comfort them in the days to come. We should tell them how much Hound loved being an officer in the Navy, how proud he was training to be a Naval Aviator. Most importantly, tell them that we know, without a doubt, that he died doing what he wanted to do."

Traffic was heavy that morning, so they didn't get to the airport until after 9. But as soon as they were in the terminal, they saw that the flight had been delayed and was now expected to arrive at 10. They saw Lt. Cmdr. Magnuson and the chaplain sitting near the gate. As they got closer, the chaplain said, "Good morning, Gentlemen. I'm Chaplain O'Reilly. My condolences for the loss of your squadron mate and friend. Before I meet his family, I'd like to know a little about him." Bulldog then told them everything he knew about Hound from the time they met to the day he died. Chaplain O'Reilly said, "I spoke to Hound's father yesterday. He was very upset, but he did tell me that, tentatively, the family wants to bury Hound next to his brother, who died shortly after he was born. If that happens, I expect one or all of you will be asked to accompany his body back to Pittsburgh."

Just then, Hound's parents, Larry and Beth Stewart, walked out of the gate and looked for anyone in a Navy uniform. Magnuson and O'Reilly offered condolences and then introduced Striker, Bulldog and Sticky as their son's roommates. Bulldog was the first to speak, "I am so sorry for your loss. Your son was our roommate through AOCS and I shared a room with him in our BOQ suite. He was a good friend and outstanding Naval Officer and was on his way to becoming an even better Naval Flight Officer, we miss him enormously. My roommates and I are available to provide you with any assistance during this terrible time." Then he handed Mr. Stewart their pager numbers.

Mr. Stewart was a big man, about 6' 5", 240 pounds and had hands like a pro football player. Hound had told Striker that his dad was an all-state high school football player who had received an athletic scholarship to play linebacker at Penn State. During his freshman year in college, Hound's father had to quit school to work at the steel plant in order to help his family. Over the years, he rose quickly through the management ranks and became the company's general manager. When the time came, his dad was able to pay for Hound to attend Duquesne University; he wanted to make sure that Hound was the first member of the Stewart family to graduate.

On the other hand, Hound's mother Beth was barely 5 ft. tall, but it was obvious that she was the bedrock of the family. Her husband was crushed by Hound's sudden death, and in no shape to make important decisions; Beth took the lead in making the decisions.

As they left the airport, Chaplain O'Reilly told Magnuson that Mrs. Stewart had requested a few hours of privacy, and then left to be with the family at Hound's sister's house. Magnuson then told Striker, Sticky and Bulldog that they should return to the BOQ and wait for instructions.

Striker and his roommates were back at the BOQ before noon. About an hour later, the XO told him that the family would not need anything until the next morning when they wanted to take a tour of the base. A van was arranged to pick up Striker and his roommates at 0830, and then the Stewart family.

With nothing to do until then, Striker said he was going to take a run to clear his mind; his roommates decided to join him. Fifteen minutes later they were jogging on the cross-country path that they had followed so many times during AOCS. Along the way they saw poopies running in formation and heard the Drill Instructor barking the same Marine Corps encouragement that both terrified and motivated them when they were poopies. They looked at each other and smiled. They knew that Hound was running with them, and he was smiling too.

When they finished and were getting cleaned up, their pagers buzzed simultaneously. It was Beth; she wanted one of them to call her. Ten minutes later Bulldog asked her how the family was doing and if there was anything they needed. Beth, "We're doing the best we can. Thanks for asking. I do have a question, but first I want to tell you what Alan wrote about you and your roommates, making it through AOCS and VT-10. He said that completing AOCS was much more difficult than he ever imagined. He even considered quitting several times, especially in INDOC, which he described as ten days of pure hell. He would have quit without you three insisting that he continue to try and encouraging him to stay with the program."

"You four guys started as complete strangers but quickly became a team of brothers. Together, you refused to let any of your brotherhood give up. He knew he was a weak swimmer, so the prospect of doing the Dilbert Dunker and water survival terrified him. But he completed both; he overcame his fear of water. Again, you simply wouldn't let him quit. When AOCS ended, he was so proud that he made it, he was commissioned, and he was going to flight training. Once he started VT-10, he knew it was worth all the effort. Again, he said he wouldn't have made it without you. Finally, he knew that if you were reading this letter, he was gone. He didn't want you to be angry or blame anything or anyone for what happened to him. He set his own course and made his own decisions. He was accomplishing what he dreamed of doing since he was a kid, and he urged you to continue pursuing your dreams as if he was still with you."

Beth was quiet for a moment before she continued, "That brings me to what I want to ask. His body will be released to us tomorrow or Friday. We are still undecided if we will take Alan back with us and bury him with our family or let him remain here in the Barrancas National Cemetery. He was born and raised in Pittsburgh but often said he loved it here and loved being in the Navy; he wanted to make it his career. If he had been able to, I'm sure he would have retired as a Naval Aviator here in Pensacola, and Barrancas Cemetery would be his final resting place. If we take him back to Pittsburgh, would you three come with us and be pallbearers? I'm sure he would want that. We'll let you know as soon as we decide. In either event we will see you tomorrow morning. We want to see where Alan lived and trained the last few months of his life."

Bulldog quickly responded, "Thank you for sharing Hound's letter. We'll be happy to show you the base and we'll pick you up tomorrow morning at about nine. If it's your decision to take him to Pittsburgh, it would be an honor to go with him and be pallbearers." Beth, "Thank you." When the call ended, Bulldog relayed what Beth said, and immediately Sticky and Striker agreed to help.

They decided to stay on base that evening to see if any classmates gathered in the Ready Room. Striker asked Wendy to join them, so Sticky decided to call Lee Ann.

Just as Bulldog arrived at the O club, his pager buzzed. It was the Officer of the Day, who told him that the Medical Examiner was releasing Hound's body on Thursday at 1300. Once in the Ready Room, Bulldog told Striker, "I hope his family decides soon what they are going to do. It's a tough decision, but knowing Hound, I'm sure he'd want to stay here, but it's totally up to them. Unless they ask, I'll keep my opinion to myself." Striker, "Me too. I sure don't want to choose sides. It's just too emotional."

Striker waved at Wendy as she walked in; she was crying. Striker, "What's wrong?" Wendy, "It's just so sad. This shouldn't happen to someone as young as Hound. I could understand it if he was a veteran aviator in combat, but not during a routine training flight in Pensacola. I feel so sorry for his family, but mostly, I'm upset because I know it easily could have been you. I'm relieved that it wasn't, and I feel guilty that I feel that way. I'm sorry, I'm such a mess."

After they finished eating, Lt. Emmet, their Class Officer, came in with Command Sergeant Major Sullivan. Emmet, insisting that they that they remain seated, "We're here to gather with Class 569 in Hound's memory. I only stopped by to give you a heads up. After VT-10 graduation this Friday, there will be a brief memorial service for Hound. If any of you want to say a few words, let your XO know." Then they excused themselves to go speak to the other members of Class 569.

As it approached 11 pm, Wendy was tired, so Striker took her to her car. As he opened the door, he said he was sorry that he had upset her and hoped she was feeling better. Wendy, "Nothing you did upset me. I was shocked by what happened, plus I won't be able to see you tomorrow, I have grades to get done." Striker, "It looks like I'll be tied up all day tomorrow, anyway. Hound's family wants to see the base and they need to decide where he'll be buried. They might take him back to a family cemetery in Pittsburgh. If they do, we'll escort him back. I may be gone for a couple of days." Wendy, "I understand, but let me know how things work out." She hugged him, said she would miss him a lot, and left.

At 0830 the next morning, Striker, Bulldog and Sticky were in a van headed to Peggy Mason's house. On the way there they decided that Sticky would be the narrator as they did a tour around the base and Bulldog and Striker would take turns showing them the places Sticky described. Two hours later, the family had been shown almost every place Hound lived or trained. Before they went to Barrancas Cemetery, they picked up Chaplain O'Reilly who escorted them to the cemetery office.

After they finished speaking to the cemetery administrator, Striker suggested that they see Hound's suite, and eat lunch at the open mess. Ten minutes later Beth remarked that the suite was much nicer than she envisioned, especially compared to the other places he lived.

As they were sitting in the open mess, Hound's father, Larry, spoke for the first time that day, "I had no idea that Naval Flight training was so rigorous, especially INDOC and survival training. I wouldn't have been able to do the Dilbert Dunker or be dragged around the Gulf, and I sure couldn't eat a raccoon. If it hadn't happened, I wouldn't believe that Alan could do those things, day after day without much sleep. I'm very proud of him; I wouldn't have lasted one day. I can see why you Naval Aviators love this place."

When they finished eating, the family was taken back to Peggy's house. On the way, Beth told Bulldog that they were having a family meeting that evening to decide where they wanted to bury Hound. Then she told him that she would let him know their decision the next day.

When Striker and his roommates got back to the BOQ, they decided to relax at the beach. An hour later, while Striker was bodysurfing on the incoming tide, he realized that he was at the very spot where he knocked Wendy down. It occurred to him that meeting her the way he did was meant to be, the same as the way Hound died.

As it got close to 6, Striker and his roommates returned to the BOQ. Soon after he cleaned up, Striker heard the pagers buzz and went to Bulldog's room. Bulldog was in the shower and hadn't heard it buzz. Striker showed him the number in the pager, Bulldog hurriedly got dressed, and they went to the front desk.

Beth Stewart answered the phone and quietly told Bulldog that the family decided to bury Hound at Barrancas National Cemetery, and that she wanted him to notify Sergeant Major Sullivan. Ten minutes after Bulldog paged him, Sullivan said he would call Beth that evening.

Bulldog, almost exuberant, "Hound's staying in Pensacola and Sergeant Major Sullivan is setting it all up. Let's go to the Ready Room and get a beer." When they arrived, Sticky raised his glass and said, "Here's to Hound, our friend and roommate. The Navy has lost one of its best and brightest. May he rest in peace."

Chapter 61

VT-10 Ends and Hound's Memorial

Early the next morning, Sergeant Major Sullivan contacted Bulldog to tell him that the funeral would be at the Chapel at 16:00 on Saturday, November 8th. Following the service, Hound would be buried at Barrancas Cemetery, and afterwards the Training Command would host a reception for Hound's family and friends at the O Club small ballroom.

In addition, VT-10 would have a brief memorial service immediately following Friday's graduation ceremony. Sullivan also told Bulldog that they would serve as Hound's pallbearers, along with Capt. Mason and two of Hound's cousins. Finally, Sullivan told Bulldog that he and his roommates would join the CO and the Chaplain to greet the cousins at the airport at 11:00.

Striker and Sticky were with Bulldog when he spoke to Sullivan. After he told them the funeral plans, they went to eat breakfast. Striker, "It never occurred to me during the grind of AOCS that being a Naval Flight Officer would involve anything more than flying. I was recently reminded that life goes on. Right after I was commissioned, my mother was almost killed in a car accident. A few weeks later, I assisted at the funeral of a legendary Marine Pilot who died in a senseless motorcycle stunt. And now Hound was killed in a routine training flight. Added to all that, I was in the wedding of two complete strangers, where I came across a girl I accidentally knocked down and who is now very special to me. Flying airplanes has almost become secondary to everything else in my life. I have always believed that the Navy would be my central focus, controlling everything else I might do. Now I know that I was wrong. The demands of being a Naval Aviator don't minimize the responsibilities of everyday life, it complicates them."

An hour later they joined Chaplain O'Reilly and Lt. Cdr. Magnuson at the airport. They soon saw Hound's cousins, identical twins, walk out of the gate. Their names were Dennis and David Stewart, and they were four years older than Hound. After introducing everyone, Magnuson expressed his condolences on behalf of the Training Command. As they walked to the parking lot, Bulldog told them about the funeral briefing, gave them his pager number, and told them to call if they needed anything.

As soon as the twins left, Bulldog asked Lt. Cdr. Magnuson if it was possible for VT-10 to present the family with a memorial plaque which included 'Hound' as part of his name. Magnuson said it was a great idea and he would look into it as soon as he got back to his office.

Later that day Sullivan conducted the briefing. When it was done, Striker took his roommates back to the BOQ, where Bulldog and Sticky went for a run. Striker called Wendy, who answered the phone after the first ring, "I hoped it was you. How's everything going?" Striker replied that the funeral would be at the Chapel, and Hound was going to be buried at Barrancas Cemetery. He said, "I wish you could attend my graduation and Hound's memorial service tomorrow, but I know you have to work." Wendy responded, "I'll certainly be at the funeral and reception Saturday, but I just can't take off tomorrow. I wish I could. What time is the funeral Saturday?" Striker, "It's at 4. After thinking about it, I can probably pick you up. I have to stick around base this evening in case the Stewarts need something, but I'm hoping that I'll be free tomorrow evening. We might be able to have dinner together."

Wendy, "That sounds like it could work, but call me either way." Striker, "You know I will." Wendy, "OK, I'll miss you." That evening, Striker and his roommates again went to the Ready Room hoping to see other classmates who had arrived for the funeral.

Early the next morning, the roommates were in their chokers and eating breakfast in the open mess. Little was said as they began to eat, but Bulldog broke the silence by saying, "I'm not sure how I'm supposed to feel. Part of me is proud that I've completed the first part of flight training, but at the same time, it seems meaningless because of Hound's death. I thought I understood that what I've chosen to do with my life is very dangerous. But until Hound was killed, the danger was just a vague concept, something that happened to someone else, not to me, or to anyone I knew. Reality hit me square in the face when Hound, doing exactly what he was trained to do, went down. Now I know that no matter how hard I train, how good I become as a Naval Aviator, my fate is out of my control." He stopped for a few seconds, and then began again. "I've never been a very religious guy, but as I continue on the path to becoming a Naval Aviator, I intend to make faith an important part of my life; it is obvious that my future is not mine to choose." No one spoke until after they returned to the BOQ.

To keep the VT-10 graduation ceremony brief, Lt. Cdr. Magnuson congratulated the class and handed each graduate his VT-10 wings. When he finished, Magnuson asked Hound's parents to come to the dais. Magnuson briefly described Hound's accomplishments in VT-10 and how he was certain to become an outstanding Naval Aviator. Then he introduced Sergeant Major Sullivan, "Hound was 'one of my guys'; someone who exceeded all the challenges I gave him in AOCS.

370

When I ordered him to bark like a dog, or PT'd him to the point of exhaustion, he did it as hard as he could, and didn't stop until ordered. I knew Hound had the 'right stuff' to succeed in AOCS and flight training. He knew it too, because when he was commissioned, he told me that 'Hound' was his badge of honor. I'll remember him for the rest of my life. His family, friends, and the Navy lost a good one. Rest in peace Hound."

Before he left the dais, Sullivan introduced Bulldog to say a few words. Bulldog was emotional as he completed his remarks with, "As well as being a promising Naval Officer, Hound was my friend and roommate; he was someone that I knew would have my back when things got tough. Without his encouragement, I wouldn't have made it through AOCS. I was lucky to have known Hound and will miss him immensely."

When Bulldog finished, Magnuson handed the Stewarts a plaque with Hound's name and rank engraved above his wings and 'Hound' boldly engraved below them. Mr. Stewart accepted the plaque, wiped tears from his eyes, and held the plaque up over his head. The class stood and applauded.

Magnuson thanked everyone for coming, announced that the aircraft assignments were now posted in the ready room, and told them that the Marine vs. Navy softball game was rescheduled until 1600 Monday. Then he wished the class well and dismissed them for the last time.

After the ceremony, Striker and Bulldog joined the rest of their classmates waiting to learn their assignments. But Sticky, who hurried out of the ceremony, was in front, and yelled to them, "All three of us got F-4s, but training won't begin for at least two months." Striker gave Sticky a thumbs-up and headed for the door with Bulldog.

As he walked out with his roommates, Sticky told them that they wouldn't find out the start date until orders were issued. In the interim, anyone who was selected to RIO training could apply for other training, including Marine Corps Weapons Qualification at Parris Island, Army Parachute School in Fort Benning, Georgia, and a short Air Intelligence Course held on base.

As they left for the BOQ, Bulldog announced that he was going to apply to Parachute Training. Sticky added, "The only thing I'm gonna do is be on the beach as much as I can before it gets too cool." Striker said he'd have to think about it but was leaning toward the shortened Air Intelligence training if there was enough time to complete it.

Sticky then said, "It's 10 am, we have nothing to do for the rest of the day; let's go to the beach." Striker agreed, but said he wanted to get back early, and Bulldog said he needed to run some errands. Not sure how long either would stay there; Striker and Sticky changed their clothes and drove separately to the beach.

With the normal crowd of young people at work or in school, Tiki Beach was practically deserted. Striker had hoped that some of their other classmates would gather there, but none did, so he didn't stay long. He wanted to run some errands and head back to the BOQ.

An hour later, Striker was on his way to the BOQ but stopped at a restaurant that he hoped Wendy would like. It was Liolio's, a steak house that featured prime beef in addition to traditional Italian food. He had never been there but heard from several people that it was outstanding. Taking a chance Wendy would want to go, he made a reservation for that evening. Afterwards, he went to the BOQ to cash a check and give her a call. As he expected Wendy was not home, so he left a message for her. When he finished, Striker did something he had wanted to do since Pless' funeral; he went to see the rest of Barrancas National Cemetery.

After parking his car, Striker went to the cemetery office for directions to Hound's grave. The administrator was a retired Navy Nurse, Commander Megan Callahan. After looking at the burial schedule, Callahan told him that the site was probably still being prepared, but he could go look at it. Then she asked him, "Are you related to Mr. Stewart?" Striker, "No, he was one of my roommates in AOCS and VT-10. We called him Hound, a nickname he got from our AOCS Drill Instructor." Callahan, "Was he the student aviator who was killed in an accident a few days ago?" Striker, "He was. Hound and his pilot were killed as they were landing during a flash storm. A sudden downwind caused a wing tip to hit the runway just as they were touching down, and they crashed in flames." Callahan continued, "I'm sorry for your loss. I know how close roommates can get in AOCS. My late husband went through AOCS, then flight school, and was the CO of a Marine helo squadron. He was killed in action almost three years ago. He's buried here, as well as several Marines I cared for when I worked at a hospital in Saigon. When I retired, I moved back to Pensacola and took a part-time nursing job. On weekends I volunteered here to help visitors find their loved ones. Then, about a year ago, they offered me a paid position doing the same thing. I accepted and quit the nursing job."

"This place is special to me. When I was in Vietnam, I saw the horrible effects of combat every day when I cared for the wounded and dying. Now I do it for those who are gone. I try to learn as much as I can about those who are buried here; they're more than just a name on a tombstone." Striker was at

373

a loss for words, and could only think of saying, "My condolences for the loss of your husband. I'm in awe of your dedication." She replied. "Thank you, but it's the least I can do for these guys. Now tell me about Hound; especially how he got that name." Striker spent the next thirty minutes describing Hound's life; from the day they met at the San Carlos Hotel until the day he died. As he did, Callahan took notes in her journal.

After he left the office, Striker drove the short distance to Hound's grave where a crew was preparing the grave and erecting a canopy. One of the workers asked him if he needed any help. Striker replied that he just wanted to see where his friend was going to be buried the next day. The worker nodded, offered his condolences, and told him to take his time. Striker remained there for about ten minutes then walked to the other side of the cemetery to see Pless' grave.

He walked slowly past rows and rows of gravestones. Striker saw that they were all the same except for a little information about the deceased. He stopped twice to see the panorama of gravestones all around him. It was the resting place for thousands of people who were very different in life, but the same in death. He then understood why Callahan chose to be there, to give meaning to their lives.

When he arrived at Pless' grave, Striker remembered that he hadn't been there since the funeral. At that time the tombstone was surrounded by flowers and American flags. Now, "Medal of Honor" was chiseled above Pless' name, but the flowers and flags were gone. It was now just the same as every other grave. Striker then realized that earning the Medal of Honor meant very little in view of all the other graves there; they were just the final resting place of those who had served their country.

As he stood by the grave, he thought about how Pless had deteriorated so much in the last weeks of his life, and probably needed help, but didn't get it. Was it because there is an unwritten code that Naval Aviators are expected to be hard-drinking risk-takers who could take care of themselves in any situation? Was seeking help a sign of weakness? Certainly, a Medal of Honor recipient didn't need help. It is a part of the program that Naval Aviators should spend their downtime partying, especially at the O Club with its nearly free booze.

Striker knew that Hound was killed doing what the Navy expected him to do, but he wondered if Pless died for the same reason. Striker left the questions unanswered; he knew that the answers would determine his fate.

When Striker got back to his BOQ room, Bulldog was asleep and Sticky was still gone, presumably with Lee Ann. Striker showered, changed into civilian clothes, and returned to the front desk. Seeing no message from Wendy, he told the desk clerk he would wait in a nearby chair for a call.

When Wendy called, the clerk transferred the call to a phone next to Striker's chair. As soon as he said hello, Wendy congratulated him, and then asked how the memorial service went and if he got F-4s. He responded, "The memorial service was sad and, thankfully, very brief. Tomorrow will be a much longer and sadder day. After saying a few words, Magnuson, our Commanding Officer, presented Hound's mother with the wings he would've received, and a memorial plaque. The plaque had 'Hound' engraved below his name. After the presentations, we went to look at the posting of assignments. I did get F-4s, and so did Sticky and Bulldog, but I also learned that the training would not begin for at least two months. In the interim, the Training Command will offer three additional training options, parachute qualification, weapons qualification, and a shortened air intelligence course. We don't have to choose any, but if we decide to take one, we have to do it by next Friday. I'm leaning toward the air intelligence course that will be here on base. The other two are in Parris Island or Fort Benning. Then we went back to the BOQ, and Sticky and I went to the beach. I had hoped to see more classmates, but none were there. After we stuck around for a while, I came back to the BOQ and then went to see Hound's burial site and Pless' grave. How was your day?"

Wendy, "Very busy, but I got all my grades done. I'm beat so I'm going to lie down for a while. Tonight, I really want to be with you. Did you plan anything?" Striker, "I did. I made a reservation for two at Liolio's. I'll pick you up about 6:45. Is that OK?" Wendy replied, "Sounds great. I'll be ready."

Striker took the opportunity to call his father since he hadn't spoken to him since Hound was killed. During the call, he asked his dad how he dealt with being a husband and father while often being deployed to combat assignments. He responded, "Obviously, not very well. I left everything happening at home up to your mother. Right or wrong, I was totally focused on my career as a Naval Aviator. Your mom accepted the responsibly of raising three kids on her own. During the times I was home, I didn't know how to deal with it. I didn't know how to be a dad; I only knew how to fly airplanes."

"When I was home, I did little to help. Over time, we often argued about the smallest things. It became clear that you kids didn't need to suffer through our crumbling relationship. Eventually we agreed that it was better if we ended our marriage rather than ruin our relationship with our children. I've never stopped loving your mom and will always help her in any way I can." Striker, "Dad, I've been dating a girl who has me thinking about exactly what you described. I'm beginning to realize that I may soon have to rethink my priorities. Thanks for your help." The call ended and Striker stopped at his room to pick up his overnight bag, then left to get Wendy.

Wendy was waiting at the entrance to her apartment when Striker arrived. As she walked to his car, he saw that she was wearing a light blue sundress that fit her like it was custom made. Her shoulder length hair glistened in the sunlight, enhancing her natural beauty. Striker almost melted as she smiled at him when he opened her door. After she hugged him, he could only think to say, "You look incredible." Wendy, still smiling, said, "Thank you. I missed you the last couple of days and I wanted you to be happy to see me." Striker, "Well, you hit a home run."

Liolio's was an old-fashioned steakhouse with white tablecloths, wood-paneled walls and an Italian flair. The maître d' escorted them to a back corner table, where their waiter quickly took their drink orders. When the drinks arrived, the waiter asked if they were ready to order or wanted to wait. Striker said, "We'll wait if you don't mind. Thanks for asking."

As they sipped their drinks, Striker told her about going to the cemetery and how moving it was to walk through the thousands of graves. He told her about Commander Callahan who, after a career of taking care of the living, had rededicated her life to caring for those who were dead, including her husband. Then he added, "Every applicant to AOCS should have to walk through the cemetery before they applied. It would peel away the romantic image of Naval Aviation and reveal its stark reality. Naval Aviators risk death every time they get into an aircraft. If more applicants knew the danger they faced, I don't think as many would apply, and even more

377

would quit before they ever got into an aircraft." Wendy listened quietly as Striker spoke. She wondered if this was his way of letting her know what she was getting herself into as their relationship became more serious.

When they finished their drinks, the waiter returned and suggested that they order the house specialty, Chateaubriand for two. Striker looked at Wendy, who said it sounded perfect. Before he left, the waiter also suggested a bottle of Italian Zinfandel to have with dinner. The Chateaubriand looked and tasted so special for such a memorable evening. They remained at Liolio's for almost two hours, enjoying the meal and each other's company. As soon as they were in the car, Wendy said, "Let's go to my place, Leah's gone for the weekend." Striker looked at her for a few seconds. He knew she needed time to heal so he had not pressured her into being intimate.

When they arrived at her apartment, she waited for him to get out, and then led him inside. As soon as he shut the door behind them, she embraced him and whispered in his ear, "I want you to stay with me tonight." Striker looked her, "Are you sure?" Wendy, "I'm positive." Striker nodded then told her that he had to get some things from his car and would be right back. When he returned, Wendy was sitting on the couch with a bottle of wine and two glasses.

After Striker opened the wine, they sat for a few minutes talking. After Wendy finished her glass of wine, Striker took her hand, pulled her to him, and kissed her. When they parted, she whispered, "Let's go to my bedroom." As they climbed into bed and embraced, she told him, "I never believed I could love someone again, but I was wrong. I've fallen in love with you, and I want to be with you always." He responded, "Wendy, I've loved you since the day you returned from Kansas, and I saw you again. I knew then that we're supposed to be together." They made love and then they fell asleep in each other's arms.

Striker woke up a little after 8 am, and he watched Wendy sleep and wondered how it was possible that she was in his life. He certainly didn't need or want a serious girlfriend or wife; he didn't even know where he would be or what he would be doing in a couple of months. Yet he did know, more than anything else, that he wanted to be with Wendy.

Later they were up and dressed. Looking at his watch, Striker said, "I have to be in uniform and at the Chapel by 3. I already planned to pick you up at about one, so how about we go somewhere for breakfast, and then we'll go to the Chapel? There's plenty of time to eat and get back to the BOQ so that I can change." Wendy, "Sure, but first, I need to put on some nicer clothes." Striker, "OK, let's go eat, then we'll head to the BOQ."

Chapter 62

Connors Faces a Difficult Choice

Even though she barely knew him, Hound's death profoundly affected Jane. She hoped to talk about it with Connors over dinner but wanted to go somewhere other than the O Club. The possibility of seeing Hound's friends there would only make her feel worse. They went to Mrs. Hopkin's Boarding House.

As they waited for their dinners, Jane told Connors how upset she was when she heard that two naval aviators were killed during a routine training flight. Initially she was in a panic but was soon relieved when Connors assured her that he was fine. Unfortunately, when she learned that one of Striker's roommates was killed, her fears reemerged. Connors, "It's not surprising that the accident upset you. Striker, his other roommates, as well as all Naval Aviators are hurting. The death of one of us reminds all of us that what we do is dangerous. Even with the extensive training we receive, unpredictable things, like wind shear, occur; and all pilots must deal with them." With tears in her eyes, Jane said, "I want to get used to these crashes happening, but I know it's not possible. You are in harm's way every time you get into an aircraft and may not come home. It doesn't matter if you are in Florida or at Yankee Station." Connors tried to console her as they ate, but she was still crying as they drove to their apartment.

When they got home, Connors found an envelope from the Naval Test Pilot School. He set everything else down and opened it. It was a copy of a letter that was sent to the Naval Air Training Command informing them that Connors application for the July 1970 class had passed its initial review. It would now be sent to the Test Pilot Selection Board in mid-January, with selections announced in February.

Test Pilot School was what Connors had worked for since he began college. As he put the letter on the coffee table, Jane came into the living room and sat next to him. "Is there anything wrong? More bad news?" Connors, "Well, it's both bad and good. The good news is my application for Test Pilot School made the first cut and I'll find out in February if I was selected. The bad news is the same thing." Jane, "What do you mean? It's definitely good news." Connors, "The bad news is that if I am selected for the July class, I'll be detailed to Pax River for about a year."

Jane was silent for a few seconds then said, "Is there any chance you could fly home on weekends?" Connors, "I don't know for sure, but I expect I could some weekends, as part of proficiency training. I can ask, but even if I can come home weekends, I wouldn't be here to help you and the baby during the week." Jane, "You would still be here until the end of June, the most difficult time for me. Plus, I have six weeks of maternity leave, and the baby will be over three months old by the time you leave. Besides, even if you were here, you would still have to work, and couldn't help me during the day. I expect my mother will be here the first couple of weeks, and your mom and sister will help after that. It's not as though I won't have any help. I know that Test Pilot School has been your goal for years, please don't think you need to turn down a chance of a lifetime opportunity for my sake. Besides, if you are selected, you'll be stateside, and we can be with you."

Connors was silent for few seconds before he responded, "OK, I won't withdraw my application, but if anything changes, I'll rethink what I'm going to do."

381

Chapter 63

Hound's Funeral

After Wendy put on a black dress, Striker gathered his belongings and walked towards the door. Wendy, seeing that he was ready to leave, "Don't you want to stay with me again. I'm not going to get many opportunities to have the apartment to myself." Striker, "You know I do, but I didn't want to be presumptive." Wendy, "The only thing that you have to presume is that I want you with me all the time." Then as she hugged him, he replied, "I want to be with you. When I change into my uniform at the BOQ, I'll get some clothes that I'll need tomorrow." Wendy, "Maybe tomorrow, but you won't need any tonight."

As Striker started his car, he asked, "Got any idea where you want to go?" Wendy, "The only place I've been to is the Gulf Breeze Diner, but it's very popular, so we may have to wait for a table." Striker, "That's where we'll go, we're not in a hurry." As Wendy warned, there was a twenty-minute wait for a table, but it was worth it. The food was plentiful and delicious. While they ate Striker said, "I told you about the training delay and the alternate training they made available. I'm pretty sure I'll apply for Air Intelligence School. It's related to what I would be doing as a RIO, and the training is here. I suspect the training delay will be a lot longer than two months; there are just not enough F-4 seats. Some people in RIO training may be reassigned out of necessity, and Air Intelligence is a logical alternative. Wendy, "I hoped that you'd choose Air Intelligence. I know that eventually you'll be transferred somewhere, so I'd like it to be later rather than sooner."

Once they left the diner, Striker stopped at the BOQ and escorted Wendy to the lobby. Striker, "I'd like to show you my suite, but female visitors are prohibited, although it is well known that it's been violated many times." Striker smiled as he added, "Sticky may be one of them. Someday I'll tell you about it. It was really off the wall." When he got to his suite, Bulldog was sitting in the living room wearing his choker. Striker, "Hey man, are you ready for this?" Bulldog, "As ready as I can be. I'm not looking forward to it at all. Sticky is in your room changing." Bulldog, "By the way, I filled out the application for Jump School. I'll submit it Monday." Striker, "I'm almost positive I'm going to apply for Air Intelligence, so I might go with you."

Before Striker could say anything else, Sticky walked in and announced, "I got accepted to suntan school at Tiki Beach. I start Monday." They all laughed as Striker went to change. When he was ready, all three roommates went to the lobby where Bulldog and Sticky spoke briefly to Wendy, and they all left for the Chapel.

Wendy went into the Chapel while Striker looked outside for the twins. He soon saw them with an Air Force officer and a minister he had never met. The three of them joined him in front of the Chapel. David said, "Striker, I want you to meet Hound's family pastor Rev. Frank Gault and 2nd Lt. Tom DeMarco, Hound's best friend from Pennsylvania. Peggy asked Tom to be a pallbearer a few days ago." DeMarco said, "Thank you. I really wanted to be here, but I told Mrs. Stewart that I didn't think it would be possible for me to get here in time. I'm stationed at Tan San Nhat Air Base in Saigon."

Rev. Gault interrupted him by saying then he had to leave so he could get ready for the service, and DeMarco continued, "Somehow your Training Command arranged a series of military flights that got me here early this morning. It was a 28-hour trip, I'm a little goofy from the time changes." Striker laughed, "Welcome to our world, just about everybody in Navy flight training is a little goofy. It helps us do what we do." Just then, Sergeant Major Sullivan, Sticky, and Bulldog joined them. Sullivan said, "You must be Lt. DeMarco. I'm Sergeant Major Sullivan. I am glad that you made it here." After DeMarco said that he appreciated everyone's efforts, Sullivan introduced Sticky and Bulldog, and added, "I helped show Hound and these guys what leadership and paying attention to detail are; both are needed to strap into a Naval aircraft." He paused for a second, smiled and continued, "It was an enormous challenge but somehow I was able to get through to them." Looking at his watch, "Gents, we've got to get ready." He told DeMarco that he needed to show him the Chapel and the protocol the pallbearers would follow during the ceremony. Twenty minutes later, they were in formation waiting for the hearse.

The funeral lasted less than an hour, including a moving eulogy from the twins, who took turns speaking. After describing several endearing antics that Hound got caught doing growing up, they spoke briefly about his intense desire to become a Naval Aviator. Dennis, "Alan was born to be a Naval Aviator. As a kid he built models of naval aircraft and the carriers they flew from. Later, he watched every movie about Naval Air battles that he could find, including old 'Victory at Sea' tapes. When he was accepted to Aviation Officer's Candidate School, he was elated that he was on his way. Drill Instructor Sullivan named him 'Hound' and from that point on that was what he wanted to be called. Hound was his badge of honor; he completed AOCS and was in flight training. Sadly, the unthinkable happened. Hound and his pilot, Fred Spiros, were suddenly killed during a routine training flight. At the worst possible moment, a freak storm hit Sherman Field just as they were touching down. When you think about Hound, please remember that he willingly accepted the danger he faced every day. He loved flying, and he is at peace."

As the organist began playing the Navy Hymn, Striker and the other pallbearers slowly pushed the coffin to the back of the church and out the front door. When they finished putting it into the hearse, they went to the cemetery.

Wendy and Striker arrived at the site before the other pallbearers. Wendy looked around at the rows of graves and said, "Now I know why you came here yesterday. The tombstones seem to go all the way to the horizon in all directions. It's moving; I'm glad you brought me here." Striker saw the twins with DeMarco and he told Wendy he had to join them.

Ten minutes later the hearse stopped as close to the gravesite as it could. The funeral director gathered the pallbearers and detailed the protocol for the last time. Then they pulled the casket out of the hearse and took it to the gravesite.

When Hound's family was gathered close to the casket, Rev. Gault made his final remarks and Bulldog removed the flag and handed it to Mrs. Stewart. Then Hound's parents put a rose on the casket, prayed silently, and left. Commander Mason thanked everyone for coming and reminded them about the reception at the Officers' Club.

When they arrived at the O Club, Wendy sat with her sister and brother-in-law while Striker joined the other pallbearers with the Stewart family. Beth Stewart hugged her nephews, Tom DeMarco, Striker and his roommates. She was fighting tears as she said, "I know why my son thought so highly of you all. You're good people who help each other when things get tough. As he told me on the day he was commissioned, he would be proud for any one of you to be his wingman. Thank you for being his friend and remember you will always be welcome in our home."

As Mrs. Stewart began to greet other people, Striker returned to Wendy. Jane hugged him and said she knew how much Hound meant to him and was saddened to hear about his death. Connors reiterated his condolences, saying it was a tragedy that he died so young. Striker thanked them and sat next to Wendy, taking her hand as he did.

When the Stewart family prepared to leave the reception, Cdr. Mason announced that everyone was invited to stay and enjoy the food and beverages. Striker asked Wendy if she would rather eat in the Ready Room, or the finger foods offered at the buffet. She said she would prefer a meal and asked her sister and brother-in-law if they wanted to join them. Jane said, "Sounds good to me. I'm starving for a cheeseburger with lots of pickles and some fries. I've gotta' feed this baby some real food." Connors shrugged his shoulders and said, "I'm with her."

Striker excused himself to tell his roommates his plans. Both wanted to stay for the buffet and have a few beers. Striker, "Then I'll see you guys tomorrow. I'll be at Wendy's place tonight. Sticky, "I think love is in in the air. Our dedicated ladies' man may have met his match." Striker, "Could be, could be, and I'm not fighting it."

Striker walked into the Ready Room just as a group of four was leaving. After Wendy and Jane sat down, Wendy pointed toward the bar, "Hound's picture is back on the bar, with flowers and a card." Striker was not able to see the picture from his seat, so he went to look at it. Next to the picture was a guest book that Striker hadn't yet signed. He waved for Wendy to sign it with him, and said, "I'm sad to say that this guest book will probably be the last connection I'll have with Hound or his family. It's hard to believe that about a week ago, Hound was living his dream, but it ended in a violent split second. Unfortunately, as things go, tomorrow this picture will be gone, but I'll remember and miss him." Connors was sitting next to Jane when they returned to the table. After everyone ordered their meals, they avoided making conversation about Hound, and talked about Jane's coming baby. Soon after Connors and Jane finished eating, they went home. Sticky and Bulldog, who had been at the bar, took the empty seats, where they remained reminiscing about Hound until the bar closed.

Later, at Wendy's apartment, she and Striker sought comfort in each other's arms. They made love until they fell asleep and didn't wake up until after 9. When they were up and dressed, they again ate at the Gulf Breeze Diner, and went to the beach.

Wendy slept while Striker swam. Nearly an hour later Striker joined Wendy on the blanket and was also asleep. As it approached 3 pm, they were awakened by nearby children and were headed back to her apartment. Striker said, "I need to get back to base early tonight to finish the application for Air Intelligence training. "I need to get home, too. I have a bunch of preparations to do for this week's classes." When they got to her place, Wendy said, "I just realized that you won't be here tomorrow." Smiling, she led him to her bedroom.

Striker got to his BOQ room just as Sticky and Bulldog returned from eating a late lunch. Sticky, "I see you found your way back, Mr. Lovestruck. I was beginning to think you and Wendy eloped." Striker, "You're partially right. Wendy is unlike any other girl I've ever met, but we haven't made any plans to get married, yet."

That evening Striker completed his application for Air Intelligence training, then joined his roommates in the suite living area, "Gents, I'm applying to Air Intelligence School. Sticky, I know you're just going to hang out at the beach. Bulldog, are you still going to Jump School?" Bulldog, "You bet I am. I got the completed application on my dresser and I'm gonna submit it first thing tomorrow morning." Striker, "So am I. Want to go together?" Bulldog, "Sure, let's meet up about 7 am and get some breakfast before we go?" Striker, "You're on. See you then." Then as they finished, Sticky, "Don't forget the squadron picnic and softball game is tomorrow at 1 pm."

Chapter 64

VT-10 Squadron Softball Game

Striker and Bulldog finished breakfast and headed to VT-10. They arrived at the CO's office just as Commander Magnuson was leaving. He greeted them in the hallway, "Good morning, Gents. Are you here to apply for training during the RIO school delay?" Bulldog responded, "Yes Sir. I'm applying for Jump School and Striker wants to go to the Air Intelligence School." Magnuson, "Good timing. I just sent a notice to everyone in the RIO pipeline. The backup is much larger than previously estimated. The delay may be six months or more, and the number of available RIO seats may be reduced, but that decision has not been made yet. In the interim, the Training Command is opening more alternative training and allowing the affected people to request different assignments. There is even a possibility that people will be discharged. And as of this morning, Air Intelligence training has been extended to 12 weeks, half the normal Air Force AI curriculum. It appears that just about everyone who applies for AI and Jump School will be accepted. Do you Gents still want to apply?" They both quickly replied, "Yes sir." Magnuson said, "OK, take your applications to the XO's office. Good luck."

As they drove back to the BOQ, Bulldog, sounding angry, "Well, that was a kick in the ass. It now appears that the reason I joined the Navy and went to AOCS may no longer be attainable. I almost quit after I was disqualified from being a pilot. I stuck with it even though I had no interest in being a RIO. It was the only way I could get into an F-4; it kept me going all those weeks of AOCS. Now, because of a recruitment

389

screw-up, those sixteen weeks don't mean shit. To think that Hound died trying to reach a goal which may be unachievable really pisses me off. The almighty needs of the Navy are all that counts. If I had to make a choice right now, I'd probably take the out." After a few minutes of silence, "I know I'm pissed, especially about Hound, so I'll wait, go to Jump School, and see how it goes the next few weeks" Striker "That's pretty much how I feel. I always wanted to be a Naval Aviator, a pilot like my dad, not an NFO. If that is no longer a choice, I'd probably request a transfer to AI. I'll wait to see how I like the first weeks of AI training before I make up my mind."

When they walked into the suite, Sticky was in civilian clothes, waiting for them to return. "How'd it go? You guys all signed up?" Bulldog, "We are, but there's a hitch. The delay is now expected to be as much as six months and could get worse. The pipeline is so backed up they may even have to cut the number of F-4 seats, and offer other choices, maybe even discharges. We're both pissed, but without any other option, the Navy is recommending that everyone in the F-4 pipeline take the additional training." Sticky, "Whoa, six months. I'm going to get a lot more beach time, 'cause I'm not going to do any other training. I'm either a RIO or I'm not. If that means I'll be booted out of the Navy, so be it. By the way, I'm going to the motorcycle dealer in town and look at a Harley-Davidson Sportster. Either of you want to go? We should be back by noon." Bulldog declined but Striker said he had nothing else to do so he'd take him there.

It didn't take long before Sticky bought a jet-black 1967 Harley-Davidson 900 cc Sportster with an aftermarket boom box. As Striker got in his car to go back to base, Sticky rode off to parts unknown. Three hours later, Striker was warming up at the ball field while Sticky was still on the road, apparently testing the limits of his bike. Striker was getting a little concerned because Sticky, who played college baseball, had volunteered to be the Navy team Captain. With not much else to do, Striker and his teammates just sat around and drank beer as they waited for Sticky to arrive.

Suddenly, everyone heard the unmistakable rumbling of a Harley as it approached the ballpark. Then Sticky brazenly rode his Harley across the open field. He was wearing gym shorts, no shirt, and a Navy Blue helmet with "Fly Navy" emblazoned across the back. All the while, his boom box blasted Steppenwolf's, *Born to be Wild*. As he reached the dugout, Sticky turned off the boom box and revved the bike's engine causing it to backfire several times. Then he shut it down, grabbed a beer, and yelled, "OK, Gents. Let's play some ball."

It only took Sticky ten minutes to choose players for each position, saying, "I did some pitching in high school and college, so I'll pitch the first three innings, after that I'll probably need some relief. Unless any of you guys have some experience at a position, I'm just going to randomly select people. Everyone will play, so if you're not on the field now, you will be soon. Now let's kick some Marine Corps butts." The Marines won the coin toss and opted to be the home team. Both teams took the field, the umpire waved the first hitter to the plate, and yelled, "Play Ball."

BOQ stewards set up a charcoal grill and a fifty-gallon barrel filled with beer and ice. It was an unusually hot October day, so there was a lot of beer drinking and very little food eaten. Many players from both teams drank almost continually, so it didn't take long before many of them were trashed, but by far the worst drunk was the second baseman, a Marine second lieutenant.

By the bottom of four innings, the second baseman was barely able to take his turn at bat. At the top of the fifth inning, he passed out on the second base bag, and no one could get him up. He became second base. The game continued with him on the bag for two more innings. When the seventh inning ended, the game was tied, but seeing the condition of most of the players, the two Captains called it a tie and ended the game.

Striker, knowing he couldn't hold a lot of beer in the hot sun, only finished two beers. Unfortunately, by 4 pm, Sticky and Bulldog were drunk, but not ready to stop partying. Sticky started his new bike and yelled for Bulldog to get on the 'sissy seat' behind him. They rode around the bases while Sticky yelled, "Anyone want to go to Barrancas Beach and jump the dunes?" Two Marines, named Larimer and Hodgkiss, yelled that they were up for it. Striker followed behind in case something happened.

There were no dunes and only mounds of sand, similar to ski moguls, on Barrancas Beach. When Striker arrived, he could see that Sticky had found a large one, almost three-feet tall, about a quarter mile from the parking lot. As Striker got closer to them, Bulldog started the Harley, drove it about fifty feet away from the mound, and sped toward it. He climbed the mound, became airborne for about six feet, and landed on both wheels. Sticky marked Bulldog's landing point with a piece of driftwood, then told the Marines it was their turn. Larimer and Hodgkiss made longer jumps than Bulldog's.

Not to be outdone by a Marine, Sticky started his approach farther away, nearly 100 feet. He revived the Harley to its maximum and sprayed a plume of sand behind him as he roared to the mound. When he went into the air, the Harley upended, throwing Sticky off. It landed directly on him. Striker and the others rushed to get the bike, engine still running, off Sticky. Sticky was writhing in pain and pointing to his right leg.

Striker didn't have to touch Sticky's leg to know that it was badly broken. It was slightly bent, and a bone had penetrated the skin above his ankle. It looked to Striker that Sticky had a compound fracture. He found out later that he was right. Striker, "He's gonna need an ambulance. No one touch him. Bulldog, stay here while I find a phone. Hodgkiss, you and Larimer take his bike to the BOQ. I'll be back as soon as I can." Then he ran to his car. When he arrived at the entrance to the beach, Striker saw a pavilion with a payphone. Luckily, it had free emergency calls, and he called for help. When the dispatcher answered, she asked where the accident occurred and who was injured. Striker told her, and she told him to wait at the entrance to Barrancas Beach so he could direct the ambulance to Sticky.

Ten minutes later, an ambulance, siren wailing, stopped where Striker was standing. He yelled, "Follow me," and got in his car to lead them to Sticky. Bulldog was sitting on the sand talking to Sticky when the ambulance arrived. "It looks like Striker got you some help. How're you feeling?" Sticky, "It hurts like hell, and it's turning blue. I'm pretty sure I broke at least one bone in my leg."

A female EMT soon knelt next to him and asked, "What happened?" Sticky, "I lost control of my motorcycle on the sand, and it fell on my leg." EMT, "OK, did you hurt any other part of your body, or do you feel any other pain?" Sticky, "I don't think I did; the only pain I feel is in my leg. It hurts like hell." The EMT gently examined his leg and said, "It is clearly broken right above the ankle, maybe in two places, and I can see a bone sticking out. Don't try to stand up. I'm going to put an IV line in and start a saline drip. It'll help prevent you from going into shock. Then we're going to put you on a stretcher and carry you off the sand and on to a gurney to get you into the ambulance. You're going to feel a little sting, then a lot of pain when we move you."

The EMT inserted the IV and attached a drip bag. The other EMT laid a stretcher next to Sticky. After he was lifted, the EMT asked Bulldog to carry the drip bag while she and the other EMTs carried Sticky to the gurney. As he was pushed into the ambulance, Sticky, with his new Fly Navy helmet at his side, smiled weakly and gave a thumbs-up. Once the ambulance doors were shut, Bulldog got into Striker's car, and they followed the ambulance to the hospital.

After being in the waiting room for over an hour, an ER doctor came out and asked if anyone was with Mr. Hickey. Both Striker and Bulldog raised their hands and the doctor said, "Mr. Hickey has fractures of both the tibia and fibula of his right leg. One of them is a compound fracture. We'll operate as soon as we can get him into an operating room. The compound fracture is about as bad a leg injury as I've seen in a long time, but I'm confident we'll be able to put it back together. He's young and in good shape, so I expect he'll have a full recovery, assuming no complications and several months of rehabilitation. My staff has notified his CO, who'll contact his family. The procedure will probably take several hours, and he'll be in post-op for several more, so you guys should go on home. He'll probably be able to have visitors early tomorrow afternoon but give us a call before you come." He paused as he gave them the phone number for the OR charge nurse, and continued, "Unless there are more questions, we'll see you tomorrow." Bulldog thanked the doctor then he and Striker went back to the BOQ.

As soon as they got to the BOQ, Bulldog went to take a nap, and Striker called Wendy. When she answered. Striker, "Hi, I'm sorry I didn't call earlier, but I've been at the hospital. Sticky had a serious motorcycle accident and is in surgery." Wendy, "I thought something was wrong. It's not like you do not call. I hope he's not badly hurt." Striker, "It could be worse. He broke his leg in two places. He was riding on Barrancas Beach and tried to make a jump over a small sand dune when his bike lost traction. It flipped, dumped him, and landed on his leg. We followed the ambulance as it took him to the hospital. Later, the doctor told us it was a bad injury but was confident Sticky would totally recover. He also said that the healing and rehabilitation process would take several months. Then they took Sticky into surgery. We'll go see him tomorrow afternoon if he's up to it."

Wendy, "My God, what's next? It seems like you guys are jinxed." Striker, "Yeah, it's been a difficult couple of months, but I'm told that bad news comes in threes. With Pless and Hound's death and now Sticky's accident, the jinx should be over. Anyway, I haven't had dinner yet, have you?" Wendy, "No, I haven't, and I'm starved." Striker, "I'll take a quick shower, pick you up, and we'll go eat somewhere. I can be at your place in about forty minutes."

When Striker knocked on Wendy's door, Leah let him in and said, "Wendy's not quite ready; come in and have a seat. How are you? I haven't talked to you in a while. Riley and I saw you at Hound's funeral and reception. I'm so sorry for your loss. Hound was such a great guy." Striker, "Thanks, I'm gonna miss him a lot. He was a great friend. Did Wendy tell you what happened to Sticky?" Leah, "Just that he had a motorcycle accident and was in the hospital. How's he doing?" Striker, "As good as we could hope. The doc said it was a really bad injury and would take months to completely heal. His training is gonna be delayed a long time."

Wendy came into the living room just as Striker finished talking. She sat next to him, took his hand, and said, "I'm glad you called. I missed you." Striker, "I really needed to see you. It was another rough day. Where do you want to eat? I prefer anywhere but the O Club. I need to get away from the base for a couple of hours." Wendy, "Somewhere on the water. I'm hungry for fresh seafood."

They ended up eating at the Sunset Bar and Grill on Pensacola Bay, north of Tiki Beach. They remained there until 8:30 p.m., when she asked him if he wanted to go to her place for a while. Striker agreed, and ten minutes later, they were in her apartment. As Wendy brought Striker a beer, she said, "I don't expect Leah to be back before 11. Let's go to my room."

The next morning, Striker got up early and went for a run. When he returned, Bulldog was waiting for him in the suite living room. Bulldog, "Wanna go to breakfast?" Striker, "Yeah, give me fifteen minutes, and we'll head to the open mess." After they finished eating, they went to the desk to call the hospital. Striker reached the OR nurse's station and asked for the charge nurse. As soon as she picked up the phone, Striker asked her about Sticky's condition. "The procedure lasted nearly six hours and he's now in post-op. The surgeon ended up attaching two rods to his tibia and one to his fibula, but the surgery was successful. He's going to be in a lot of pain for several weeks and will have to be in rehab for at least three months. It'll be at least six months before he regains normal use of that leg. Call back this afternoon, and we'll let you know if he can have visitors."

When they returned to the BOQ, Striker had a message from his sister. He was worried and called right back. When Lizzy answered, he immediately asked if everything was OK. Lizzy responded, "Everything is good. I have great news, but I first want to tell you that I'm so sorry that you lost your roommate. My prayers are with him." Striker, "Yeah, it was tough. He was a great guy and close friend, but I need to hear some good news. What's going on?" Lizzy, almost yelling, "I'm getting married. My boyfriend Jerry, who has been a policeman for a couple of years, was accepted into the FBI Academy and he leaves for Quantico in less than three weeks. It's what he's always wanted, and I told him he had to accept. We've been talking about getting married for about a year and decided that now is just as good a time as any. I went to my parish priest, and he arranged for us to use St. Nicholas, the base chapel, next Saturday, November 15th, at 4 p.m. It will be a pretty small wedding with just a few friends and family in attendance. I'm thrilled to death. I hope you can be there." Striker, "I'll find out soon and let you know. Congratulations, I'm happy for you."

It wasn't yet 10 am, so Striker decided to go to VT-10 to ask the XO, Lt. Santoro, if he could take leave to go to the wedding. Then he changed into the uniform of the day and told Bulldog what he was doing. He also told Bulldog that he should be back around noon to call the hospital. Bulldog said he would be out running errands but would be back about the same time.

Fifteen minutes later, Striker knocked on Lt. Santoro's office door. He casually yelled, "Come on in." Then as Striker approached him, Santoro told him to be at ease and have a seat. "How are you, Mr. Striker? You've had a lot on your plate recently. My condolences on the death of your roommate. It is so sad when they are young and just starting a career. What can I do for you?" Striker, "Well Sir, first, did you receive any information about Mr. Hickey?" Santoro, "I did, yesterday afternoon, but I haven't heard anything since that time. Do you know how he's doing?" Striker, "I only know that the surgery was complicated but successful. He really broke his leg badly. The doc said it would take several months before he's back to normal. I'm gonna try to see him later today." Santoro, "I guess we'll get the doctor's report late today. It sounds like he'll be rehabbing during the entire training delay. I'll try to go see him later. Now, what can I do for you?"

Striker, "Sir, I came to ask for leave to go to my sister's wedding in Pax River on Saturday, November 15th. I'd like to leave Friday and return Monday. This is a wedding being planned at the last minute." Santoro, "I tell you what, you've been putting a lot of time in recently. Let me see if I can get you on a MATS (Military Air Transport Service) flight as a crewmember. You'll just need to sit near the cockpit and observe what's going on. It will take longer to get there than flying commercial, but you'll be on duty and won't need to take any leave. Does that sound OK?" Striker, "Yes Sir, that sounds great." Santoro, "Then I'll call you as soon as I find out something. You'll have to excuse me now; I have to go to a staff meeting." Striker, "Thank you sir."

It was still too early to call the hospital, so Striker went to visit Hound's grave. When he arrived, he was encouraged to see that it was still surrounded with flowers and American flags. He also wondered how long it would be before it was just another forgotten grave in the midst of thousands of others. As he reflected on Hound's sudden death, he heard the occasional roar of aircraft flying overhead and the distinctive sound of Marine Drill Instructors barking orders at fledgling officer candidates. It was the sound of college boys being transformed into the men who were to become Naval Aviators. Hound was very proud to have been one of them; it was the most important thing in his life. Now it was over, Hound was dead. Almost out loud, Striker whispered, "Hound, I'm glad your family decided to keep you here. This is where you spent the most challenging, yet happiest, days of your life." Then he crossed himself and said a silent prayer.

Striker returned to his car and drove slowly toward the cemetery exit. As he did, the sheer number of tombstones again overwhelmed him. He realized that in just the short period of time he had been in the Navy, Hound and Pless died, Sticky suffered a life-changing injury, and his own future as a Naval Aviator was in jeopardy. As he approached the gate, he saw still another internment taking place on a small hill, about a quarter mile off the road. He thought he saw a familiar figure standing nearby so he stopped to look; it was Commander Callahan. She was again taking notes as she spoke to those who were gathered to say goodbye to a friend or loved one. Watching her brought him to tears, and for the first time, he wondered if becoming a Naval Aviator was worth the risk, and if it was what he really wanted.

Chapter 65

Striker Goes to His Sister's Wedding

Striker went back to the BOQ. When he checked for messages, there was one from Lt. Santoro, "Mr. Striker, the meeting was cancelled so I went to base flight ops. There are several flights to and from Pax River on Friday and Monday. You need to go there ASAP and sign up for the ones you want. Let me know how it goes." Striker left a note for Bulldog and left for the flight ops office at Sherman Field.

An hour later, Striker walked into the living room of his suite. Bulldog, who was on the couch reading a Jump School manual, asked, "Did you have any luck getting flights?" Striker, "I sure did. I just called Lt. Santoro to tell him. I'm on a regularly scheduled MATS reservist run. It's a R6D that leaves Sherman at 8 am, November 14, stops at Eglin, Pope Field, Oceana, and then Pax River. With decent weather, the flight should take about eight and a half hours, getting me to Pax River at about 3:30 pm. Then on Monday, I'm on the return flight of the same aircraft. It leaves Pax River at 6 pm, only stops once, and arrives here at 11 pm. The great thing is they'll let me sit in a jump seat in the cockpit, both ways. All I have to do is watch and listen."

It was a little before 1 pm when they called the hospital. The charge nurse told them they could see Sticky, but he was in a lot of pain and falling in and out of sleep, so they had to limit their visit to an hour. Striker said they would be there in fifteen minutes.

Sticky was sitting up with his right leg in an elevated sling. When Bulldog asked how he was doing, Sticky grimaced and said, "Like I ejected from twenty thousand feet without a parachute. I hurt everywhere, but especially my leg which feels like it's being pounded by a gremlin with a six-pound sledgehammer." Then as he smiled, "Otherwise I feel great. You guys have any idea what happened to my Harley? Also, I haven't talked to Lee Ann, could one of you tell her to call me? I'm gonna ask her to move in with me at the house I rented. She's been staying there a lot with me, so I'm pretty sure she will. I'll sure need her help, 'cause I refuse to go to a rehab hospital." Bulldog, "Yeah, I'll call her, and Larimer parked your Harley at the BOQ. He dropped the key off to me earlier today and I put it on your dresser, but I don't think you're gonna be riding it any time soon." Sticky, "Yeah, I know. The doc told me that it would be a couple of months before I could even walk without crutches. Riding that Harley was the most fun I've ever had with my clothes on. Since I won't be able to ride it for a while, you guys can use it anytime you want. By the way, other than asking how I was, I haven't heard a word from the CO about my training status. The doc, who was a flight surgeon, said that I'm not going to be able to fly for a long time, maybe as much as a year." Striker, "I saw Lt. Santoro yesterday. He told me he was waiting to find out what your prognosis is, and then he'll come to see you. It might be today." Twenty minutes later, when a nurse came to check Sticky's vital signs and administer a painkiller, Striker and Bulldog went back to the BOQ.

When they got there, Striker called a couple of airlines to see if there were any convenient flights to Baltimore or DC on Friday and returning to Pensacola Monday. The travel agent reminded him that the schools would have Monday off, so Striker told her to look for flights in the afternoon both days.

With that in mind, Striker decided that he was going to ask Wendy to go.

There were two flights, one to Baltimore Friendship and the other to DC National. Either one of them was scheduled at times when Striker could take Wendy to the airport. The only real difference was that National Airport was closer to Pax River and Friendship Airport was an easier drive. No matter which one she took, he would be there.

Striker then called Lizzy to see if he could bring Wendy to the wedding. Lizzy had quit her job the week before and was home preparing for the wedding. When she answered the phone, Striker asked her how the preparations were going. Lizzy, "Good, the Chapel is all set and dad has reserved a private room at the O Club for the rehearsal dinner and the reception. Even better, he said he would pay for both, as a wedding present. When you called, I was completing the final list of guests." Striker, "Then I called just in time. I'd like to bring a date. Her name is Wendy Carmody and we've been seeing each other for several months." Lizzy, "Is it serious?" Striker, "Very much so. I've never met anyone like her. She is very special to me, and I'd like to introduce her to you and the rest of the family. Your wedding would be the perfect time to do it." Lizzy, "Then of course you can bring her. I'd love to meet her. I'll add her name to the list for both events." Striker, "Well you'd better wait a couple hours. I wanted to find out if it was OK before I asked her. I'll call you back when she gets home from work, about 4:30." Lizzy, "I hope she can come. I'm looking forward to meeting her. I have to run; I've got a boatload of things to do and very little time to do them."

Later Striker called Wendy. Almost as soon as she answered, he asked if she wanted to go with him to his sister's wedding in Maryland the coming weekend. He apologized for the late notice but explained he had just learned that she was getting married. Striker, "I've been approved to be a crew member on a Navy flight to and from Pax River, so I'll be going separately. The commercial flights I found for you are going to either Baltimore or DC National, but I'll have plenty of time to pick you up and take you back to either one. I'll even pay for everything. I really want you to meet you my family, and this is a perfect way to do it."

Wendy, "I'd love to go. I've wanted to meet your family. I have Monday off and can take a personal day for Friday. I hope I'm not imposing on them this close to the wedding, and you don't have to pay for the flights." Striker, "I already talked to Lizzy, and she's thrilled to have you there. Since I was allowed to go on a MATS flight, I don't have to pay for any flight. Paying for your tickets is no big deal." After a few seconds, Wendy responded, "I'll go, but I want to pay half." Striker, "That'll work. I'll make the reservations as soon as you pick the airline." Wendy, "Either is OK with me; I can take half a day off and be ready any time after 1 pm. Book the one which is the most convenient for you." Striker, "OK, I'll take care of everything, and I'd like to take you to eat so we could talk about the details over dinner. Are you up for it?" Wendy, "You know I am. I'll be ready in an hour."

Before he left, Striker called his sister. As she answered she said, "If Wendy can come, there's something else I need to tell you. Mom's house is already filled with out-of-town family, but she reserved a few rooms at a motel about two miles from the Chapel. It's the Patuxent View Motel and I'll give you their number. There's also the Navy Lodge on base, which is for VIPs and visiting families. I'm told it's really nice. You might be able to book a room there, but don't mention that Wendy isn't your wife; it's supposed to be for families. I can give you

403

their number as well. Striker, "She wants to come, so give me both phone numbers." He thanked Lizzy and told her he'd see her on Friday.

After he hung up with Lizzy, Striker called the Navy Lodge and reserved a room for two people for three nights. They didn't ask if Wendy was his wife, and he didn't mention it. Then he made reservations on Eastern Airlines for Wendy to fly to Friendship Airport in Baltimore and return to Pensacola.

When he arrived at Wendy's apartment, Connors and Jane let him in. They had come over to visit Wendy and Leah, but Leah wasn't there; she was still at a school workshop. Connors said, "Wendy just went to her room to get ready, and we were just leaving. Before we go, how are you doing? How is your friend Sticky? Wendy told us that he was injured badly in a motorcycle accident." Striker said, "I'm fine, thanks, and Sticky's doing pretty well. I saw him earlier today. His surgery was successful, but he's going to be out of commission for several months. The docs had to use three metal rods to put his leg back together so he's in a lot of pain. As bad as it is, Sticky was lucky that it wasn't worse. Typical Naval Aviator, he really likes to live on the edge."

As Wendy came out of her bedroom, Connors and Jane opened the door to leave. Striker, now standing, asked them, "Would you guys like to join us? We're going out to dinner." Connors, "Normally we'd love to, but Jane isn't feeling well, so we'll take a pass. You guys enjoy yourselves. We'll meet you another time."

As soon as Wendy got into Striker's car, he told her that everything was set for her to go to Maryland. Then he added. "Since my mother's house is full, I made a reservation for us to stay at the Navy Lodge. They may think that we're married.

Is that OK with you?" Wendy, smiling, "Do you mean being your wife? Or just being with you for the weekend." Before he could answer, Wendy laughed as she added. "You don't have to answer that, either way sounds great to me. I just want to be with you."

Chapter 66

A Surprise at Lizzy's Wedding

Striker's flight took longer than expected. The old aircraft had to plow through a strong headwind and several storms all the way up the Coast. The weather also caused delayed departures from their planned stops. Luckily, even with all the delays, the flight still arrived in Pax River with enough time for Striker to pick up Wendy in Baltimore. Still in a flight suit, he took a shuttle to an on-base car rental agency, picked up a car and headed to Baltimore. Less than two hours later, Striker parked in a short-term lot and went to the arrival gate.

Wendy's flight was delayed by the same bad weather that delayed Striker's flight. Thirty minutes later, she cleared the gate, saw Striker and waved. Striker hugged her, took her bag, and walked toward the exit, Striker, "I hope your flight wasn't bumpy; mine sure was." Wendy, "Only briefly, mainly as we left the Pensacola area. The pilot did a good job flying around the storms." Striker, "You were in a state-of-the-art Boeing 727, which can go above a lot of weather, and make up time for the storm delay. We just trudged through it all in a much slower prop aircraft. It was tedious, but it was free. We have three hours to check into our room, change, and get to the rehearsal dinner. Luckily, it's at the O Club, just about a mile away."

The Navy Lodge was much nicer than Striker expected. The lobby was elegant with a sitting room that looked like an old English clubhouse and had a large dining area for breakfast. The clerk checked them in without any questions and called a bellhop, who took their bags to their one-bedroom suite. As

406

soon as the bellhop left, Wendy embraced Striker and said, "I sure didn't expect anything like this. It's wonderful. I love it, and I love you." They took a shower together, but as Striker began to embrace her Wendy whispered, "We better slow down before we can't stop. We have to get ready to go. We will have lots of time later. I promise. OK?" Striker made a face like a spoiled child and whispered "OK." Twenty minutes later, they were ready to go.

Before they arrived at the O Club, Striker said, "I don't think I mentioned to you that my older sister, Anne Marie, is expecting a baby, her first, about the same time as Jane is due. They've been trying to have one for almost four years and Anne Marie is thrilled. With the baby coming, my parents, who are divorced, are getting along well. Like your parents, they can't wait to be grandparents. I hope you get a chance to talk to Grandma Nonna, my mother's mother, who is one of my favorite people on earth. I grew up spending time at her house in Solomons, right through college. She is very special to me."

The rehearsal was done early, and all the guests were already at the O Club when Striker and Wendy arrived. They were the center of attention as they walked into the room. Wendy was wearing a simple navy blue dress, and Striker was wearing the uniform of the day, but most eyes in the room were focused on her. She was gorgeous and smiling broadly; it was obvious to everyone that she was thrilled to be with Striker and meet his family.

Striker's two sisters helped his mother, who was in a wheelchair, over to Striker and took turns hugging him. A few seconds later, all three of them turned to Wendy, and Lizzy said, "You must be Wendy, I've heard so much about you and I'm happy you were able to come to my wedding." A few seconds later, Striker's dad, in his Captain's uniform, took his turn hugging Striker, then Wendy, saying, "You have to be Wendy, you're exactly as Jonathan described. I'm glad you were able to join us."

Soon it was time for everyone to take a seat for dinner, and Wendy was seated between Striker and his maternal grandmother, Nonna. Wendy soon learned that Nonna had immigrated from Italy with her parents and five older siblings right after WW1 began. Her father, Nick Antonelli was an experienced deep-water sailor who enlisted in the U S Navy almost as soon as they settled in Brooklyn, NY. He had learned English while working on American fishing trawlers and as soon as he completed boot camp, he was designated a Seaman Third Class and assigned to the Atlantic fleet.

Nonna's father retired as a Chief Petty Officer after twenty years in the Navy, and the family moved to Solomons Island, Maryland, across the Patuxent River from Lexington Park. After retirement, he built a small charter fishing company into a very lucrative business. Nonna grew up and was married on Solomons, and eventually raised four children there. One of them was Francesca, Striker's mother.

Nonna was totally charmed by Wendy and was immediately convinced that Wendy was the one for her Johnny Boy, which she had called Striker since he was little boy. Before Striker's parents bought a house near Lexington Park, they spent most holidays with Nonna and her late husband in their waterfront home. Striker adored Nonna, and often spent weekends with her when he was home from college.

When Striker's table was called to the buffet, Nonna took him aside and asked, "Johnny Boy, I need to know how serious you are with Wendy. I have to say this. She's the one for you, I know it in my heart." Striker, "Nonna, I haven't told anyone else, but I'm going to ask her to marry me." Nonna, "Wonderful. I have a ring I want to give you. It's an emerald ring your Grandpa Nick gave to me on our 50th anniversary. I love it as much as my engagement ring. I already gave your sisters the engagement ring and my 25th anniversary ring. It would really mean a lot to me if you used this ring as your engagement ring. I'll give it to you at the wedding tomorrow." Striker, "I don't know what to say except thank you, Nonna." Then he kissed her cheek, and they joined the buffet line.

The rehearsal dinner was over by 9 pm and Striker's dad invited everyone to the bar, which had a large private room. While they were there, Striker and Wendy talked to his family, some of whom he had not seen for years. Later, while Wendy was away from the table, Striker's dad told him, "Wendy is the star of the show. Everyone I've spoken to thinks she's a doll. You hit a home run with her, son." As he finished, his mother joined them and added, "Your dad is right. I feel as if I've known Wendy for years. She was totally at ease with us. She's a wonderful girl, don't let her get away." Not knowing what else to say, Striker simply thanked them and admitted that Wendy was very important to him, more than any other girl he had ever met.

When Wendy returned, Striker asked her, "Are you ready to go? I'm bushed and I'm sure you are too." She nodded that she was, they said goodnight to his parents and went to find Lizzy. They soon found her, talking to Anne Marie. Both sisters quickly hugged Wendy and Anne Marie said, "It was an absolute pleasure meeting you, Wendy." Then Lizzy added, "I'm so happy my brother brought you. I can see why he wanted us to meet you." Wendy, slightly embarrassed, responded, "Thank you so much for inviting me; I really enjoyed meeting everyone."

When they arrived at their suite in the Navy Lodge, Wendy said she was so tired she just wanted to sleep, "I'm sorry, but I promise I'll make up for it tomorrow morning. Striker kissed her goodnight; ten minutes later they were asleep in each other's arms. They slept until after 8 am, when the smell of fresh coffee and frying bacon woke Striker up. After he shaved and brushed his teeth, he climbed back into bed. Wendy was still asleep, but she soon woke up as Striker kissed the back of her neck. She turned over and whispered, "Now I'm gonna make good on the promises I made last night."

Afterwards Striker fell back to sleep, and Wendy got up to shower and wash her hair. After drying off and wrapping herself in a robe provided by the Lodge, she kissed his cheek. As he started to wake up, she said, "Poor Mr. Flyboy, did this little science teacher wear you out?" Striker, pretending he was still sleepy, slowly turned over and hugged her. "Did I make good on my promises?" Striker, "You sure did. Do you want to make more promises?" Wendy smiled, "Only if you promise to stay awake."

After breakfast they went back to their suite, and Striker saw the message light blinking on the phone. It was from his dad, who wanted to know if Striker and Wendy wanted to take a boat ride on the Patuxent River. He added that they would be back in plenty of time to get ready for the wedding.

When asked if she'd like to go, Wendy enthusiastically agreed. She had heard a lot about the Chesapeake Bay and wanted to see it while she was there. Striker called his dad at the BOQ and agreed to meet at the marina in an hour. Before they left, Striker suggested that Wendy buy something warmer to wear just in case it was colder on the water. They stopped at the Base Exchange and bought hooded sweatshirts.

On the way to the marina, Striker drove by the Navy Test Pilot School where many aviators trained before becoming Gemini and Apollo astronauts. As they drove past the famous facility, Wendy said, "Don't tell anyone, but my brother-in-law, Connors, was just notified that he was nominated to attend test pilot school, but because the baby is coming, he's waiting to find out when he'd begin before he decides whether or not to accept." Striker, "That's quite an achievement. Only the best of the best pilots is accepted, and most of them are engineers, usually aeronautical engineers. I'm really impressed. I understand Connors wanting to be by Jane's side the next few months, but attending the Test Pilot School is a once in a lifetime opportunity. That's going to be a tough decision."

Just as Striker finished talking, they drove into the marina parking lot. Striker's dad was waiting for them on his boat. The 25-foot Grady White, with its twin 150 HP outboard motors, could get almost anywhere on the bay in less than two hours. After helping Wendy aboard, Striker's dad showed her around the boat. Even though there were a couple of passenger seats, it was obvious to her that the boat was designed for sport fishing, not pleasure cruising. After she put on a life jacket and found a place to sit, Striker removed the mooring lines, his dad fired up the engines, and they slowly left the marina.

It was a little more than three miles across the Patuxent River to the entrance of Solomons Island, marked by the Drum Point lighthouse. Once there, they cruised by the waterfront homes, oyster and crab packing plants, and an old pier that once was a dock for commercial fishing vessels. Then they made their way to Back Creek and then to Mill Creek, where during WW II, soldiers and Marines practiced amphibious landings, and after the war was a popular place for boat races.

411

Wendy, now standing, remarked, "What a beautiful place, I'd love to come back and walk around town, maybe have dinner. I bet you can get great seafood here." Striker, "Fresh oysters and crabs are sold almost everywhere, even at the gas station." Wendy, "I'm not too big on oysters but I've had Maryland crab cakes, and I liked them a lot. I'm sure what you get in Kansas is not the same as what you get here." Smiling, Striker replied, "Well, stick with me and we'll be back here as often as you want." Wendy kissed him on the cheek and replied, "I intend to. I'm going where you're going."

Striker's dad, pretending not to hear their conversation, thought, "I think we'll soon have another wedding in the family. I hope it happens." On the way back to base, Striker's dad showed Wendy where Nonna lived in Solomons Island and where she took the launch to Lexington Park to shop. As they got closer to the base, they cruised by a few of the many creeks that fed into the Chesapeake Bay. When they slowed down at the entrance to the marina, Wendy said, "Captain Striker, thank you so much. I had no idea how beautiful the Chesapeake Bay is. I hope to be back soon to see more of it." Striker's dad responded, "I certainly hope so. Maybe next time my son will show you Annapolis, St. Michaels and Easton. You could easily spend a week cruising the bay and only see a small part of it. I love it here." Striker, smiling, "Dad, we'll be back soon."

Striker's dad took them to the O Club for a quick lunch before they had to get ready for Lizzy's wedding. When they finished, Striker's dad went back to the BOQ, and Striker took Wendy back to the lodge. When they arrived, Wendy said, "You wore me out this morning. If you don't want me to fall asleep early, I better take a nap." Striker replied that he could use some rest, and quickly fell asleep next to her.

412

Later Striker got up, took a quick shower, came back to bed, and kissed Wendy on the back of her neck. When she woke up, she said, "You can either keep that up for the next hour or so and we'll be late for Lizzy's wedding, or you can take a break until tonight and we'll start where we left off." Striker, "We could do both. I'm sure Lizzy will understand if we're late, but since you made tonight sound so great, I'll take a break."

St. Nicholas Catholic Church was on the base, and they were soon outside of the Chapel, waiting for others to arrive. Wendy wore the same stunning dress that she had worn when they went to Liolio's. Since most of his family had never seen him in uniform, Striker wore his choker. Striker's mom soon arrived and slowly walked on her crutches to them. Wendy greeted her, "Mrs. Striker, is this your first day using crutches? You certainly look like you are making a great recovery." His mom responded, "Wendy, please, call me Fran. I'm doing much better than the doctors thought possible. By the way, you look incredible; that dress is gorgeous."

Nonna soon joined them. "Wendy, you look like a movie star. My Johnny Boy is so handsome in his uniform. I bet he has to scare away all the girls with a stick." Wendy, "Believe me, Nonna, I know, but I'm gonna be right next to him and make sure that doesn't happen." While Wendy continued to talk with Fran, Nonna stepped toward Striker and gently put a small velvet bag into his hand and said, "Here is the ring, give it to her. She is the one for you Johnnie Boy, you can trust your Nonna." Then as she kissed him on his cheek, he said. "Thank you, Nonna. I promise I'm ready to take your advice." As Nonna turned away, Striker saw that she was crying.

Lizzy was escorted to the altar by her dad. Waiting for them were two groomsmen, Jerry's cousin and his college

413

roommate, and two bridesmaids, both Lizzy's cousins. Next to Jerry was his brother Paul, his best man, and Anne Marie, the matron of honor. At the end of the wedding ceremony, the priest introduced the obviously happy bride and groom. Later, as the couple walked to their waiting limousine, the raucous crowd cheered and pelted the newlyweds with rose-petals and rice. Striker watched Wendy as she cheered as if she had known them for years. He smiled and thought, "She's already become a member of my family. Now I just need to make it official."

The reception was delayed while the wedding party was photographed, but as soon as the newlyweds were introduced, the bar opened, and the party began. After a buffet dinner of Italian food and fresh seafood taken straight from the Chesapeake Bay, the band started playing. Striker and Wendy joined family and friends on the dance floor and danced every song.

Wendy was getting a little tipsy from the Chianti at dinner, champagne, and two glasses of Prosecco in between dances, but she was radiant as the band played *Unchained Melody* for the last song. Even after the band stopped playing, Striker held Wendy in his arms in the middle of the empty dance floor. Finally, she kissed him on his cheek and whispered in his ear that she loved him. Almost impulsively, Striker went down on one knee and said, "Wendy, I don't know what will happen to me and my Navy career in the days ahead, all I know is whatever happens I want to be with you." Then told her that he loved her, took the ring out his pocket, and handed it to her. "Wendy, will you marry me?" Totally surprised, Wendy nervously took the ring, began to cry and said, "Of course I will," and hugged him. After she gathered herself, she put the ring on and said, "This is beautiful. Is it an emerald? Where did you get it?" Striker, "It is an emerald, Nonna gave it to me earlier today. She said she knew in her heart that you're the one for me and wanted me to use it as an engagement ring. It's very special to her. It's her 50th anniversary present from my late grandfather." Wendy started crying again as she looked at it and said, "It fits perfectly; Nonna must be right."

Striker's sister Anne Marie was one of the few people in the room who saw what happened. She immediately went to her brother and asked, "Did you just propose to Wendy, or am I seeing things?" Wendy, with tears rolling down her cheeks, raised up her left hand, and shook her head yes. Striker, smiling, added, "And she said yes." Anne Marie hugged her brother, saying, "I'm so happy for you." Then she embraced Wendy as Fran, and then Nonna came over to join the rapidly growing crowd. Nonna embraced Wendy, and quietly told her, "I told Johnnie Boy that I knew you were the girl he should marry, and I wanted him to use that ring. Now as I see it on your finger, I'm overjoyed that he did, and that I could be here to see you when he proposed. You are perfect for him, and he loves you very much."

Seeing a crowd quickly growing, his dad and several other relatives gathered around the couple, congratulating them and wishing them well. Finally, Lizzy and her new husband, Jerry, broke away from a photo shoot and virtually ran to Striker. She was crying and asked, "Did you just do what I think you did? Did you ask Wendy to marry you? You did, didn't you?" Striker, smiling, "I did, and she said yes." Lizzy shaking her head, said, "I knew when I met Wendy that she was the one for you. When I saw you dance with her, I knew that you felt the same way. You asked her on my wedding day and I'm so happy I could explode with joy." Then she cried while she hugged Wendy and her brother.

Finally, Striker's dad, also with tears in his eyes, approached him, "Son, when we were on the boat, I saw the way you looked at each other. I knew then that you belonged together, and I'm thrilled that you are engaged. I couldn't be any happier. It's great that you asked Wendy to marry you on such a joyous day for our family. Congratulations."

Wendy and Striker remained at the reception until Lizzy and Jerry left. When they got back to their suite, Wendy prepared for bed while Striker took a shower. When he returned to the bedroom, Wendy was waiting, wearing only the emerald ring.

Chapter 67

Jane's Health Problems and Connors Ponders His Future

The phone ringing early awakened Jane. She had been sick most of the night and had finally fallen asleep on the couch at about 5 am. The episodes of nausea and weakness were happening more often, and she was very concerned about her baby. During the night, Jane decided she needed an appointment with the doctor as soon as possible.

When Jane answered the phone, Wendy screamed with delight that she was engaged. Jane asked, "When did this happen, and where?" Wendy, almost crying, replied, "We were at Striker's sister's wedding last night in Maryland. As the last dance ended, he got down on one knee and proposed. We were the only people on the dance floor. I was beside myself. I love him so much. I said yes immediately. The ring he gave me is a beautiful emerald that was a fiftieth wedding anniversary gift to his Nonna. He told me that she knew in her heart that I was the one he should marry, and she wanted him to use it. I'm so happy. I have no idea when we'll get married but when we do, I want you to be my matron of honor. Will you?" Jane, "Congratulations, I'm so happy for you. Striker is a wonderful guy and it's obvious that he's crazy about you. I know you're just as crazy about him. I'd be proud to be your matron of honor. When you decide the date, just let me know and I'll do everything I can to help." Wendy said that she needed to make a lot of calls, so she told Jane she loved her and ended the call.

Not wanting to spoil Wendy's news, Jane had not mentioned her concerns about her pregnancy.

Before Wendy could make another call, the phone rang. It was Fran, who called to say how happy she was about the engagement. Then she added, "I'd like to invite you and Jonathan to come to my house for dinner tonight. Nonna wants to make one of her Johnny Boy's favorites, clams and linguini, with fresh bay clams. She is also making lasagna, his other favorite. We'll eat about 6, so I hope you can come." Wendy. "We would love to, and I am sure that we can be there. It will be great to spend more time with the family."

After Wendy's call ended, Jane was feeling worse, so she went back to bed. Connors, who had not heard the phone conversation, let her sleep until the afternoon. As he gently rubbed her back, Jane slowly woke up, and asked, "What time is it? I was really asleep." Connors replied that it was about one and he didn't want her to sleep any more or she would be unable to sleep that night. Jane held her face in her hands and shook her head, "Something's wrong. Nowhere in any of the literature I've read is there anything like my symptoms. I'm not waiting any longer. I am calling Dr. Wiegand's emergency number."

When she got off the phone, Jane forced a smile, "I almost forgot. Wendy called. She and Striker are engaged. He asked her last night at his sister's wedding in Maryland. I was so happy that I didn't mention how bad I felt. Striker is the only guy that Wendy has had any real interest in since Roger died. I remember how she looked at him when they ran into each other at Gina's wedding. She couldn't take her eyes off of him. At the reception, it was obvious that Striker was crazy about her. I'm so glad they somehow found each other. It's as if they were meant to be together. "

Connors added, "He's a great guy with an outstanding record. Unfortunately, the Training Command is apparently way over-recruited, and there is a delay in RIO training that is expected to last over 6 months. Unless a lot of guys are allowed to change their pipelines and take different career training, there is a good chance of a reduction in force, and even discharges. Morale is really low, but if anyone can come out of this OK, it's Striker. I just hope their wedding plans are not affected."

Twenty minutes later, Dr. Wiegand, a Navy OB/GYN, called and said that he was on duty at the hospital and could see her in an hour. She quickly replied, "I'll be there." then asked Connors to take her. Forty-five minutes later, Connors dropped Jane off at the entrance, and parked the car. Jane had already seen the doctor when Connors joined her in the examining room. She had a concerned look on her face as Connors asked, "Everything OK?" She answered, "Let's talk in the car."

As soon as they were in the car, Jane was crying but still managed to say, "Doctor Wiegand did some blood work but may need to do more tests. From my symptoms, he's pretty certain there's something more than normal prenatal fatigue and nausea happening. I'm running a low-grade temperature and losing weight, both of which are out of the ordinary, but he also said that the baby is developing normally, and he sees no sign of distress." Connors, "Did he discuss the range of possibilities?" Jane, "Yes, it could be anything from a virus or bacterial infection to some form of cancer, but he wouldn't speculate on which one it is. It'll take a day or two before he knows what the test results are. In the meantime, he wants me to rest as much as possible, and to let him know if the symptoms get worse."

Back at the apartment, Jane was feeling a little better and they ate an early dinner. Jane asked, "Have you thought about what you're going to do about Test Pilot School?" Connors, "Like I said, I'm gonna wait to see what other dates are available before I decide. I should know in a week or so." Jane, "You know how I feel; this is something you can't turn down. I'll be fine. Wendy will be around if I need something, and I know my mother will come here whenever I ask." Connors, "I know. Before I agree to go, we need to find out what's making you sick."

Chapter 68

Nonna's Dinner

Since both had a lot of calls to make, Striker and Wendy decided to eat a quick breakfast at the Lodge. When they finished eating, Wendy used the suite phone and Striker used the one in the lobby to make calls. Wendy called Leah, who was getting ready to go to the beach with Riley. Leah screamed with delight when Wendy told her that Striker had proposed, and she had said yes. Leah, "I'm so happy for you, Striker is the best. I thought he was special when he was so nice after he knocked you down in the water. Then when you guys miraculously met up again at Gina's wedding, I saw the way you looked at him. You were hooked, and I knew then that somehow the two of you were meant to be together. Now you're engaged. Congratulations."

Wendy paused then said, "Thanks Leah. I love you so much and you're my best friend on earth, but I've asked Jane to be my matron of honor. I hope I'm not hurting your feelings. I do want you to be a bridesmaid." Leah, "You know I will. You did the right thing asking Jane. Without her, we wouldn't have moved to Pensacola, and you wouldn't have met Striker. No matter what my title is, I'll be with you to do whatever I can." Wendy said, "Thanks, I'll be home tomorrow, and we can talk more then. Now I have to call my parents, so I'll see you when I get there."

Over the next two hours Wendy called her parents, grandparents, several other relatives and friends. Then, after thinking about it a while, she called her late fiancé's parents. In an emotional exchange, she described how she and Striker met and a little about him. Roger's mother then told Wendy that she was happy for her and that it was good that she was going on with her life. Wendy ended the conversation by telling Roger's parents that she hoped they would be able to come to the wedding.

As soon as she finished the call, Wendy returned to the suite. Striker told her that he had just finished talking to Sticky. "Before I told Sticky the news, I asked him how he was doing. He said that he's on extended rehab leave and is slowly getting better but is still confined to a wheelchair or crutches. His goal of walking unassisted will not be possible for several weeks. Finally, he told me that Lee Ann agreed to move in with him at the rental house when he gets discharged. Now she can help him a lot with meals and taking him to doctor's appointments. Otherwise, he'd have to go to the rehab hospital." Then Striker also told Wendy that he had talked to Sticky about their engagement, and that he wanted him to be his best man. "Sticky said he was not surprised, and I was smart to not let you get away. Sticky also said that if he ever met someone like you, he would do the same thing. That's coming from a guy who's avoided marriage like leprosy."

When Striker told Bulldog that he was engaged to Wendy and wanted him to be a groomsman, Bulldog said that he suspected Striker was going to propose to Wendy and that he would be honored to be in the wedding. Then, as he laughed, "Now, with you out of circulation, it might be possible for me to get a date. It seems like every girl in Pensacola wanted to go out with you, and you almost did." After a short pause, "By the way, I've also signed up for the Marine Corps weapons training, which starts the week after Jump School ends. Don't tell anyone. I had a couple of beers with Sergeant Major Sullivan the other night and asked him if it would be possible to transfer to the Marine Corps. He told me it was, but my chances would be better if I went to both schools. He said that once I finished, he would call some folks he knows to see if it could happen. I'll meet with him when the training ends. We'll see what happens."

Striker, "Bulldog, ever since you were medically disqualified from pilot training, I thought you might consider transferring to the Corps. I've always thought you have the grit to be a good Marine. It was obvious that Sergeant Major Sullivan thought so too." As the conversation ended, Bulldog thanked Striker and told him he would help any way he could.

After he called some more old friends, he asked Wendy, "How about we take the launch over to Solomons Island and I'll show you all the places we saw from my dad's boat yesterday? Maybe go to a waterfront cafe that has the best crab cakes and crab soup on earth." Wendy enthusiastically said, "That sounds wonderful."

It was a gorgeous fall day with a 75-degree temperature and clear skies. The ride over in the WWII era launch lasted only twenty minutes, but the moderate chop on the Patuxent River made it seem longer. Wendy stood near the bow almost the entire trip and got splashed by an occasional two-foot wave. Striker stood next to her, making sure she was steady and protecting her from some of the saltwater spray. When they approached the dock on the Solomons Island side of the Navy Base, the launch slowed to a no-wake speed and gently glided to the dock. With the assistance of two sailors, the passengers departed the launch and walked to a nearby bus that would take them to the center of town.

As they rode the bus to town, Wendy said, "Solomons Island must be a kid's paradise." Striker, "It is. My sisters and

I spent a lot of summers here with Nonna. Almost every day we went crabbing or fishing, and when we weren't doing that, we went snorkeling in the river. I miss it a lot."

Later, in town, they walked by Our Lady Star of the Sea Catholic Church and school. Striker, "My mother went to school here; it's something out of the past. It only has four classrooms, first through 12th grades, three grades per classroom." Then they went into the Bowen's Inn, built in 1918. It had 40 rooms, including a third-floor suite with a balcony that overlooked the marina. It also had a first-class restaurant and bar which was frequented by many celebrities. Down the street was Bowen's Market, which was a general store with a soda bar and cafe. It sold take-out containers of freshly shucked oysters and live crabs by the bushel. Then they visited several boutiques and walked onto the pier which used to house a movie theater and a crab house.

About noon Wendy said she was hungry, and Striker suggested they try Bowen's Inn. Wendy, "Absolutely, that place is charming." Luckily, it wasn't crowded, and they got an outside table adjacent to the marina. Wendy watched the many boats cruising on Back Creek, and said, "This place is something out of a movie. Maybe the next time we come; we can stay here in the Inn." Striker replied, "I'm sure we can, and we also have to stay at Nonna's house. It's a restored Victorian home on three waterfront acres, complete with a pier and a boathouse. You will love it."

They both ordered crab cake sandwiches and Maryland crab soup. Striker ate his entire sandwich and half of Wendy's. As he finished eating, she asked, "Did you forget that Nonna's making an Italian dinner for you tonight?" Striker, "I didn't, but don't worry, I'll be able to eat more than my fair share. Nonna can really cook."

424

As they rode the launch back to the base, Wendy again stood near the bow so that she could see the watermen checking their crab pots. As they approached the base marina, she told Striker. "This has been a wonderful day. I can understand why you love this place so much; I can't wait to return."

Anne Marie, her husband, dad, and other family members were at Fran's house when Striker and Wendy arrived. Nonna met them at the door with open arms and told Wendy that the ring looked beautiful on her. She invited them into the living room for a glass of wine before dinner. After Anne Marie poured everyone a glass, Striker's dad proposed a toast, "To my son and his beautiful fiancée, Wendy. Here's to a lifetime of happiness and endless love. I couldn't be happier that Wendy will soon be a member of our family." Then Fran hustled everyone to the table.

Nonna had prepared a traditional Italian dinner with an antipasto, thick-crusted Italian bread, two main courses, wine, and dessert. Wendy was already full before the main courses were served, but still took small portions of both the linguini and lasagna. Striker ate like it was his first meal in a week as Nonna smiled and repeated, "Mangia, Mangia, Johnny Boy," When everyone was finished, Nonna brought out a platter of bomboloni, coffee, and a bottle of Amaretto Liqueur.

When the meal ended, Wendy was stuffed and a little tipsy. Striker, who was just as full, was well beyond tipsy. Wendy brought him a cup of coffee and told him they should leave soon. Twenty minutes later they thanked Nonna, and Wendy drove them back to the Navy Lodge. Once in the suite, Wendy went to the bathroom to prepare for bed. When she came out, Striker was asleep on the bed.

Chapter 69

Jane's Diagnosis

Doctor Wiegand's nurse called Monday morning when Connors was at the commissary and Jane was taking a shower. When she returned the call, the nurse told her the doctor wanted to see her at 10 am. Jane replied that she'd be there and waited for Connors to return home. When he did, he dropped off the groceries and came to her as she started to cry. "What's wrong?" Jane replied, "The doctor wants to see me at 10. Will you take me?" Connors said, "Of course. I'll be ready in 15 minutes."

Neither of them said a word on the way, and Connors could see that Jane was crying. As they got out of the car, she started shaking, and held Connor's hand tightly as they walked into the hospital. She stopped him in the hallway and whispered, "I'm so scared that there's something wrong with the baby. I want you to come in with me." Connors, "I'll be right next to you."

As soon as they got to the nurse's desk, she took them into a small conference room. A few minutes later, Dr. Wiegand came in and sat down facing them. He took Jane's hand and said, "I've seen the blood work and talked to the pathologist. We both agree on the diagnosis." Then he paused for a few seconds, "I'm sorry to tell you that I have some bad news." Jane started crying, "Please don't tell me there's something wrong with the baby." Dr. Wiegand. "No, your baby is normal, but it looks like you have leukemia." There was silence in the room, and then Connors asked, "Are you sure?" Dr. Wiegand's response was brief, "Yes, all the tests show leukemia. We're still trying to determine what strain you have; there are several. We'll run some more tests as soon as possible." Jane asked, "What happens next? Can it be treated? When will I start treatment?"

Dr. Wiegand, "Normally you would start treatment immediately, but pregnancy is a complication. The most effective treatment is chemotherapy. Unfortunately, chemo is often damaging to the baby in the first two trimesters of pregnancy. Since you just began the second trimester, and won't begin your third trimester until mid-December, chemo is not recommended yet. It's just too dangerous for your baby. Waiting until the third trimester seems to prevent damage and allow a normal gestation. So, unless you choose to end the pregnancy, we'll have to wait before beginning chemo treatment."

Jane, "I won't even consider abortion, even if it means I get worse." Dr. Wiegand, "Every case is different, but the data shows that delaying chemo will significantly reduce the chance for a full remission. In any event you will probably have to be hospitalized to avoid getting an infection; your immune system is weakened, but we'll wait to see what the oncologist says. You should make an appointment with one as soon as possible. I'll give you the name of a doctor who specializes in cancer treatments for pregnant women. I have worked with him several times. His name is Doctor Livingston, and my scheduler can set up an appointment. Again, I'm sorry to give you such bad news, but I believe you can beat the cancer, and have a normal baby. Do you have any questions?" Jane and Connors looked at each other, and she responded, "Not now, but I'm sure we will later." Dr. Wiegand shook both of their hands and said, "If you do, don't hesitate to call me at any time."

They sat silently in the conference room for several minutes after Dr. Wiegand left. As Jane wept, Connors held her tightly and tried to offer words of comfort, but she was inconsolable. Finally he said, "We have to go, Jane." He took her hand and led her to the car. As they drove home, Jane, almost thinking out loud, whispered, "Dear Lord, what am I supposed to do, begin chemo and hurt the baby or don't begin chemo and possibly die?" Connors, now with tears in his eyes, responded, "I don't know, but whatever you decide, I'll be at your side." Jane, now calming down, looked at him and said, "All I know is that I will not harm our baby, no matter what the consequences are for me. I would rather die than risk our baby's health. Can you understand how I feel?" Connors, "If that's your decision, it's mine as well. No matter what happens, I'll be with you."

As soon they got into the apartment, Jane, still crying, went to lie down. Connors called Dr. Wiegand's office to set up an appointment with Dr. Livingston, the oncologist. The scheduler said that a tentative appointment with Dr. Livingston was set for Tuesday at 1 pm. Connors said they would be there, and then made a list of people he needed to call.

Connors let Jane sleep for a couple of hours then reluctantly woke her up. Without saying a word, Jane embraced Connors and began to weep again. Finally, she was able to whisper, "I'm so sorry. You don't deserve this to happen to you. I keep hoping that I'm having a terrible dream that will soon end, but it's not going to, and I'm devastated. Now, when I'm back to reality, I don't know if I have the will to continue." Connors, "Jane, we'll face this together. I won't let you give up, and we'll fight this every day, an hour at a time. I know that together we'll beat this terrible disease and celebrate the birth of our child together. Now we have to let our families know

428

what we have in store. Their support will make it easier for us to make it through the next few months." Jane calmed down, shook her head in agreement, and then went to the bathroom to wash her face.

While Jane was cleaning up, Connors made a call to his CO. With his voice breaking, Connors told him Jane's diagnosis and that there would be days he would have to be at home to help her. Then he paused and said, "As time goes on, it will get worse." His CO was silent for a few seconds and said that he would be as flexible as he could with Connors's flight schedule to allow him to be home as much as possible. If Connors agreed, the CO would ask for volunteers to take some of Connor's flights. Then in a moment of real concern, the CO told Connors that he would be praying for them and would be available to help anyway he could.

Jane was still in the bathroom, so Connors called his parents, his sister, and Riley. Then, not wanting to endure another emotional encounter, Connors decided to wait before calling anyone else. Jane had not yet made any calls; she dreaded having to do it. She calmed herself as much as she could and called her parents. Still, she could barely talk when she began her conversation with her mother, and soon they were both crying uncontrollably. Eventually they calmed down and her mother said that she would fly there whenever Jane wanted her to come. Jane started to call Wendy, but remembered she was on her way home, so she called her boss, Professor Williamson. He was speechless after Jane told him the bad news. Almost whispering, he slowly responded, "Jane, I don't know what to say, other than this is just terrible news. I'm so sorry it's happening to you and your husband. I'll do everything I can to help you." Jane, crying, replied, "I just want to continue teaching as long as I can. I love my job and the students will help me have hope for the future, but I also realize that eventually I'll have to take a leave of absence." Dr. Williamson replied, "I don't want you to worry about taking a leave of absence. You just continue to teach your classes as much as you can, and I'll take care of the rest."

Connors sat next to Jane and told her that he was going to call the CO of the Test Pilot School to tell him that he couldn't accept the position. Jane reluctantly agreed but hoped that they could move him to a later date, after the baby was born. Connors said he would try, and he made the call. The CO of the Test Pilot School agreed to remove Connors' name from the class list, but to Connors' surprise, the CO said that even though entrance into the school is very competitive, he still wanted Connors to attend future training. So, in view of the extraordinary circumstances, he would put Connors name on the list for the next available class beginning in 1971.

On Tuesday morning, Jane and Connors met with Doctor Livingston in his office. After reviewing Jane's blood work and test results, he told her that they indicated that she had an acute form of leukemia. To protect her from infection, she needed to be hospitalized as soon as possible and he would check her condition every day. Assuming there were no complications, she would probably be able to begin chemotherapy by mid-December. Finally, Dr. Livingston assured her that this was the best treatment with the least impact on the baby. He gave Jane and Connors time to ask questions and reassured them that he was available at any time they had more questions, and then he left Jane and Connors alone.

Chapter 70

Planning Ahead

Monday morning, Wendy and Striker slept late and had just enough time to eat breakfast before leaving for the airport. Luckily, traffic was light, and Striker arrived at the Friendship departure gate before 2 pm. After he took Wendy's bag out of the trunk and handed it to her, they embraced long enough for the cars behind them to start honking. Striker quickly promised to call her when he got to Pensacola, and she went into the terminal. A little after four he was in the Pax River terminal, where he changed into a flight suit and bought a sandwich and a soda. The plane was a half hour early, so as soon as it emptied, he got on board, introduced himself to the pilot and copilot, and took his position on the jump seat.

Unlike the trip to Pax River, the return flight to Pensacola was smooth. Since they only stopped once, the plane landed at Sherman Field about a half an hour early. After checking out, Striker was in his car and on the way to the BOQ. As promised, he called Wendy as soon as he got there.

Wendy's flight stopped in Atlanta, was delayed because of a thunderstorm, and arrived in Pensacola almost an hour late. Leah greeted her as she walked out of the gate. "Welcome back engaged lady. I'm so happy for you. Striker is a gem, you two are perfect for each other." Wendy was smiling and crying at the same time, but still replied. "It was so romantic. I never expected him to do what he did. We were alone in the middle of the dance floor when he got down on one knee and proposed. I was so surprised I almost passed out. I'm so happy I could explode."

After they got into the car, Leah said, "Now you have to start making wedding arrangements. Any idea where or when?" Wendy, "Just some vague ideas, but since it would be difficult to set up something in Kansas while living here, I'm leaning toward doing everything here, on base, in the spring. Both families live about the same distance away, and the O Club is much cheaper than any place I know, and the Chapel is a beautiful place to have a wedding." Leah, "Especially if it's a military one with the guys in chokers, like Gina's and Jane's wedding." Wendy, "The chapel is also where Striker and I met the second time, but I won't make any decisions without talking to Striker and our families." Neither had eaten dinner so they stopped at the Castle Bar for a sandwich and a beer. Soon after they finished, they went to their apartment, and Wendy waited for Striker to call.

Wendy was asleep on the couch when Striker called, "Hi, it's me. I just got to the BOQ. How was your trip?" Wendy, sounding sleepy, said, "We had a weather delay in Atlanta, otherwise it was good. How was your flight?" Striker, "It was great. Only one stop and then it was smooth sailing all the way into Pensacola. What's your week like? I'm not scheduled for anything. I could be at your place when you get home tomorrow, and we could grab some dinner and talk about wedding plans." Wendy responded, "Sounds perfect. My week is just a routine one, so I can be ready at 6. I'll sure miss you tonight, especially after such a wonderful weekend together," Striker, "I'll miss you too, but we'll have a lifetime of wonderful weekends, I promise," Wendy, "OK. I love you and I'll see you tomorrow." Striker, "Tomorrow can't come soon enough." Ten minutes later, Striker was in bed, but remained awake thinking about being engaged to Wendy.

The next morning, Striker got up early and completed a three-mile run. When he returned to the BOQ, Bulldog was in the living area completing an application for Marine Corps Weapons training. Striker. "I see you're lining up more training. I haven't heard if I've been approved for Air Intelligence, but I'm going to check later this morning. Then I'm going to visit Sticky at the hospital, but first, do you want to get some food?" Bulldog, "You bet. I'll go with you then I'm going to the beach. It's supposed to be a nice day, I have nothing else to do, I might as well enjoy myself until I start Jump School."

After they finished eating, they went to the VT-10 admin building. While Bulldog dropped off his application at the XO's office, Striker checked the bulletin board to see if any training assignments were posted. Just as he did, Mrs. Jenkins, the squadron secretary, was opening the glass case to tack up a new list of assignments. She looked at him and asked, "You're Mr. Striker, aren't you?" Striker said, "Yes ma'am." Mrs. Jenkins responded, "Congratulations, you've been selected for Air Intelligence training, which begins Monday, November 24 at 0800. It will be a 12-week school, Monday through Friday, 0800 to 1600, and may require some airborne reconnaissance training. We need to know if you want to accept this assignment by 1600 on October 24." Striker, "I'll do it now, where do I sign?" Mrs. Jenkins, "That's what I thought. Come with me and I'll prepare the papers."

As Striker was walking out of the office, Bulldog walked in and dropped off his acceptance papers. Bulldog, "It turned out they had plenty of vacancies for weapons training, so the XO offered me a spot as soon as I handed him my application. I'll start Monday, November 24. It looks like you got accepted to Air Intelligence School. That is just what you wanted. We

433

both hit home runs." Striker, "Yeah, I still wish it was RIO school, but that's probably not going to happen. Air Intelligence is the best alternative and I feel pretty good about it. Now, let's go see Sticky."

Twenty minutes later, the hospital information desk gave them Sticky's room number and said that he could have visitors. When they walked into his room, Lee Ann was adjusting his bed. His leg was still elevated in a sling and had a "Fly Navy" sticker and several signatures on the cast. He had had a drip bag hanging next to him. Striker, "How are you feeling?" Sticky, "Ok, I guess. The doctors are concerned about infection in the compound fracture, so they are going to keep me here on antibiotics longer than they originally thought. So here I remain, living the dream." Sticky, now smiling, "Congratulations again, Striker. Wendy is a super girl. I wish I could be more involved with your wedding plans, but it's gonna be a while before I can be of any assistance," Striker, "Don't worry about it. We haven't even begun to think about what we're going to do. First, I need to figure out what I'll be doing in the next few weeks and months, but I did get accepted to Air Intelligence training."

Sticky said, "Yeah, it's a real screw up. All those weeks of getting our butts kicked in AOCS and now we just sit around and wait. Welcome to Naval Aviation, lads. As soon as I'm able, I'm going to take full advantage of the delay and sit on my ass on the beach until they make up their minds what they're gonna do. The way I feel right now, if I stay in flight training, it's OK, but if I don't, that's OK, too. It's totally up to them."

Bulldog, taking advantage of the moment, looked at Lee Ann and asked, "I haven't seen Julie for a long time. How's she doing? She still single?" Lee Ann, "Since I'm gonna move

434

in with Sticky when he gets out of the hospital, Julie's moved back into her parents' house. As far as I know, she's not dating anyone regularly. If you're interested, I can fix you up with her." Bulldog, "That'd be great. Beginning next week, I'll be away in training for about a month, so it'll have to wait until I get back." Lee Ann, "Just let me know when you're ready, and I'll give her a call."

When Striker returned to the BOQ, there was a message from Wendy; she wanted him to call as soon as possible. When he did, she could barely speak. He tried to calm her down and finally she said, "Jane called me about an hour ago," She tried to calm herself down again, then quietly continued, "She found out yesterday that she has leukemia and is being hospitalized. She didn't tell me she was sick on Sunday because she didn't to want to spoil my news about getting engaged. She had some tests done and yesterday morning the doctor told her that she had leukemia. I can't believe she was going through all of this while we were having such a good time in Pax River."

Striker, not knowing what else to say, asked, "What happens now? When does she start treatment?" Wendy gathered herself, "Since Jane is pregnant, there is nothing they can do until her third trimester. Chemo in the first two trimesters could harm the baby. There is no way Jane would do anything that could endanger her baby. She refused any chemo until her third trimester began, and she had to be hospitalized to protect herself from infection. I need you to come over, will you?" Striker said he would be at her apartment in half an hour. Wendy was sobbing as she rushed into Striker's arms. He tried everything he knew to calm her down, but nothing worked. Finally, he suggested that they take a long walk on the beach. For the next two hours, they walked along the Gulf and talked about the unfairness of Jane's illness. Striker could only suggest that they pray that the baby would be born healthy.

After they left the beach, Striker and Wendy went out to dinner. They agreed that they would avoid talking about Jane and focus primarily on wedding plans. First, he wanted to tell her that he was accepted to Air Intelligence School and had signed the papers to go. Wendy was thrilled. But I was not sure how being an Air Intelligence officer would affect Striker's career in the Navy. Wendy, "I know that this means that you probably will not be a RIO. What future do you have in the Navy? After all, you didn't join the Navy to brief pilots; you joined the Navy to be a pilot. Do you think you will still want a career in the Navy?"

Striker, "That remains to be seen. Right now, I'm not willing to admit that AOCS was a waste of time. Earning a commission proved to the Navy that I had what it takes to become a pilot. Finishing first in my class proved that I could be a good officer, no matter what I did. At this point, if I'm offered a chance to continue in the Navy as an Air Intelligence Officer, I'll take it." Wendy then asked him, "Where would you be stationed? Will you still be flying?" Striker, "From what I've been told, about a third of Air Intelligence Officers are assigned to an aircraft carrier or some other sea duty. The other two-thirds are assigned to Naval Air Intelligence commands somewhere on shore. As far as I know, the only flights I'd be assigned would probably be reconnaissance missions, and I expect there would only be a few of those."

Wendy, "Well, if you make the change, at least you wouldn't be constantly flying combat missions, and I could sleep at night." Striker, "It's also possible that I'd only do one tour as an Air Intelligence officer, and then I would probably want to go to Law School. We'll have to see what happens."

436

Wendy changed the subject, "I've been thinking a lot about possible locations for the wedding, and I think that having it here makes the most sense. The two weddings I've been in, or attended here have been wonderful. The Chapel, while not a typical parish church, is more than adequate. After all, who even notices what a church looks like at a wedding? But the great facilities the base provides are what really convinced me. The Officers' Club is as nice as any reception venue I've been to, and the price is maybe one-third less. Plus, if we got married in the spring, hotels are still reasonably inexpensive. Finally, the distance my family and your family would have to travel is about the same. What do you think?"

Striker, "You took the words right out of my mouth. I totally agree with you." Wendy, "Well, that was a lot easier than I thought. Since Jane just went through it, maybe I'll ask her advice. I know she really wants to help." Striker responded, "Sounds great. Sticky's gonna be unavailable for a while, but I'll certainly ask him what he thinks." Then laughing, Striker continued, "Realistically, asking Sticky for advice about a wedding is like asking a monkey how to fly an F-4."

They finished eating and returned to the apartment. Leah heard them coming and met them at the door. She hugged Striker, telling him that asking Wendy to marry him on the dance floor at a wedding was the most romantic proposal ever. Wendy, "It was the best weekend of my life, something out of a happy dream." The three of them spent the next few hours drinking wine and talking about wedding plans. Then Striker, knowing that Wendy had to get up early, went back to the BOQ. After he did, Wendy told Leah about Jane's illness.

Chapter 71

Wedding Plans Continue

In late November, Lisa Scalise would finish the required coursework for Nurse Practitioner certification. She already had over five years of clinical experience but needed another six months of pediatric work to be eligible for the certification exam. Even though she had several months to go, Lisa began to think about where she wanted to be stationed when she finished. Pensacola was high on the list.

One evening, Lisa's mother called her to tell her about Jane's diagnosis and the complications of her pregnancy. After the call ended, Lisa wondered if it was wise to go back to Pensacola. She loved living and working there, and she wanted to help Jane make it through the rough time she was facing, but she was realistic about Jane's prognosis; delaying chemotherapy made a recovery highly unlikely. On the other hand, if Jane survived and had a normal delivery, she would need a lot of help.

Lisa lived in an upscale high-rise apartment complex located about two miles north of the hospital. It was a two-bedroom unit that she shared with another Navy nurse, Debby Stein. Debby's father owned the apartment, and Lisa rented the second bedroom on a month-to-month basis. Before she requested a transfer, Lisa told Debby about her cousin and what she hoped to do. Debby, understanding the dire nature of the situation, told Lisa that she could leave at any time.

During the months Lisa was in Bethesda, she rarely had time to date, and most of the single men she knew were more interested in local college girls or student nurses. In addition, she refused to date interns or doctors from the Naval Hospital because she didn't want to be in another difficult work situation. Friends introduced a few men to her, but none of them really interested her. She had no compelling reason to remain in Maryland, and she wanted to help her cousin. Even though things could get complicated with Tony, her ex-husband, and Connors, she decided to return to Pensacola as soon as she could.

The next morning, Lisa submitted a hardship transfer request to her CO, Captain Lillian Newsome. That afternoon, Newsome called Lisa to her office to explain the basis of the hardship. Lisa, hesitating for a moment, told Newsome that her cousin Jane, a Navy wife who lived in Pensacola, had an aggressive form of leukemia but could not start chemo because she was pregnant. Newsome knew that without the use of chemo, Jane would probably not survive because she was pregnant. Newsome then said, "Lisa, helping your pregnant cousin in her terrible situation is doing the right thing for the right reason. As far as I'm concerned, it qualifies as a hardship. I have to get your request cleared, so I'll get back to you as soon as I hear something." Then she added, "By the way, my closest friend lives in Pensacola. Her name is Commander Megan Callahan, and I worked with her in several field hospitals in Vietnam. She's the best nurse and person I've ever known. Her devotion to her patients was amazing; she often sat up all night consoling a dying soldier. When Megan's husband was killed, the stress of her job, plus her husband's death, left her emotionally drained. A few weeks later, she retired and moved to Pensacola, where her husband was buried at Barrancas National Cemetery. Even though she was retired, Megan still wanted to help people in any way she could. Up to that point, she only took care of the wounded and dying, but when she retired, she decided to care for the ones who did not survive. She is now the caretaker of Barrancas Cemetery and all those who are buried there. Megan's one of a kind. If your transfer is approved, you should go introduce yourself and tell her Lillian sent you. She'll have a lot of stories to tell about our days together, most of which I don't tell many people."

That evening, Lisa called Jane. After a long, emotional discussion, Lisa told her that she hoped to be stationed back in Pensacola NAS hospital, where Jane would be a patient. Lisa ended the conversation with, "I'll be by your side as much as I can."

Following Jane's leukemia diagnosis, Striker and Wendy still hoped for a spring 1970 wedding. Even though her health had deteriorated significantly, Jane insisted that Wendy should not change her plans. Jane talked to Wendy almost every day to offer advice and reaffirm that she would stand up for Wendy at the wedding and deliver a healthy baby. After checking with both families, Striker reserved the small O Club ballroom for a rehearsal dinner on May 8, the base Chapel for a 2 pm wedding on Saturday, May 9, and the large O Club ballroom for a reception.

Striker began Air Intelligence School on Monday, November 24. There were only 16 people in his class; all of them were caught up in the RIO training delay. As Striker suspected, the curriculum in Pensacola was the same as the curriculum of the first 12 weeks of the Air Force Air Intelligence program. Striker believed it was done intentionally to make the Navy's AI program an alternative career pipeline for stranded RIO students. Later, he would find out he was right.

Chapter 72

Lisa Comes Home

Lisa's transfer request was approved, and she had to report to the Women and Children's Department of the Pensacola NAS Hospital by December 15. She was released from her assignment at Bethesda Naval Hospital and left for Pensacola the next day. She decided to visit her parents in Jacksonville for a few days and then drive to Pensacola. When Lisa arrived at the Naval Air Station, she checked into the Nurses' Quarters. Beginning early the next morning, she visited Jane at least once every day and then spent most afternoons preparing for her assignment in the neonatal unit.

In mid-December, Lisa was just walking out of Jane's room when she was suddenly face-to-face with Connors. Nothing was said for a few seconds, and then Connors awkwardly stammered, "Lisa, I thought you were in Maryland. When did you get here?" Lisa, forcing a smile, "About a week ago. I transferred here to finish my clinical work and to help Jane. I've been coming to see Jane early in the morning and when my shift is over. I hope you're not uncomfortable with my being here." Connors, "Lisa, you are always welcome here. I really appreciate your help and hope you continue to come anytime you want." Lisa thanked him and quietly left.

Chapter 73

Sticky Improves

In early November, Sticky was released from the hospital and was supposed to begin rehab, but he ignored the doctor's recommendations. His leg did not improve, and at his next appointment the doctor told him if it did not substantially improve in two months, Sticky would be medically discharged.

He was then determined to get better. He religiously went to rehab and used his crutches, even at the beach. He even stopped riding his motorcycle, which required him to put his full weight on his leg. By the end of February, he was cleared to return to flight status.

Later that month, Bulldog finished first in his Jump School class, earning him the Iron Man physical fitness award, in addition to his parachutist badge. Three weeks later, he earned an Expert badge in Marine Corps weapons training. With these accomplishments in hand, Bulldog made an appointment with Command Sergeant Major Sullivan to discuss a lateral transfer to the Marine Corps. When they met, Sullivan was not surprised by Bulldog's performance in the two schools. "I knew what you did in AOCS. You did everything I hit you with and made it look easy. For a swabbie, you are one tough son of a bitch, and your awards prove it. I'm going to call an old friend of mine; we did two tours in Nam together. When I met him, he was my Battalion Commander. Now, he's a three-star general in charge of the Marine Corps Training and Education Command. I'll give him a call and ask how hard it is for a recently commissioned ensign to transfer to the Corps. I'll personally vouch for you being the best badass that I have trained in Parris Island, AOCS, or the Basic Officers' Course (BOC). I'll let you know as soon I hear from him. While you're here, how are Mr. Striker and Mr. Hickey doing? I heard about the snafu that backed up RIO Training and knew all three of you were in that pipeline." Sullivan's assistant then called and said he had to accompany the CO to a reception in fifteen minutes. Sullivan told Bulldog he had to leave, shook hands, and said, "I think you've got a good chance of being transferred to the Corps. There's no doubt in my mind that you'd make a great Marine. I'll get back to you as soon as I hear something."

A week later, Sullivan told Bulldog that he would have to request a transfer from the Training Command to the Marine Corps. He would also have to pass a physical and then submit an application to the Marine Corps Training Command for acceptance to the next Basic Officers' Course (BOC). Then Sullivan added, "Give me your transfer request, physical exam results, and your application for the BOC, and I'll see to it that they get to the right people." Bulldog now elated, said, "Sergeant, that's the best news I've had since I was commissioned. Thank you."

Chapter 74

Striker, Bulldog, and Sticky Move Forward

Sergeant Major Sullivan called Bulldog at the BOQ and left a message that his request to transfer to the Marine Corps and subsequent assignment to the 28-week Basic Officer's Course was tentatively approved. He also explained that the Training Command still had to approve the release date of January 15, 1970 and that the next available BOC was not until June 1st. Until BOC began, Bulldog would be sent to the training Marine recruits normally got at Parris Island. He needed training that was not included in the AOCS program: Advanced Weapons Training and hand-to-hand combat. If time allowed, Bulldog would also go to advanced parachute training. So, before he even began BOC, Bulldog would have more training than most of the people in his class.

When he got the message, Bulldog was so overjoyed that he ran to his room hooting and hollering all the way. Then he celebrated even more by doing a handstand on the balcony outside his room, got to his feet, and sang the Marine Corps hymn as he walked to the beer machine. He put a quarter in the machine and got a Jax beer that he chugged in less than thirty seconds. Unknown to Bulldog, Sticky was asleep in his room when Bulldog started making all the noise. Now wide awake, Sticky came out on the balcony, and saw Bulldog chugging a beer and yelled, "Bulldog, it's kinda early to start partying, isn't it? What's the occasion?" Bulldog, "My transfer to the Corps was approved. I'm gonna be a Jarhead in a couple of

444

weeks." Sticky, "Holy shit, I knew you were thinking about it, but I had no idea it could actually happen, especially so quickly." Bulldog, "Me either, but Sergeant Major Sullivan got it done." Now chuckling, he continued, "Ever since I told him how I bit my wrestling opponent, he's thought I would make a good Marine. When the RIO pipeline collapsed and we were left with our thumbs up our butts, I thought seriously about transferring to the Corps. I talked to Sullivan, and he told me what I had to do. I got it all done, and then he wrote a letter of recommendation for me and submitted my application to his friend. A week or so later, it was approved."

Sticky, "I'm glad it worked out for you. I guess you know that Striker's in AI training and he's pretty sure he's going to make a move. With Lee Ann's help, I've been rehabbing at my house, and Striker's been spending most of the time at Wendy's place. Since you've been at parachute and weapons training, we haven't seen each other in a while." Bulldog replied, "That's for certain. The last time we were together, you were using crutches. Now, it looks like your leg has healed up pretty well; you were barely limping when you came out to see me chug that beer. Have you been cleared to return to flight training, if and when it starts again?" Sticky, "Yes, but I still have to see the doctor again before I can fly. They want to make sure it has healed properly. Who knows if or when RIO training will start again? I may look at other options if it goes on much longer. Just sitting on my ass in my house all day is getting old, especially when it's too cold to go to the beach. Last night was the first time I hadn't stayed there in weeks. I came to the BOQ because Lee Ann and Julie had a girl-only bridal shower at the house. As soon as I eat some breakfast and get some groceries at the commissary, I'm heading back. Want to go get some food?" Bulldog, "Yeah, I better; chugging that beer made me a little woozy." Sticky, "Ok, Let's head to the open mess."

While they ate, Bulldog asked Sticky about Julie. "Do you know if she's seeing anyone?" Sticky, "Not to my knowledge, but as soon as I get back, I'll ask Lee Ann. I'd take you there now, but I'm sure they'll be asleep until at least 10 or 11. I'll call you as soon as I find out."

Chapter 75

Jane's Cancer Struggle Continues

Jane's condition continued to worsen, and she was too weak to get out of bed. Once she began chemotherapy in mid-December, family and friends were only able to do limited visits with Jane and they tried to bring some holiday spirit to the room. Connors visited her twice a day and talked about anything but her condition.

The week before Christmas, Wendy, in an attempt to raise everyone's spirits, put up a Christmas tree and decorated Connors' apartment. She even put a Christmas wreath on the door of Jane's hospital room and placed poinsettias on the windowsill near Jane's bed, but Jane's rapidly worsening condition and Connors' obvious despair negated her efforts. Most of the family, including Connors, did attend Christmas Eve mass, and continued to pray for a healthy baby and a miracle for Jane. Connors spent most of Christmas Day with Jane, talking quietly about Christmas memories and the new baby. He tried to keep Jane's spirits up, even while he was at an extremely low point. He did not even participate when the rest of the family exchanged a few gifts on Christmas Day, making it a holiday without joy.

Everyone was encouraged again when Jane rallied in mid-January and showed signs that the chemo was working. She even got out of bed and showed Connors her large baby bump, but it was the last time he saw her on her feet. A week later, she contracted pneumonia, and daily, she got weaker. One day Jane told Connors that she knew she was getting worse and said, "I know that I am dying, but before I do, please promise me that

I can hold our baby at least once. Connors, I want you to go on with your life without me. Find someone else to help you raise the baby as I would. Always let the baby know that I did all of this for love. I love you and I love our baby." Connors could not speak; he just held her, and they wept together.

As Jane's condition deteriorated, Connors became more and more despondent, but he still managed to visit her and go to work every day. After months of watching Jane suffer and knowing that her prognosis was grim, Connors couldn't control his emotions any longer. He couldn't accept the fact that Jane was dying, and he became bitter. He was easily angered and often yelled at his flight students for little or no reason. He finally realized that he was putting himself and his students in danger, so he took some time off. The first day he was off, he made an appointment to see Father O'Reilly, the Catholic Chaplain who officiated at their marriage.

At their first meeting, Connors could barely talk about Jane. Over the next couple of days, O'Reilly was gradually able to get him to talk about her without breaking down. Then at the beginning of their third meeting, O'Reilly said, "Connors, everyone I have ever counseled about the loss of a loved one has asked this question, "How can it be that so many bad things happen to good people? You may have already asked yourself that question." He paused as Connors nodded in agreement. "The only answer I can offer is that it's part of God's unpredictable and sometimes unacceptable plan." He paused again, then added, "In every tragic situation, including Jane's, there is reason to be comforted. I'm convinced that good things emerge from bad things. In her case, Jane has faced a life-threatening disease that has required treatment that might hurt the baby, but she has refused to do anything that could endanger the baby, even at the cost of her own life. Now, as a result of her selfless act, she's dying, but her goal that the baby would remain healthy will soon be reached. A joyous event, the birth of a child, will happen in spite of Jane's terrible suffering. Jane's sacrifice is a heroic act, and you should always be comforted that she has had the courage to do it." For the rest of the time Jane was sick, and through the difficult time that would follow, Connors relied upon Father O'Reilly's words to make it through each day.

Jane's prognosis continued to worsen. In early March, Dr. Livingston privately told Connors that Jane would probably not survive more than two weeks, so he stopped the chemo. He added that the baby was still growing normally, but Jane's body could not sustain a normal delivery. With little else he could do for her, Livingston shared that he had met with Dr. Wiegand, and they both strongly advised Jane and Connors to allow them to perform a Caesarian Section. Since they both had been working with Jane throughout the pregnancy, they would both be in the delivery room to closely monitor her condition. They agreed but wanted Connors to talk to Jane and her parents before it was scheduled. That night it was agreed that the baby would be delivered on March 16, as recommended.

Chapter 76

Striker and Wendy Make Decisions

During Jane's hospitalization, Striker tried as much as he could to comfort Wendy and still help with their wedding plans. Every day after class, he finalized all the wedding arrangements except ordering the bridesmaids' and Wendy's dresses. In addition, he brought Wendy food when she visited Jane in the hospital and picked up family and friends at the airport.

On the last day of the first 12 weeks of AI Training, Cmdr. Thomas Christopher, the CO, announced that the program would be extended another 12 weeks, beginning on February 17th. More importantly, he said that the Aviation Training Command also announced that those who successfully completed all 24 weeks of the AI program would be offered a lateral transfer into Air Intelligence. Finally, Christopher announced that whoever was first in the class would be allowed to pick his next assignment if he opted to transfer. After class was dismissed, he told Striker that they needed to talk.

When Striker arrived at his office, Christopher said, "Mr. Striker, you did a great job in the first half of the program, and it looks like you will finish first. I also know that being an AI Officer was not the reason you joined the Navy, and you're now in this program because you were caught up in circumstances beyond your control. I have to assume that you're here because you want to continue your career in the Navy. I've been told that you grew up in a Navy family and that your dad is a Naval Aviator, a Mustang who made Captain. The Navy wants people like you, and I'm going to do all I can to keep you. After talking to the CO of the Training Command, I've been authorized to tell you that if you do finish first, you will be recommended for an early promotion." Striker was ready to accept the offer, but he asked for time to talk to Wendy. Cmdr. Christopher knew that they were facing a family crisis, so he allowed Striker a few days to make the decision.

Most weekdays, Wendy and Striker went to the hospital as soon as they both got off work, but since Jane was so sick, only Connors was allowed to visit her. On February 13th, Striker asked Wendy if she wanted to get away from the hospital for a while. He needed to talk to her about continuing AI training. Wendy agreed and said that she also wanted to discuss their upcoming wedding.

While they ate in the Ready Room, Wendy and Striker reviewed what they needed to do for the wedding. As soon as they agreed that the plans were in good shape, Striker said, "I finished first in my class for the first half of AI training. Commander Christopher said if I continue at the top of the class, I am up for an early promotion. The second session of AI School starts next Tuesday, so I have to decide by Monday. What do you think?" Wendy, "You know I want you to stay stateside if at all possible, so I'm all for it, but I'm with you, whatever you decide." Striker, "Then I'm going to stay with the AI program. It may not be the reason I joined the Navy, but it's a good reason for me to stay in the Navy." Wendy, elated, kissed Striker and said, "I'll always love you, whether you're a Flyboy or not."

Wendy teared up and said, "I know I promised not to discuss Jane, but I'm so worried that she won't even be able to be at the wedding, much less be my Matron of Honor. I can't stop thinking about the baby and what Connors will do if Jane passes away." Then as she started crying, she said, "It's just so unfair."

Chapter 77

A Child is Born

Connors Assesses His Future

Early on the morning of March 16, Connors was at the hospital to reassure Jane of his love before she went in for surgery. When she was taken into the delivery room and prepped for the C-Section, Connors went to the fathers' waiting room to await the birth. After what seemed like hours, Dr. Wiegand entered the room to tell Connors that he was now the father of a beautiful and healthy baby girl. Sadly, he also told him that Jane was weakened by the surgery and was in the recovery room. They would be watching her carefully over the next few hours. After Connors briefly looked at his daughter in the nursery, he and Dr. Wiegand went to tell the family.

Connors announced with tears in his eyes, "It's a girl, Sarah Jane is her name, and she's just as beautiful as her mother." Everyone surrounded Connors, hugged him, and offered congratulations. Dr. Wiegand then shared that Jane was in recovery and was being carefully monitored. He would have more information about her condition when she came out from under the anesthesia. He suggested that Connors needed time to go to visit the baby, and the pediatrician would be in to see the family.

A few minutes later Connors was in the nursery's observation room, watching a nurse take the vitals of his infant daughter and place her in the incubator. He didn't notice that the nurse was Lisa Scalise. Connors remained in the observation room, watching his daughter sleep and taking her picture with a Polaroid camera. Then another nurse told him that the pediatrician would soon meet him and the family in the waiting room. Connors went back to the waiting room and gave out Polaroid pictures of Sarah in the incubator. Wendy and her mother cried as they looked at the pictures and could not wait to see Sarah Jane in person. When the attending pediatrician came into the waiting room, he said the baby displayed normal vital signs, but as a precaution, they were going to keep her for a few days to run more tests. He also said that Jane had been moved to a nearby room but wouldn't be able to have any visitors except Connors until the next day. He also told them they were welcome to see the baby from the nursery observation room.

Connors left immediately to see Jane. She wasn't awake yet, and despite her condition, Connors held her hand and talked to her as if she was alert. As Jane started to wake up, a nurse brought Sarah into the room and allowed Connors to place her next to Jane. They both had tears in their eyes as Jane cuddled their newborn daughter. Connors knelt by her bed and held Jane's hand until she fell back to sleep. Then he moved to a nearby chair and held Sarah until the nurse took her back to the nursery. Later the nurse came in and said that Jane would be asleep for the rest of the night, so Connors kissed Jane, told her again that he loved her, and went to get some rest.

Connors was in the nursery observation room early the next morning. Just after he arrived, Lisa took Sarah out of the incubator and began to feed her. She saw Connors and brought Sarah close to the observation window. She motioned for him to come to the door. Connors, in surgical scrubs, entered, but remained motionless. Lisa waved Connors towards her and asked him if he wanted to feed Sarah, saying, "You have to learn how to do this sometime, so you might as well start now."

Connors hesitated for a few seconds, then nervously took Sarah and looked at Lisa for help. She showed him how to hold and feed the baby, then a few minutes later, how to burp her. The whole process took about 20 minutes, but to Connors, it was a lifetime. Finally, Lisa said, "You did great. Later I'll let you feed her again, and tomorrow, you'll learn how to change her diaper and give her a bath. Sarah is doing fine, except for being a little jaundiced, she should be able to leave in a day or two. I have to take her vitals and put her back into the incubator now, but you can come back later." As Connors started to leave Lisa said, "By the way, I checked on Jane earlier this morning. I wish I could do more for her; I've been praying for her every day." Connors waited a few seconds, thanked her, and went to see Jane. She was still sleeping, and the nurse told him that she was getting weaker.

Dr. Livingston, the oncologist, came into Jane's room and briefly examined her. Then he said to Connors, "I hoped you would be here; I need to talk to you. Let's step into a conference room down the hall." Once they were in the conference room, Dr. Livingston paused to gather his thoughts, and said, "Jane's condition has deteriorated significantly, and her organs are beginning to fail. Dr. Wiegand and I feel that unless she rallies, the only thing we can do is put Jane on life support. Please understand, without the life support she will only survive a couple of days. With life support, she could live about two more weeks, maybe longer, but there will come a time when you have to decide when further medical care is no longer appropriate. She did a wonderful job of delivering a strong, healthy baby, but she sacrificed her life to do it. It saddens me greatly to advise you that there is nothing more that we can do for Jane."

Connors had been preparing himself for this prognosis since the day leukemia was diagnosed. When it came from Dr. Livingston, Connors sat silently for a minute then calmly said, "Thank you for all you have done for us. I know what Jane wants, but I'll let you know our decision as soon as I have spoken to her family." Livingston, with tears in his eyes, replied, "I wish to God there was something else I could do, but the sad truth is there is not. I did the best I could, and I'll pray for you and Jane. I hope you can find some comfort from the birth of your daughter, for which Jane made the ultimate sacrifice. I'll leave now and tell the charge nurse to let you and Jane have total privacy for the next hour."

Back in the room, Connors spoke to Jane, held her hand, and thanked her for bringing Sarah into the world. Then he prayed, "Dear God, what am I going to do with a baby daughter? Please give me guidance. Today was only the second time I've ever held an infant and I've never held and fed a baby. I have no idea how to take care of her. I really need your help." When the hour ended, Connors kissed Jane's cheek and left. Connors drove home knowing that he had to have a horrible conversation with the family. To prepare himself to tell everyone that Jane was near death, Connors sat in his car and prayed that he could do it without breaking down.

Both sets of parents, as well as Wendy, were talking in the living room when Connors entered. He spoke before anyone could ask how Jane and the baby were doing. "This is the hardest thing I've ever had to do, but I have to tell you that Jane is dying. Doctor Livingston told me that she would die in a few days without life support and maybe a couple of weeks with it. Months ago, Jane and I talked about this because she worried that she would probably not survive Sarah's birth. I'd like to hear what you each think. Please understand if we put her on life support, we'll also have to decide when to shut it down. Jane always put the baby's health ahead of hers and as much as she wanted to see Sarah grow up, she knew from the beginning that this day would come. Her wishes have always been that we needed to let her go." For a few minutes, no one said a word. The only sound was their sobs.

Finally, Jane's dad calmly said, "There is no good choice; Jane will be gone soon regardless of what we decide. I see no compelling reason to prolong Jane's suffering by putting her on life support. As I understand it, there is no hope that she will get any better on life support. As much as it rips my heart apart, I agree with you and Jane that we need to let her go naturally."

Connors saw his family nod their heads in agreement and he waited for the others to respond. Finally, Wendy and Jane's mother agreed, as tears ran down their faces. Connors then said, "It's what Jane wants, and I want to do as well. Thank you for reinforcing the decision. I'm going back now to tell Dr. Livingston what we decided and to be with Jane. I'll also ask him to allow all of you to visit her as much as you want in her last days."

When Connors got to Jane's room, he asked the charge nurse to page, Dr. Livingston; then he went to see Sarah Jane. The baby was still swaddled and peacefully asleep, a picture of joy in the midst of sorrow. Then he went to see Jane, who was still heavily sedated. Connors eyes teared up, as it was now apparent to him that Jane could go at any time, but he continued to hold her hand and talk to her as if she were alert. He told her how much he loved and needed her, and promised to learn to take care of Sarah like Jane would have done.

As he was telling Jane about how beautiful Sarah was, Dr. Livingston came into the room, and said, "Mr. Connors, I admire you for the unending dedication you have given Jane, even when she is so incredibly ill." Connors nodded and responded, "Thank you. She is the most important person in my life and has been since I met her a few years ago." Then softly, "I don't know what I'll do without her, especially with a newborn daughter coming home in a few days." Connors then collected his emotions and continued. "I've spoken to both families, and we've agreed that extending Jane's suffering is not what Jane or we want to do. Jane definitely did not want to be placed on life support and we all agree. If it's possible, I want to stay with her in this room until it's over." Dr. Livingston shook his head and replied. "I'll see to it that a recliner is brought in here and you and your family are allowed to stay with Jane around the clock."

An hour later, a reclining chair was placed next to Jane's bed and Connors remained by her side until the next morning. Exhausted and hungry, he went to the cafeteria to get some breakfast. As soon as he finished eating, the charge nurse found Connors and told him that he needed to return to his wife's room as soon as possible. When he arrived at Jane's room, Dr. Livingston and two other doctors were attending to her. A nurse quickly asked him to step outside and Dr. Livingston would soon come out and talk to him.

A few minutes later, Dr. Livingston approached Connors, "Mr. Connors, Jane's taken another turn for the worse. Her kidneys are now failing, and her blood oxygen and blood pressure are dangerously low. Unless she improves soon, her heart will not be able to function." Connors interrupted him, "That means she's going to die soon, doesn't it?" Dr. Livingston, "Yes, without significant improvement, Jane will not survive much longer. If you wish, a nurse will contact her family and page Chaplain O'Reilly." Connor, understanding

458

that the end was near, replied, "Yes, please do that. Will I be allowed to stay with her?" Dr. Livingston, "Of course. We should be done in about fifteen minutes, and then you can go back in." Connors leaned against the wall, closed his eyes, and prayed.

Father O'Reilly was by Jane's side before her family was. "Before everyone else arrives, let me ask if there's anything I can do for you." Connors, "Padre, besides miraculously curing Jane, which I believe is not going to happen, you can pray that she is at peace and that I'll find a way to properly take care of Sarah. Right now, I'm so emotionally drained, I'm not sure that I can carry on." O'Reilly replied, "Connors, I certainly can't produce a miracle. I can only tell you that if you focus on the miracle child that God has already given you, everything else will fall into place. There is now nothing more important than caring for that little girl. I know from your background that you've overcome tough times before, and with God's help, you'll find the strength to overcome this one as well. If you need help along the way, I'll always be available to you." Connors nodded and then sat as close to Jane as he could, held her hand, and prayed.

Once the family arrived, Father O'Reilly led everyone in prayer for a few minutes and then gave Jane the Last Rites, the Commendation, and the Anointing of the Dying. Then he spoke quietly with each member of the family, blessed them and prayed silently to himself.

Less than an hour later, an alarm sounded, indicating that Jane had stopped breathing. The charge nurse, followed by Dr. Livingston, quickly came into the room and examined Jane. Minutes later, Dr. Livingston solemnly said, "I regret to tell you that Jane has passed." The charge nurse asked everyone but Connors to leave the room. Connors sat next to Jane, held her hand, and wept. Then he prayed for her, whispered that he loved her, and kissed her.

After he left, a nurse prepared everything for the family to come in for their last visit with Jane. As the family began to leave, the charge nurse told Connors that Father O'Reilly would be able to help him make the arrangements. Connors, obviously very upset, thanked her and then stayed with Jane until she was taken out of the room.

Father O'Reilly was waiting for Connors as he left Jane's room. O'Reilly comforted Connors as best he could and then suggested they go to his office for a few minutes. They prayed together for a while, and then O'Reilly began to help Connors through some of the difficult next steps. O'Reilly suggested that Jane's funeral mass be held at 11 a.m. the following Saturday, March 21, at the Chapel. Connors agreed, and then O'Reilly contacted the funeral home and made an appointment for Connors for that afternoon.

Connors returned to the waiting room, but could not speak to anyone without choking up, so he quietly said, "Thank you for being here." Each person there offered a few words of condolence, and Connors just nodded or whispered, "Thank You." Lisa cried as she said to him, "I know how much you loved Jane, and I cannot imagine the pain you're suffering. If there's anything I can do, even changing Sarah's diaper, please don't hesitate to call me. "Connors managed to say, "Thank You" but added, "I still have so much to learn, so that would be greatly appreciated."

It was clear to Father O'Reilly that Connors needed to be alone with his thoughts. He quietly suggested that Connors seek comfort at the hospital chapel. He agreed, and O'Reilly told everyone that Connors was going to the chapel for a little while, but they were welcome to go to the apartment. At the chapel, Connors sat in the back pew trying to put his life back together. Now that Jane was gone and he would soon be alone with Sarah, he couldn't see how he could be a Naval Aviator and care for her. But he soon realized that if he resigned from the Navy and found another job, he would still be alone with her. As he began to feel sorry for himself, he remembered O'Reilly's words and was confident that with the Good Lord's guidance and family support, he would find a way to raise Sarah.

Chapter 78

Sarah Comes Home

When he arrived home, most of his family as well as Riley and Leah were there. Sheila hugged him and said that she developed a schedule for Sarah's care. First, Jane's mother, Wendy and Leah would rotate staying at his apartment, and Lisa would examine Sarah if she appeared to need medical attention. Next, Jane's parents would be at his place for a month, followed by their mom. She continued, "When school is out, I'll be here with the twins to take care of her; they've been begging to meet their new cousin Sarah. Pat is very busy at work, but he may be able to come for a while."

Connors's eyes welled up, and he said, "Sheila, Thank you. You're a godsend. I've been worried about taking care of Sarah for the last couple of weeks. I don't even know how to prepare a bottle for her, much less what to do if she gets sick. I even considered resigning from the Navy and prayed that the Good Lord would show me the way. Now, with your plan, I feel sure that I'll find a way." Connors thanked everyone for their prayers and support during Jane's last days.

Connors then took Riley aside and said, "I'm beaten, my reflexes are shot, and my mind is mush. Would you take me to the funeral home so I can set things up for Jane?" Riley, "Sure, when do you have to be there?" Connors replied, "At 4 pm. Father O'Reilly recommended Morris Funeral Home, it is near the base. It's almost 2:30, so we better leave in about half an hour."

On the way to the funeral home, Connors told Riley, "Assuming Morris can get everything done, Jane's funeral is scheduled for next Saturday at 11 am, but I haven't decided whether to bury her at Barrancas or back in Overland Park. I'm leaning towards Barrancas because that's where I want to be buried. I'm pretty sure I can reserve the gravesite next to her, or I could also take her to Kansas, where a lot of her family is buried, and buy a place for me. I'm really torn between the two. I've already decided that I'm not going to have her cremated, and the cancer really took its toll on her, so it'll be a closed casket viewing and Mass. Do you have any advice?" Riley thought about it and responded, "I can understand why Jane's family would want her in Kansas, but I also think that for the next year or so, they'll be here a lot to visit Sarah and Wendy and could also visit Jane's grave. To be frank, you're not even thirty, so in a year or two you may find another woman, get married again, and your new wife will adopt Sarah. More importantly, assuming you've been married for many years, you may change your mind about being buried next to Jane, or your second wife will decide to bury you somewhere else. So, if it were me, I'd choose to bury Jane here, reserve the plot next to her, and not be concerned about what happens sometime in the future."

Connors replied, "I'm going to do exactly what you suggested." Riley, "While we're talking about making decisions, I've made a couple myself. First, I've requested to be reassigned to VT-10 for another year, and second, I'm going to ask Leah to marry me. As you know, we've been seeing each other exclusively for the last several months, and recently we've been talking about getting married. I've already bought a ring and next week I'm going to ask her. I want you to be my best man when we do get married." Connors, "I think that's great. Leah's definitely a keeper; you're perfect for each other.

463

I'd be proud to be your best man. Any guess when you'll get married?" Riley, "It will either be next summer or Christmas break when school is not in session."

Later, at Morris Funeral Home, the director set up Jane's arrangements exactly as Connors requested, except for the Barrancas burial sites. "You'll have to see Megan Callahan at Barrancas to do it, but there shouldn't be a problem." After Connors did everything at the funeral home, they left for the cemetery. Megan Callahan had just finished reserving two burial sites for an elderly veteran and his wife when Connors walked in with Riley. Connors and Riley introduced themselves, and Connors suddenly choked up and couldn't continue. Riley patted Connors on the back and said, "My friend just lost his wife Jane this morning, just days after she gave birth to their first child, a baby girl. Her funeral is scheduled for this Saturday at 11 am. He needs to reserve two sites next to each other. Is it possible that it can be done by then?" Callahan, "I'm so sorry, how old was she?" Connors, now calmed down, "27, she had leukemia and because of the pregnancy, she refused chemo until it was too late. They had to do an early C-section on the 16th, and she died this morning."

Callahan, "My God that's terrible. Your wife was a very brave woman. She must've have been an incredible person." Connors, "She was. She just earned her PhD in theoretical math and was in her first year as an assistant professor at West Florida. I just decided this morning to bury her here and I'd like to reserve the place next to her for me." Callahan, "We'll get it done, I promise, but we have to make some quick decisions. Will she be cremated or in a casket?" Connors, "Casket." Callahan, "OK, let me show you what we have available on this map of the burial sites. Pick out a couple then we'll go take a look at them." Connors studied the map and chose three locations. Twenty minutes later he had seen all three and picked the graves in between a pond and a wooded area. When they got back to the office, Connors signed the reservation agreement, thanked Callahan, and left. When they got into Riley's car, they went back to Connors' apartment to pick up anyone who wanted to go see Sarah.

When Connors walked into the observation room, the attending pediatrician was placing Sarah back under the ultraviolet light. Recognizing Connors, the pediatrician waved for him to come to the nursery door. As soon as he got there, the doctor asked, "Mr. Connors? I'm Doctor Samuels. I'm sorry I didn't have a chance yesterday to express my condolences for your loss. I know that Jane delayed chemo to minimize any harm to your baby. Her courageous act worked for the baby. I just finished examining Sarah and, except for a mild case of jaundice, she's doing great. I expect that after one or two more days under the ultraviolet lights, she'll be ready to go home. Now, if you put on some scrubs, you're welcome to come in and see her. Just don't be alarmed by her slightly orange skin. That's the jaundice; it is caused by incompatible blood types. It's nothing to be worried about; we see it all the time. I have to go now, but I'm glad I had a chance to meet you. Again, I'm sorry about Jane. I wish I could have met her; I understand that she was one of a kind. If you have any questions, ask the charge nurse, soon-to-be Nurse Practitioner Lisa Scalise."

As Dr. Samuels left, a nurse brought Connors some scrubs, and he immediately put them on. When he got to the nursery, he pointed at his daughter, gave a thumbs-up, and smiled at the people in the observation room. It was the first time in weeks that he smiled about anything. While Connors watched Sarah sleep, he thanked God that she was healthy. Then he thought,

465

"Jane, this is the miracle child that you loved so much that you sacrificed yourself for her. Because of what you did, she is perfect. Now, even though you're not here, I promise that I'll raise her as you wanted."

Lisa interrupted his thoughts as she tapped Connors on his shoulder. He was a little surprised, "Lisa, I didn't see you come in. Thanks for your help. I hope you continue to do it; I sure need all I can get." Lisa replied, "It's absolutely my pleasure. Just let me know if you need anything and I'll do what I can. I'll give you my pager number; don't hesitate to use it, even in the middle of the night." Connors, "Thank you. My sister Sheila has developed a schedule for family and friends to care for Sarah when I'm at work. I'll ask her to page you if she needs more people." Lisa, "Please do. In fact, if you need someone to take care of Sarah during Jane's viewing and funeral, I'll be happy to do it." Connors, "I don't think Sheila has any coverage for the viewing or the funeral. I'll ask her about it." Lisa, "Just let me know, I'll be there."

It was almost 7 pm when Connors left Sarah and returned to the observation room. As he walked in, he said, "I'm sure we're all tired and hungry, but there's no need to go to the apartment and fix dinner. How about I take everyone over to the O Club to eat? It's just down the road and Wednesday nights are usually pretty quiet. I'm sure none of us are interested in partying but a couple of hours away from the house will do everyone some good."

Just as Connors hoped, it was quiet in the Ready Room. While they ate, there was very little said about Jane's illness and death. Instead, they concentrated on the good times of years gone by. Finally, at about 9 pm, Connors said he needed to get some sleep, and he got up to leave. As soon as he did, everyone else followed suit.

When he went to bed that night, he easily fell asleep and slept soundly until 5 a.m. the next morning. Then, feeling refreshed, he dressed and went to see his daughter. Connors was watching Sarah from the observation room when Lisa came into the room. She told him that the jaundice had cleared up and Sarah could go home at noon.

Connors, still unsure of what he was doing, was briefly in a panic. Seeing his reaction, Lisa said, "It's time you learned some more basics of caring for a newborn baby. As I promised, I'm going to show you how to feed, burp, and bathe a baby. Then you'll learn how to change her diaper, swaddle her, put her in her crib, take her temperature, and what to look for if she cries for an abnormal length of time. Now, put on some scrubs and we'll begin."

After Lisa showed him what to do on a lifelike doll, she gave it to Connors to practice. About an hour later, Sarah woke up and started crying. Still not sure what to do, Connors looked at Lisa for help. Instead of doing anything, Lisa said, "She's all yours. It's time for you to feed her." Connors was very timid initially, but after Sarah finished eating and quieted down, he began to gain confidence. With Lisa carefully watching, Connors tried to do everything just like Lisa had taught him. Then, after he swaddled Sarah and put her back in bed, he looked at Lisa and proudly said, "That was the scariest thing I've done since carrier qualifications. Did I do OK?" Lisa took a large diaper pin out of her pocket, pinned it on his shirt, and said, "Mr. Connors, you've earned your daddy pin. Welcome to fatherhood."

It was nearly 9 am when Connors went to the waiting room to call his sister Sheila, "Sis, Sarah's being released at noon. Can you arrange for somebody to help me bring her home? As soon as I hang up, I'm going over to the Base Exchange and

467

buy diapers, a car seat, and a baby bath. I'll be back in about an hour." Sheila, "Marianne Carmody and I were just getting ready to head over there, and others will be coming later, so you'll have plenty of help. Don't go to the Base Exchange. I figured you wouldn't have time to buy anything, so I bought almost everything you'll need, and Jane's parents bought more. We've already set up the furniture, including the bassinette, and I have a baby carrier and a car seat in my car. How about we meet for breakfast in the hospital cafeteria to talk about the schedule we've set up? Afterward, we'll go with you to the nursery. We'll be at the cafeteria in about a half hour." Connors, "That sounds great. I really appreciate you guys getting all those things done; I didn't even think about what Sarah needed until ten minutes ago, I have a lot to learn. I'll see you soon."

Connors was drinking a cup of coffee when his sister and Marianne Carmody walked into the cafeteria. As soon as they sat down, Connors asked, "Are you guys OK with the schedule?" Marianne, "Yes, at least until August. After that, assuming it's working out for everybody, we'll just repeat the rotation."

Connors, "You guys are angels. There is no way I can ever thank you enough for what you're doing." Sheila then pointed at Connors' shirt and asked, "I have to ask, why do you have a diaper pin on your shirt?" Connors, "I forgot to tell you. With Lisa's help, I fed and burped Sarah. Then I changed her diaper, swaddled her, and put her back to bed. I've earned my daddy pin, and now I'm a certified father." Sheila, laughing, "Now, you have to start your first assignment as Mr. Daddy, and it's gonna be the toughest thing you've ever done."

After they had been in the observation room for about an hour, Lisa came in holding Sarah. "OK, Connors, let's see how well you've learned to be a daddy. Come take Sarah. I want to watch how you hold her when you sit, stand, and walk. Once you've done that, I'll give you a car seat that the hospital requires for you to use to transport Sarah home. Put Sarah in the car seat, take her to the car, and I'll show you how to buckle her incorrectly." Ten minutes later, Connor, who was too anxious to drive, sat next to Sarah in the back seat as they took her home.

Connors' parents, Striker, and Wendy were there. As Connors carried Sarah into the apartment, he saw a new rocking chair with a pink ribbon around it in the living room. Then, when he went into the bedroom, he saw that it was painted pink, a crib was next to the bed, and a bassinette was sitting on a new dresser. Hanging across the back wall of the room was a handmade sign that read, "Welcome home, Sarah." Connors, with tears in his eyes, turned to everyone and said, "Again, I'm overwhelmed by your kindness. I'll never be able to thank each of you enough."

On Friday, Connors endured the agony of attending Jane's viewing. While he stood by her coffin, he was barely able to say thank you to the dozens of people who came to offer their condolences. Then, on Saturday, he had to endure it again at her funeral and internment. As much as he wanted to give a eulogy for Jane, he was too emotional to attempt it. Instead, Wendy volunteered to speak for him, and Connors wrote some things he wanted her to say.

The funeral Mass was over in less than an hour, but to Connors it never seemed to end. During the internment, he wept when the casket was lowered into the ground. Before they left, Sheila held Connors' right side, and his dad had his left side as he dropped a rose into the grave. At the following reception, his father was again next to him as he thanked everyone for coming. As soon as he finished, Connors went to his apartment. He needed to hold Sarah, Jane's gift of love to him.

Connors took leave for the next two weeks to acclimate to Sarah's sleeping and eating patterns. He quickly learned that she woke up every three to four hours, either hungry or needing a diaper change. Connors got up every time she cried, either to help Marianne or take care of Sarah by himself. A few days after he started, Connors realized that Sheila was right; he was as tired as he had been in AOCS. By the end of Connors' first week back at work, Marianne insisted that she take care of Sarah at night so that he could get some sleep. Connors agreed, but when he got home after work, he took care of her until he went to bed.

Chapter 79

Connors Works out a Schedule

After Jane's death, Wendy asked Leah to be the maid of honor and Gina Zimmerman to take Leah's place. Still wanting Jane to be part of her wedding, Wendy asked Connors if she could wear Jane's wedding dress. Connors eagerly agreed, saying that Jane would have been thrilled that she did.

At the same time Wendy, Striker asked Sticky to finalize wedding arrangements over dinner at the O Club. When they did, they quickly decided that everything was in place, so they caught up with their lives. Striker told Sticky that unless something totally unexpected happened, he was going to transfer to Air Intelligence. Sticky said that he was still unsure what he wanted, so he was going to wait until the Navy decided what it was going to do. Striker then asked, "I haven't spoken to Bulldog in weeks except for a few minutes at Jane's funeral. Have you seen him?" Sticky, "Yes, He was staying at the BOQ, waiting to see if he was selected for Advanced Parachute training. He wasn't and he had to report to Quantico. He'll still be at your wedding, so don't be shocked when you see him in a Marine Corps choker. The big news about Bulldog is that Lee Ann finally introduced him to his dream girl, Julie, and they've been seeing each other a couple times a week. As you know, she's very young and really pretty. He'll be gone, and there will be a lot of new officers chasing her. I have my doubts that her relationship with Bulldog will last very long." Striker, "Even though I think Julie is too young for Bulldog, I hope that somehow, they can work it out. I hate to see him get hurt." A few minutes Wendy said she was getting tired, and they called it an evening.

When Air Intelligence training ended. Cmdr. Christopher announced that, as expected, Striker finished first in the class. After everyone else left, Christopher told Striker that his transfer was approved and handed him the transfer papers. Before he signed, Striker reflected on how much he wanted to be a Naval Aviator. Even though he did everything required of him to become one, it wasn't going to happen. He was angry and disappointed, but he still wanted to be in the Navy; Air Intelligence was the best way to do it, and he signed the documents.

Cmdr. Christopher congratulated Striker, and as promised, he asked him what his first choice of duty stations was. Striker, "As you know, sir, my fiancée Wendy and I are getting married Saturday. We had planned to visit potential duty stations, but the birth of Wendy's niece and her sister Jane's death prevented us from doing it. We want to stay as close to Pensacola as possible to help her brother-in-law, Tim Connors, take care of his newborn daughter. He has very few family members nearby and must rely on people from out of the area for help. I know that advanced jet training includes an AI segment, so I was hoping to be assigned to the Training Command. If that is not possible, our second choice is Jacksonville NAS. We'd also be interested in Eglin Air Force Base, where I've been told Navy AI officers are sometimes detailed. I apologize for the indecision, but sometimes family problems must be considered when career decisions are made, even in the Navy."

Christopher replied, "I've heard about Lt. Connors' terrible situation, and I can't imagine how he's going to continue on his own. I didn't realize that he was your fiancée's brother-in-law, so I understand that you want to help him. In fact, it's not

472

just understandable. It's the right thing to do. I'll do my best to honor your request. I have to tell you that the Training Command only takes AIs with experience with a deployed air wing squadron. Nothing surpasses first-hand experience when it comes to briefing pilots about going on dangerous missions. I don't think staying here in Pensacola will happen. Of the other two places you listed, I think that you will learn the most at Eglin. Before I was stationed here, I spent a couple of years with Air Force AI in Washington. Their emphasis is mostly on land-based air intelligence assessment, while the Navy provides the best intelligence to aviators who are going into battle from aircraft carriers. We always share intelligence with the Air Force, and they do the same for us. A tour with Air Force AI will make you a better AI officer. Any comments or questions?"

Striker, "Eglin would be great. What are the chances I could get an assignment there?" Christopher, "I don't know for sure, but I do know they are always looking for more help, just like every other AI Command. I know the CO of AI at Eglin. I'll give him a call and see if he can use someone who just finished first in his AI class, and I bet he does. By the way, Mr. Striker, your promotion was approved. Beginning the first of July, you'll be Lt. JG Striker. Congratulations, you've earned it."

Chapter 80

Roommates Go Separate Ways

Striker wanted a low-key bachelor party. Since most of his AOCS and VT-10 classmates would soon leave for their next assignment, he wanted to have a couple of beers with them before they left; Sticky set up a gathering at the Ready Room. Compared to most bachelor parties, Striker's was tame, He did what he wanted: spend time with the guys he had lived and trained with for the better part of a year, When the Ready Room closed at midnight, they wished each other the best knowing that it would probably be the last time they would ever be together.

On Sunday, April 26, about two years after they became roommates, Sticky, Striker, and Bulldog checked out of their BOQ suite. Striker was living with Wendy, and Sticky, who spent most of his time in his rented house, kept a small BOQ room. Bulldog decided to stay with Sticky until after the wedding, when he would report to Quantico.

As they packed their belongings, it occurred to each of them that being roommates during the most challenging time of their lives was over. They would never be able to rely on each other to survive AOCS or make it through Hound's death, but the bond between them would never be broken.

Chapter 81

Connors Begins Again

Connors worked out a schedule to take care of Sarah with the help of family and friends. He got up at 5:30 am and fed and changed the baby before someone relieved him. The Carmody's were scheduled first, followed by his mother Anne, who would remain there until Sheila finished the school year. In addition, Lisa came to check on Sarah at least twice a week and babysat her whenever she was needed.

In the Fall of 1970, Lisa, now a Pediatric Nurse Practitioner, became the CO of a new Well Baby Clinic and Childcare Center. The facility accepted children from newborn to six years old, so Connors enrolled Sarah. The need for family help ended, but Lisa continued to babysit Sarah after hours. Inevitably, Lisa's strong feelings for Connors were rekindled, but she refused to show any indication that there was anything between them. She focused on caring for Sarah, who she soon began to think of as her daughter.

As the months passed, Connors noticed the special bond between Lisa and Sarah. Lisa became the missing piece in the life that he shared with Sarah. She wasn't Jane and never would be, but he knew that she would always put him and Sarah first. In late November, the CO of the Test Pilot School notified Connors that there was a spot for him in the April 1971 class. He wanted to accept the offer, but he realized he could not leave Lisa behind.

One Saturday evening, Lisa was babysitting Sarah while Connors went to the commissary. When he returned, Sarah was asleep, and Lisa was reading in the living room. Connors offered Lisa a glass of wine, which she accepted, and he got a beer. They talked briefly about Sarah, and then Connors told her about his offer to go to Test Pilot School. She was immediately worried about them leaving her, but she knew that it was Connors' dream. With tears in her eyes, she told him to accept and that she would help Sarah as long as she could. Now crying, she said she would transfer to Pax River if he wanted. Connors knew that Lisa was in their lives for a reason and that Jane would be happy that she was. He also knew that it would be much easier for her to transfer if she was his wife.

Connors dropped to one knee, proposed to her and she immediately said yes. A few minutes later, they found themselves in his bed, where they made love for the rest of the night. For the next few weeks, they spent as much time together as possible but hid their relationship as much as they could. When Christmas came, they broke the news of their engagement. Their families were surprised but understanding; they knew that this was the best thing for Connors, Lisa, and Sarah.

On Valentine's Day, 1971, Connors and Lisa were married in a small Catholic ceremony at the base chapel. A week later, both of their transfers were approved, and Lisa began the process of adopting Sarah. It was finalized on March 16, 1971, Sarah's first birthday, a week before they moved to Pax River.

Chapter 82

Striker and Wendy Wed

It was their wedding day, and as she put on Jane's wedding dress, Wendy felt Jane's presence surround her. She almost began to cry but held back tears until after Father O'Reilly introduced Mr. and Mrs. Jonathan Striker. Striker was now her husband, and Jane was at peace. Striker also had tears in his eyes as they reached the Chapel exit. He was abandoning his dream of becoming a Naval Aviator through a canopy of swords, the entrance to his destiny, his life with Wendy.

Epilogue

The week after Striker and Wendy were married, Striker learned that his first assignment was two years at Eglin Air Force Base. They moved to an apartment in Fort Walton Beach and then honeymooned in Key West. When they returned, Wendy got a teaching job in the Okaloosa County school district, and Striker reported to the AI commanding officer. During the next few months, they often went back to Pensacola to help Connors with Sarah, but that ended when Connors moved. Toward the end of his tour, Striker was accepted to the JAG program at the University of Florida Law School. Three years later, he was a JAG officer stationed at Jacksonville NAS; they had a daughter named Jane, and Wendy was expecting again.

About a month after Striker's wedding, Bulldog started the Marine Corps Basic Officer's Course. When he graduated, he was assigned to RECON training in Camp Pendleton, California. Soon after he was designated a RECON, he was deployed to Vietnam for the first of two tours. When he finally returned to Camp Pendleton, he was a Major and was wearing a Silver Star, two Bronze Stars, and three Purple Hearts. Julie visited Bulldog several times while he was in BOC and went with him to Camp Pendleton. They were married the week before his first deployment to Vietnam. She gave birth to a son, Stewart, shortly before he returned.

Two months after Striker's wedding, Riley and Leah were married at sunset on Tiki Beach. Connors was the best man, and Wendy was the matron of honor. Eight months later, Riley was transferred to North Island NAS and then again deployed to Yankee Station. Six months into the deployment, shrapnel from a SAM-3 near miss severely wounded Riley's back. After several operations and six months of rehab, Riley was given a full-disability discharge. He and Leah remained in San Diego, where he became a very successful Real Estate Broker and the father of four children. The first, a boy, was named Alan.

Five months after Striker's wedding, Sticky finally started RIO training. Six weeks later, he finished and completed a week in the mandatory Survival, Evasion, Resistance, and Escape (SERE) training. When he finished, he reported to the RAG in Miramar, where he was assigned to an F-4 squadron and deployed to Yankee Station. During his tour in Vietnam, he completed over 200 carrier traps and 100 combat missions. In mid-1972, his F-4 was shot down; he and the pilot were captured and imprisoned. When the war ended, he was released from the Hanoi Hilton. He spent 2 months rehabbing at Bethesda Naval Hospital and was subsequently reassigned to Glynco NAS as a RIO Instructor. While he was there, he and Lee Ann reconnected. They continued to see each other for years, even during her marriages to other people.

The roommates were never together as a group again in Pensacola, but over the years, they stayed in touch and occasionally visited each other. When they did, they spent most of the time reliving the happiest and most memorable time of their lives, their Pensacola days.

Acknowledgments

First, I need to thank my wife, Sandy, who, in addition to her encouragement to write this book, has spent hundreds of hours editing and offering suggestions to make it a more readable document. Without her, *Pensacola Days* would not have been written.

Many thanks to John E. Crouch, 1st Sergeant, USMC, Ret. whose great book, *The Pressure Cooker*, reminded me of my days in Aviation Officers Candidate School (AOCS). He is also the administrator of the Facebook blog AOCS Alumni Pensacola. Once I read *The Pressure Cooker*, I knew that I had a story to tell. Then, as I was finishing the manuscript, John was instrumental in my efforts to publish the book, and he graciously allowed me to use photographs from his collection.

In addition, my thanks go to Thomas S. Wolfe, who is an administrator of the Facebook blog Exploring Pensacola NAS. He also allowed me to use photographs from his collection for my book cover. Other photographs, to the best of my knowledge, are from the public domain.

As anyone who completed AOCS will readily express, the Marine Corps Drill Instructors' strict discipline and motivational training transformed us from college boys to self-confident men and Naval Officers. They made us do things we never thought we could do. As tough as it was, I will always be thankful that they did. AOCS was disbanded in 1994, but it is my hope that *The Pressure Cooker* and *Pensacola Days* provide chronicles of the most intense officer training that ever existed.

Finally, I need to apologize to all my fellow AOCS graduates for all the errors and omissions I made in my narrative about AOCS and flight training. The more than fifty years since I finished AOCS have fogged my memory but did not alter the effect that it had on my life.

Made in the USA
Middletown, DE
21 February 2025

71558789R00272